CW01337174

ARTHUR JAMES
BALFOUR

First Earl of Balfour, K.G., O.M., F.R.S., Etc.

By His Niece

BLANCHE E. C. DUGDALE

1848–1906

*

With Seventeen Illustrations

G · P · PUTNAM'S SONS

New York

Printing Statement:

Due to the very old age and scarcity of this book,
many of the pages may be hard to read due to the
blurring of the original text, possible missing pages,
missing text and other issues beyond our control.

Because this is such an important and rare work, we
believe it is best to reproduce this book regardless of
its original condition.

Thank you for your understanding.

ARTHUR JAMES BALFOUR
From a drawing by George Richmond, R.A.

Contents

CONTENTS

fast. Second Home Rule Bill. Balfour's views on oratory. Balfour visits Hawarden. Balfour's first encounter with Mr. Lloyd George.

CHAPTER X

CHAPTER XI

CHAPTER XII

CHAPTER XIII

CHAPTER XIV

CHAPTER XV

CHAPTER XVI

CHAPTER XVII

CHAPTER XVIII

CHAPTER XIX

List of Illustrations

ARTHUR JAMES BALFOUR

Chapter I

THE FIRST TWENTY-ONE YEARS

Home and Ancestry. His father's illness and death. His mother. Whittingehame. Private School. Eton. Cambridge. Canoeing round Skye.

ARTHUR JAMES BALFOUR was born on July 25th, 1848, at Whittinge-hame in East Lothian, the home of his branch of the family.

Whittingehame House stands on the edge of one of the loveliest of the deep, heavily timbered glens down which the streams from the Lammermoor Hills flow to the North Sea. It is made of fine white stone in the Greek style, and was designed by Robert Smirke, who was also the architect of the British Museum.

Arthur Balfour used to speak gratefully of the good sense and taste of his grandfather, founder of the Whittingehame line of Bal-fours, who, building as he did in the first quarter of the nineteenth century, yet left his descendants a good country house which bears no resemblance whatever to a castle.

The painting of old James Balfour, which hangs on the staircase at Whittingehame, is certainly not the portrait of a man likely to be tempted by the battlemented exuberances of the romantic revival. The forehead is high and narrow, the mouth long and tight, the eyes shrewd. The picture shows him for what he was, a man of good breeding and conspicuous business ability. A younger son of the family of Balfour of Balbirnie, in Fife, he came of an old stock which traced descent from Robert the Bruce, and held a leading place in the county for many generations before James Balfour's day. He went to India in his youth and made a considerable fortune as a contractor for military material in the days of "John Company's" wars. Thus equipped, he proceeded, on his return to Scotland, to marry the daughter of the 8th Earl of Lauderdale, Lady Eleanor Maitland. After much deliberation they bought the Whittingehame estate from its ancient and impoverished owners, the Hays, and there set themselves to establish a new branch of the Balfour family.

At Whittingehame, in 1820, their eldest son, James Maitland Balfour, was born, and from Whittingehame in the year 1843 Lady Eleanor wrote to a friend announcing the engagement of the heir: "James is very ardently inspired in love towards a lovely and intelligent girl."

The marriage in question was of a kind so gratifying to the parents that this description of the young couple might be read as nothing more than an expression of Lady Eleanor's general sense of suitability. In fact, it was perfectly accurate. The young man was ardently in love, and remained so until the end of his short life, through thirteen years of marriage. The "lovely and intelligent girl" was Lady Blanche Gascoyne Cecil, daughter of the 2nd Marquis of Salisbury and sister of Lord Robert Cecil, afterwards 3rd Marquis, and Prime Minister of the Queen.

Arthur James Balfour's father was twenty-two, his mother eighteen, at the time of their wedding. In the next eleven years nine children were born. First three girls, of whom one died at birth. James Balfour died before the birth of his first grandson in 1848. The boy was named Arthur after his godfather, the great Duke of Wellington, and James after his father and grandfather.

Five more children followed, four boys and a girl. Then in 1854, a few months before the birth of the youngest son, James Maitland Balfour broke a blood-vessel in a paroxysm of coughing. According to one story it happened when he was playing golf; according to another, when he was putting on the uniform of the East Lothian Yeomanry before going to Edinburgh to sit for a portrait to be presented by the regiment. The hæmorrhage was the symptom of the end of a cheerful, active life. His wife nursed him for two years with passionate devotion till his death in 1856.

On a ridge of high ground on the Whittingehame estate, visible for many miles round, there is a column of red sandstone, set up as a monument to him by the subscribers of the money for the portrait that was never painted. It is a memorial to a country gentleman, popular with his neighbours, full of zest for sport and all the proper occupations of a good laird. His father, James Balfour, had represented the County of Haddington in Parliament from 1831 till 1835. James Maitland Balfour also entered the House of Commons, where he sat from 1841 till 1847 as Conservative Member for the District of

Burghs of Haddington, Dunbar, North Berwick, Lauder and Jedburgh.[1] But he made no mark in politics. Balfours as a rule develop
late, and only one of his five sons (Frank the biologist) was acknowledged by the outside world as of outstanding ability before he
reached the age of thirty-five—the age at which James Maitland
Balfour died.

Arthur, although he was seven at the time of his father's death,
remembered nothing whatever of him, and even the elder daughters
very little. The long illness may partially account for the father's dis-
appearance from the daily life of a nursery full of babies. Certain
striking episodes they did connect with him, such as voyages on
large ships to Madeira, where he wintered twice, the elder children
being taken each time. At Whittingehame, too, strange and unfamiliar things occurred. Once his daughter Evelyn saw a live turtle
crawling on the flagstones outside the kitchen door, brought, she
was told, to be turned into soup to make her father better.

Everything that could be done in those days to save his life was
tried. Tuberculosis had a strong hold on that generation of Balfours,
one of James Maitland's sisters, and a brother, also dying of it. The
fact that the disease never reappeared among his own children is
probably largely due to their mother's extremely enlightened ideas
about health. Lady Blanche was highly critical in after years of the
medical treatment of her husband, and she applied her own theories
and beliefs with courage. Good feeding and fresh air were by no
means the articles of faith in the fifties that they are nowadays, but
she held them strongly, guided by the advice of that great physician,
Sir James Simpson, on whom she relied in all these matters. Several
of her eight children, most notably Arthur, were delicate in youth,
and as a family they had more than an average share of serious ill-
nesses in their early years. But they all grew up healthy, and the
father's constitutional weakness developed in none of them.

James Maitland Balfour died during his second stay in Madeira.
He was buried there in February 1856. His death affected his children far more directly than his life had ever done, for it left them
under the sole and concentrated influence of a very remarkable
woman.

Lady Blanche Balfour had a powerful personality even before the
illness and death of her husband produced the conditions which
nourished the strength of her character. One impression of her

[1] See *Return of Members of Parliament*, Part II.

belongs to a date just before the approaching break-up of her husband's health. The following letter was written at the beginning of the year in the course of which James Maitland Balfour's lung disease first showed itself.

Lady Victoria Talbot, daughter of the 8th Earl of Shrewsbury, to Lady Waterford, January 4th, 1854.

I have heard pretty often from Lady Salisbury, always interesting her letters, and whenever you come here again, I have one or two of hers to show you, and several of Blanche Balfour's which will interest you perhaps even more than Lady S. In some things she does me. For whereas in Lady S. it would be impossible to be five minutes in her society and not see there was something, in Blanche there is such a wonderful power of command and duty that to know her slightly you would think she was a healthy-minded, happy wife, a mother of children, doing all the good she could, and consequently at peace with God and man. But you never could suspect the intense funds of feeling, dashing and flashing and bursting and melting and tearing her at times to pieces. And she looks so quiet, and pure, and almost cold, aye cold; about as cold as Hecla under its crust of ice. She is a glorious character.

This is how Blanche Balfour appeared to penetrating eyes during the happy period of her life. Her husband's death left her own health shattered by child-bearing followed by exhausting sick-nursing, and the eighteen years that elapsed before her own death at the age of forty-seven were a perpetual struggle against allowing weakness or pain to interfere with the single remaining purpose of her existence —the training of her children. On them she now concentrated the whole of her dominating personality and powerful mind.

The effect on them all was naturally tremendous, although the reactions she produced differed widely in every case. With her eldest son, they were flawlessly happy. Through twenty-four years, till her death in 1872, her great heart and strong head worked, where he was concerned, in absolute harmony and drew from him eager response.

A very early record of him is in one of her letters, written when the family had settled down at Whittingehame after the father's death. "Chickens prosperous," she wrote, "I look in at their meals. Last night proverbs as usual. Arthur the questioner. He put himself astride my lap and gave his question: 'Can you tell me why I love you so much?'"

Mother and son were alike in many ways, not least in their ex-

LADY BLANCHE BALFOUR
About the time of her marriage

treme reserve about emotional matters. She was intimate with very few, and during her widowhood she withdrew so much from ordinary society that hardly anyone came near her who could speak of her in terms of absolute equality. I recollect one illuminating conversation about her quite late in Arthur Balfour's own life. He had been reading a sketch of her, written by an old friend, Dr. Robertson, Minister of Whittingehame parish from 1865 to 1918. The book emphasises the self-abnegation of her character, the vivid reality of her religious life, and the awe and admiration with which her little circle at Whittingehame looked up to her.

"It's all quite true of course," said Arthur Balfour, "but for Heaven's sake don't get the idea that she was goody!" Then with increasing vehemence he went on: "She was very amusing. She was brilliant. Looking back now I can see she was one of the most brilliant talkers I ever knew."

Lady Blanche did not live to see any of her children's children. One of these once asked what she would have thought of her descendants of the second generation. The aunt to whom the question was put said: "It is quite impossible to tell you that. If any of you had known her you would have all been so different from what you are that I really cannot say." When this was repeated to Arthur Balfour, he burst out laughing and said: "Absurd!" But he added thoughtfully: "Still, you know, there's something in it."

There is at any rate this in it, that the impression of a great and vivid personality cannot be handed down by description, but only through studying the people who have drawn it into themselves. There is no doubt that his Cecil mother had more to do than any other human being with forming Arthur Balfour's ideas of duty, with training the independence of his judgment, and laying the uncompromising foundations of his character. In the development of these is the truest indication of the atmosphere which surrounded him in youth. One remark made by Lady Blanche he sometimes quoted in after years as having impressed him so deeply that it may have been a turning-point in his life. She made it at some period of his young manhood when he was half-seriously considering renouncing the active duties of his position, and spending all his time in studying and writing metaphysics. "Do it if you like," she said, "but remember that if you do, you will find you have nothing to write about by the time you are forty."

The five brothers and three sisters formed a very close corporation, early exhibiting the lively appreciation of each other's society which grew with the years. This highly vitalised family existence struck its roots deep into Whittingehame itself.

The place lies where the broken country at the foot of the sheep ground and heather of the Lammermoors meets the ten-mile belt of plough-land that stretches between the hills and the sea. The landscape is full of colour all through the year, owing to the rarity of grass fields and to the vivid red of the soil, varying from purple almost to scarlet. All the green is hidden in the depths of the glens. East Lothian is the very centre of the granary of Scotland. Its most characteristic season is early autumn, when the teams begin to plod up and down the big fields the moment the stooks are lifted, ploughing the silver-grey of the stubbles back to red. The throb of the threshing machines, whose chimneys rise above the farms, drifts across, and makes an undertone for the squawking of the sea-gulls scuffling behind the plough. Along the horizon lies the blue strip of the Forth; the Bass Rock and North Berwick Law rising suddenly from the flatness. Beyond them is the outline of the coast of Fife, its own cornfields pale in the clear autumn light.

From Whittingehame old James Balfour looked across the water to his native county. From the top of the Lomond on the Balbirnie property the other Balfours could see Traprain Law, the landmark of Whittingehame. The two Lowland counties are near to each other and much akin. It was not difficult for the younger branch to strike root on the south side of the Forth.

When Whittingehame was bought by Arthur Balfour's grandfather it was a fine property of about 10,000 acres. In those prosperous days of agricultural ownership the public burdens on the land were less than £2000 out of a rent-roll of some £13,000. Cottage-building and planting went on actively under Lady Blanche's regency and for many years after Arthur Balfour came of age. To spend money on Whittingehame was always his delight, and after the bad times came he fell back on plans for doing what still remained to be done for improving and beautifying the place.

During his childhood however the family life was on a very simple scale. In his grandfather's days the drawing-rooms, hung with yellow damask and filled with French furniture and Sèvres china, were constantly open and filled with guests. So too they had sometimes been in the early days of Lady Blanche's married life. But after 1856 the dust-covers were drawn over the buhl cabinets and the ormolu clocks. For years the life of the house centred first in the nurseries, then in the schoolrooms.

Just before his eleventh birthday Arthur Balfour went to his private school at Hoddesdon in Hertfordshire. He was thoroughly happy there. The following reminiscences of him, written years later by his schoolmaster, the Rev. C. J. Chittenden, leave an impression of an atmosphere not common in educational establishments even in these days; unique one may suppose in the 'sixties of the Victorian era.

A. J. B. came to the Grange 13th May, 1859. He was a peculiarly attractive boy, with a look of bright intelligence when he was well; but his health was far from strong, not from any definite tendency to disease as far as appeared, but from lack of vital energy. He would sometimes, by the doctor's advice, lie down in the afternoon when he felt languid, and try to get to sleep. On these occasions he liked to have the organ softly played in the hall below. He was always very fond of music, but did not get sufficiently through the drudgery of the elements to enjoy playing himself.

As he grew stronger he disliked exercise less, but we never could succeed in developing in him any love for athletic games. He would *endure* a game of cricket conscientiously, as he would anything that was prescribed by lawful authority.

When we found that there was no prospect of his ever entering into games I ceased to insist on his constantly attempting it, and he often walked with me while his school-fellows were at cricket or football. He was a delightful companion, and his conversation was much more like that of an intelligent youth of eighteen than that of a boy of twelve.

I soon discovered that not only the best way, but the *only* way to teach him the subjects necessary for Eton was to help him constantly to general principles in everything, and not to try to get him to remember isolated facts beyond what was absolutely necessary. When he had gained a principle which explained a number of instances that had appeared unconnected, his satisfaction would amount (judging from appearances) to a feeling of pleasure.

He had an uncommon power for a boy, of taking in the purport of a number of connected facts and seeing quickly any apparent inconsistency between them.

His interest in anything he learnt varied in proportion as it gave room for reducing chaos into order. He did not care much for mathematics, yet his love for logical correctness gave him some interest in Euclid and arithmetic. For the same reason he was interested to some extent in Latin Prose; he never showed much interest in Latin Verse. He cared most for history, and this most in its political, social and economic aspects. He did not seem to care greatly for a pictorial rehabilitation of the past, and it was difficult to rouse in him any enthusiasm for antiquity as such. He seemed not to have much of that "historical imagination" which can call up a vivid picture of bygone persons and things.

A. liked poetry; he appreciated Tennyson, and later became a great admirer of Pope.

One characteristic of A.'s mind was that he never could persuade himself, as boys generally do, that what he wished for would happen— he could never live in a "fool's paradise." He was generally liked by his school-fellows for his good-humour and unselfishness, but they laughed at his abstraction. Several of them, including A., were travelling with me by railway and one of them remarked, on stopping at Ponder's End, that it would be a good place to leave A. as he was always pondering.

A. was amenable to reason to a greater extent than any boy with whom I have had to do, though, I may add, this characteristic was largely shared by most of his family. Where no question of right or wrong was involved it was enough to show him that a course was most reasonable for him to adopt it at once.

One of his greatest trials was the necessity for punctuality and order. Lady Blanche was much amused by finding that the frequent entries in his account book of "Lateness ½d." were the record of fines for unpunctuality which he was pleased to enter under this abstract form.

A. was generally so much occupied with his own thoughts and with questions that suggested themselves to him that he had no time or attention for the little personalities which occupy the attention of many boys. If he was laughed at he would join in the laugh, often shutting up his assailant by some witty repartee.

Everyone who knew Arthur Balfour in his maturity will recognise his features here. The description shows how early his tastes were fixed, with the one great exception of the later development of his love for games. For purely physical reasons the keenest of his pleasures as a man was nothing but boredom to him as a boy. Low vitality and short sight made him hopeless at cricket and football. Spectacles were among the taboos at Eton in his day, and it was not till he went to Cambridge that he got a chance to play a game which suited him, on equal terms with other people. There his passion for Court Tennis developed. Lawn Tennis was not yet invented, and he only began golf later. In spite of the nearness of Whittingehame to the chain of magnificent links that border the Forth from Musselburgh to Dunbar, neither he nor his brothers ever played as boys.

ARTHUR JAMES BALFOUR
About nine years old

Their father had been a golfer, and Arthur Balfour always thought that if he had lived, his sons might have been taught young enough to become really first-class players. As things were, riding, and natural history collections, were their chief out-door occupations in the holidays.

Lady Blanche Balfour's brother, Lord Robert Cecil, afterwards 3rd Marquis of Salisbury, was trustee for the Whittingehame estate during Arthur Balfour's minority, and came there from time to time. He possessed by nature the power over young minds enjoyed by those who can treat them as intellectual equals. Arthur Balfour looked back through life to the stimulating effect of one particular conversation with his uncle while he was still an Eton boy. The fact that he used to try in vain to recall what it was about is a very early example of the way his memory discarded unessential facts, so to speak, in spite of himself. The interest of the episode is mainly in its effect upon his own mind at this stage. Sooner or later it was inevitable that sympathy should be established between these two whose lives and characters were cast for the most part in the same grooves, and who in age were only separated by eighteen years. In Arthur Balfour's boyhood, however, current politics did not enter much into his home life. Lady Blanche's natural tastes lay more in history, literature and theology.

The distress in Lancashire during the cotton famine of 1862 and 1863, that followed from the American Civil War, was however used by her for educational purposes with characteristic ruthlessness for her own personal comfort. The staff of servants at Whittingehame was reduced and the wages thus saved were given to the Famine Fund. Two mill-girls were imported to do the roughest work, and the cooking and other jobs were performed by the children themselves. Arthur, aged fourteen, was supposed to black the boots. There is no record of how long this curious episode lasted, nor of how it was brought to a close.

In 1861 Arthur began his outwardly placid and uneventful Eton career. He went first to Mr. Birch's House, who in 1864 was succeeded by Mr. Thackeray. The impressions of the Eton masters are remarkably like Mr. Chittenden's. Mr. Birch, in a letter written years after, describes "a delightful sort of openness in all he said and did, and a beautiful purity of mind and ways." He adds: "Had you asked me in 1864 what I thought of his future, I should have said:

'mind too restless for the frame it is set in, and he will be very short-lived.' "

It is clear that very few of the masters realised the quality of intellect that was ripening during the years at Eton. The school work hardly drew it to the surface. Once indeed "Billy Johnson," that remarkable scholar better known to the world as William Cory, set a paper on general subjects outside the ordinary curriculum, and Arthur Balfour found himself second among the competitors. This he never forgot, for, as he wrote: "scholastic failures unrelieved by any flashes of appreciation began, as boyhood drew to its close, somewhat to discourage me, and tended to make me doubtful of myself." [1]

Nevertheless by the time he left Eton his acquaintance with English history and literature, especially in the seventeenth and eighteenth centuries, was pretty wide. His passion for general reading was fully developed, largely through his love for Macaulay's Essays, which his mother had given him while he was still at his private school. He read and re-read them, setting himself to follow up as many as possible of the allusions they contained.

In 1866 he left school and went to Cambridge as a Fellow Commoner of Trinity. He calls this "a period of almost unmixed satisfaction." The fragment of autobiography written sixty years later recaptures the atmosphere of a rising vitality. The serene fragile schoolboy disappears. Instead there is a young man in good spirits from morning till night, with his natural love of games made more acute by repression, and capacity for playing them raised to the normal—revelling in the first opportunities for listening to good music, and making friends in half a dozen sets.

One of these friends, the Hon. Hugh Elliot, recorded in a letter the only occasion when Balfour ever appeared in a police-court.

There was a certain Dr. Ransome at Cambridge, who lived in Jesus Lane. This gentleman had somehow or other contrived to make himself objectionable to us undergraduates, and in retaliation for his supposed offences it became the fashion to ring his bell at night and run away before the door was opened.

One night I was walking down Jesus Lane with Kinnaird [2] and

[1] This is a quotation from Balfour's own *Chapters of Autobiography* (Cassell & Co.) upon which I have drawn freely in the early chapters of this volume.

[2] Afterwards Lord Kinnaird.

A. J. B. It was suggested that we should pull Dr. Ransome's bell. A. J. B. put out his hand as if to pull the bell, though he did not touch it, nor as a matter of fact intended to ring it. As he stretched out his arm a policeman who was concealed behind a doorway sprang out and charged him with ringing the bell. A. J. B. denied the accusation and as the best way of testing its truth proposed that we should wait and see whether the bell was answered. As it was not, the policeman rang the bell himself when the door was at length opened. The inmates of the house declared the bell had rung twice. The very next morning we all appeared in the police-court. The Mayor of Cambridge was on the Bench. The charge, directed against A. J. B. alone, was for offensively and wantonly ringing Dr. Ransome's door-bell. Both he and Kinnaird swore the bell had never been pulled. A. J. B. stood condemned on the perjured testimony of a policeman. He had to pay £1, I think, in the shape of a fine, and I shall never to my dying day forget the awful solemnity with which the Bench in passing judgment upon him told him that he might think himself lucky that he had got off so cheaply and that if he did not regulate his conduct more carefully he would some day find himself in prison.

Often have I sat in the House of Commons, and heard A. J. B. founding an answer to some Irish question on the unimpeachable word of a policeman; often have I wondered what the Irish members would have said had they been aware that the Chief Secretary had himself fallen an innocent victim to the hard swearing of one of these officials!

Arthur Kinnaird and another Cambridge friend, Reginald MacLeod,[1] were Arthur Balfour's companions in an amusing expedition to the Hebrides in the Long Vacation of 1867. Starting from Dunvegan Castle (the home of Reginald MacLeod's father, the chief of the Clan) in Rob Roy canoes, they coasted down Skye, and crossed sixteen miles of open ocean to the island of Rum. Even in summer this was a risky journey among coasts where the waves, if they beat at all, beat against rocky precipices.

On looking back [wrote Balfour] the whole thing seems a very harebrained adventure. A Rob Roy canoe was no proper sea-going craft. Three Rob Roys are very little safer than one. If a canoe at sea be swamped it can scarcely be re-entered by its late occupant; nor can he seek refuge with a friend, for no canoe can by any contrivance hold more than one.[2]

[1] Afterwards Sir Reginald MacLeod of MacLeod.
[2] *Chapters of Autobiography*, p. 48.

As a matter of fact the weather kept calm all through the week or ten days that they spent among the islands, sometimes camping, and endeavouring, not too successfully, to cook their own suppers, but more often as guests of MacLeod's kinsmen and clansmen. The only actual risk they met was from the levelled rifle of one of the latter, who for the moment mistook the bobbing canoes for sea-monsters of an unknown species. The whole affair was however considered dangerous enough by their elders for expostulations to be made by somebody beforehand to Lady Blanche. "Would you have me spoil a character?" she answered. This episode of undergraduate days stuck pleasurably in Arthur Balfour's mind to the end of his life, and he was delighted when, sixty years or so after the date of it, his own grand-nephew and niece, and the grandson and grand-daughter of the two friends who had shared it, found themselves all together on a visit to Dunvegan.

Another Cambridge friend, Walter Durnford, describes more of College life:

We used to meet in Balfour's rooms (at the corner of the New Court adjoining the Library) almost every Sunday evening and discuss in moderation his excellent claret, with much talk of men and books. We were conscious, I think, that we had among us a man of unusual ability, whose tastes lay in a direction different from our own, namely, philosophy and metaphysics, but whose opinion was worth having on all literary subjects. But I do not think we had any idea that there was the stuff in Balfour which would make him one of the foremost politicians of our time.... On the contrary, as I remember him then, there was an unusual disregard, and almost contempt for current politics; he was emphatically not one of the show young men who come from the Union or the Canning and take their place as it were by right in the House of Commons. But it was observable that in the rather prim society of the High Table he held his own with the Dons, some of them men of undoubted genius, as R. L. Jebb, H. Jackson and W. J. Clark.

Probably the only one of Balfour's Cambridge friends who was fully aware of Balfour's absorption in metaphysics at this time was Henry Sidgwick, his tutor, later to become his brother-in-law. Hugh Elliot, in his retrospect, says:

Balfour was not reputed to be a great reader, but to have a wonderful facility for picking the brains of other people.... I believe however that he read far more than most people imagined.

He undoubtedly did, and it is equally true that he enjoyed drawing out other people's ideas. The love of listening was one of the
chief qualities of his charm. Adaptability to the interests of his company was another, and perhaps it is only to an intellectual solitary
that these social gifts come naturally. Certainly eagerness for self-
expression interferes with them both, and such eagerness Balfour
never had.

He went down from Cambridge in November 1869, after taking
a Second Class in the Moral Science Tripos. He felt no particular
disappointment at the mildness of this success. "Before it took place,"
he wrote, "I was planning the future course of my speculative efforts;
after it was over the plans, such as they were, remained unchanged."

The "plans" culminated some ten years later in his first book,
A Defence of Philosophic Doubt. No one can understand Arthur
Balfour who forgets that interest in speculative thinking was part
of the fabric of his everyday existence, wherever he was, whatever
he was doing. It was a natural taste, like music, games, and general
reading, and like these, he never let it be crowded out, even at the
point in his life when interests, duties, and pleasures first began to
press upon him. Never again perhaps did he find the opportunity
to concentrate upon it, as he did during the years between leaving
Cambridge and his serious entry into politics; but by that time his
philosophical standpoint was fixed, and his later work is a development of the same challenge to a purely rationalistic conception of
the Universe, which is contained in the *Defence of Philosophic
Doubt.*

Chapter II

MANHOOD

Mr. Gladstone visits Strathconan. Family events. Death of Lady Blanche. A love affair. Entry into Parliament. Travel. Family portraits. Balfour's maiden speech. Berlin Congress. Music. "Defence of Philosophic Doubt." Balfour's attitude to religion.

BALFOUR came of age in 1869, the same year that he left Cambridge. The event gave him possession of an estate in Ross-shire, bought by his grandfather and let during his minority. Strathconan was a lovely Highland place, with a deer-forest and salmon river. The family revelled in it. Balfour, who never cared for shooting, rather enjoyed deer-stalking. In the autumn months he kept the Lodge full of guests. In 1872 one of them was the Prime Minister, Mr. Gladstone himself. The entertainment must have pleased the great man, for he stayed till the very eve of a Cabinet Meeting. His actual departure proved excessively agitating to his young host. Mr. Gladstone was being escorted by row-boat, and on pony-back, across five miles of moor and loch between Strathconan Lodge and the railway station at Ach-an-Alt. While a great expanse of heather still stretched in front of the party, the smoke of the train was seen across it. Waving frantically, Arthur Balfour flew forward, splashing through pools, reflecting gloomily as he ran on the awful possibilities of the Prime Minister missing a Cabinet Meeting and his own unescapable responsibility for the results. But he caught the engine-driver's eye— and when the train left the station he thankfully saw two wet woollen socks waving from the window of a first-class carriage.

The Balfours' circle of friends was enlarging now that the brothers and sisters were all grown up. In July 1871, Evelyn, the second sister, married John Strutt (afterwards Lord Rayleigh), a Senior Wrangler who was to become one of the most distinguished men of science of his time. The marriage which brought him inside the family ring caused great rejoicing, for he was already one of Balfour's best friends. Mr. Gladstone's daughter, Mrs. Drew, in her Diary, speaks of "B. and S., as we call Messrs. Balfour and Strutt, the two Cambridge inseparables."

One great shadow lay over the family round the turn of the seventies. Lady Blanche was dying, slowly, and with suffering. The end came in May 1872, not at Whittingehame, but in a house in Eaton Terrace in London. Balfour had just bought the lease of Number Four Carlton Gardens, which remained his London house for the rest of his life. He was busy with alterations in the rooms for his mother's comfort when she died. It was a lasting disappointment to him that she never inhabited them.

With the opening of the London house new elements entered Balfour's life.

His friendship with Miss May Lyttelton, daughter of the fourth Lord Lyttelton, began in 1870. He was drawn that summer, originally through his Cambridge friendship with Spencer Lyttelton, one of her elder brothers, into the midst of the Lyttelton-Gladstone clan. Lady Lyttelton and the Prime Minister's wife were sisters, and the immense cousinhood formed by their families grew up as close a corporation in its own way as were the Balfours themselves. But they possessed an ebullient vitality which the Balfours lacked. Rollicking spirits, boisterous jokes and chaff, were rather new to Balfour. He enjoyed them now among contemporaries who shared many of his own tastes, and pursued them with energy far greater than his own. He loved listening to music; they loved performing it. He liked watching a first-class game as much as joining in a second-rate one. The Lyttelton brothers were famous already at tennis as well as at cricket, although Alfred, the star of their extraordinary team, had not left Eton when Balfour first knew them. The warm social atmosphere of Hagley, their home in Worcestershire, supplied something that he needed, perhaps needed especially just then, when his mother's illness was the permeating fact at Whittingehame.

Intimacy and ease came quickly. One of Miss Lyttelton's sisters, Mrs. Talbot,[1] has thus described for me the beginning:

Spencer brought Arthur Balfour to Hagley in the summer of 1870, feeling sure he would be liked by us all. Mary Gladstone was there too. Both she and May played on the piano as much as possible, and

[1] Wife of the Rev. Edward Talbot, afterwards Bishop of Winchester.

A. J. B. sat wherever there was music going on. I remember being amused at my brother Neville saying: "I don't know that I like this friend of Spencer's,—he seems to do nothing but hang about the girls." I told him it was the music he was enjoying first and foremost.

This may have been true in June. In December the Gladstones gave a ball at Hawarden, and at that house-party it was clear that Balfour was attracted by May Lyttelton. She was about twenty at that time, not beautiful in any strict sense, built on a large scale with masses of shining hair, and brown eyes wide set. She was full of vitality, highly responsive, eager, keenly interested in intellectual things, revelling in friendships, a central figure wherever she came. She and Balfour became intimate friends quickly, and on that basis their friendship remained apparently static for some years. Just as it was quickening it was defrauded by fate of its climax. Miss Lyttelton died when Balfour was on the point of asking her to marry him.

I can recall May's happy face [wrote Mrs. Talbot many years later] when I saw her for the last time before her terrible illness, on January 4th, 1875. She had just been at Latimer where A. J. B. was, and he spoke to her, as he afterwards told me, in a way which she must entirely have understood, of his feeling for her. It would have been best if he had proposed to her then, but he was in deadly fear of a refusal, and thought he had spoken quite plainly of his attachment, and would propose at the next opportunity.

It may seem strange that he had not done so earlier. There were certain obstacles no doubt, and reticences characteristic of the period in which they were brought up. A definite check occurred in 1872, the year of Lady Blanche's death, when Balfour was kept a good deal at Whittingehame by business. Miss Lyttelton became engaged then to someone else. Lord Lyttelton insisted upon a year of hard work before there was any question of marriage. This period was hardly begun when the young man died.

This episode naturally set back the development of Balfour's relations with her, but it seems as if he had failed to realise the nature of her feelings for himself from a much earlier stage. If he had been a more decided wooer the other engagement might never have taken place. Hesitation is the easiest thing in the world to rationalise, but the real barrier here was hesitation itself. This he only learned for certain after her death. To a man of his temperament, more tolerant of most things than of bungling, this discovery, made too late, must

have been an almost insupportable aggravation of grief. Mrs. Talbot
writes:

> May was to him the embodiment of strength and spirit. The news of
> her death staggered him to the last degree. He has told me he walked
> for hours about the London streets, where—he never knew. He came to
> Hagley the day before the funeral, after having written a passionate little
> note to my brother Edward, enclosing a beautiful emerald ring of his
> mother's, which he was looking forward to give May as the engage-
> ment ring. He asked Edward to have it placed in her coffin.

Mrs. Talbot goes on to describe Balfour's utter breakdown during
the funeral service. Afterwards

> he made us promise not to tell others of his great attachment, not, I
> always felt, because he did not want others to know, but because he
> could only get along by not having sympathy because, if really moved,
> he could not restrain tears, and that would have been dreadful to him.

Mrs. Talbot was almost the only human being to whom Balfour
thereafter ever alluded to the subject. Till the end of his life she was
accustomed to speak freely to him about her sister. No one who witnessed his reactions in later life to sorrows, his own and other people's, will be surprised by her account of his behaviour at this time.
To such friends the theory that Balfour was cold at heart is ludicrous.
But he loathed display of emotion; fundamentally he was afraid of
it—it was one of the few things of which he was afraid—and this
coloured his reception of it in other people on all ordinary occasions.
In addition to the discomfort of stirred-up feelings he objected very
much to the waste of energy they involved. Energy was something
to be husbanded and harnessed to produce results. He never had it
in superabundance, and it ebbed quickly whenever he was mentally
or physically ill.

For some time after Miss Lyttelton's death, his active interest in
life flagged. In his Autobiography there is a parenthesis referring to
the years between 1875 and 1880, almost certainly a distant allusion
to this subject, possibly the only one that he ever put on paper.
Speaking of his long delay before taking part in debate during his
first Parliament he speaks of the flatness of contemporary politics,
and of other preoccupations. Then he adds: "Such excuses (and there
may have been others) sufficed for the moment."

Balfour had been a member of the House of Commons for a year before Miss Lyttelton fell ill. He drifted into the arena without effort. His entry was made in acquiescence to Lord Salisbury's suggestion, and his constituency was the Borough of Hertford, a seat traditionally swayed either by the Whig influence of the Cowpers at Panshanger, or by the Tory House of Cecil. At the General Election of 1874, which put Disraeli's last Ministry in power, the Hatfield candidate was unopposed. An Election Address, one speech, and a little personal canvassing, made up the sum of necessary activity. Here is the Address, the first essay of its kind from the pen that produced in time to come some of the famous State Papers of British history. Between those and this rather jejune document lay some fifty years of laborious, painful practice in the art of political writing.

Mr. Balfour's Election Address, 1874.

4 CARLTON GARDENS,
26/1/74.

GENTLEMEN

The sudden dissolution of Parliament again throws on you the responsibility of deciding what policy you mean to support. There is on the one side that Party, which during the term of its power has threatened every interest which it has not directly injured; which has passed measures, which, bad as they are in themselves, are yet worse when regarded as precedents, and whose declared policy, will, if carried out, destroy the political existence of this Borough.

On the other side there is the party, which, while aiming at social improvement, does not believe that that can be attained by the reckless subversion of existing institutions or the reckless destruction of existing interests.

Between these two you have now to make your choice, and it is in the hope that you will choose the latter that I venture to offer myself as a successor to your present respected representative. I earnestly trust that, as you were constant to the fortunes of the Conservative Party in the hour of its greatest adversity, you will not desert it in what we hope may be the hour of its triumph.

Should you do me the honour to elect me, it will always be my endeavour to promote, to the utmost of my ability, the local interests of the Borough.

As far as time will permit before the Election I hope to wait on every Elector and to explain personally my views on the Political Questions of the day.

I remain
your obedient servant
ARTHUR JAMES BALFOUR.

The speech took more out of its author than did the composition of these rounded sentences. It was the third or fourth of his life, the earlier ones having been made at tenants' dinners or the like. In his Autobiography, Balfour says that on all these occasions his "preliminary sufferings were acute," and proceeds to criticise his own style of oratory throughout life, deploring the lack of verbal memory, which "after half a century of speech-making" still left a "lamentable difference between the written and the spoken word." It would be very premature to discuss in this chapter the justice of this self-made criticism, for in the Parliament of 1874–1880 he gave the world little material for judgment. In the first two sessions he never opened his mouth, and when the House rose at the end of 1874 he set out with Mr. Spencer Lyttelton, for a tour round the world, which lasted six months. Apart from the Madeira journeys of his childhood and a short trip to Egypt in 1873, this was the first time he had travelled outside Europe. It was also the last for forty-two years. He had proved to his own satisfaction that no pleasures lay on the other side of any ocean which were worth, to him, the misery of crossing it. When next he faced the Atlantic it was as Chief of the Allied Mission to Washington in 1917.

"Comatose most of the time," is the first entry about him in Spencer Lyttelton's diary, written off Sandy Hook on August 7th, 1875. Even on land Balfour was a disappointing sightseer. They did not stop long in New York, for by August 11th they were at Lake George, "struck by advertisements of Vinegar Bitters painted all over the rocks and hill-sides." Then at Niagara, putting on bathing dresses and mackintoshes to go under the Falls. Then on their way to Chicago in Pullman cars, new experiences, "which A. J. B. hated, because he cannot rest his head against the low seats, and read his book instead of looking at scenery." Then they went to San Francisco and "walked through the Chinese quarter and were on the whole bored and hated the dust." From there they drove out to see the Big Trees, which were among the few things on this journey which Balfour used to talk about afterwards with enthusiasm. So too was the Yosemite Valley. After that they very soon embarked for New Zealand, where they spent about two months of an exceptionally cold wet spring. There was hardly any railway in those days, and conveyance over atrocious roads was mostly by coach. The two young men always travelled outside when they could. Spencer Lyttelton's diary leaves the impression that they were usually wet to the skin during these journeys, and that if the leaders did not kick over the traces, the wheelers broke the splinter-bar to pieces. The coaches were always overcrowded, and once Balfour failed to get a seat at all, and rode the fifty-six miles between Ohinemutu and Lake Taupo by himself, on a very indifferent horse. At Ohinemutu they ran out of money and borrowed £10 from an innkeeper. On arrival at Napier, they borrowed more money from someone unspecified, oddly contenting themselves this time with £5. From Napier they sailed for Wellington and separated for a fortnight, after which Balfour returned, "having had a successful and amusing expedition." It was probably then that he bought the property of Pahiatua near Christchurch, a stock-run which is still in the possession of his heir, and was one of the most successful investments of money that he ever made on his own initiative.

At the end of November, 1875, they spent six dull days at Invercargill, waiting for a steamer to take them to Melbourne. Balfour lay in his bunk on board this vessel from Monday till Saturday. Lyttelton relates that he sang at intervals on such occasions, but unfortunately the diary does not endorse a family legend that he was wont also to play melodies by Handel on a concertina in his recumbent position. Certain it is, that he did perform on the concertina at home at this period of his life, using it to supply the tenor part in glees and choruses sung in the privacy of the family circle. Four elaborate concertinas known as "the Infernals" were in existence at Whittingehame a generation later, and were distributed by him eventually to his younger nephews and nieces. When he presented them he swung the instrument and pressed the keys with old familiarity, remarking that his fingers had got stiff.

To return to less inspiring facts. The travellers stayed a few days at Melbourne, and then set out for Sydney, Balfour travelling overland alone. But the swinging seas could not be permanently dodged, and by Christmas they were on board ship again. On January 23rd, 1876, they reached Singapore. In the diary of this part of the journey a first mention is made of "A. J. B.'s servant, who got very drunk on voyage about January 16th." Balfour's instinct would undoubtedly have been to ignore this lapse, but a repetition of it while they were staying with Sir William Jervoise at Government House forced him to take steps. He gave the man his ticket back to England, where (a note in the diary states) he re-engaged him. Subsequently he got drunk once more, and enlisted.

This domestic episode probably ran its course during the only in-
terregnum in the management of Balfour's household by one or
other of his sisters. It was while he was at Singapore that he learned
of the engagement of his eldest sister Eleanor to Henry Sidgwick.
The news decided him to cut short his projected tour in India, and
return to England immediately. Eleanor's marriage, like that of his
sister Evelyn to John Strutt five years before, was to a close friend,
whom he rejoiced to welcome inside the family. But it caused more
disturbance to his own life. It involved, in the first place, rearrange-
ments, for Eleanor had acted as head of his house since their
mother's death. All through their lives (she outlived him) the
sympathy between them was very close. He was always alert for
the sound of her low voice in general conversation, and could often
be observed catching her eye. They would wink at each other, this
sister being the best exponent of an art much practised in the family
of closing one eye without the slightest contortion of the facial
muscles.

Eleanor Balfour was in intellect and in character one of the most
remarkable in a family whose average in these things was high.
After her marriage she took a leading part in the movement for
women's University education, and in later life in the scientific
work of the Society for Psychical Research. Investigation of psychic
phenomena was only beginning in the late seventies. All the Balfours became much interested in it, together with the brothers-in-
law, Lord Rayleigh and Professor Sidgwick. This had important
results later, both upon research into the subject and on Balfour's
own attitude towards the problems of survival.

It would be difficult to find a parallel among any group of relations, all under middle age, for the intellectual driving power assembled round the Whittingehame dinner table at this date, now
that Sidgwick the philosopher and Rayleigh the physicist had been
added to the party.

Arthur Balfour's third brother, Francis, was already a Fellow of
the Royal Society. In 1876 he was at work on the book on Comparative Embryology which made him the greatest authority on
that subject. A very few years later he was Professor of Animal
Morphology at Cambridge—a Chair which he was the first to hold
—which indeed was created largely as the result of the advancement
his work had brought about in that branch of biological science.

Gerald, the fourth brother,[1] afterwards to be Arthur Balfour's colleague in two Cabinets, shared his eldest brother's interest in metaphysics, and was besides a good classical scholar. He took a First at Trinity, and became a Fellow and Lecturer of his College. Gerald did not follow Arthur into the House of Commons until 1885, and his interest in politics, keen enough while it lasted, waned far sooner. He never sought re-election after 1906.

Eustace, the youngest of the family, became an architect. He would perhaps have been equally happy as a soldier, but the Army was one of the few spheres of life that lay rather outside the wide ranging interests of Whittingehame. Eustace later found scope for that side of himself in the Volunteer Movement, and before the end of his life (he died in 1912) had commanded the London Scottish for many years. He was the tallest of the brothers, not one of whom was under six feet, Arthur a little above it. They were long-legged, slender, and rather loose-limbed, all of them, except Gerald (whose features were of classic regularity and beauty), sharing the family characteristics, short noses, rather large mouths, eyes very wide apart, set flush with the face, hazel or brown, very expressive and luminous.

It was a very self-sufficing group, highly trained in the habit of independent judgment, immensely respectful of the freedom of the individual, declining to criticise conduct, ruthless in criticising ideas. Accuracy was a passion. The family would. dispute as long and as eagerly over the posing of an argument as over the point itself. They possessed in common a strong sense of humour, all of them, for example, finding anything irrational in behaviour or speech irresistibly comic. Personal chaff or personal remarks were not very popular with them. They were united by intense interest in each other's opinions, and intense pleasure in each other's society.

The atmosphere of such a circle is the most difficult of all things to reproduce. To strangers it seemed sometimes hard to breathe; to those accustomed to it it seemed the most invigorating to every faculty. It remained an active influence in the lives of three generations of the family in a way that could hardly have happened if Arthur Balfour had had a wife and children of his own.

After the marriage of Mrs. Sidgwick, Miss Alice Balfour, the youngest of the sisters, took her place as mistress of Whittingehame

[1] Afterwards second Earl of Balfour.

House and at 4 Carlton Gardens. This arrangement was never afterwards changed.

Balfour returned from abroad in the spring of 1876. His aunt, Lady Salisbury, told him that it was time he took some active part in politics, and he saw that Lord Salisbury, though he said nothing, agreed with her. Indeed it was undeniable that after two years in Parliament a maiden speech was overdue. Nevertheless some months passed before it was delivered. On August 10th, 1876, Balfour first addressed the House of Commons. In his Autobiography he thus describes the occasion:

The object of a full-dress "maiden speech" is to show members of the House of Commons how admirably one of their untried colleagues is able to address them. But this was no object of mine. I knew well enough that I was no heaven-born orator. What as yet I did not know was how far, on a stage so unfamiliar and so alarming as the House of Commons, I could maintain unembarrassed the thread of my discourse, pursue an argument without the aid of notes, and find on the spur of the moment words more or less adequate to my ideas. Until I learned something from experience on points like these, I could not make up my mind whether it was worth my while to make politics my profession. I did not doubt that I had capacity, for modesty was never my worst fault. But I had some misgivings as to whether I had capacity of the right kind; and my object, therefore, was not to impress the House with my eloquence—a task far beyond my powers—but to convince myself that I possessed, in however rudimentary a form, the qualities required in an assembly which lives by debate.

How could this task be best accomplished? It seemed to me that the Parliamentary environment in which I should be most at my ease would be one in which the occasion was informal and the audience small. Informality could best be secured by choosing a period when the House was in Committee. How about a small audience? At first sight nothing could seem easier of attainment. The art of emptying the Chamber is widely diffused, and requires no special cultivation. But then, unfortunately, the House I dreamed of addressing was not one already thinned by my own eloquence, but one where the audience had been rendered "fit though few" either by the exertions of previous speakers, or by the unattractive character of the subject under discussion. How was this to be secured? The surest and most dignified expedient was to select as my theme a question undeniably important, but intrinsically dull; perhaps with a technical side, and in any case recalcitrant to rhetorical treatment.

These strategic principles were supplemented in actual practice by judicious tactics. On August 10th, the business of the House was the

Committee stage of the Indian Budget. It dealt with an immense variety of subjects only connected with each other by the fact that they all related to India. No Party issue was raised; no division was expected; the House was ill attended; and of the members present the majority were kept in their places not so much by the desire of any individual to hear what the others had to say, as by his fear of missing a chance of saying something himself. This at least was my case.

But though in this respect I resembled my neighbours, in another I probably stood alone. They wanted an audience, I on this occasion wanted none. I desired security, not success; and when the House was in Committee, when the attendance was poor, and no dramatic developments were possible, security was within my reach. Should I feel myself on the brink of failure, I had only to sit down, and in all probability no one save the next speaker would notice the event, and he would probably be grateful!

Even these precautions did not content me. In order to complete the story, let me add that my chosen theme was Indian silver currency, and my chosen hour was about eight o'clock. The reader least experienced in House of Commons habits will realise that in these conditions I enjoyed to the fullest extent the advantages of speaking in a silent and friendly solitude.

So much for my first appearance on the floor of the House. Some may be inclined to ask what purpose is served by this circumstantial account of a dull speech, on a dull subject, delivered in an empty House by an anxious beginner. It contains no hints on the arts of debate. It says nothing either to warn or encourage intending orators. It certainly does not present the speaker himself in an interesting, still less in an heroic, light. Wherein, then, lies its interest?

Its sole interest is autobiographical, and its sole importance for me lies in the fact that it marks the real beginning of my Parliamentary career. To be sure, my success was but a modest one; yet it sufficed. No one will ever know what I said on this (to me) all-important occasion; for I have forgotten all the details myself, and there is little in Hansard to remind me of them. I remember only that I spoke on Indian currency, and that in my own opinion I made my case. I had thus taken the first step in my Parliamentary adventure, and taken it without disaster. For the moment this sufficed.[1]

Balfour's strong Parliamentary instinct surely had the upper hand of him when he wrote this. Setting out to describe his own maiden speech, the atmosphere of the House of Commons overwhelms it. The master of Parliamentary technique cannot give his mind, after

[1] *Chapters of Autobiography,* p. 91 *et seq.*

the lapse of fifty years, to recalling what a back bencher said during the dinner hour. He can and does remember what it is to address the House for the first time. He can still sympathise with the tyro's qualms, and approve of his preparations. But for the result he has nothing but a withering epitaph, "A dull speech on a dull subject."

After the Indian Currency debate of 1876 Balfour was silent in the House until the Universities Bill of 1877 was in Committee. At that stage he joined in, proposing one or two Amendments, the most important being one to empower the Universities to give degrees to women, on the ground that women's importance as educators was increasing. The proposal of course had no chance, and he withdrew it on the same night, but not before Mr. Beresford Hope, his uncle by marriage, had opposed it on the ground of what it might lead to, and Lord Edmond Fitzmaurice had observed that he thought there was a great deal too much discussion about women both inside the House and out of doors. "It was disgusting to hear so much of it," he said.

After this excursion into Committee work Balfour tried his hand at legislation, and in the spring of 1878 brought in a Bill for reform of the Burials Law. He sent it in draft to Lord Salisbury. "A very good Bill," wrote his uncle, "but, if you bring it in, you will probably find yourself pretty well protected from the curse that attaches to those of whom all men speak well."

This was a true prediction. The Nonconformists, one of whose grievances it was to remove, had no particular wish to see an argument for Disestablishment weakened. The High Church Tories disapproved for tactical reasons. The member for Cambridge University, Mr. Beresford Hope, was the wet blanket again. He argued with his nephew in private. "To make concessions anywhere," wrote Balfour, "was, in his opinion, to weaken the defences everywhere. Nothing should be freely given lest all should be taken away. I was little moved by this theory of political dynamics, but I recognised that it would appeal to many of my friends."

The Bill was none the less brought in, and "talked out" the same day by Mr. Beresford Hope.

These various efforts make up the sum total of Balfour's mild experiments into his own fitness for a political career in the last Disraelian Parliament. They left him more than sceptical upon that

point. In the meantime, life was gaining in attraction for him outside the House of Commons.

These were years when the "Eastern Question" preoccupied the
country. In 1876 Lord Salisbury had represented the British Government at the Conference of the Powers in Constantinople, and
there "international politics had gripped him with a hold never
again to be loosened." [1] In March 1878, he succeeded Lord Derby
as Foreign Secretary. As soon as he took his new office he invited
his nephew to become his parliamentary Private Secretary. As such
Balfour went with the British Delegation to the Congress of Berlin.
His memories of this, his first contact with international affairs,
were chiefly of the parties and banquets, which were anathema to
Lord Salisbury, but far from that to his nephew, unweighted with
any responsibilities, and already developing the unaffected pleasure
in society which stayed with him to his old age.

Forty years after, when the Peace Conference of Paris was closing
the epoch of history that opened at Berlin in 1878, and Balfour in
his turn held the office of British Foreign Secretary, he still liked
to end his day's work with some sort of social gathering. In Berlin
these occasions were the best opportunity for a Private Secretary to
have at least a look at the great Europeans, Prince Gortchakoff the
Russian, Count Andrassy in his gorgeous Magyar dress, and Bismarck. Balfour was introduced to Prince Bismarck by Lady Odo
Russell, wife of the British Ambassador in Berlin.

"Are you a descendant," the great man asked him, "of the
Balfour of Burleigh who plays his part in Sir Walter Scott's *Old
Mortality?*" Balfour had to disclaim that ancestry, but told the
Prince how much he felt gratified, as a Scotsman, by his knowledge
of Scott's novels. "Ah," said Bismarck, "when we were young we all
had to read Sir Walter. He was considered so very proper." [2]

In the years 1877 and 1878 Balfour had more leisure to dispose of
than ever again after the end of that Parliament. He spent much of
his time in hearing music, and took pains to hear the kind of music
he liked.

There were the Saturday and Monday "Pops" at the St. James'
Hall, the Orchestral Concerts at the Crystal Palace, and the Richter
Concerts. He attended all these pretty constantly, and arranged
besides for music in his own house. For years there were two pianos

[1] *Life of Lord Salisbury,* by Lady G. Cecil, Vol. II, p. 126.
[2] See *Chapters of Autobiography,* p. 110.

in the large drawing-room at No. 4 Carlton Gardens, and Balfour provided the eight-handed scores for those who came to play. He loved Beethoven and Bach, and in varying degree the other great classical composers; but the *grande passion* of his musical life was for Handel. This love he never deserted or outgrew. It was concentrated on the Oratorios, perhaps chiefly upon *Israel,* and, a shade less, upon the *Messiah.*

Of these two immortal creations [he wrote] it is hard to say which is the most perfect. But there can be no doubt, I think, not only that *Israel* is the most characteristically Handelian, but that it stands out amid all creations of the last century, whether of poets, painters or musicians, unique in its unborrowed majesty.

This quotation is taken from his Essay on Handel, published in 1887.[1] This Essay is a most finished piece of work, both from the critical and literary point of view. It shows the writer's deep familiarity with Handel's music, and the age in which Handel lived and for which he wrote. The polished beauty of the style is thrown into relief every now and then by a break into the personal warmth which occasionally shot through Balfour's writing when his subject was something that really touched his affections. As regards Handel, it appears as the article approaches the subject of his defects.

It is not, perhaps, very easy to say it, and it is not rendered much easier by the fact that the writer is obliged to confess to a degree of affectionate devotion to the great composer which it is not possible, or I had almost even said, which it is not desirable that the majority of readers should show....In art as well as in life it must be given us sometimes to judge as lovers, and not with the chill impartiality of mere intimate acquaintance.

The Essay on Handel is an enduring tribute. Balfour offered another to the fame of his beloved musician. In 1873 *Belshazzar* was performed in full at the Albert Hall for the second time[2] in the nineteenth century, on his initiative, and with his financial guarantee. Why he chose this particular Oratorio for revival is not on record, but it may well have been because of the number of

[1] See *Essays and Addresses,* by the Rt. Hon. Arthur James Balfour. Edinburgh. David Douglas. 1893.
[2] The other occasion was Exeter Hall, in 1847.

good choruses it contained, and the great variety of their treatment. The Albert Hall was fairly full, but the success of the performance was mainly a *succès d'estime*.

Music was a sphere—one of the few—in which Balfour did not, or could not, move with his times. He never loved Wagner, though he went in 1895 to Bayreuth. Modern composers seldom gave him much pleasure.

The first instalment of *The Defence of Philosophic Doubt* appeared in *Mind* in 1878. In 1877 it was being put on paper. To Balfour literary writing was always a slow, painful, exacting process. Heaps of manuscript heavily erased testify to the toil which went into the final limpidity of his style. The invention of the typewriter did little to relieve even the manual part of the labour. He seldom dictated anything except letters. First drafts of his books, pamphlets, and memoranda continued to be made in his own hand, and he worked over the typed copies again and again, transposing phrases, substituting words, working up towards his own very high standard of compression and lucidity.

Talking, many years later, about the period of his youth, Balfour said:

I took *Defence of Philosophic Doubt* very seriously. I thought I was making a contribution to religious thought of an original kind, and whatever may be its merits it *was* the solid background of twenty years of my life. In my youth it was my great safeguard against the *feeling* of frivolity. This is much more important now—biographically—than the book itself.

The first book, although it was composed at greater leisure, probably entailed greater effort than any of its successors. All these started from the original standpoint marked out in *Defence of Philosophic Doubt*. That standpoint is not unconcerned with a question vital to the understanding of any life—his personal attitude towards religious belief. The title, *Defence of Philosophic Doubt*, led to some misunderstanding. It was all that the great majority of people knew of the book, and its meaning was hardly self-explanatory. It was easily assumed that the "Doubt" referred to creeds, and that the author was unorthodox to the point of agnosticism. This notion was very wide of the mark. The Doubt here defended is doubt of the principle that everything which cannot be proved by scientific means is incapable of proof, and that everything inconsistent with science is thereby disproved. The book is an attack on the "advanced thinkers" who claimed to speak in the name of science. It is an examination of the bases on which belief in science and belief in religion should properly rest, leading to the conclusion that their foundations are distinct, and that neither of them is built solely upon proof or reason. Convinced of this, the "conflict between religion and science," which still continued to trouble many minds, could not exist for Balfour. "I, and an indefinite number of other persons, if we contemplate religion and science as unproved systems of belief standing side by side, feel a practical need for both."

It follows from this that he had little sympathy with those "apologists" for religion, "the end of whose labours appears to be to explain, or explain away, every appearance of contradiction" with science. Consistency can be bought at too high a price. Religious truth cannot always be so expressed as to be consistent with itself. Why then should it necessarily be expressed so as to be consistent with science? If it were so, what would become of religious mysticism?

This is not the attitude of an agnostic, nor is this the language.

Even could I command the most fervid and persuasive eloquence, could I rouse with power the slumbering feelings which find in Religion their only lasting satisfaction, could I compel every reader to long earnestly and with passion for some living share in that Faith which has been the spiritual life of millions ignorant alike of Science and Philosophy, this is not the occasion on which to do so. I should shrink from dragging into a controversy pitched throughout in another key, thoughts whose full and intimate nature it is given to few adequately to express, and which, were I one of those few, would seem strangely misplaced at the conclusion of this dry and scholastic argument.

In later writings Balfour makes absolutely clear his belief in the existence of a personal God.

The influence of his definite faith upon some of the friends of his young manhood is shown in a letter from one of them, dated 1916.

MY DEAR ARTHUR,

...When I look back on the troublesome and most critical time of our making up our minds whether we could intellectually accept Christianity or not, in our vast ignorance it was a grand support to us to know that in your case faith in the Creed was compatible with clearness of thought; and if ever you are inclined, as most people are at times, to look upon your efforts for good as often frustrated, don't forget what real help you gave to two wanderers, without probably suspecting it at the time.

Direct allusions to his private feelings on this most intimate of subjects were not often made in conversation even with those nearest to him. But none who shared his daily life ever doubted the importance in his eyes of the things that are unseen and eternal. The dogmatic differences which divide some Christian bodies from each other were not however considered important. He was confirmed in the Church of England while he was at Eton, and was ever afterwards a communicant in that Church, as well as in the Church of Scotland. He held himself to be member of both and had no sympathy with the point of view that found this difficult of acceptance. Communion was held quarterly at the Parish Church at Whittingehame, and he always attended it when he was at home. At Whittingehame every Sunday evening family prayers were read by him. They consisted of the Lord's Prayer, the General Confession, and prayers from the Anglican liturgy, including often the Collect for the Sunday, and a chapter from the Bible, which he always chose himself; Isaiah, or the Psalms, or St. Paul's Epistles were perhaps drawn upon most. To some who knew his renderings of them, certain passages of the Bible must always be associated with the scene. The large dining-room entirely in shadow, the family, guests, and household, sitting round the walls; the only light coming from a pair of candles on a small table in the middle of the room, at which he sat. His reading was rather slow, without dramatic emphasis, but bringing out every inherent shade of beauty and meaning. It deeply impressed all his hearers. It was impossible for attention to wander from it for a moment.

Chapter III

REAL POLITICS

1880–1885

Balfour and Lord Beaconsfield. The "Fourth Party." Ireland and the "Kilmainham Treaty." Death of Balfour's brothers. Francis Maitland Balfour. Balfour and Churchill. Lady Frances Balfour. "Elijah's Mantle." Fall of the Liberal Government.

MARCH 6th, 1880, was the moment chosen by Lord Beaconsfield for dissolving the Parliament, whose natural life was running out. A bye-election had cheered the hearts of the Party organisers, who were deluded enough to imagine that a continuance of Conservative government was in the category of probabilities. The Tory Party were as much taken aback by the wholesale rejection now preparing for them at the hands of the country, as the Liberals had been by their defeat in 1874.

Members dispersed to their constituencies. Balfour took up his abode in the Salisbury Arms at Hertford. The county town was an easy seat to hold, as seats went just then. There was a Liberal candidate in the field, Mr. Edward Bowen, then a master at Harrow, and author of "Forty Years On," and other famous Harrow songs. This brilliant but whimsical man was not so adapted for political controversy as to make him a very formidable opponent, but the tide ran his way, and good speakers supported him. Balfour had to work harder for his second return to Westminster than for his first. However, on April 1st he was elected by a majority of 164, a result with which he felt quite satisfied.

Hertford polled early in the contest, and its Member's services were needed at once in Midlothian, where Lord Dalkeith wanted help in his hopeless struggle against the overwhelming personality of Mr. Gladstone. Balfour, as a Lothian man, was bound to be thrown into the central battle the moment he had won his own. But before going north he stopped at Hatfield for an hour or two.

Lord Salisbury and most of his family had gone abroad for the period of the General Election, in which peers were then precluded from taking any part. But Hatfield was not deserted. As Balfour drove up to the house, he saw, standing on the steps of its majestic north front, closing the long vista of the avenue, a solitary figure gazing towards him. It was Lord Beaconsfield. Hatfield had been placed at his disposal because it was an accessible, yet quiet, headquarters for the Prime Minister at such a time. So it happened that the first congratulation after the victory which formed the real prelude to Balfour's political career was his greeting from the veteran leader of his Party. For a fraction of time the two stood together and alone in the doorway of the mighty House. The little episode dissolved almost as soon as it took shape. Nevertheless it stamped itself on the elusive memory of the younger man. "I recall him," wrote Balfour, "a strange, almost a picturesque figure, dignified and calm, though not, I thought, unmoved. We exchanged electoral news, little of it good, and I hurried off without unnecessary delay." [1]

The scene had no traceable consequences, and no practical importance. It was neither the first nor the last time that Dizzy and Balfour met and talked. But it may not seem too fantastic, perhaps, to imagine that, in the emotions generated by the time and place, some virtue passed that day from the old man to the other, a virtue that Dizzy possessed still in superabundance, in spite of age, a virtue in which Balfour, in spite of youth, was deficient still—that priceless gift for Parliamentary success—eagerness for the fray.

Be that as it may, the first authentic sparks were soon to appear. It is probable that on that April afternoon Balfour put away for ever any lingering intention for a purely meditative career. Certainly in the latter years of his life he talked about the General Election of 1880, and said that he had then made up his mind, if defeated at Hertford, to leave politics for philosophy.[2] When defeat was refused him, he did not, it is true, determine to abandon philosophy altogether for politics. But nevertheless he now came to the real parting of the ways.

In this Parliament of 1880–1885 the amateur bound himself apprentice, and began, by regular attendance in the House and constant practice in speaking, to acquire style and mastery in the art

[1] *Chapters of Autobiography*, p. 123.
[2] My authority for this remark is Professor G. M. Trevelyan.

of debate. Naturally it was some time before the House itself noticed that the gulf which separates the trained man from the most gifted dilettante had been crossed, but before the first Session was over, one expert observer had perceived the small beginnings of the transition. At the end of August, 1880, Henry Lucy wrote:

> The member for Hertford is one of the most interesting young men in the House. He is not a good speaker, but he is endowed with the rich gift of conveying the impression that presently he will be a successful Parliamentary debater, and that in the meantime it is well that he should practise. He is a pleasing specimen of the highest form of the culture and good breeding which stands to the credit of Cambridge University. He is not without desire to say hard things of the adversary opposite, and sometimes yields to the temptation. But it is ever done with such sweet and gentle grace, and is smoothed over by such earnest protestations of innocent intention, that the adversary rather likes it than otherwise.[1]

The House in which Balfour began to make a name happened to offer perfect conditions for developing his parliamentary gifts. The lack of talent for Opposition leadership on the Conservative Front Bench was as great a piece of luck for him as for Lord Randolph Churchill, though in a different way. For the maturer and more ambitious genius of Lord Randolph it cleared the field for the exercise of his tactical ability, and enabled him to create a group of freelances whose services he could lend or withhold from his official chiefs. It was this, more than his brilliant speaking, which made him a Parliamentary force, and one of the rare examples of a man who built a great Parliamentary reputation solely on his record in Opposition. It is not a belittling of this achievement to say it was made possible only because the heavy guns of the Conservative Party were concentrated at that moment in the House of Lords, and that the leader in the Commons was "no more a match for Mr. Gladstone than a wooden three-decker would be for a Dreadnought...."[2] In his Autobiography, Balfour observes that "there would surely never have been a Churchill had there not also been a Northcote." What Northcote was to Churchill, so was the Fourth Party—Churchill's creation—to Balfour: a gift of Fortune.

Nevertheless, his connection with it was semi-accidental in the

[1] See Henry Lucy. *The Gladstone Parliament*, 1880–1885, pp. 84-5.
[2] See *Chapters of Autobiography*, p. 141.

beginning, and never close at any time. Lord Randolph and his two friends, Mr. Gorst and Sir Henry Drummond-Wolff, had chosen seats on the Front Bench below the gangway on the Opposition side of the House as the best base for their frontal assaults on the Government, and their flank attacks on their own leaders. Balfour took his place beside them because, as he said, he had room there for his legs. So he drifted into their neighbourhood, just as throughout life he drifted so often, but so seldom into any position where he did not wish to be. He found this one very congenial. It involved no commitments. In the first two years, at any rate, the Fourth Party stood for no principle beyond those common to the Conservative Party as a whole. The absence of serious purpose is perhaps what distinguishes this famous little group from its predecessors and successors in the history of Party politics inside the House of Commons. As Balfour himself wrote:

it possessed no distinctive creed; its very name was an accident of debate; it consisted at its gayest and best of no more than four friends who sat together in the House, supported each other in difficulties, consulted freely on points of tactics, and made it their business to convince the Government that large majorities did not adequately cover a multitude of sins.[1]

There was a freedom in this programme of pure ginger which suited Balfour's temperament. Like a poker-player whose hand is not to his taste he could stand aside from the game whenever he chose, without prejudicing his power to return. The controversy which raged over the attempts of Mr. Bradlaugh, the atheist, to take the Parliamentary Oath were a case in point. In these Debates the Fourth Party first tasted blood, and through more than one Session they delighted in intensifying the passions aroused, for the embarrassment of the Government. Balfour however never spoke on any Bradlaugh night. To profess horror at any man's opinions about religion may have been beyond his powers.

At all events, when talking about it many years later, he said:

I see it remarked that I left it to the others out of indifference. I'm quite sure I never did make a speech about Bradlaugh, but I'm not so sure it was because of indifference. It doesn't seem to occur to people that I might not be prepared to entrust my theological views to that partnership. However, that's a detail. My point is that as the question of Party

[1] *Chapters of Autobiography*, p. 135.

leadership became a practical one, a second phase set in. Randolph himself realised what my attitude would be and never expected me to act differently from the way I did.

The fact is that neither liberty nor stimulating company, much as he liked both, would have enticed Balfour into association with the Fourth Party if his position there had conflicted with his personal loyalty to Lord Salisbury. In its first phase, however, it did not, and both the great Conservative Chiefs in the Upper House had a soft spot in their hearts for Lord Randolph and his group. Whatever may have been the opinions held by Sir Stafford Northcote and his lieutenants, "Marshall and Snelgrove" (as Lord Randolph called Sir Richard Cross and Mr. W. H. Smith), about the relative merits of decorum and pugnacity in Opposition, the preferences of Lords Beaconsfield and Salisbury were hardly veiled. In the autumn recess of 1880, at the end of a Session in which the Fourth Party had flustered their leaders in the Commons almost as much as they had annoyed the Government, Lord Beaconsfield told Sir Henry Drummond-Wolff that he sympathised with their feelings about the representatives of respectability in the Party, because he had never been respectable himself. Lord Salisbury went down to speak at Woodstock, Lord Randolph's own constituency. Balfour was the go-between in fixing the engagement, and his way of approaching his uncle shows how frank and easy their intercourse already was, on political, as on personal, matters.

AUCHNASHELLACH,
Ross-shire,
September 29, 1880.

MY DEAR UNCLE ROBERT,

I enclose a letter from R. Churchill requesting me to ask you to make a speech to his constituents on the occasion of your visit to Blenheim. The proposal strikes me as a cool one; and if you do not feel inclined to accede to it, you have only to let me know, and I will get you off in a manner that will cause no awkwardness. It is possible that you may wish to deliver yourself on things in general during the autumn, and if so, perhaps this would be as convenient an opportunity as any other....

On the other hand, what Randolph says about your speaking to his constituents being an honour to the "Fourth Party" may really be an argument against your doing so. Northcote certainly dislikes us. Why he should do so is not very clear. A so-called Party which (if it is to be taken seriously at all) consists of only four persons, which has no organisation, no leader, and no distinctive principles, cannot be regarded as dangerous, though it may be useful.

Wolff has always asserted that Northcote's hostility is owing to a scheme he is cherishing of forming eventually a junction with the Whigs. But putting aside the fact that Wolff always suspects everybody of everything, I fail to see how the present action of members below the gangway can either help or hinder any such political combination. I can hardly believe Northcote such a fool as to think that the Tory Party can purchase the future support of the Whigs by showing present incapacity to resist the Liberals. My own view of Northcote's attitude is that he has a constitutional dislike to decided action, and that he objects to, and feels himself incapable of, using independent action in his followers— a trait of character quite as obvious to his own Front Bench as his behaviour is to ours.

Lord Salisbury, accepting the Woodstock invitation, wrote:

I am disposed, with you, to doubt that Northcote expects any coalition with the Whigs. He may hope by adopting a moderate attitude, to lure one or two Whig rank and file to become Tories, and this, if Gladstone is violent, is not unlikely to occur. I think his tactics so far are wise. The leader even of a diminished Party must behave as the arbitrator between its various sections, and if he has fair ground for hoping to attract a new section they must come within the scope of the arbitration. But that attitude involves no censure or slight on any one of the sections, who are not in the least bound to adopt the same attitude. If there is any feeling in his mind against the Fourth Party (which I see no ground for believing) it is probably due to the great impudence with which Wolff talks about him.

In the Parliament of 1880–1885 the development of Balfour's relations with Lord Salisbury in public life is the most interesting thread to follow. His connection with the Fourth Party has little importance to-day, except as it serves to bring out his loyalty to his kinsman and political Chief. This was met by a growth of confidence on Lord Salisbury's side, which, through time, became almost unbounded, and thus was produced that closeness of co-operation between the two which left its mark on twenty years of our political history.

Some months after the Woodstock Meeting the event happened which divides the life of the Fourth Party into two distinct phases. This event was Lord Beaconsfield's death on April 19th, 1881. After that, the Conservative leadership remained for a time in commission between Lord Salisbury in the House of Lords and Sir Stafford Northcote in the Commons. The Party being in Opposition, no urgent necessity arose to decide on a Commander-in-Chief, and (as Balfour wrote):

neither the practice of the Constitution nor Party loyalty debarred any Conservative from endeavouring to obtain a position which, when the time came, would justify him in hoping for the place left vacant by Lord Beaconsfield's death. No such ambition was ever explicitly avowed by Lord Randolph as far as I am aware. But that he resolved to reach, either in one step or two, the summit of the political ladder, I do not doubt; nor do I see in such an ambition anything to criticise.[1]

These sentences were written some forty years after Lord Randolph's meteor had completed its rapid curve and perhaps they hardly represent Balfour's contemporary view of its rise. He looked on with a sardonic eye at the bid for "Elijah's Mantle" and the subsequent effort to get control of the Party organisation. Meantime, his own star was mounting in less spectacular fashion during the two years of opposition work.

The day came at last when he was roused, and on that day for the first time he really held the House. On May 16th, 1882, the subject of Debate was the terms on which the Government had suddenly released Parnell and two other Irish leaders from Kilmainham Gaol, where they had been sent seven months before on warrants for intimidation and suspicion of treason. Mr. Winston Churchill, in his Life of his father, writes that "Mr. Balfour, speaking with altogether unexpected power, denounced the Kilmainham Treaty as 'an infamy.' This was the first speech that he had ever made that commanded general attention, or gave any promise of his future distinction."[2]

Balfour comments on this remark in his Autobiography:

On the particular occasion I was exceedingly indignant, and this may have improved my oratory. But what doubtless improved it still more was the debating practice I had enjoyed during two years of vigorous opposition.

Whatever the explanation, there is no doubt that he got between the joints of the Prime Minister's harness. Mr. Gladstone rose as

[1] *Chapters of Autobiography*, p. 152.
[2] *Life of Randolph Churchill*, by Winston Churchill, I, p. 211.

soon as Balfour sat down, and showed himself deeply incensed. His reproofs reverberate out of the old Hansard still, alive with the anger of an old man who has been hit to hurt by a young one. Years were to pass before Mr. Gladstone forgot or forgave the word "infamy," and Balfour rather regretted afterwards that he had used it. To understand the provocation and Mr. Gladstone's sensitiveness, it is necessary to recall what had happened.

Ever since the Liberal Ministry had taken office its impotence to uphold law and order in Ireland had been more and more demonstrated. In September 1880, Mr. Parnell had explained to the Irish people the use of a new weapon of terrorism:

When a man takes a farm from which another has been ejected, you must show him on the roadside, you must show him in the streets, you must show him at the shop counter, you must show him in the fair and in the marketplace, and even in the house of worship, by leaving him severely alone, by isolating him from his kind as if he were a leper of old—you must show him your detestation of the crime he has committed, and you may depend on it that there will be no man so full of avarice, so lost to shame, as to dare the public opinion of all right-thinking men, and to transgress your unwritten code of laws.

The Anglo-Irishman had taken the correct measure of his Celtic followers. The "right-thinking" men received his sinister instruction with roars of applause, and three days later peasants in Connaught were putting it into practice against Lord Erne's agent, Captain Boycott. Before the end of the year "boycotting" had become, as a Land Leaguer boasted, "a better weapon than any eighty-one-ton gun ever invented." In November, the Government staged a public display of their powerlessness to put down the Organisation which was terrorising the land. They decided to prosecute the Land League. An information was filed against its officers, the name of Parnell heading the list. The charge was conspiracy to prevent payment of rent, etc., and to create ill-will among Her Majesty's subjects.

Everybody knew beforehand that no Irish jury would give a verdict against the Land League. It was thought extraordinary that two men out of the twelve who sat in Dublin in January 1881 were found brave enough to hold out against an outright acquittal. When the disagreement was reported to the Judge, he said: "Let the jury be discharged. We shall not force an agreement." Bonfires were lit on every hill that night to acclaim the triumph of the League. The Government suspended the Habeas Corpus Act, and Mr. Gladstone moved in the House of Commons that a new Coercion Bill should take precedence of all other business.

Then ensued the famous sitting of forty-one hours which was only ended by the Speaker acting on his own responsibility. It was one of the deadliest of the blows through which the organised obstruction of the Irish Party forced the House of Commons to self-mutilation of its rights of Debate. But by March 1881, a Coercion Bill was through, and the Lord-Lieutenant of Ireland was thereby enabled to arrest all persons suspected of treasonable practices or agrarian offences, and keep them in prison for eighteen months.

Soon Kilmainham Gaol was full of Land Leaguers, but the Land League in the country waxed fat on this form of coercion. Ireland fell into such a condition that the Government actually considered whether they could afford even to try to break up the body which had almost become the only effective authority. As the Lord-Lieutenant pointed out to the Cabinet:

It must be remembered that the Land League has now taken very deep root, and that bad characters of every description take advantage of its organisation, and are enrolled in its local branches. If the restraining influence of the central body were withdrawn, and the local branches driven to become Secret Societies, crime, particularly assassination, might increase, for though the central body gives unity and strength to the movement, it does to a certain extent restrain crime.[1]

Mr. Gladstone now (February 1881) introduced a Land Bill. It was based on the tenants' "three F's"—Fair Rent, Fixity of Tenure, Free Sale. It set up Land Courts to determine the first, it enacted the second, and as for the third, it made sale free only on the tenants' side. Thus it deprived the landlords of all control over their property, and was as repugnant in principle to the Whigs in the Cabinet as it was to the Conservative Opposition. But the Irish landlords were not prepared for resistance. They were as much under the shadow of the Land League terror as the Government from which this Act was wrenched.

Mr. Gladstone's Land Act, in point of fact, was riddled with the

[1] Barry O'Brien, *Life of Charles Parnell*, Vol. I, p. 287.

imperfections of hastily contrived, perfunctorily discussed legislation. The attitude of the House of Commons (apart from the Irishmen) was summed up by the man who said that if the Prime Minister had asked the House to pass the Koran or the Nautical Almanac as an Irish Land Bill, he would have met with no difficulty. Its most glaring deficiency was its failure to settle the question of arrears of rent. Nevertheless it removed too many genuine grievances of the Irish tenant population to suit the political agitators. Mr. Parnell found himself in a quandary. The "uncrowned king of Ireland" knew himself really the vassal of the American organisations who financed the Land League. Therefore he dared not support the Bill. On the other hand he had neither the power, nor the will, to wreck it in passage through Parliament. He never took the view that the movement for independence fattened on unsatisfied grievances. "My opinion is," he once said, "that everything they give us makes for Home Rule, and we should take everything. The better off the people are, the better Nationalists they will be. The starving man is not a good Nationalist."[1]

He could not lead a united Party for the Bill. So he took a middle course. Knowing the Bill was safe he abstained (with rather more than half his followers) from voting on the Second Reading, but in Committee brought his men to the rescue of certain clauses. Then, when the Act became law, he began in Ireland a series of brilliantly conceived moves to control its operation. To keep up the agitation, he forbade a rush of rack-rented tenants to the new Land Courts, but sent up instead a few selected cases, none of them examples of particular hardship. He caused the Land League convention to pass this Resolution:

That, pending the result of the test cases, no Member of the League shall apply to the Courts to fix his rent without obtaining the consent of the branch of the League to which he belongs.

On this the Government had a spasm—of exasperation rather than of courage. On October 12th, 1881, Mr. Parnell and two of his lieutenants were arrested and sent to Kilmainham Gaol. The instant result was the issue, from Kilmainham, of the Manifesto calling on the tenants of Ireland to pay no rent till the Government had restored the constitutional rights of the people.

[1] Barry O'Brien, *Life of Charles Parnell,* Vol. I, p. 292.

The command was generally obeyed. Moreover the leader's prophecy of the consequences of his imprisonment was fulfilled. "What will happen if they arrest you, Mr. Parnell?" one of his followers had asked. Lifting a glass of champagne to his lips Parnell answered: "Captain Moonlight will take my place." He said it gloomily. He was not personally enamoured of the terror that walks in darkness. But Ireland was given over to that through the winter of 1881–1882. Boycotting, houghing of cattle, burning of farm buildings, beating and torturing of people who paid rent, went on unchecked. Actual murder was kept under to some extent by police protection. Thirteen hundred people were receiving this in February 1882.

Mr. Parnell became uneasy at the success of "Captain Moonlight." Like some other monarchs he grew jealous of the power of his appointed Regent, and determined to resume control. On this the Cabinet in London were as keen as he was himself. Their dislike of coercion had been sharpened by its ill-success in the form in which they had applied it. They were more than ready to give concession a turn. Therefore the negotiations opened by Mr. Parnell in the middle of April, through the medium of an Irish Member of Parliament, Captain O'Shea, were sympathetically received. The basis was that Parnell should abandon the "No Rent" Manifesto and declare against outrage, if and when the Government announced a plan for dealing with arrears of rent satisfactory to the Irish leaders. On this understanding Parnell, Dillon and O'Kelly were to be at once released. The bargain was really struck on these terms. It was not embodied in writing, at any rate not in any single or binding document. Mr. Gladstone's biographer says that Mr. Gladstone was "always impatient" of any reference to "tacit understanding" in respect of the dealings with the prisoner in Kilmainham. Still, "the nature of the proceedings was plain enough."[1]

It certainly was so to the Conservative Party, and to Mr. Gladstone's own colleague, Mr. W. E. Forster, the Chief Secretary for Ireland, who resigned office rather than be responsible for the release of the prisoners except after a public declaration by Mr. Parnell that he would not in future aid or abet any form of intimidation, including boycotting. No declaration was exacted. On May 2nd, the day the three left Kilmainham, Mr. Forster wrote:

[1] John Morley, *Life of Gladstone*, Vol. III, p. 64.

Either the release is unconditional, or it is not. If unconditional, I think it is at the present moment a surrender to the law-breakers. If conditional, I think it is a disgraceful compromise.[1]

The Chief Secretary's resignation greatly weakened the case on which Mr. Gladstone took his stand in the House of Commons. Briefly this was that there had been no compact between Mr. Parnell and the Government. The release of the prisoners had been in the interests of Ireland. The Government had determined before it took place, to deal with arrears, and they had received trustworthy information that if they did so along certain lines the trio in Kilmainham would find themselves able to take the side of law and order.

This was the gist of the Prime Minister's statement on May 4th, 1882. The impression that all had not been revealed was heightened by some corrections of facts and dates which Parnell, back in his seat among his followers, interrupted Mr. Gladstone to supply. Balfour had run downstairs from a Committee room on learning that the Prime Minister was up. His speech suited the rising temperature of the House.

When he was angry he could be pitiless. He was very seldom really angry. But he had a vast natural contempt for inconsistency and ineptitude, and in the Kilmainham Treaty he saw their apotheosis. The crowning touch was added by Mr. Gladstone's asseveration that there had been no treaty, reiterated in face of the correspondence which Ministers had been forced to produce in the course of Debate.

The House [Balfour said] seemed to have a tolerably clear notion of what had passed. The Government were to give Hon. Gentlemen their liberty and a Bill with regard to arrears. The Hon. Gentlemen were going to give the Government peace in Ireland and support in Parliament. However that transaction might be disguised in words there was no doubt whatever it was a compact.

No other such transaction could be quoted in our political history.

It stood alone—he did not wish to use strong language but he was going to say—it stood alone in its infamy.... The Government had been degraded by treating on equal terms with men ... whom they had asserted to be steeped to the lips in treason.... They had negotiated in

[1] T. Wemyss Reid, *Life of W. E. Forster*, Vol. II, p. 441.

secret with treason, and, almost worse than all, it appeared that one of
the things the Government had, in their own words, reasonable grounds
for believing, was that they would obtain the Parliamentary support of
men they had put in prison for the gravest crime.

Mr. Gladstone's answer contained an indignant rebuke against
distrust of the word of men who had grown grey in the service of
the State. For the rest it was a bold passionate denial of the "treaty"
accusation, which however left the convictions of the House much
where they were before on that subject.

Among Balfour's papers there exists the draft of an incomplete
letter meant probably for some correspondent in Mr. Gladstone's
circle. But whether it, or anything like it, was ever sent I do not
know.

May 1882.

If you intend to write to any of the Gladstones on the subject of our
yesterday's conversation, there is no harm whatever in your alluding to
the other thing on which we are agreed, that I am sorry that the word
"infamy" should have slipped out in the heat of the debate. The *reason*
I am sorry is, not that I think it inapplicable, or that I think Gladstone
has any right to complain of it, but that I am of opinion that very
violent words should be excluded from debate. I hold that it is better
to describe a man as having "feloniously appropriated other people's
property" than to describe him merely as a "thief": though in meaning,
the two accusations are indistinguishable; and though it is difficult to
believe that the accused person should seriously prefer one form of words
to another. I must add that Gladstone's attitude seems to me very strange
in the matter. I understand that he thinks that an old friend should not
have attacked so vehemently. Now this is in itself a position which,
whether right or wrong, is capable of defence. But it seems to me wholly
inconsistent with the character of his reply to my speech. No man should
claim *both* the privileges of considering himself injured by an attack
and the privilege of replying to that attack with a violence which
greatly surpassed it. Gladstone in his answer hit as hard as he could.
I am far from complaining. I think he was quite right. But I am a
little irritated that after recouping himself in this perfectly legitimate
manner he should consider me still in his debt.

The history of the Kilmainham treaty has been sketched here in
detail disproportionate if it were merely the background for a private member's first Parliamentary success. But it is rather a setting
for a demonstration of Balfour's quality which still lay five years
ahead. Not by the annoyance of his opponents, or the applause of

his friends should the speech of 1882 be judged—the measure of its importance must be sought in the records of his methods of dealing with political crime when he in his turn ruled from Dublin Castle.

In 1881 and 1882 Balfour lost two of his brothers. Cecil Balfour, the next in age to himself, died through the results of an accident in Australia. In July 1882 Francis Maitland Balfour perished on Mont Blanc. Exactly how the fatal fall occurred will never be known, for when his body was found there lay beside it the body of the guide who had accompanied him on many far more dangerous climbs. His death at the age of thirty-one was a loss greater than can be measured. Among his papers was found a letter from Charles Darwin, thanking him for the gift of the book on Comparative Embryology which had made Frank Balfour already a prime authority on that branch of research. The letter expressed Darwin's gratitude "to one who I feel sure will one day be the first of English biologists."

> How can I describe to you [said another friend soon after his death] his keen intellectual curiosity, his capacity for the reception of large and fertile ideas, his noble courtesy, never more strikingly shown than when circumstances led him into argument with one who was plainly his inferior in the subtle force of intellect, his generosity, his disinterestedness, his pure and supreme love of truth.[1]

These characteristics might be made the foundation of a description of Arthur Balfour's own personality. Here were two men whose genius touched grandeur, although manifested along different lines. The one matured slowly, the other with extraordinary rapidity. If it had been Arthur who had died at the age of thirty-one, and if his brother Frank had lived, the family name might still have been no less illustrious.

Frank Balfour's body was brought home by his brothers Eustace and Gerald, Gerald the nearest to him in age, and up to that season always his mountaineering companion. He was buried under the beech trees in the family burial ground at Whittingehame, in the same grave as his mother.

One or two letters from Balfour to Lord Salisbury, written in the autumn of 1882, survive. The first is from Whittingehame on Sep-

---

[1] Mr. J. E. C. Welldon at the Balfour Memorial Meeting at Cambridge, October 30th, 1882.

tember 19th, just before his uncle's arrival there to speak at a Conservative meeting.

MY DEAR UNCLE ROBERT,

I am going to Edinburgh to-morrow to make arrangements for your Demonstration. I am sure you are right to accept. I am glad you have declined Belfont. As it is quite impossible to say anything which shall be both new and agreeable to the audience, I am clearly of opinion that Northcote is the man for the place. His peculiar gift for platitudes will at last find its use. I am going to attend that confirmed stump orator at his Glasgow meeting. It will look well.

As orator, I made some feeble efforts at the Haddington Borough Election; but the Liberals were so displeased at what I said at Haddington and Dunbar that they gave notice I should not get a hearing at Jedburgh! We did, I think, fairly well all things considered. But W. E. G. is still The People's William in these parts.

There was an autumn session that year. Parliament was called for the sole purpose of reframing its Procedure. Parnell had by now so trained his Party in the art of obstruction that he seemed on the verge of achieving his object of stopping the progress of all public business at will. One of the finest Parliamentarians of his generation had, in fact, nearly succeeded in wrecking parliamentary government in these islands. For self-protection the House of Commons was forced to initiate sacrifices of its own rights of free debate. The most drastic check was the closure, now introduced under Mr. Gladstone's new rules.

The Conservatives decided to limit their opposition to this innovation to an Amendment proposing that debate should only be closured by consent of a two-thirds majority of the House. Lord Randolph Churchill spoke with vehement brilliance against the line his Party were taking. His own would have been to resist the closure altogether, to make such use of the rights of parliamentary minorities, before the new rules destroyed their powers for ever, as to bring about a Parliamentary deadlock and force an appeal to the country on the cry of "freedom of speech for the Commons." As for the compromise that would substitute a two-thirds majority for a simple majority, it was a Radical, a foreign, innovation more alien to the spirit of British constitutional history even than the closure itself. He imagined that those who supported it secretly believed the palmy days of Tory government were over, and that in this Amendment the Tory Party were building themselves a little dyke for shelter through long years of endless opposition. But how long would Mr. Gladstone be likely to allow the Tory Party to refuse him the necessary two-thirds majority for getting on with his business? Twice. Possibly three times, but no more, and this miserable safeguard would be swept away.

Balfour rose the next night to answer Lord Randolph. It was the first time he ever opposed him in full-dress debate.

His noble friend [he said] had pointed out how by a majority of one, the greatest of changes, such as the change of the English monarchy into an English Republic, might be introduced into the Constitution. His noble friend however forgot that when our forefathers permitted a majority of one to decide such important matters, such a thing as *clôture* was unknown, and there was no limit to free discussion. Therefore, the reason that it had never been found necessary to introduce government by two-thirds majority before, was because they had never lived under a Liberal Government who were anxious to put a stop to free speech. The last argument of his noble friend was that the safeguard of the two-third rule would be wasted away under the pressure of a powerful Radical Minister. He [Balfour] however preferred the most slender protection to none at all. In his opinion it would not be easy for a Radical Minister to get rid of such a safeguard, because he would then have boldly to announce to the country that his object was not to put down merely illegitimate obstruction but legitimate opposition.

The duel of the two young men was the outstanding feature of the Debate. On November 6th, 1882, Balfour's sister-in-law, Lady Frances Balfour, wrote to his brother Gerald:

An interesting week in politics. The Irish voting with the Government, and Arthur's answer to Randolph's speech being the main points. I hear Arthur spoke very well; it was a subject where he would, being a matter of logical argument. He was much knocked up after his speech, and a day of Committee in the House. When I saw him he was naturally rather low about his "constitution," and unless he gets stronger I don't see how he could stand Office work, which he inevitably will have if the Conservatives come in again.

Balfour's reputation as a coming man was establishing itself. Towards the end of 1882 a bye-election impended at Preston, and he was approached with a suggestion that he should stand. He knew that the Borough of Hertford would disappear as a separate constituency at the next redistribution, and he was prepared to accept the Lancashire seat, but eventually another candidate was preferred.

To Lord Salisbury.

HOUSE OF COMMONS,
Nov. 10th, 1882.

MY DEAR UNCLE ROBERT,

On arriving in town I found the enclosed. Decision must be come to at once, and it is very awkward not being able to communicate with my Hertford people. I have been obliged to allow my name to be submitted by telegram to the Preston Committee, but if you see any decided objection to the course I am taking it would not be too late to change it if you will let me hear from you before 11.30 to-night.

I am doing my best for the Party I believe; but I do not feel either in spirits or in health for a fight. The whole thing should be over by the end of next month, so that it ought not to interfere with Whittingehame. Yours in greatest haste,

A. J. B.

The depression of his brother's death hangs about his letter, and his desire to get home is expressed again in the next, to Lady Frances Balfour.

MY DEAR FRANCES,

Preston is at an end: the story is too long to tell you, but it appears that the Chairman at Preston has thrown over the plenipotentiaries of the Preston Committee in London, and has closed with one Hanbury. I have a great grievance, which is rather agreeable; but I am somewhat awkwardly placed with regard to my Hertford friends. No matter—I shall save £2000 and be at Whittingehame. yours affecly

A. J. B.

Lady Frances was more successful than most people in drawing answers to her letters from her brother-in-law, whose ideas of correspondence, especially with his own family, were very one-sided. He liked being written to, but detested answering, therein not differing perhaps from the majority of men, except that in this, as in many other matters, he got his way without apparent exertion. Lady Frances was a brilliant and provocative letter-writer. Her father was the Eighth Duke of Argyll, friend and Cabinet colleague of Mr. Gladstone's. Through her mother she was a granddaughter of one of the great Whig hostesses of the mid-Victorian era, Harriet Duchess of Sutherland. In 1879 she had married Eustace, the youngest of Arthur Balfour's brothers. She threw herself with zest into the life of her new family, but she brought from the Whig houses which cradled her, political views very different from the Cecil traditions of Whittingehame, and also a passionate delight in Party politics and the dramatic and personal aspects thereof, which the cool reflective Balfour temperament was incapable of sharing, though not incapable of enjoying. When she entered the family at the age of twenty-one she considered her new relations lamentably tepid about most of the important things of life.

With none of the Balfours [she wrote in her own Reminiscences a generation later] were politics a vital interest. None of them had that exclusive and inclusive interest in state-craft that marked the great Whig families.[1]

Lack of interest in politics was not the criticism which most people would have passed upon Arthur Balfour and his family, even in the eighties. But there is no doubt that the inclusion in his home circle of a vehement, stimulating and very feminine personality had its effect. Lady Frances must be classed among the forces that vital-ised his interest in the political side of his life while it was gathering momentum.

Happily for their intercourse, she was able soon after her marriage to reconcile her loyalties, at any rate for the time being. Her father, the Duke of Argyll, as a great landlord and upholder of the rights of property owners, had been unable to swallow the principles of the Irish Land Bill of 1881, and had quitted Mr. Gladstone's Cabinet in consequence.

No great issues came to a head in the year 1883, and as often happens at such times political interest was apt to descend upon questions of personalities and first principles. The Conservatives in-deed were almost bound to consider the first of these topics, for the question of their leadership had remained in abeyance ever since Lord Beaconsfield's death. Neither Lord Salisbury nor Sir Stafford Northcote had the least desire or intention of forcing the question of the succession to a settlement. But a vacant throne breeds fac-tions. Moreover the general political situation might well make the Conservative Party anxious to get its domestic problems settled. A new power was disintegrating the Liberal Government through Mr. Joseph Chamberlain, personifying the growing strength of Radical-ism in the country. No wonder if there was talk in Tory circles of the necessity for a leader and a popular appeal, before the General

[1] Lady Frances Balfour. *Ne Obliviscaris,* Vol. I, p. 201.

Election came any nearer. Mr. Gladstone's Government was in its fourth year, and although the fall of Khartoum and the death of Gordon were still in the future, Majuba Hill and the bombardment of Alexandria lay behind. And Ireland continued to be governed by the help of a Coercion Act.

Many people must therefore have agreed in their hearts with this *résumé* of the situation given by Lord Randolph Churchill in a letter to *The Times* on April 2nd, 1883:

> The position of the Conservative Party is hopeful and critical. Everything depends upon the Liberals keeping their leader, and upon the Conservatives finding one. An Opposition never wants a policy: but an Opposition, if it is to become a strong Government, must have a leader. The country, though it may be disposed to dispense with Mr. Gladstone and his colleagues, is not likely to exchange them for an arrangement which would practically place the Premiership in commission. The Conservative Party must at once decide upon a name. This is more important with the modern electorate than a cry, but at the present moment, when the battle may be joined any day, we have fixed upon neither.

Lord Randolph then named three possible leaders.

> If the electors are in a negative frame of mind they may accept Sir Stafford Northcote. If they are in a cautious frame of mind they may shelter themselves under Lord Cairns; if they are in an English frame of mind they will rally round Lord Salisbury.

Nature as a rule resents interference with her processes, which are never more mysterious than in the fashioning of a Party leader. It is unlikely that Lord Randolph's impatience hastened by an hour the emergence of Lord Salisbury as the accepted Head of the Conservatives. The only immediate effect was to produce in the House of Commons a demonstration of loyalty to Sir Stafford Northcote, and of irritation against Lord Salisbury's self-appointed champion. Undaunted, however, Lord Randolph returned to the charge. Another letter appeared in *The Times,* and then, in the *Fortnightly Review* for May, the article "Elijah's Mantle," which, while still calling upon Lord Salisbury to place himself in a position to receive the floating garment on his own shoulders, indicated that rather than let it fall to the ground, Lord Randolph himself was prepared to wear it. He went on to describe it as he saw it. In "Elijah's

Mantle," Lord Randolph outlined for the first time his conception of the inheritance of Disraeli, and labelled it "Tory Democracy."

The central proposition covered by this phrase was (according to Mr. Winston Churchill):

that the Conservative Party was willing and thoroughly competent to deal with the needs of democracy, and the multiplying problems of modern life; and that the British Constitution, so far from being incompatible with the social progress of the great mass of the people, was in itself a flexible instrument by which that progress might be guided and secured.[1]

In the case of a first-class popular orator, such as Lord Randolph, it is idle to try to distinguish between the appeal of the man, and the appeal of the message. The message may seem a little nebulous, but the personality of its champion produced the clearest of impressions. Here was a challenger. The Tory electorate was delighted with him, and by the end of 1883 Lord Randolph had begun to base his political power on his popularity in the country, a far surer foundation, as he well knew, than a reputation in the House of Commons.

Lord Salisbury and his nephew watched all this with vigilance. The majority of people were either scandalised by Lord Randolph's audacity, or impressed by his brilliant initiative. It was never easy however to scandalise, or to impress, Balfour. His affection for Lord Randolph was genuine, but he knew him very well. Probably no two men were less surprised than he and Lord Salisbury by the suggestions of "Elijah's Mantle." It seems indeed quite possible that they perceived the entry of a new candidate for the Conservative leadership almost before the new candidate had consciously decided to come forward. A month before the publication of Lord Randolph's article, Lord Salisbury wrote to Balfour: "I entirely agree with you, all this fuss is so much grist to R. C.'s mill."

The date of this letter is April 3rd, 1883, the day after Lord Randolph, through *The Times,* had called on the Conservative Party to rally round Lord Salisbury himself. The "fuss" referred to must therefore, have been the sensation created by the proposal. The immediate reaction in favour of Sir Stafford Northcote took shape next day. Balfour wrote to Lord Salisbury on April 5th:

[1] Rt. Hon. Winston Churchill, *Life of Lord Randolph Churchill,* Vol. I, p. 293.

I enclose the form of testimonial to Northcote which is to be signed by the Conservative Party! It is absurd (in my opinion) but not offensive. I have of course announced my willingness to sign.

He could do no less, but the touch of acidity is not surprising, for he suspected that his own desire to see Lord Salisbury at the head of the Party was more sincere than was Lord Randolph's.

By the autumn this was clear. Lord Randolph, conscious of his growing popularity, attempted to capture control of the Conservative Party machine. The National Union was an advisory body, whose roots were in the constituencies. The Central Committee had its seat in London, and was the organ through which the Party leaders controlled policy and Party funds. Lord Randolph, elected Chairman of the National Union in October 1883, demanded for it a share in the executive power. The dispute with the Central Committee lasted till the summer of 1884. It ended by leaving the function of the National Union unchanged, and Lord Randolph's immediate objective to that extent defeated. Nevertheless there was a reconciliation between him and the Party leaders, and Lord Salisbury's cautious handling of the negotiations was hailed by Lord Randolph's supporters, not without reason, as a tacit admission of his power. The avoidance of a break had, as a matter of fact, been Balfour's intention from the beginning, and he had probably more influence than any man in preventing it, for Lord Salisbury relied much on his advice and guidance throughout the affair. But his letters to his uncle show that the determination to compromise was not entirely inspired by respect for the strength of his opponent.

I am inclined to think [he wrote, on January 14th, 1884] that we should avoid, as far as possible, all "rows" until R. puts himself entirely and flagrantly in the wrong by some act of party disloyalty which everybody can understand, and nobody can deny. By this course we may avoid a battle altogether, but if a battle is forced upon us, we shall be sure to win it.

Thus calmly he arrayed himself against his contemporary—not however without giving due warning. Here is an extract from another letter to Lord Salisbury, dated January 8th, 1884, from Whittingehame:

I think I fully explained my view of Randolph when you were here. He is, I think, quite capable of denouncing in a public speech the existing organisation. At least he told me so the other day when, having asked me whether it was to be peace or war between us, I said that if peace meant yielding to his pretensions on the subject, it was war! We are excellent friends otherwise! My idea is that at present we ought to do nothing, but let Randolph hammer away.

A month or two before this Balfour had appeared on Lord Randolph's platform at a Mass Meeting in Edinburgh. The Liberal Government's Bill for extending the franchise to the counties was already before the country. The Conservative Party were offering no objection to it in principle. Their fierce opposition which developed in the ensuing year was on the score of Mr. Gladstone's refusal to couple with franchise reform a Bill to redistribute seats. On the question of extending the franchise the views of individuals varied considerably. Oddly enough the champion of Tory Democracy ranged himself, in the beginning, among the opponents, and in his Edinburgh speech declared that the time for reform was not yet ripe. The audience visibly froze. Balfour had the presence of mind, when he rose to propose a vote of thanks, to take the unusual course of expressing his dissent, on this particular point, from the principal speaker. The incident did not increase his receptivity for the catchword of Lord Randolph's campaign.

Do you want to know [he said to me in 1928] what I thought about Tory Democracy? The words sound all right, but they never meant what *I* mean by them. Democracy. What's Democracy? It's government by the people. I'm all for that; but in 1883 I was all for the extension of the franchise, though Randolph wasn't, which is comic. But I saw no point in resisting what was bound in logic to come. Therefore I was always for Women's Suffrage as you know. But the theory of Tory Democracy, held by those Tories, I never held. They said they believed in letting certain classes rule—classes quite unfit through ignorance and lack of experience. But I did believe that the more you extend responsibility to the *whole* community the more Tory the result is likely to be. By Tory I mean averse to changes—inclined to continuity. There is a famous speech of Macaulay's in the Debates on the great Reform Bill, which begins by saying that if there was universal suffrage this country would be doomed. I have never believed that for a moment—and in fact the countries where there is real universal suffrage prove my point—look at Switzerland—where the referendum is used and always in a Conservative sense.

That's my idea of Tory Democracy, which you will see was very different from Randolph's.

Parliamentary time in 1884 was mostly taken up with the fight over redistribution, and attacks on the Government's Egyptian policy, growing in vehemence as the public uneasiness about the safety of General Gordon increased. Balfour took his due share in these debates, but his two most interesting speeches were on social subjects, London slums and Highland poverty. In the first of these his interest had been roused by Lord Salisbury; who had concerned himself deeply with the question. In the second case his knowledge was personal. Strathconan, his own Ross-shire property, had been, when his father succeeded to it, one of the congested areas in the north of Scotland, owing mainly to overcrowding. In a few years, by temporarily foregoing rents, by expenditure of money on improvements to benefit the remaining tenants, but above all by making arrangements for large-scale emigration, the situation of the people was transformed. Balfour spoke of what he knew when he insisted that diminution of population was the only cure for poverty in the crofter districts. The subject interested him, for the welfare of the Strathconan people had absorbed a great deal of his mother's thoughts, and he was very fond of the place. His personal connection with it was however near an end in 1884. A year later it had to be let on lease, for Balfour's income had been so diminished through agricultural depression and other causes that it became impossible to keep the sporting estate in the Highlands without contracting the way of life at Whittingehame. After that he never revisited Strathconan. When the lease came to an end it was found necessary to sell the estate.

On February 5th, 1885, the news of the fall of Khartoum and the death of General Gordon reached England, and a bitter cry went up against the Government who had sent him, and left him, to his fate. Mr. Gladstone's Ministry met Parliament on February 19th with the remnants of its reputation in rags about it. The Soudan tragedy was only a part of the foreign policy which was bringing down our prestige among the Powers. Russia advanced on Penjdeh over the Afghan frontier. Bismarck sneered at us openly in the Reichstag. For the first time the representatives of the Germanic Empires sided with France in demanding the multiple control over Egyptian affairs.

The Opposition in the House of Commons closed on the harassed Government like hounds round a beaten fox. Exasperation against the ineffectual methods of Sir Stafford Northcote ran through their ranks. Gone were the days when Lord Randolph's dangling of the crown before Lord Salisbury had called forth a manifesto of devotion to his partner! Lord Salisbury himself was torn by the difficulties of the situation. He appreciated the risks of the Government's continuing in office better than any man, for in his judgment of foreign affairs he stood above them all. On the other hand, in his capacity as Party leader he saw the difficulties existing at that moment if the Government fell. These arose out of the agreement which had ended the Party conflict over redistribution of seats. The Bill left the House of Lords on June 7th, 1885. It brought the old constituencies to their legal end. New ones could not be brought into being before November. Therefore it would be impossible for the Conservatives to make an immediate appeal to the country if Mr. Gladstone's Ministry was defeated that summer. Somebody would have to carry its embarrassing heritage for five or six months, by which date the electorate might easily have become confused as to who was to blame for the embarrassment. This was a leader's dilemma. The rank and file were not troubled by it. Nor, this time, was Balfour. The old Fourth Party drew together just once more, and planned the *coup* which brought the Government down. The exhilaration of that last act of back-bench life rings in the description of it in his Autobiography.

With two additions, Sir Michael Hicks Beach and Sir Cecil Raikes, we all lunched at my house in Carlton Gardens, and there discussed and drafted an Amendment to the Budget, which, when approved by our leaders, was moved by Sir Michael. We four had on countless festive occasions combined business with pleasure (or was it pleasure with business?) by contriving Parliamentary pitfalls for the common enemy. But this particular effort was destined to be historical. A somewhat languid Debate, apparently leading to its too familiar end, then a slowly growing sense that something unusual was about to happen.... The Division was close. Not till the tellers walked up to the table was the result assured. The Government was beaten by 14.

The shouts of the victors were the measure of their surprise as well as of their satisfaction. But the most exultant figure of all was Lord Randolph. In defiance of all Rules of Order he leapt on to his familiar seat, waving his handkerchief in triumph. Such was the last gesture of the "Fourth Party" made by its most brilliant member. Born to oppose Mr. Gladstone, it necessarily perished with his Government; and on the next day Mr. Gladstone resigned.[1]

[1] *Chapters of Autobiography*, p. 175.

Chapter IV

1885–1886

*The "Caretakers" Government. Balfour President of the Local Gov-
ernment Board. Home Rule becomes an issue. General Election
of December 1885. Gladstone approaches Lord Salisbury through
Balfour. Home Rule Bill. Chamberlain talks to Balfour. Defeat of
First Home Rule Bill. Lord Salisbury takes Office.*

THE defeat of Mr. Gladstone's Government took place on June
8th, 1885. On June 12th Lord Salisbury was summoned to Balmoral,
whence he returned convinced that it was the duty of the Conservatives to take power for the five months which intervened before
the inevitable dissolution of Parliament in November. He well
knew the tactical disadvantages of picking up the heritage of the
Liberal Government's failures at such a juncture, but his eyes were,
as always, fixed on the European horizon, and he believed that in
the time at his disposal before the General Election he might do
something to restore strength and coherence into foreign policy.
So the "Caretakers" Government came into being. Its very nickname shows how far the political prophets were from foreseeing
that it was destined to be a curtain-raiser on twenty years of Conservative and Unionist rule, interrupted by only two relatively brief
interludes.

Cabinet making on this occasion took longer than was normal,
and was even fuller of the distressing personal incidents that fall to a
Prime Minister's lot at such a time. The most painful of them was
the sacrifice demanded by Lord Randolph Churchill as the price of
his support. On June 14th Lord Salisbury telegraphed as follows to
the Queen on the results of a meeting with some of his principal
colleagues:

Beach and Hamilton were against acceptance of office unless we get the consent of Churchill. Churchill will not consent unless Northcote is excluded from the lead, and Cross [1] from the Ministry. Some time for negotiation is necessary.

That such a demand should have been made, thus crudely, by a man who had never yet held even a minor office, and that it should have been accepted almost immediately by the Prime Minister, is the measure of Lord Randolph's influence in the country, and of Lord Salisbury's realism. Sir Richard Cross was retained, but within a few days Sir Stafford Northcote went to the House of Lords as Earl of Iddesleigh. He held the office of First Lord of the Treasury, and was acknowledged as the second man in the Ministry; but Lord Randolph and his friends had not been scrupulous to conceal the terms of their bargain. Sir Stafford's feelings were wounded, and Lord Salisbury himself felt "sore all over" before the matter was settled.[2] His private emotions however did not betray themselves in his correspondence with Lord Randolph, who, as his biographer relates, was filled with gloom almost as soon as his terms were stated. "In the last five years I have lived twenty," he said to a friend; "I have fought Mr. Gladstone at the head of a great majority. I have fought the Front Opposition Bench. Now I am fighting Lord Salisbury. I have said I will not join the Government unless Northcote leaves the House of Commons. Lord Salisbury will never give way. I am done."

Thus Lord Randolph may have been as much surprised as relieved when he received from the Prime Minister a courteously worded note, offering him the Cabinet post of Secretary of State for India. It was a spectacular triumph.

Lord Salisbury's telegram to the Queen reporting Lord Randolph's conditions and his invitation to Lord Randolph himself to join the Ministry are both dated June 15th. Late that night Balfour scribbled a note to the Prime Minister which shows him to have played some part in the events of the day and to be contemplating the outcome with a tranquillity not entirely due to philosophic indifference. In dealing with Lord Randolph, Lord Salisbury and his nephew were in the habit of taking long views.

[1] Sir Richard Cross, afterwards Lord Cross.
[2] Lady Gwendolen Cecil, *Life of Lord Salisbury*, Vol. III, p. 140.

CARLTON CLUB,
June 15th, 1.15 a.m.

MY DEAR UNCLE ROBERT,

Of course the line I took to-night with R. C. and the line I suggested for to-morrow are based on the supposition that it was better to have him with us than against us. This is, I think, certainly true if we only consider the period up to the end of the next General Election; if we look beyond, it may well seem doubtful. But this is not my affair.

As regards the Under-Secretaryship of F.A., I hope I made it quite plain that I would do anything that most conduced to the smooth working of your arrangements.

yours affectionately but sleepy,

A. J. B.

Lord Salisbury had decided to combine the offices of Prime Minister and Foreign Secretary in his own person, and had evidently considered for a moment the idea of his nephew as his own subordinate at the Foreign Office. Eventually however the Under-Secretaryship was given to Mr. Bourke, and Balfour's official career was begun as President of the Local Government Board.

Perhaps no politician has ever installed himself for the first time in his own ministerial room without some curiosity about the future, some desire to know in what other of the historic buildings round Whitehall he will play his part, and what kind of part he is destined to play. If such speculations were ever entirely absent from the mind of a man taking up his first office, they were assuredly absent from Balfour's, whose ranging curiosity never seemed to linger for an instant upon his own career. Neither did it ever occur to him to see himself as the centre of any stage, or to dramatise any personal experience. In later life he was rather apt to mistake this lack of interest in himself for a deficiency of memory, and to deplore it. "If I could only remember the things I have seen and done," he said, not long before he died, "I should be a much more interesting fellow than I am." As a matter of fact his memory was very accurate, but it failed almost consistently on the scenic side.

Although the maze of technicalities surrounding the subject of Local Government had not fully developed in 1885, it would even then have taken a Minister more than half a year to form his own opinions, and the "Caretakers" knew themselves only engaged for five months. The record of Balfour's first office would be almost a blank if it were not for a rather instructive failure to add to his Parliamentary reputation. Some slight opportunity of doing so offered itself through the Medical Relief Disqualification Bill, which he piloted through the House in July. The measure was to enable persons in receipt of assistance from Poor Law funds to exercise electoral rights. It was on the same lines as an Amendment to the Redistribution Bill supported by Mr. Jesse Collings, henchman of Mr. Chamberlain, which had been rejected by the Peers in May. Balfour should therefore have met with little criticism when he introduced his Bill, except possibly from the high Tory wing of his own Party. Actually, however, in his Second Reading speech, he so trailed his coat under Mr. Chamberlain's nose that the Radical leader bestirred himself to retort with a sneer at the sudden conversion of the Conservative Party on a question which might appeal to the new agricultural labourers' vote. The impression left at the end of the Debate was that the dashing habits of the Fourth Party in opposition needed some unlearning on the part of the President of the Local Government Board. The incident did not pass unnoticed by Balfour himself. Six months later, when the question of his taking office in Lord Salisbury's second Administration arose, he was not free from doubts as to his own fitness for a ministerial post.

In the meantime Irish Home Rule had become the dominating issue in Party politics. The General Election that put Mr. Gladstone into power was held in November 1885. The big guns had opened fire on political platforms all over the country early in the autumn. The first pronouncement was Mr. Parnell's on August 24th, declaring that the great and sole work of his party in the next House of Commons would be the restoration of an Irish Parliament. The challenge was taken up in the speeches of all the Party chiefs, with the single exception of Mr. Gladstone. Whig and Radical, Lord Hartington and Mr. Chamberlain, harmonious on this as they had seldom been in the five years of their uneasy fellowship in the Liberal Cabinet, vied in refusing support to a settlement of the Irish question involving a separate legislature. "If these," said Mr. Chamberlain, "are the terms on which Mr. Parnell's support is to be obtained, I will not enter into the compact." Local self-government, in the form of Provincial Councils, Mr. Chamberlain advocated warmly, and this was really the proposal to which Lord Salisbury devoted most attention at Newport, where he made his chief pronouncement in respect of Irish affairs. On local self-government he went so far as to point out in detail some of the difficulties of insti-

ARTHUR JAMES BALFOUR
1885

tuting it in Ireland. On Home Rule he merely repeated in a general, but emphatic, way the unalterable opposition of the Conservative Party. No more was required from the Prime Minister in his then state of knowledge of the movements of Mr. Gladstone's mind.

Mr. Gladstone's Election Address had been issued on September 17th, but on the Irish question it contained only a number of sentences described by his biographer as "large and profuse, undoubtedly open to more than one construction, which either admitted or excluded Home Rule as might happen." [1] In speeches he exhorted his followers to no duty in respect of Ireland, except to return a Liberal majority large enough to settle its problems independently of the Parnellite vote. And when Parnell asked him for a pronouncement on Nationalist aspirations he specifically refused.

Mr. Gladstone's strategy of silence has been defended and criticised in many books. The last and warmest apologia is made in his son's book, published in 1928.[2] Mr. Gladstone's conversion to Home Rule is there fixed as complete by August 1885, and his refusal to disclose it before the General Election in November is eulogised as the only "square and honest" course, on the ground that to bid for the Irish vote would have been "inconsistent with honour and duty. Ireland must make a free choice at the Election."

The margin of Balfour's copy of Lord Gladstone's book is scribbled all over with sarcastic little comments. A pronouncement of Mr. Gladstone's intentions with regard to Irish policy would certainly have violently disquieted Liberal opinion. Yet English and Scottish voters were kept in ignorance of a matter which deeply concerned them. Their freedom of choice was preserved at the price of their freedom to make an intelligent choice. "Such reticence," noted Balfour, "may easily, from Mr. Gladstone's point of view, have seemed capable of defense. But were I hunting for the words that would most fittingly describe it, I have to own that 'square' and 'honest' are not those that would first occur to me." Here, across the years, is an echo of the mocking laughter with which the monopoly of political morality proclaimed from Hawarden was wont to be greeted at Hatfield.

The Tories repaired to their constituencies before the middle of November—Balfour not this time to Hertford, where his old borough constituency had been abolished, but to East Manchester, be-

[1] John Morley, *Life of Gladstone*, Vol. III, p. 237.
[2] *After Thirty Years*, by Viscount Gladstone.

ginning his connection of twenty-one years with that seat, which was broken only at the defeat of 1906. His Election Address dealt firstly with extension of local government; secondly with Ireland, a topic on which the sequence of his ideas is worth noting.

To secure order, freedom and safety, for the minority as well as the majority of the Irish people, and to do so as far as possible by the administration of equal laws, should be the first object of any Ministry responsible for the government of the country. But I shall resist to the uttermost any attempt to loosen the connection which has subsisted so long between Ireland and Great Britain, under whatever disguises that attempt may be made.

Within eighteen months he was translating words into action in Dublin Castle. Seventeen years later it fell to him to frame and carry the Education Bill of 1902, which established on an enduring basis the next of the political principles which he emphasised in this Election Address:

I shall offer uncompromising resistance to any measure which may throw obstacles in the way of the teaching of religion in elementary schools. I will not consent in the name of religious freedom, to banish religion from education; or, in the name of religious equality, to plunder the Church.

To switch the torch of knowledge forwards and backwards across a life is apt to confuse the picture, and—more unforgivable—to distort it. But every now and then it is irresistible to pause and throw a light round the years behind and before. This Election Address of 1885 is a case in point. The value of such phrases as "resist to the uttermost," or "uncompromising resistance" can only be tested by the record of the fighting period now beginning.

By comparison with Hertford, Balfour found electioneering in Manchester exhausting. He wrote to Lady Frances Balfour on November 20th:

Very tired, and endless walking about. Why don't you come here if you are so anxious to discuss the situation with me? Gerry's election is Wednesday, Manchester is Thursday; come over and bring him with you.

The reference is to his brother Gerald, standing for Parliament for the first time in Central Leeds.

The redistribution had given Manchester six representatives in place of two, so that Balfour's division of East Manchester was new. It returned him by a majority of 824. But in the country the Liberals had a majority, though not large enough to fulfil Mr. Gladstone's hope of being independent of the Irish vote.

The new House was summoned for the middle of January, and meanwhile the "Caretakers" carried on in Whitehall. Now that the Election lay behind him Mr. Gladstone was preoccupied with the problem of finding support for the policy which he must soon unfold and for which he had abstained from preparing his Party. Happening to meet Balfour at a country-house about Christmas time, he made him the bearer of overtures to the Conservative leaders.

I was enjoying the hospitality of the Duke and Duchess of Westminster at Eaton [wrote Balfour in his Autobiography]. The gathering was intimate and purely social.... Into our midst there suddenly appeared no less a person than Mr. Gladstone. Eaton Hall and Hawarden Castle were sufficiently near each other to be described as neighbours. ... There was therefore nothing surprising in the afternoon visit, and to this day I do not know whether Mr. Gladstone's primary object in calling was to use me as a connecting link with Lord Salisbury, or whether this was a happy thought which occurred to him when he found me among the guests....

The conversation consisted chiefly of statements made by Mr. Gladstone to me respecting the serious condition of Ireland, and the urgency of the problem which it presented to the Government. He told me that he had information ... which caused him to believe that there was a power behind Mr. Parnell which if not shortly satisfied by some substantial concession to the demands of the Irish Parliamentary Party, would take the matter into its own hands, and resort to violence and outrage in England for the purpose of enforcing its demands. "In other words," I said, "we are to be blown up and stabbed if we do not grant Home Rule by the end of next session." "I understand," said Mr. Gladstone, "that the time is shorter than that." [1]

Balfour never supposed that such threats, or any other argument which Mr. Gladstone could bring to bear would have the smallest effect on Lord Salisbury. But his personal interest as the chosen intermediary for such a communication between the Party leaders

[1] Four letters passed between Mr. Gladstone and Balfour following up this conversation. They are printed in Viscount Gladstone's *Through Thirty Years*, pp. 396-398.

stimulated him to investigate for himself the causes behind Mr. Gladstone's overtures. They were not very far to seek, but it is probable that the following letter to Lord Salisbury contained the first definite information about the lines on which the Liberal front was about to be rent asunder, and the Unionist Party come to birth.

4 CARLTON GARDENS, S.W.

23 *Dec.,* 1885.

MY DEAR UNCLE ROBERT,

Since writing to you yesterday I have received a good deal of information about the "situation" as it appears to the other side, which I believe to be accurate. W. E. G. is, it is true, not committed publicly to H.R.; but he has corresponded with so many persons, among others Stead, in a H.R. sense that it will be difficult for him now to withdraw, even if it were consistent with his character to do so. I hear from more than one source that he goes about saying that his desire is to settle the question in concert with you: in other words his letter to me of yesterday is an echo of his conversation to his intimates. He gets no support from any *important* member of his late Cabinet except Spencer:
...

Hartington has publicly declared himself and in so far as he can ever be trusted to adhere to any of his expressed opinions (not very far) he may be trusted now. Goschen is also firm.

Chamberlain, Dilke and Morley nearly ceased to pull together on the subject. Morley is a Home-Ruler by conviction: Chamberlain and Dilke are anti-Parnellites partly by calculation and partly by temper. Chamberlain—the most vindictive of men—finds it (at present) impossible to forgive the Irish Party for the way in which they have treated him and his Radical following, ... He was only with difficulty restrained from denouncing the G.O.M. in his last speeches. Without Hartington, Goschen, Chamberlain, or Dilke it is manifest that even the G.O.M. cannot frame a Government—and I understand that the calculation is that we shall be forced to go on whether we like it or not. Parnell is the only person who will move an Amendment on the address, and no Amendment moved from that quarter will have any chance of success. All these considerations, I think, go to strengthening the view that we must get out of office, and at once. Even if we have to return in consequence of no one being able to fill our places, it is all important that that fact should be driven well into the minds of the public.

yrs. aff.,

ARTHUR JAMES BALFOUR.

Lord Salisbury could not persuade all his colleagues to the immediate bringing in of a Coercion Bill to suppress the National

League's activities, so the Queen's speech only contained a general statement repudiating Home Rule, which effected nothing beyond rousing impatience in the Conservatives, and suspicion among the Whigs. The temper of the House quickly showed the blunder, and five days after Parliament met, the Chief Secretary for Ireland, Mr. W. H. Smith, was sent hurrying to Dublin to prepare a Coercion Bill. On the same evening the Opposition divided the House on an Amendment to the Address embodying a measure of rural reform beloved by Mr. Chamberlain and the Radicals. The House was hardly in the mood that night to weigh arguments for or against "three acres and a cow." The vote to be taken would lay open the fate of three kingdoms. So much members knew, although the Union had never yet been openly defended or attacked from either Front Bench. When the Division was called, eighteen Whigs followed Lord Hartington into the Government Lobby, and seventy-six other Liberals abstained from voting. Lord Salisbury's Government was nevertheless beaten by 79, and next day it resigned. On January 29th the Queen sent for Mr. Gladstone. He undertook to form a Government and sought a basis on which to rest his invitations. Home Rule could not be left out of them, though the mere mention of the word had proved too much for Lord Hartington and the Whigs. Mr. Gladstone's Ministry of 1886 was the first Liberal Government in our history in which the great Whig aristocracy formed no element. But a more fiery star was rising, and it was to the address of Joseph Chamberlain that Mr. Gladstone framed his proposals to "consider" the question of Irish self-government. The Radical leader accepted office, and held it for ten days after the plan of the first Home Rule Bill was presented to the Cabinet. Then he resigned—the date was March 26th, 1885. In the interval a conversation took place between him and Balfour, which (owing to Lord Salisbury's absence from England) was put on record in a letter. It gives a glimpse behind the political scenes on the eve of the last great upheaval of Party politics in the nineteenth century. From it dates the beginning of that relationship between Balfour and Mr. Chamberlain which was to prove to the uttermost the political genius, the forbearance, and the power of mutual understanding, of these two most diverse characters.

The occasion that produced the letter to Lord Salisbury was a dinner given by Mr. Reginald Brett, afterwards Lord Esher, a friend whose great influence upon the events of his time was often exercised by such intelligent application of his brilliant social gifts.

Wednesday, March 22nd, 1886.

MY DEAR UNCLE ROBERT,

I dined on Monday night with the Bretts, a small man's dinner: present our host, N. Rothschild,[1] Chamberlain, Albert Grey[2] and myself. Ch. talked with his usual "engaging frankness" and to do him justice, very pleasantly and without "pose." I thought it might amuse you if I were to Boswellise our friend. So while the conversation was still fresh in my recollection I dictated some reminiscences of it which I think will give you a better idea of the real Chamberlain (at least as I have always found him) than either speeches or newspaper criticism. I need not say that I should not have ventured to send you so long an epistle in my own vile handwriting, even if I had time to pen it, which I have not.

You will note that throughout all that was said it was openly assumed that Ch. was going to leave the Government. I myself have little or no doubt that he will, but it must be remembered that Gladstone has not, or had not till then (Monday), communicated his scheme to the Cabinet, but only enough of it to convince Joe that he at all events could not swallow it.

Now for my fragments of Chamberlainiana.

Rothschild. "A great city man, who has never gone against Gladstone before, came to me this morning to consult me about holding a big anti-Home Rule meeting in the City. I advised him not to do it at the present time."

A. Grey. "I have just come from the House, and hear that the meeting is to take place in a fortnight."

Chamberlain. "This is perfect madness. For the City to oppose a measure is as fatal as for the House of Lords to throw it out. It is enough to set up the back of the caucus from one end of England to the other. Whether we like it or dislike it, the Tories are in a minority in the country, and it is only by the help of the Radicals that anything material can be done. As soon as this scheme is declared I shall go down and make a speech to my Two Hundred. They say the caucus is not representative in other places. Perhaps it is not. In my borough it is absolutely representative. If I can get a unanimous vote, or nearly a unanimous vote, of confidence, the thing is done; but the condition of it being done successfully is that the whole affair should not be supposed to be part of a Tory-Whig manœuvre."

.   .   .   .

[1] Lord Rothschild.
[2] Afterwards 4th Earl Grey.

A. Grey. "I think this time we shall defeat the G.O.M."

Chamberlain. "Don't be so sure. I agree with what Harcourt said, 'We shall never know how strong he is until he has got rid of every one of his colleagues.' Consider what the situation is. He has a majority at this moment of about 160. Of the seats of the present minority at least 25 were won by the Irish vote. I think it is more, but put it at 25. That makes 210 seats to be won at a General Election in order to equalise the Parties. Such a thing has never been done."

A. Grey. "At this moment if you were to poll the Northern Counties I believe you would find a majority of Home Rulers."

A. J. B. "If that be so, the prospect, if we are driven to an Election, seems dark indeed!"

Chamberlain. "Well, part of my democratic creed is that if a scheme is truly absurd (and, unless we are all in a dream this scheme is so) people can be made to understand its absurdity."

. . . .

Chamberlain. "Yesterday, in the House, a moderate Liberal, as he called himself, came up to me and said, 'I hope you are going to stand firm.' 'Stand firm,' I said, 'I always stand firm. But what does it matter to you?' 'Oh,' he replied, 'if you stand firm, seventy or eighty moderate Liberals will vote against Mr. Gladstone.' 'I am a Radical,' I replied. 'Why should their action depend on me?' 'Oh! they wish to shelter themselves,' he answered, 'behind you!' There is your Whig all over! They dare not follow out the dictates of their own conscience, except under the shadow of a Radical!"

A. Grey. "The reason is that they know that the majority of their constituents are Radical."

Chamberlain. "No doubt that is so, and it indicates the extreme difficulty we shall have in managing the constituencies at an Election."

A. J. B. "In this new cave there are many mansions, and it will be hard to make them all live in harmony together. But it may be possible, I think, to prevent those who are united on this question, though differing on others, from cutting each other's throats at the poll."

Chamberlain. "The difficulties will be enormous, since the mere suspicion that a Radical is going to get Tory support would of itself ensure his defeat.

"I get, and have for a long time got, a large number of political letters every day. There has been no increase in their number in the last week or two; they are not couched in more violent language either way, and about the same proportion as formerly express approval of my conduct. How do you interpret this? I interpret it as showing that the public have not yet made up their minds, and are still waiting for a lead.

"Now, Balfour, let us make a joint attack on the Whigs. The Tory policy I understand with regard to Ireland, and the Radical policy I understand. The Tories go in for coercion. I believe that if that could be carried out consistently for five years it would succeed. The Radicals go in for very large measures of Reform and Local Government. They are ready to allow the Irish to manage and mismanage their affairs as they please, up to a certain point, with a determination of coming down and crushing them if they go beyond that point—just as the North left the South alone year after year, but finally imposed their will by force. But the Whigs are too frightened of the Radicals to support the Tories, and too frightened of the Tories to support the Radicals. It is no particular secret now that what destroyed the last Liberal Government was not the Budget, but the proposal of a National Council for Ireland. The Whigs of the Cabinet would not accept it, and now we see them in the shape of Spencer and Grenville, going in for Home Rule!

"The great bulk of the London newspapers—of course I am talking of the Liberal newspapers, including *Reynolds'* and *Lloyds'*—are going against Home Rule, but the majority of the country newspapers are evidently preparing to support Gladstone.

"You do not approve, I hope, of the absurd system of double ownership of land which your people introduced in Ireland, and are now introducing in Scotland. Of course I am now speaking without prejudice, and across the dinner-table.

"Without prejudice, then, and across the dinner-table, holding myself quite free in an official capacity to use opposite language, I do not approve of it. My view about land has always been to municipalise it— a barbarous word, which, however, expresses my substitute for the absurd scheme of Land Nationalisation.

"I think the look-out is alarming. Any important relaxation of outdoor relief would produce most serious consequences. State Public Works are absurd. Yet if this distress goes on for three more years, we may find ourselves *en pleine révolution*. I may be wrong, but that is my instinct.

"I think a democratic government should be the strongest government from a military and imperial point of view in the world, for it has the people behind it. Our misfortune is that we live under a system of government originally contrived to check the actions of Kings and Ministers, and which meddles far too much with the executive of the country. The problem is to give the democracy the whole power, but to induce them to do no more in the way of using it than to decide on the general principles which they wish to see carried out. My Radicalism at all events desires to see established a strong government and an Imperial government."

The only observations which it occurs to me to make on those portions of the foregoing which relate to the present crisis are:

(1) That Chamberlain means, if possible, not to let Hartington be the man who is to throw out Gladstone's scheme.

(2) That we shall find in him, so long as he agrees with us, a very different kind of ally from the lukewarm and slippery Whig, whom it is so difficult to differ from, and so impossible to act with.

What results will ultimately follow in the impending reconstruction of Parties from this Radical move, I cannot conjecture. "In politics," said Chamberlain on Monday (in words with which in Randolph's mouth, I am familiar), "there is no use looking beyond the next fortnight."   yours aff.

A. J. B.

Lord Salisbury's reply was characteristic. Neither he nor Balfour ever wrote to one another except from necessity, but their letters often draw aside the curtain from their inmost thoughts on men and things.

Private.

March 29th, 1886.

MY DEAR ARTHUR,

Many thanks for your very interesting précis of the conversation with Chamberlain. I quite agree with you that—so long as we *can* work with them—they are much more satisfactory allies than the Whigs. I am glad to see Chamberlain coming to the idea that a representative body interfering with every detail of executive is incompatible with strong government. But before you have a strong democratic government freed from this thorn in the flesh, you must follow the example of the U.S. and have "fundamental laws," which could only be altered by special machinery. With us the feebleness of our government is our security— the only one we have against revolutionary changes of our law. The conversation gives me the impression of Chamberlain's character expressed by the *Pall Mall* that he is "as touchy as a schoolgirl and as implacable as Juno." The personal element is very strong. He will never make a strong leader. He has not yet persuaded himself that he has any convictions; and therein lies Gladstone's infinite superiority.

The look-out is gloomy enough from the point of view of Chamberlain's numerical calculations. But it is a consoling reflection that if we can reduce the majority to the Irish 86, the moral force for innovating purposes is gone. I have been summoned to England in mysterious language by Randolph—but I have been unwell, and cannot stir before Thursday.

Ever yours affecly.,

SALISBURY.

On April 8th Mr. Gladstone presented the Home Rule Bill to the House of Commons. Exactly two months later—two months vibrant with political passion—the House of Commons rejected the Bill on Second Reading by 341 votes to 311, a majority of 30. Ninety-three Liberals, between one-third and one-fourth of the full Liberal strength in Great Britain, passed with the Conservatives into the Unionist Lobby on this night.

Lord Salisbury had decided not to await the result of the Division in London. It was taken at a little after one o'clock in the morning on June 8th, so the family at Hatfield had to sit up through the greater part of the short summer night to know the result. Lord Hugh Cecil, then a boy of sixteen, waited at the post-office, kept open for the receipt of a telegram. The note of triumph in his shouts as he ran up to the House with the paper was the first intimation they had of what had happened. They gathered at the North Door, Lord Salisbury emerging from his own room with Bulbul, the Persian cat, seated on his massive shoulder, the only totally unmoved participator in the scene. "It's too good," Lord Salisbury observed when he heard the figures. "They might resign on that. I want them to dissolve." And repeating "I want them to dissolve," he retired to bed.[1]

At about the same hour Mr. John Morley went into the Prime Minister's room in the House of Commons, and it seemed to him that Mr. Gladstone for the first time was bending under the crushing weight of the burden he had taken up.[2]

Two or three weeks had to pass for the winding-up of parliamentary business, before the appeal to the country could be made. During the interval it behoved the Conservative leaders to consider the relations in which they should stand towards their new Liberal Unionist allies, Whig and Radical. Again it was Balfour who went into consultation with Mr. Chamberlain. They were fellow-guests of Mr. Ferdinand de Rothschild at Waddesdon on June 13th and Balfour embodied their talk in a Memorandum for his uncle.

Chamberlain. "Our great object must be to get rid of Gladstone. If the Conservatives come in he will probably go. But if a Liberal

---

[1] This scene was described by Lady Frances Balfour, who was at Hatfield at the time.
[2] *Life of Gladstone,* by John Morley, Vol. III, p. 341.

Unionist Government is to be formed he probably cannot resist the temptation of staying to make mischief."

A. J. B. "We may assume as almost certain that if Gladstone is beaten at the Election no single Party will have an absolute majority in the House. Do you think under these circumstances that a Coalition Government could be formed?"

Chamberlain. "So far as I am concerned it would be impossible for me to form part of such a Government, and though I cannot of course speak for Hartington I doubt whether he would join one."

A. J. B. "Then what would occur?"

Chamberlain. "My idea is that you should form a Government with a definite and complete understanding with Hartington, and an adequate though less complete understanding with me."

A. J. B. "Our experience of carrying on a Government in a minority was not of so agreeable a kind that we should be anxious to repeat it."

Chamberlain. "I believe it will be inevitable, but it will be done under far more favourable circumstances than it was last year. There ought to be no difficulty in obtaining a sufficient unity of action by means of consultations behind the Speaker's Chair.... Hartington is difficult to deal with. He does not realise that if he is to be leader of a double Party he must consider the claims of both its sections. I am indifferent about being the nominal leader. I do not care about the appearance of power; what I desire is the reality; and though I know many people would not believe me, I think you will, when I say that I have no desire to be Prime Minister...."

The result of the General Election—held early in July—was as Balfour had prophesied. The new House was composed of four Parties, instead of the old three, but none of them had a clear majority. Conservatives numbered 316, Liberal Unionists 78, Gladstonians 191 and Irish Nationalists 85. Balfour himself was returned for East Manchester by 644, a slightly reduced majority, but on this occasion, on the simple Home Rule issue, he seems to have practised his favourite form of economy—the economy of energy.

Tell Gerald [he wrote to his sister-in-law, on the eve of his own poll] not to waste too much brain on his speeches: it is enough to strain one's vocal chords without straining one's intellect at all. Things seem pretty satisfactory here ... don't let the Leeds people bother about Gladstone's reception here: I cannot make out that it has produced the slightest effect. Let them imitate our indifference.

yours affcly.,

A. J. B.

Events turned out much as Mr. Chamberlain had predicted. Lord Salisbury, determined above all things to assure himself of Liberal-Unionist co-operation, offered to serve under Lord Hartington in a Liberal-Unionist coalition, but the Whig leader refused the suggestion, one of his reasons being that the inclusion of himself and his group in the new Government would leave Mr. Chamberlain and his Radical following so isolated that they would have no choice but to slide back into the Gladstonian camp. Upon this Lord Salisbury informed the Queen that he was prepared to form a purely Conservative Administration to carry out the country's mandate to resist Home Rule. He kissed hands on July 25th.

The day, as it happened, was Balfour's thirty-eighth birthday. He passed it by himself in a hotel at Great Malvern, where he had gone as soon as the General Election was over. Thence he wrote to his sister, Lady Rayleigh, to congratulate her on the birth of her third son:

July 22nd, 1886.

MY DEAREST EVE,

...I am delighted that all is going smoothly....I should rather have liked a niece—they tell me girls are cheaper in the long run (no unimportant consideration with wheat at 32/-)....

Life is moving very agreeably with me here...all the views are lovely, and all the women hideous. It does not much matter, to be sure, as I don't know any of them, but the fact is curious and distressing.—Talking of not knowing—conceive my disgust at receiving an MS. book from a gentleman at Worcester with the modest request that I would put some quotation in it with my autograph! He pointed out he had recently got the signatures of the Bishop of Worcester and Sir Charles Dilke,—strange collection! Most of the quotations were of a highly moral and improving kind, but Dilke, I noticed, contented himself with a simple signature.

your affec. brother,

ARTHUR JAMES BALFOUR.

Another letter of about the same date was to his sister-in-law.

ABBEY HOTEL,
GREAT MALVERN.
Wednesday, July/86.

MY DEAR FRANCES,

I am having one of the nicest times I ever remember. My days are spent in playing golf, walking by moonlight, writing an article on

Handel, and dictating a letter (which is practically a long review) to my friend Seth [1] on the first series of his "Balfour Lectures." I shall hope to finish these various undertakings before I am thirty-eight; but the only rule I have found invariable in this world of change is that everything from shaving to literary composition, takes longer than one expects! I am therefore not sanguine, though I am working as hard as a man can do who is in the open air six hours a day.

I am always thinking of you all which prevents my feeling solitary.

yours affly.,

A. J. B.

[1] Mr. Seth afterwards took the name of Pringle Pattison. He was the author of the chapter on Balfour as a Philosopher which is an Appendix to Volume II of this Biography.

In the year 1882, Balfour endowed for three years a "Balfour" Philosophical Lectureship at the University of Edinburgh. Mr. Seth was the first holder of the appointment.

Chapter V

THE SCOTTISH OFFICE

1886

Doubts. Acceptance of Scottish Office. Crofter Agitation. Balfour enters the Cabinet. Lord Randolph Churchill resigns. Mr. Goschen enters the Government.

On July 25th, 1886, Lord Salisbury kissed hands, and set about forming his second Ministry. Balfour, still lingering at Malvern, was passing through a phase of doubt about his fitness for an official career. The little failure at the Local Government Board, related in the last chapter, had left its impression, and determined him to make certain that, whatever happened, he should not owe further advancement to the accident of family connection. In this mood he wrote to his sister-in-law on July 23rd.

> I hear that Uncle R. goes to Osborne to-morrow: . . . I want you, *if* you can, to find out whether you think it would be desirable, having regard to all the circumstances, that I should come back to London at once. . . . *Unless I can be of use* I do not wish to be mixed up in the formation of the new Government. One man has already written to me asking me to get him a place! Ludicrous as it is, seeing that I do not know that *my* services will be required in the new Administration, still no doubt his example will be followed. I feel no natural vocation for being a Great Man's Great Man, still less for being thought to be so, therefore there are obvious motives for not leaving these solitudes; but of course they would not for a moment stand in the way of my coming up if I thought I could be the slightest use to Uncle R.

The offer of the Secretaryship for Scotland, which must have reached him soon after this letter was posted, only increased his determination to get at the facts. He knew that the Prime Minister had thought rather poorly of his performance at the Local Government Board, for Lord Salisbury had said as much in the family circle, and Lord Cranborne [1] had thought it right to pass on his father's comments, although with hesitation, for he was much younger than Balfour, and his respect for his cousin was equal to his affection. Balfour naturally took the communication in the same spirit in which it was given. But, when office was offered him a second time, he wrote to Lord Cranborne, demanding the "unvarnished truth." His letter unfortunately has disappeared. Lord Cranborne answered it as follows:

20 ARLINGTON ST., S.W.
July 30. 86.

MY DEAR ARTHUR,

I feel very diffident in answering your letter. However here goes.—

The reasons you are to be Sec. are sufficiently obvious, e.g., you were chosen to lead the Party in the Crofters Debates instead of Macdonald to whom it would naturally have fallen, and most wisely so chosen. In a word there is every reason to suppose you will be a good appointment in that Office.

For the rest it was evidently necessary you should have an Office with which you would readily be put into the Cabinet, where Papa, I know, considers you will be most useful to himself and the country. Lastly Papa knows quite well what he is doing—there is, I feel sure, no misapprehension. Under these circumstances I hope that nothing I have said will make you take the suggested course.

That you can increase your usefulness is true of all men—I venture to think particularly true of you. If you don't quite agree with me, it is at any rate very natural I should be keen about it, especially as I am undoubtedly convinced that it is a most important moment in your career.

I must apologise for what to anyone else would be "confounded cheek."   yours affly.,

CRANBORNE.

Upon this Balfour accepted the Secretaryship for Scotland without more demur. He held it for seven months, a period very little longer than his tenure of the Local Government Board, but far richer in interest, for he had to deal with a Scottish crofter agitation, which was like a rehearsal, on a miniature scale, of the far sterner struggle against agrarian crime that awaited him in Ireland.

The Scottish Office, when Balfour went to it, had only been in existence as a Department of State for a year. It was largely due to

---

[1] Succeeded his father as 4th Marquis of Salisbury in 1903.

Lord Rosebery that the Bill separating it from the Home Office had been introduced by the Liberals in 1885. The "Caretakers" passed the Bill into law, and therefore the first Scottish Secretary (the Duke of Richmond) was a Conservative. His successor was Sir George Trevelyan, who resigned from Mr. Gladstone's Cabinet with Mr. Chamberlain, at first sight of the Home Rule scheme. His post in the Scottish Office (though not in the Cabinet) was filled by Lord Dalhousie, to whom Balfour succeeded.

The Scottish Land League, following its more formidable Irish model, was running a No Rent campaign in selected spots in the Highlands and Islands. A military and naval force had been stationed for weeks in the Duke of Argyll's island of Tiree to protect the police in their efforts to enforce the law. One of the first papers which Balfour examined at Dover House was a letter sent to him by the Duke from a reliable correspondent in Tiree.

July 30th, 1886.

My dear Duke,

I do believe that most of the crofters are for peace and quiet, but it is impossible for them to declare themselves in the present state of matters as the Land Leaguers have perfect control over the Island.

The Island is under the rule of savagery and there is neither freedom of speech nor action.

If a person, no matter who he is, says or does anything against the League he is brought to task by an infuriated mob. This has quite paralysed everybody, and those who never joined the League, I really do believe, have come to the conclusion that the law cannot protect them.... There is scarcely a Township in the Island but there are some of the Tenants against the League, but, as I have already explained, they dare not speak or act against it, because there is no protection for them against those outrageous crowds that gather, and pass all manner of resolutions, and no doubt use language which would not be tolerated in any part of the Kingdom....

I beg to add that a detachment of soldiers must be kept here until this rioting is thoroughly crushed out.   (*Unsigned.*)

There were 250 Marines encamped on Tiree, and the *Ajax,* a big turret ship, was lying off. The population of the little island, including women and children, being not much more than two thousand, there was reason in the anxiety expressed by Lord Dalhousie, in a parting letter to his successor, lest an air of ridicule should be cast over the whole thing by the continued presence of this impressive force. The *Ajax* was accordingly sent back to her station as guard-ship at Greenock, and the number of Marines reduced.

On August 23rd the Duke of Argyll wrote to Balfour, warning:

You will have need of some force soon in Skye. The late Government told me they meant to enforce the serving of writs there for Poor Rates, School Rates, etc. All serving of writs can probably only be effected by protected police, for the barbarous doctrine has been instilled by the League that the police represent the landlords only. That means that the people will yield to military force only, but not to law and its representatives. I wish you would point out in the House the necessity of employing military.

The Debate on the Queen's Speech took place on September 1st, before the crisis in Skye had come to a head. There was however an Amendment on the general crofter question, and Balfour made an effective reply. He had been well coached in Tiree affairs by the Duke, and his own knowledge of Highland conditions and of the misery caused by allowing subdivision of crofts was of long standing. As far as the House of Commons was concerned he remained easily master of the Debate. But from the far-off Hebridean island came a sterner repartee to one of his thrusts than anything produced on the Opposition benches. Balfour had remarked that the Scottish Land League based itself partly on misinterpretations of Mr. Henry George, and partly on misinterpretations of Scripture, but that, as the head of the Tiree branch of the League had lately been imprisoned for theft, his views on holy writ were not authoritative. The House of Commons laughed, but a meeting convened in a crofter's cottage in Tiree immediately despatched the following rebuke:

It is evident that the Secretary for Scotland, in a fit of passion, forgot that St. Paul was the Chief of Sinners.

By critics on the mainland however Balfour was held to have made a good showing. Scottish newspapers began to clamour for his inclusion in the Cabinet, although they failed not to point out that this was a recognition primarily due to his office.

Meanwhile the arrangements for serving writs in Skye were begun. On September 15th Balfour wrote, for the information of the Government, a Memorandum on the situation in the Island. The document is the first of that long series of Cabinet Memoranda which he prepared during the next forty years, and which always represented, as he once said, "the best that his mind could do."

Analysing the crofter agitation he fastens on his central difficulty —the demoralisation of the police consequent on five years of ill-usage at the hands of the Island population never adequately punished. Therefore the military had to carry out the ordinary enforcement of the law, a duty which it was utterly objectionable for them to perform. To restore respect for the police in their own eyes and in the eyes of others was the first essential.

This was his earliest preoccupation, and there is no doubt that the experience in the Hebrides contributed later on to his determination to keep up the morale of his Constabulary in Ireland by supporting them through thick and thin.

Two or three letters illustrate his problems and his attitude towards them. He wrote to his cousin, Lord Robert Cecil:[1]

Private.

BASS ROCK HOTEL,
NORTH BERWICK.
Oct. 2nd, 1886.

MY DEAR BOB,

You said you would like to have a dictated letter—I now fulfil your wish—not that I have much news; my whole time having been taken up, during the last week, with arranging the details for Skye, and playing golf.

As regards the former, there was nearly a crisis at the beginning of the week, owing to the refusal of the Admiralty to give me the ship I wanted. I am sure it was very ungrateful of them to raise difficulties in the way, as I only put in a request for about a quarter of the force that Harcourt and Dalhousie obtained the disposal of! But the meek do not inherit the earth, just at present! All, however, is now going smoothly—ships, Marines, policemen and Sheriffs are all to rendezvous on Monday at Portree, and then to proceed at once to deal with the successive stages of the two or three hundred writs that have to be served in the different parts of the Island.

We have been trying to keep the whole affair as secret as possible— I do not suppose we shall succeed. And one of the means which we have taken to effect our object has not produced very happy results.— The telegraph clerks in the Highlands are supposed to be in the interests of the crofters; so I got the Foreign Office to provide us with copies of

[1] Lord Salisbury's son, then aged twenty-two, and acting as his father's Private Secretary. Afterwards Viscount Cecil of Chelwood.

one of their disused cyphers. The consequence (and as far as I know, the only consequence) of this has been that we have all spent weary hours in trying to decypher telegrams, which were so hopelessly inaccurate in delivery that they kept their secret not only from the police, but from us! ...

So much for Skye— The plot, as Shakespeare says, is a good plot; though I dare say the whole thing will come to grief over some unfortunate trifle.   yours aff.,

A. J. B.

A day or two later the foreboding looked like coming true.

Private.

Bass Rock Hotel,
North Berwick.
Oct. 4th, 1886.

My dear Bob,

My key must be changed to the minor; and if I write to you now, it is not to send you as before mere gossip, but in order that you may let your father know the latest events of the Skye business;—though the whole thing is, in a sense, a storm in a tea-cup, it is one that may give us trouble.

Yesterday, Sunday morning, a special messenger arrived here from Sheriff Ivory with·a letter stating that he (Sheriff Ivory) had just learnt that writs for payment of rates had not been taken out by ——— against defaulting landlords—but only against defaulting tenants; and asking instructions.

In not applying for the writs against the landlords ——— was acting in direct contradiction to the instructions which I have given to Ivory, and which Ivory had given to him. ——— is a kind of factotum in Skye. (He·is known at Dover House as Pooh-Bah!) Among his other functions he is agent for almost all the landlords, and all the local authorities; and it is, I am afraid, only too clear that acting in the latter capacity he has deliberately refrained from issuing writs against his clients in the former capacity, keeping the fact secret until he thought we were too far committed to be able to draw back—a proceeding, I regret to say, extremely characteristic of the Highlands.

I at once sent instructions to Ivory restating some of the conditions under which the Government were prepared to give military assistance to the local authorities, and telling him categorically that, unless landlords and tenants were treated on exactly the same footing, I should not allow writs to be served under military escort.

I have also telegraphed advising him to go to-day to Skye to explain matters to ——— (over whom, of course, we have no direct authority) and to show him my despatch in confidence. This will, I hope, bring him to reason. But even if it does, he will have greatly interfered, if not with the success, at all events with the dramatic effect of the expedition. For instead of the Marines and the police being able to set instantly to work, they will now have to sit kicking their heels at Portree, until the writs against the landlords are ready.

I confess that I am more angry than I care to say. Mere stupidity I could have forgiven. Treachery on the part of a man, whose views were opposed to our own, I should have regarded as in the natural order of things. But ——— without doubt knew exactly what he was about, and he and his clients have more to gain than anyone by the action the Government have initiated. The truth is, I fear, that he thinks he can presume on our known desire to restore law and order, and that once having got the troops, he can force us to use them in his way and for his use. I have a suspicion, indeed, that this is not the only trick he is prepared to play us. In the list of the writs to be issued, which we have obtained with the utmost difficulty, there are suspiciously few for the recovery of rent; the majority being for the recovery of rates. Now we know that the arrears of rent in Skye are enormous and I have a suspicion that Mr. ——— thinks that for some reason it would be more convenient to have the rate question settled first, and that then he would spring the rent question on us, and tell us we must keep the Expedition in Skye for two more months. It is to stop this game that I have introduced the last paragraph in my despatch to Ivory.

My grounds for taking up, however, the decided position I have, are not merely founded upon brag. I think, indeed, that by the course I have adopted I shall bring ——— to reason; but if I do not, I am still of opinion that, in spite of all the ridicule that attaches to an abortive expedition, we should adhere to the principles that we have laid down from the very beginning. If we do not, we shall find ourselves, among other difficulties, in this position:—that our troops will be occupied in protecting the police while the goods of the crofters are being distrained for rates, while the landlords next door, who have committed the very same offence (no doubt with more justification) are left untouched. I need not develop at length the full results both in Skye and in the House of Commons that might follow from such a course. I am horribly annoyed, but I do not think that there is anything more to be done.

I remain,

yours affectionately,

A. J. B.

The third letter is more cheerful, and written to the Prime Minister himself.

SUDBURY HALL,
DERBY.
Oct. 19th, 1886.

MY DEAR UNCLE ROBERT,

The Skye business has so far gone exceedingly well. A considerable number of crofters have paid up:—and the organisation of the expedition seems to have worked as well as my most sanguine anticipations led me to expect. But the critical time will come when the next stage—distraining the stock—has to be taken. There are two possible dangers: (1) resistance, (2) boycotting the stock when put up for sale.

I hope the first is most unlikely. As regards the second I have been privately urging Sheriff Ivory to provide means (if necessary) of conveying the stock to Midland markets. I don't know yet whether he will do it.

I have been spending a happy week with my constituents. Loathsome but necessary.

I shall come up to London on the 8th Nov. Currency Commission begins on the 12th. I have not been able, between Skye and constituents, to do quite as much so far as I would have wished on one or two points I had hoped to think over during the holidays:—but there is still time. I mean to avoid just now any political speeches. But I have to deliver one on Education (rather ticklish) on the 3rd—and to receive three or four Deputations on more or less awkward questions —land, licensing, etc.

I have also got to appoint a Professor of Ecclesiastical History in Glasgow. How I hate Patronage.   yours affecly.,

A. J. B.

From these letters the Prime Minister may have formed an impression of his nephew's administrative methods that was not without influence on the appointment to govern Ireland, which presently roused the doubts of friends and the derision of foes. Soon after the Skye expedition was successfully finished, Lord Salisbury wrote:

10 DOWNING ST., S.W.
Nov. 17th, 1886.

MY DEAR ARTHUR,

I informed the Cabinet to-day that, in view of the fact that much of our impending legislation had a Scotch side, and Scotland being in no way represented in the Cabinet, I thought it expedient that you should become a member of it. The announcement was very cordially received.   yours very truly,

SALISBURY.

That same night came the reply:

4 CARLTON GARDENS, S.W.
17.11.86.
Wed. night.

MY DEAR UNCLE ROBERT,

I was so taken by surprise this evening that I had nothing very appropriate to say in answer to your announcement. Of course I was much pleased, but apart from that, which is a small matter, I am glad on one or two public grounds. The Scotch, moved not by liking for me but by national susceptibility, will highly approve—and (which is of more importance) it will make the administrative machine work more smoothly. The present Lord Advocate is an excellent fellow and a personal friend. But *no* Lord Advocate likes being subordinated to a Minister *not* in the Cabinet; the tradition of the Office, according to which the principal Secretary of State was the only official superior to the Scotch Law Officers, is too strong at the Edinburgh Bar.—I do not take a very sanguine estimate of my political capacities, but *if* I am to be of any use in the House it can only be as a Cabinet Minister —no other can be asked, without a slur on the Cabinet, to take part in general Debate. And also it may be that I shall prove of some use as a counterpoise even though a feeble one, to Randolph. But this I say, not as rating myself high (Heaven knows it!), but as rating the rest of my colleagues from this point of view, low.—This however is a speculation which, if not wholly visionary, relates to the "dim and distant future"; by that time we may be all too sick of politics to find further courage to take part in them.   yours affecly.,

A. J. B.

As "a counterpoise to Randolph" Balfour's services were not long needed. They were colleagues in Cabinet for not more than a month before Lord Randolph resigned on the policy of the forthcoming Budget. This time he was suffered to go, and the vacant Chancellorship was promptly offered to a Liberal Unionist, Mr. Goschen, and eventually accepted after some heart-searchings. Lady Frances Balfour's letters to Gerald Balfour, written from Hatfield, show how seriously this step was regarded by the Liberal Unionists. Public opinion was far from ripe for the full coalition which Lord Salisbury had offered, and Lord Hartington refused, a few months earlier.

HATFIELD.
New Year's Day, 1887.

Uncle Robert has offered Goschen the Chancellorship of the Exchequer, and Hartington undertook to urge him to take it. There is much amusement over Hartington making poor old Conservative-hating Goschen go over when he won't. Goschen has answered he must have till Monday to consider it, and the betting here is that he will take it. Arthur says "the statesman who hesitates is lost." Uncle Robert has told him they will find room for any other Whig he may wish to bring with him.

January 2nd.

The Queen has written urging Goschen to take office and Hartington is pressing it strongly. Arthur thinks he cannot well refuse if he means to continue in public life. It was Henry Cowper's [1] idea making Uncle Robert offer him office. He said it would not shock the public as the head of the Cavendishes turning Tory would, and that Goschen had no real Party ties. The Whig he has been offered to bring in with him is to be a Peer and Arthur gave me to understand that in this event one would have to go out of the Cabinet, and he has been pressing Uncle Robert that it should be himself, both on the grounds of his relationship and footing, and because his office can be held in or out of the Cabinet. But I don't think Goschen or Hartington will wish to bring anyone in at the expense of any member of the present Cabinet.

Jan. 5th, 1887.

Uncle Robert came back very tired last night, and it was not till the end of dinner that he remarked "you know we have landed our fish." Goschen asked him to go over the whole field of contemporary legislation, and Uncle Robert was struck with his "timidity," which, as somebody remarked, merely means that Goschen is more Tory than Uncle Robert! He had stipulated that on taking his seat he should be introduced by a Liberal Unionist and a Conservative. The Carlton is not pleased with his admission.

It was impossible, under these circumstances, that Mr. Goschen, in succeeding Lord Randolph at the Exchequer, should also fill his place as Leader of the House of Commons. Nor did he wish to do so, and Mr. W. H. Smith was chosen. The Government's programme of legislation for 1887 was however violently dislocated by fresh eruptions of crime in Ireland. The Nationalist Party left no choice open between Home Rule and coercion. In the first week of March a new Crimes Bill was introduced. It opened the period in which the evolution of Arthur Balfour as a Parliamentarian and an administrator was accomplished.

[1] Earl Cowper.

Chapter VI

"BLOODY BALFOUR"

1887

State of Ireland. Parnell's "Plan of Campaign." Resignation of Sir Michael Hicks-Beach. Balfour appointed Chief Secretary for Ireland. His Crimes Act. His Land Bill. "Remember Mitchelstown." Difficulties of Administration.

In March 1887, when the Unionists had been seven months in office, law and order in Ireland were vain words in an increasing number of counties. Irish people had lost faith in the power of the Government to punish terrorism, or to protect against it. The history of the Home Rule Bill, though ending with defeat, had nevertheless taught the Nationalists how large a body of support they had in England, and their hopes were higher than ever before. Moreover, a bad season, producing great hardship in the congested districts in the south and west, offered a brilliant opportunity of enlisting sympathy, and embarrassing the Government. The question of rents was the weak point for the Administration, and bound so to remain while Irish land was held in dual ownership of landlord and tenant. Mr. Gladstone's Land Courts had not succeeded in evolving machinery that protected either class against injustice or hardship, and the defects were most obvious in seasons when the landlords' legal dues involved a pinch to the tenant. Under Sir Michael Hicks-Beach, Lord Salisbury's first Irish Secretary, the Government's policy was so far formulated that it was being embodied in draft Bills. They had set up a Commission of Enquiry into rents, to be a basis for a Land Bill. But Mr. Parnell meanwhile introduced a Bill of his own, making an all-round flat cut of fifty per cent on the rents. The moment the House threw out this Bill a scheme had been launched in Ireland to force landlords to accept a reduction in rents to a percentage fixed by the Nationalist leaders. The tenants were directed to pay the specified sum into a common fund. This was proffered to the land-

82

lord, and if he refused to accept it and proceeded to evict the tenant, the fund was used for "defence," which including boycotting and other forms of terrorism, generally stopping short of murder. This was, in brief, the famous "Plan of Campaign." It was operated on certain large estates where distress was real, and the landlord reputed harsh.

Lord Clanricarde's property of Portumna, in Galway, was well chosen for the first experiment. The owner was a millionaire. He exacted the uttermost legal penny of his rents. The execration in which his name was held affected him not at all, as he was a perpetual absentee. It was he who wrote: "If you think you can intimidate me by shooting my agent, you are mistaken." He was no less impervious to the expostulations of the Government, who were forced to spend considerable sums of public money in giving police protection to the said agent. Few Irish landlords were as hard of head or of heart as Lord Clanricarde. He never overstepped the law, and therefore he was a more abiding embarrassment than any law-breaker.

The Portumna estate office was guarded by police on the November rent-day, 1886, when the Plan of Campaign was opened. The scene had been carefully set by an artist in political melodrama, Mr. William O'Brien, M.P. Lord Clanricarde's four thousand tenants thronged into the town by all the country roads. They converged to the music of brass bands, marched past the estate office where Lord Clanricarde's agent sat solitary at his table, went up the street to the roll of kettle-drums, and stopped in front of the little hotel, where Mr. O'Brien and Mr. John Dillon, M.P., were awaiting them. Thence a Deputation went back to the estate office to offer seventy-five per cent of the legal rents. After this had been refused they returned to the hotel, where for the next few hours the queue of tenants filed past the two Land League organisers who sat collecting the little rolls of dirty bank-notes eagerly deposited before them.

A few days later similar scenes took place on another of the great estates in Clare, Lord Dillon's. This time a well-known priest was presiding over the public meeting that made part of the proceedings.[1]

The Plan was launched. It kept Parnell's men busy, though Parnell himself never appeared on its platforms. He was not very enthusiastic about it. He foresaw difficulties in keeping up the people's

[1] William O'Brien, *Evening Memories*, p. 174.

payments into the Fund if the landlords did not give way in the first winter. When the Plan was first proposed he was nervous about its effect upon English Liberal opinion, which it had become his primary duty to study. Possibly he would have been relieved if Mr. Gladstone had put a veto on the "Plan"; but Mr. Gladstone only wrote to Mr. Morley:

> Upon the whole I suppose that he [Parnell] sees he cannot have countenance from us in the Plan of Campaign. The question rather is—*how much disavowal.* I have contradicted a Tory figment in Glasgow that I approved.[1]

As soon as he was satisfied that the Plan was not alienating the sympathy of English Home Rulers, Parnell let his lieutenants proceed, and it became the fashion for Gladstonian Members of Parliament to go to Ireland and appear at "Plan" meetings, even after these had been prohibited by law. Not till now had an Irish Secretary had to contend against Englishmen in the struggle with agrarian agitation in Ireland.

In the early autumn of 1886 Sir Michael Hicks-Beach had despatched Sir Redvers Buller, then Permanent Under-Secretary for Ireland, to investigate conditions in the disturbed counties. His report from Kerry and Clare emphasised two points: first, that the forces of the law were impotent, secondly, that agrarian discontent was an abiding inducement to the people to endure the tyranny of the National League. If the Land question were to be so dealt with as to satisfy the majority of the occupiers, he was convinced that the fulcrum of the League's power would disappear. Meantime order could not be restored until the people regained confidence in the power of the law.

This Report confirmed the impressions which Lord Salisbury's Cabinet had formed of the line along which the Irish problem could be solved by Unionists. They believed that the root of the Separatist Movement was social discontent, with the system of land tenure as its principal source. Abolition of dual ownership, by buying out the landlords, must therefore be their goal. But the Tory Government and their Whig supporters well knew that this gigantic and costly revolution could only be carried out gradually, and in favourable circumstances. In actual fact it took the Unionist Party sixteen years

---

[1] John Morley, *Gladstone,* Vol. III, p. 370.

to accomplish. From 1886 to 1902, drastic land reform was a fundamental part of their policy. They set themselves now to prepare for it within the framework of Lord Salisbury's "twenty years of resolute government."

Our generation has watched the course of Nationalist movements too often to understand readily the confidence of the Unionists of 1886. Their belief was shared however by many of the Nationalist leaders of that date. There were few of Parnell's Irishmen who were not afraid of the results of a land settlement upon the political agitation—except indeed Parnell himself. When he declared that no limits could be set to the march of a nation, he was so convinced of the truth of what he said that he grasped at everything, no matter whence it came, that ministered to the social well-being of the Irish people.

Before the end of 1886 it had become clear that unless the Plan of Campaign was quickly countered, Irish rents would be at the mercy of the National League before the Government's legislation was through the House of Commons. Therefore in December the Plan of Campaign was proclaimed a criminal conspiracy. The only immediate result was that the tenants' money was collected after dark, by the light of tallow dips, in the cabins of the "mountainy men" instead of in country inns at noonday. Mr. William O'Brien ate his Christmas dinner in the Archbishop of Cashel's house at Thurles, and there attended the Midnight Mass. Then, fortified by the archiepiscopal blessing upon his enterprise, he travelled through the frozen night to pounce upon Lady Kingston's estate in County Cork. He and his colleague, Dr. Tanner, beat up sleeping cardrivers and hotel-keepers by the magic or fear of their whispered names and business, and had collected a good deal of the money belonging to the Kingston estate before the police heard of their being in the neighbourhood.[1] The odds were all on the side of the Campaign men in the districts they chose for their operations.

In January, five of the leaders put themselves within reach of prosecution by speeches inciting against payment of rent. But the Dublin jury disagreed, and they were discharged without a verdict. While the trial was proceeding it became known that two big landlords had accepted the reduced rents offered them by the Plan of Campaign. The power of Government was evidently still on the ebb.

Parliament met on January 27th, 1887. The Debate on the Address

[1] William O'Brien, *Evening Memories*, pp. 69 and 195.

was prolonged by the Irishmen over three weeks, opening a grim prospect for the Crimes Bill, when it should be introduced. On February 27th the first draft of it was printed. It already incorporated one of the two features which distinguish this Act—the last Irish Crimes Act ever put on the British Statute Book—from the long line of its predecessors. In all these, special powers for suppressing political crime had been given for a limited period only. But in this House of Commons, it was clear that the Conservative Crimes Bill would be resisted through every stage of its passage, while English and Scottish business waited, and Irish agitation flamed with the fresh fuel of Parliamentary debates. The Government consequently determined that this first struggle should also be the last in respect of powers to deal with crime. The Bill contained no time-limiting clause. The principle of permanence was there in the first draft.

Between its consideration by the Cabinet and the printing of the second draft, Balfour had become the Minister in charge. All through a fierce debate on the Irish Constabulary vote on March 3rd, 1887, Sir Michael Hicks-Beach had obviously been in severe physical pain. On the 5th his resignation, on account of acute eye trouble, was announced. Great was the speculation during the next two days as to whom Lord Salisbury would choose to fill his place. It was a key post, for the Chief Secretary for Ireland in that Parliament carried more than the Government's credit in his hands. He carried the Union.

The political world received with stupefaction the appointment of the Prime Minister's nephew. Nepotism could hardly suggest itself as an explanation of this choice of a practically untried man, still reputed a brilliant *flâneur,* delicate in body and mind, to the hardest post in the Ministry. There was fierce glee on the Irish benches. "We have killed Forster, we have blinded Beach," they said. "What shall we do to Balfour?"

Balfour meanwhile had been consulting his doctor.

There could be no question of declining [he wrote] except possibly for reasons of health. On this subject I had some slight misgivings. It was easy to foresee that we had an Irish session before us, and that in an Irish session the chief burden must fall on the Irish Secretary. The history of Irish Secretaries, since Mr. Gladstone came into office in 1880, was not wholly encouraging. Mr. Forster had never concealed the fact that if he had known what the office involved he would never have taken it. His successor was murdered.[1] Sir George Trevelyan, who followed, temporarily broke down under the strain. Putting all personal considerations aside it would surely be very inexpedient that yet another Chief Secretary should be driven from office by the combined effect of tireless obstruction, bitter invective, and administrative perplexities. From my youth up I had never been robust. It therefore seemed wise, before undertaking new and onerous duties, to show myself to Sir William Jenner. Fortunately, after careful examination he "passed" me, and without further delay I crossed St. George's Channel and was duly sworn in by Lord Londonderry, Lord Lieutenant of Ireland, long my friend, and once my fag at Eton [2]

This first visit to Ireland lasted four days. Before starting he wrote to his sister-in-law.

4 CARLTON GARDENS, S.W.
6/3/87.

MY DEAR FRANCES,

Accidents have occurred to a Chief Secretary for Ireland and (though I think it improbable) they may occur again. If the worst (as people euphemistically say!) should happen, cut open the accompanying pouch ...I leave unsaid through want of time all the things I would have said to you and all the other dear ones whom (in the highly improbable event alluded to) I should leave behind. I do not at all feel in the situation of a soldier going on a forlorn hope, but one cannot be sure in this weary world of *anything*—not even of the competence of the police force.   your affec.,
A. J. B.

This letter written, Balfour dismissed its topic from his mind. Physical courage is not an uncommon quality, but the amount of nervous strain it entails varies in different people. Balfour possessed it in its least exacting form. He got no thrill out of personal risks, but they never weighed upon his mind, nor deflected his thoughts or his steps from their natural courses. The reasonableness which his schoolmaster had noted in the little boy prevented him now from feeling bothered by the precautions thought necessary for his safety. For some years after he became Chief Secretary he was followed everywhere by two detectives. The only mishap that ever befell him in Dublin was in fact caused by his brougham being run into from

[1] Lord Frederick Cavendish, in Phoenix Park, Dublin, May 6th, 1882.
[2] This passage is quoted from the opening of a chapter on Ireland in the Autobiography, left too incomplete for publication in that book.

behind by their jaunting car. He was moreover desired always to carry a loaded revolver, even within the policies at Whittingehame. His submission to this edict involved certain risks, for he was apt to forget that he had the weapon on him. I remember feeling impressed as a child at hearing it thump on the table from inside his overcoat pocket when he flung the garment off.

The Irish Office in London was in Queen Anne's Gate. From his room overlooking St. James's Park, Balfour wrote his first letter on Irish policy to his Permanent Under-Secretary, Sir Redvers Buller, on the day after his return from Dublin.

IRISH OFFICE.
March 12th, 1887.

MY DEAR SIR REDVERS,

I laid at great length before the Cabinet to-day my general views of what ought to be done from the legislative point of view in the immediate future. Probably our programme will be as follows:

The Criminal Law Amendment Bill strengthened by clauses giving the venue to London, and the power of suppressing the National League, or any other dangerous combination, either in any part, *or* over the whole of Ireland, under certain Parliamentary restrictions.

We do not, as at present advised, propose to ask for powers to suspend the Habeas Corpus Act, because it is understood that anybody imprisoned under such a suspension would have the privileges of a man sent to gaol for a first-class misdemeanour, and experience under Forster's Act appears to show that they rather like this than otherwise.

In our Land Bill ... we are inclined to think that any arrangement for fixing rent according to prices will be found unworkable, though we are not opposed to it in principle. The questions of Land Purchase and dealing with congested districts are too big for this Bill, and will be reserved for future legislation.

I horrified my colleagues by a plan for which I still confess I have a lingering regard. In view of the danger that when the process of eviction is made easier a bad landlord might exercise unjustly his legal rights, I proposed that in certain cases where too great a strain was put on the resources of the Executive by such action, it should be in the power of the Government, acting perhaps by the advice of a Court, to throw the estate into the hands of the Landed Estates Court precisely as if the estate was bankrupt. ... My own opinion is that the mere threat of this would keep in order the few unreasonable landlords. It is possible that this proposal may be accepted, to this extent, that in those districts where the National League is proclaimed, these exceptional powers should also be given against the landlord, thus holding as it were an even balance between the two classes. All this, however, is at present very vague and incomplete.

I think this will make you sufficiently acquainted with the present position. Of course it is most important that nothing of this should get out.

This letter is instinct with the spirit in which Ireland was to be administered for the next four years. It discloses not only the bent of its writer's mind, but the balance of his policy. If he had had a perfectly free hand, "coercion" would have been meted out impartially against anyone who obstructed the progress of peace. Lord Salisbury's Cabinet never brought itself to sanction the form of pressure foreshadowed here against "unreasonable" landlords. Nevertheless Balfour did not readily drop the idea, and later on he wrote a Cabinet Memorandum on that subject with special reference to Lord Clanricarde, whose indifference to seeing public money spent on preserving the lives of his agents did not diminish with time.

In respect of the denial of privileges to prisoners arrested under the Crimes Act, Balfour got his way, and Irish gaols ceased to be centres of social life and political activity. The letter shows that the idea which completed the development of the Crimes Act had taken root already in Balfour's mind. The Bill gave very wide powers to the Executive when he took it over. He made them no less strong, but more elastic, through clauses which permitted exemption of parts of Ireland from application of the Act. His draft enabled the Lord-Lieutenant by proclamation to prohibit Associations wherever they were proving dangerous, and likewise to remove the ban at will. In "proclaimed" districts there was also to be summary jurisdiction for specified crimes. From every point of view these new clauses proved a success. They permitted innocent Associations to keep their freedom, they were a bulwark to the Government against criticism on the score of unnecessary severity, they were a formidable weapon against the worst activities of the National League, and before long they became a barometer of progress made in subduing crime.

Balfour had hardly come back to London from Dublin when an incident in Ireland produced from him an initial demonstration of the kind of backing on which the constabulary might now rely. Captain Plunkett, Divisional Magistrate for Cork District, had received information that an attack was to be made on a small force of police which had been sent to Youghal to deal with disturbance there. He was in Dublin, having come there by Balfour's desire to discuss the general state of his district. On his own responsibility Captain Plunkett despatched to the County Inspector at Youghal a telegram, destined to be quoted and misquoted far and wide as Balfour's own. It ran: "Deal very summarily with any organised resistance to lawful authority. If necessary, do not hesitate to shoot them. Plunkett."

The telegram was purposely not cyphered, and the expected leakage occurred. "I have little doubt it helped to prevent a riot," wrote Sir Redvers to Balfour on March 13th, warning him that the telegram was published in the Nationalist Press, and that he might soon expect a Parliamentary Question. "I mean to give a very decided answer about Plunkett to-night," Balfour answered on March 15th, and did so, giving unqualified approval to action "best calculated in the long run to prevent the injuries and loss of life which must ensue, if it is supposed that the police, in the execution of their duty may be attacked and maltreated with impunity. The Government approve Captain Plunkett's action, though they greatly regret its necessity."

A week after this there opened between the opposing forces in the House of Commons the first engagement of the hot and long-drawn Session. On March 22nd the Government asked precedence for the Crimes Bill over all other business. The Debate on this point was carried through four nights, and a Division on the Main Question only accorded then at a signal from Mr. Gladstone to the Irish benches.

On March 28th the Chief Secretary rose to move for leave to introduce a Bill "to make better provision for the prevention and punishment of crime in Ireland, and for other purposes relating thereto."

From that date until July 8th, apart from the Budget, practically the whole time of the House of Commons was taken up by the Crimes Bill. After it was through, the ordinary business of the Session, Supply, etc., had to be taken. The House sat that year till the middle of September. It only rose twice before midnight in all those months, the average hour of rising being a quarter past two.

The mere physical tax which such a Session exacted from every member of the House of Commons was heavy. For the Chief Secretary it was tremendous, and still the least part of the burden. He was obliged to be almost continuously in his place. Every day at Questions he had to face a fierce, skilful, prolonged bombardment. Every day when business opened, there were over eighty Irishmen, all more or less competent to attack the Crimes Bill, whereas he was almost the only man on the Treasury Bench equipped to argue in its defence.

Forty years afterwards he described to me the position. "I had the luck to do it all myself," he said. "There was literally no one to help me. Night after night I had to stand up in the House and defend myself to that raging lot opposite, and no one to say a word for me. Old W. H. Smith would put in some generalities occasionally, but nobody knew the facts but me. So you see I had luck in that way. There was a lot of fun to be had in those days. I don't think there is so much fun now."

In these words may be sought one explanation of Balfour's leap to Parliamentary fame. No one could have stood the strain to which he was now subjected who was not enjoying himself. Ease, bodily and mental, was undoubtedly the foundation on which his debating technique now flowered suddenly to its perfection. How was it done? It is impossible to suppose that his use of mannerisms as combative weapons was not deliberate. His serenity under invective was a natural gift, highly cultivated for offence and defence, and it served him well against the Celtic Irish. No public man has ever been better aided by cartoonists in producing a desired effect. Languor, and a pair of pince-nez drooping down his cheeks or dangling in a long nerveless hand, quickly became his symbol, more piquant, if more misleading, than Mr. Gladstone's collar or Mr. Chamberlain's eyeglass and orchid.

Cartoons follow great reputations, to enhance or to damage. They do not precede them. Balfour's nonchalant air was an asset, but his Parliamentary strength lay in lightning quickness of dialectic and argument, in scorching power of sarcasm, and in the flexibility born of hard practice in preparing the subject and leaving unprepared the phrase. But, above all, in the first period of his career, his force derived from harmony between his views and the work he had to do. Never again, perhaps, till the post-war generation began to catch up with his forward ranging mind, was he so well in step with his Party and the times as in the years of Lord Salisbury's second Administration. Free from perplexities within himself, or over-much interference from outside, he developed his policy in Ireland and expounded it at Westminster. Successes on either front reacted on the other.

For the first quarter of an hour of his first speech on the Crimes Bill, the Irish Party stared in silent curiosity, as he sketched his general picture of the state of the country. It contained one word for the Nationalists: "They should know the condition of Ireland," he said, "as an artificer recognises his own handiwork." Then he entered into detail about the counties where Irish judges in their Assize Charges had declared crime rampant, and trial by jury a farce. In Mayo, Galway, Clare, Limerick, Kerry and Cork, in fact in half Ireland excluding Ulster, the National League was imitating with "terrible fidelity" the processes of the paralysed law. Every instance he gave of its punishments for disobedience raised angry clamour from the Irish benches, but they listened to his outline of the provisions of the Bill. There were to be summary powers for magistrates to send to prison for six months with hard labour persons guilty of the lesser crimes in which the League specialised, such as boycotting, cattle maiming, and pouring pitch over young women. For arson, aggravated violence, and murder, trial by jury would remain, but the place of trial might be in England if the Government so decided.

Then came a few observations for Mr. Gladstone's followers. "It is quite true that for the first time in the history of this country the victims of oppression, of outrage, of murder, have called upon the Government to protect them, and that Government has not been supported by the English minority." "There are those who talk as if Irishmen were justified in disobeying the law because the law comes to them in foreign garb. I see no reason why any local colour should be given to the Ten Commandments."

Before the Bill came up for Second Reading the Government began to experience the difficulties familiar to those who work with allies. The Liberal Unionists disliked the proposal to change the venue of trials to England. Nevertheless Balfour wrote to Sir Redvers Buller on April 6th:

I have no intention of dropping the venue, though it is possible we may be beaten on it. I entirely take your view as to the advantage of retaining it. I shall be very glad to have any material illustrating the dangers which jurymen have had to undergo from the persecution they have been subjected to.

In the end the removal of trials to England had to be given up. On June 11th Balfour wrote to Sir Redvers Buller:

A careful analysis of the figures proved that we could not carry the English clause. Partly in consequence of defection among the Liberal Unionists—partly by defection among our own men. The former were extremely anxious not to be placed in the position of allowing the Government to be beaten, and still more anxious not to see Hartington go into the Lobby with only fifteen of his own special followers. They were of opinion that it would have a very serious effect on the future action of the Party.

Gladstone's speech last night indicates very clearly that his Party are losing very heavily in the country on the charge of obstruction. I am inclined to think that the speech which he made was extremely dexterous from his own point of view, though it gave at the time very little satisfaction to his own followers.

The speech in question was delivered at an important moment in Parliamentary history. The Government without warning brought in a Resolution that, on that day week, the discussion of the Committee stage of the Crimes Bill should be compulsorily ended, any clauses still outstanding to be put without amendment or debate. Nineteen Committee nights had been spent on the Bill, and only five of its nineteen clauses were through. The power of Parliament was being killed by obstruction and the Government took the only way open to renew its vitality.

Owing to Mr. Gladstone's decision not to record his protest in the Division Lobby, the Motion was carried that same night, and the "guillotine" became a permanent part of the machinery of the House of Commons. The Irish Nationalists voted against the last curtailment of the right of debate, to which they had themselves compelled the hated Assembly. When the guillotine fell for the first time at 10 P.M. on June 17th in the middle of a speech by Sir Charles Russell, they rose in a body and filed slowly out of the House.

On May 16th Sir Redvers Buller had written from Dublin:

So far as I can see the shadow of the Crimes Law Amendment Act is steadily spreading over Ireland, and the country is getting decidedly quieter.

He was however hailing a false dawn. The Crimes Act, by itself, could not produce a healthy quiet in Ireland while the Land Law remained as Mr. Gladstone's Act of 1882 had left it. This was demonstrated a month later by the evictions on Colonel O'Callaghan's estate of Bodyke in County Clare. The land was notoriously rack-rented, and the evictions of defaulting tenants involved thirty-six families. The whole country-side was up against the police who were called in to turn the people out of their houses. They were bombarded with stones, vitriol and boiling water by a mob while they carried out their odious task. They behaved with great self-control, and their defence was not the really troublesome problem for the Chief Secretary when the affair was debated in Parliament. Balfour did not try to defend the business he had sent the Constabulary to do. His disgust at Colonel O'Callaghan's proceedings was made nearly as clear as the point that Colonel O'Callaghan was within his rights as the law stood. The Government's new Land Bill was before the House of Lords at the moment. There was a pledge to bring it down to the Commons before the Crimes Act left that House. Nothing but the slow passage of the one Bill was hanging up the other which would put a stop to harsh evictions. Meanwhile the remedy for a harsh law should not be a broken law. That was subversive of civilisation. "It is because I firmly believed that, that I am determined, not cheerfully indeed, but with a firm resolve, to support Colonel O'Callaghan in these cases of eviction without expressing any opinion myself as to whether his action was morally justified or not."

The Crimes Bill Debates were now dragging towards their end, and the House thankfully heard the last rumble on July 8th. Balfour had only a respite of three days before presenting the Land Bill, newly down from the House of Lords. True to his principle, Mr. Parnell allowed no obstruction to this Bill, though he criticised it bitterly as inadequate. It was in fact not much more than an Amending Bill, but it had rather a rough passage in both Houses, and behind the scenes. The lease-holders who abounded in Ulster demanded, and got, with Liberal-Unionist backing, extension to themselves of judicially fixed rents. The landlords in vain fought against the revision of rents on a sliding scale operating for three years, instead of the fifteen-year security that Mr. Gladstone had given them. While the Bill was in debate, Balfour wrote to Sir Redvers Buller:

As regards the coming evictions I wish you would consider how far it would be possible to defer at least those in which the landlord is acting harshly until after our Land Bill has become law. Reasons of humanity suggest such a course, and in addition I should be unwilling on grounds of policy to use the powers of the Coercion Bill in the first instance to crush the resistance of tenants who, whatever be their faults, have not been well treated by their landlords.

The Bill was through in the first week of August. It gave the tenants an appeal to County Court Judges, which, it was maintained, would put a stop to oppressive evictions. Balfour's two weapons were now forged.

As far back as June 11th, a letter to Sir Redvers shows that he meant to "proclaim" the National League. The first advantage now appeared of that limitation of the Crimes Act by space, though not by time, which Mr. John Morley had sneered at as a metaphysician's idea. Proclamation would give power to suppress the League anywhere by Order in Council, but no knowledge got out as to where the Government would strike. Balfour went over to Dublin for a day or two to discuss matters. The assault on the League was a delicate business, as the following letters show.

Confidential.

4th August, 1887.

MY DEAR SIR REDVERS,

My view with regard to proclaiming the League, or rather to the Parliamentary defence of such Proclamation is that it will hardly be expedient to rely even upon the most forcible generalities. Generalities can always be opposed by generalities; and when I say, as I certainly shall, that the Land League is practically ousting the established Courts of Justice; that it is interfering with the legitimate exercise of the most ordinary rights, and so on;—Gladstone, Trevelyan, or some other master of political commonplace, will get up and say that the Land League is the one protection of the tenants, that it corresponds to Trades Unions, and so on round the old familiar circle of well-worn arguments. What comes home to people's minds are specific examples of gross tyranny; and I should like to get a very strong case resting upon well established details especially as regards the particular branches of the Land League that we propose to deal with by order. If I can get this, and I am sure that the Authorities on the spot can easily furnish it if they can be made to understand precisely what is wanted, I should be placed in a very strong Parliamentary position.

yours very sincerely,

ARTHUR JAMES BALFOUR.

Confidential.

13 *August,* 1887.

MY DEAR SIR REDVERS,

There is an argument being used by some of the most influential Liberal Unionists with regard to the Proclamation of the League, which I mention not as shaking my own opinions on that subject, which are entirely made up, but because I am anxious that we do all we can in Ireland to meet it. The argument is something of this kind.—It is said that the Act has now been on the Statute Book, and that under the first four clauses of it a large part of Ireland has been proclaimed, for about three weeks, but that nothing has been done under it during that time to suppress the intimidation which, it is alleged, exists over a large part of the proclaimed area. This, it is said, can only be interpreted to mean either that the Irish Government decline to exercise the powers which they have obtained, or that there is no evidence of crime which will justify them in exercising those powers. And the inference is drawn that the Irish Government ought not to be entrusted with the further powers claimed under Section VI, since they are either incapable of turning those powers to account, or there is no occasion for their use.

Now this reasoning, though in my opinion eminently unjust to a Government which has only possessed the powers referred to for three weeks, is undoubtedly effective from a Parliamentary point of view; and I think it is most important, both on account of English and Irish public opinion, that we should as soon as possible make it clear that steps will be taken to diminish intimidation even under the powers which we already possess....

You will observe that this letter is written with the same motives as some others that I have been obliged to trouble you with, i.e. to provide myself with Parliamentary defence against Parliamentary attack.

In great haste, I remain,

yours very sincerely,

ARTHUR JAMES BALFOUR.

On the same day he wrote this, Balfour received an appeal from the Leader of the House of Commons, very hard to resist. Mr. W. H. Smith wrote that the Speaker and the Chairman of Committees were worn out by the terrific work of the Session. They were both of opinion that if it were known that the League would not be proclaimed, the business of Parliament would be permitted to proceed. To postpone proclamation till October would moreover show the country that the Government did not strike before it was absolutely necessary. Mr. Smith was uneasy about the Parliamentary case for

proclamation, and he had heard that Mr. Chamberlain would vote
against it, and carry some of the Liberal Unionists with him. A
majority would doubtless be forthcoming, but it would be narrow.
Balfour put all this aside, and four days later announced the proclamation of the League to a violently demonstrative House. The
result of the Division was a Government majority of 77 (the maximum possible being 113). Though Mr. Chamberlain did go into
the Opposition Lobby, Lord Hartington voted with the Government.

The first prosecution of an individual under the Crimes Act led to
the most advertised incident of Balfour's war upon crime. "Remember Mitchelstown" became Mr. Gladstone's chosen war-cry for the
autumn, and all the eloquence that had once made Turkish atrocities
fuel for Party passion, now inspired his version of a riot in County
Cork. Thus Mitchelstown was long "remembered," and frequently
"remembered" inaccurately. Mr. Gladstone's biographer has given a
highly selective account of the facts, which were, briefly, these. A
day or two before the Land Bill became law, evictions were due to
take place among Lady Kingston's tenants at Mitchelstown (the
same estate where, during the previous Christmas, Mr. William
O'Brien had directed the Plan of Campaign). Following Balfour's
policy, the evictions were postponed, but not before Mr. O'Brien had
again visited the place, and at a public meeting incited the people to
resistance. A summons was therefore served upon Mr. O'Brien to
appear before the new Court set up under the Act, which was convened at Mitchelstown for the morning of September 9th. Mr.
O'Brien stayed in Dublin, but two of the Irish Parliamentary Party,
Messrs. Dillon and Mandeville, went to Mitchelstown, together with
various English members, including Mr. Labouchere, and some
English women who had espoused the cause of Home Rule—all for
the purpose of attending a meeting to be held in the market square
during the hours when it was supposed that Mr. O'Brien's trial
would be taking place. Thither also went a Dublin barrister lately
appointed to as difficult and dangerous a post as any in Ireland in
those days: Mr. Edward Carson, prosecuting for the Crown. The
following account is given from notes which he sent to the Chief
Secretary the day after the riots.

Upon driving into Mitchelstown I observed to Rice, the Crown
Solicitor, who was with me, that all the persons going into the town
were armed with heavy sticks. I also observed a great number of per-

sons on horseback, also armed with sticks. During the sitting of the
Court, although a large crowd assembled outside, no noise or demon-
stration was attempted. At this time the "Members" had not arrived.
When the warrant was granted I walked out of Court amongst the
crowd, and was asked by several if the warrant for O'Brien's arrest had
been issued, and I said yes, and even then there was no jeering or attempt at demonstration of any kind. I walked up to Mitchelstown
Castle, and when there I heard cheering, and bands in the distance.
This turned out to be the procession which had formed to meet the
Members, returning to the town. It consisted of about 4000 persons, and
about 15 bands. There were about 150 men on horseback. The procession marched up to the gates of the Castle; when passing (I was standing
at the gates) they indulged in the usual booing and shaking their fists
and sticks at the Castle. I was standing with Captain Seagrave [1] near
the temporary police barrack at the upper part of the town, when a
police constable came running up and said the County Inspector required Captain Seagrave to go down, as there was a scuffle. He immediately went, and just at this time shots were fired. I walked down to
the Square and met people running away in every direction—a good
many with signs of having been severely handled by the police. When I
came to the Square the whole mob were dispersed, and I found about
40 police drawn up across the Square, and the remaining police near the
barracks. They presented a very battered appearance. Most of them were
bleeding, and a great many seemed to have been knocked down, their
backs and shoulders covered with mud. I observed the windows of the
priest's house all broken, and I was informed by a constable that some
of the police had been driven to take refuge there, and that the stones
fired after them had broken the windows. Mr. Dillon was standing in
the Square; he appeared very much cowed and looked more wretched
than usual. He came over to me and asked me if I was the R.M. I said
not. He complained there was no officer in charge, but as a matter of
fact the Sub., and County Inspector, and Seagrave were with the other
police near the barracks. . . . I went down to the barrack; the police were
drawn up in front of it. I saw a man lying dead within two or three
feet of the door, and the windows were broken, and the door was battered. The police here were also very badly injured, and some had lost
their helmets. I saw them ask some of the bystanders to remove the dead
body to the nearest public house. They refused to do so, and the pub-
lican refused admittance. I think this was in some way owing to the fear
and confusion existing. The police were perfectly calm. It can only have
been eight or ten minutes from the time the shots were fired, and yet
the whole mass of people had fled away through the county in all direc-

[1] The Resident Magistrate.

tions. There was no attempt at congregating again, and it struck me that there was the utmost consternation inspired by the firing of the police and I am inclined to think the people will be slow again to molest them in this district. The conduct of the "Members" was very bad. They kept walking up to everybody engaged with the police, asking their names and their ranks, and attempting to interfere. The carman who drove me gave a very good account of the actual row which I did not see. He looked on it as a triumph for the people, and spoke freely. He said that when the police went up with the reporter in the first instance (they were then only armed with batons) the people on the fringe of the crowd attacked them with stones. The reinforcement then came up and the mounted peasantry rode down on the police and trampled them underfoot. This is entirely borne out by the condition in which I found the men.

This independent Memorandum agreed with the official Reports on which Balfour relied for his first contradictions of the stories given to the House by Irish eye-witnesses. According to these the R.M. was "refreshing himself in the hotel" when the shooting began. The police "having fired and wounded and killed ... sallied out and batonned indiscriminately with furious passion every man and woman they found." There had been no assault on the barracks. Mr. Dillon had examined its windows and found only three panes broken, and those, he believed, from inside. And much more to prove that the police shot only for "retaliation and revenge."

Balfour, replying, said that a dark picture had been drawn of the sufferings of the wounded, and the tragic effects of the police fire. "The deaths!" ejaculated Mr. Sexton. Balfour went on: "There were two deaths. Three were wounded, two killed. The Hon. Member has omitted all reference to injuries upon the police. Fifty-four police were hit, twenty-nine injured, one very seriously, eight severely. Now when an attack of that kind is made, are the police, who are men, to be said to have exceeded their duty when they resort to what should be resorted to only in the last necessity, but which, when the last necessity occurs, no officer should shrink from using?"

By September 12th, two days later, the Chief Secretary had received more official details and the Opposition a rich variety of newspaper reports from which to select; Balfour continuing his defence of the police, said:

It is impossible to say, when the order to fire is once given, who will be the victims. That no doubt is a conclusive reason for deferring to the last dread necessity the act of firing. It has never been a reason, and if I have my way, will never be a reason for not firing when self-defence, and the authority of the law, actually require it.

At this, sarcastic cheers from the Irish were taken up by the Front Opposition Bench, and Balfour turned on Sir William Harcourt. "I am amazed that the Right Hon. gentleman, who was Home Secretary, who was responsible for five years for the peace of the community, should cheer that sentence ironically."

The eagerness of the Liberal leaders to encourage on hearsay any sort of accusation against the Constabulary is a testimony to the Party rancour of the time. As Lord Randolph Churchill remarked later in the Debate: "the serried ranks of ex-Ministers have bustled up to lend their sanction to every species of abuse and disgrace being poured on the officers of the law and the officers of the Crown." Sir William Harcourt had "poured the whole vials, nay, the whole cellar of his wrath" upon Balfour's defence of his subordinates. But in spite of all this, no Vote of Censure was moved, the Gladstonians preferring to reserve their denunciations for their platforms after the Session closed. Their attitude added immensely to the difficulties of the man responsible for the government of Ireland. It even complicated the problem of discipline as regards the police force itself. At Mitchelstown the officers in command were not above criticism, though the police fired only in self-defence, and to shield the injured constable who was crawling to shelter in the barracks. An original mistake was in not escorting the Government reporter within earshot of the speeches before the crowd thickened round the waggonette on which the agitators were standing. Balfour instituted an enquiry into the affair, though he took no notice of the verdict of murder returned against five policemen by a Coroner's Jury. A letter to Sir Redvers Buller shows the Scylla and Charybdis he had to avoid.

It has to be borne in mind that if we are never to enquire into or punish failures of duty because the police happen to be the objects of denunciation by the dominant party in Ireland there would be as great danger to the efficiency of the force on that account, as there would be from any feeling among the police that the Government were not giving them all the countenance and support that they deserved.

On September 15th, 1887, Parliament was prorogued at last. Lord Salisbury wrote that day:

Supplement Gratis with

Saturday, September 17th, 1887.

GOVERNMENT BY MURDER.—FRUITS OF THE COERCION ACT

BLOODY BALFOUR (to Policemen): "Well done, boys. That's a good day's work."
CHORUS OF POLICEMEN: "But look at our heads! They are not as hard as Tipperary blackthorns."
BLOODY BALFOUR: "Never mind: don't hesitate to shoot."

My dear Arthur,

I congratulate you heartily on the close of a Session which must have been trying enough,—but in which you have enormously added to your reputation and influence.... I suppose you will now issue Orders against the League, especially in those districts which contributed the blackthorn brigade at Mitchelstown.

Yours affecly.,

Salisbury.

After a month's holiday at home Balfour moved to Chief Secretary's Lodge in Phœnix Park, with Miss Balfour and his entire establishment. Dublin was his headquarters till Parliament met again in February 1888. He appointed Mr. George Wyndham, one of a family who were among his most intimate friends, as his Private Secretary. Mr. Wyndham had not yet begun his own brilliant Parliamentary career, but he now made his first acquaintance with Dublin Castle, where fourteen years afterwards, during Balfour's Premiership, he, as Chief Secretary, was to work out his Land Purchase Bill, the greatest contribution of a Unionist Government to the future stability of Ireland.

Early in October Balfour lost Sir Redvers Buller, who felt impelled to go back to the War Office, where great charges were impending under Lord Wolseley. Balfour was sorry to part with him, and Sir Redvers wrote in his farewell letter: "I have taken up my military duties to-day, and feel rather as if I had deserted my ship." His place was filled by Sir West Ridgeway, who remained Permanent Under-Secretary for Ireland until after Balfour had left the Irish Office.

The winter of 1887–88 was the first test of the Chief Secretary and his legislation. Could he, before the House met again, prove himself an administrator as well as a Parliamentarian? Dublin Castle was a less familiar, less congenial atmosphere than Westminster. He could not have the "luck" to do everything himself, though at first he had to try. "There is nothing for it," wrote Lord Salisbury on October 14th, in answer to a letter about timidity and inefficiency in certain departments, "but for you to form your own judgment on every question of procedure, of law, of drafting, etc."

Lord Salisbury was, as in Scottish Office days, the confidant of many difficulties. The correspondence of this winter shows how he pondered them from the English end, and how he kept Balfour in touch with a point of view which was easy to lose across St. George's Channel.

The timidity of some of the Irish Law Officers afflicted both uncle and nephew. The tone in this respect improved after the appointment of Serjeant Peter O'Brien to the Attorney-Generalship. "Peter the Packer" was the name his friends took over from his enemies, who disliked his determined use of the power given by the Crimes Act to object to jurymen whose presence in the box would ensure the usual acquittal of prisoners.

Then there was the Attorney-General's Counsel—"Coercion Carson." I have heard from Lord Carson's lips, as from Balfour's, the first impression that each formed of the other.

It was Mitchelstown [Lord Carson told me in 1928] that made us certain we had a man at last. That affair was badly muddled. But Balfour never admitted anything. He simply backed his own people up. After that there wasn't an official in Ireland who didn't worship the ground he walked on. He never boggled about anything. He made up his mind to the "Kicks and ha'-pence" policy from the beginning. The ha'pence were very well done too. Look at the fund he raised, and the arrangements he made, when the potato crop failed. That was what made them call it "Balfour's famine."—Thanks be to Mary and all the saints, and to Bloody Balfour, ould Ireland will be saved yet!—as an old woman said at the time—and she was right.

These notes of Lord Carson's conversation a little outrun chronology. "Balfour's famine" was still two years ahead in 1887, though "Bloody Balfour" he was already to Nationalist Ireland. He said to me in 1928:

I made Carson in a way. I made Carson and Carson made me. I've told you how no one had courage. Everybody right up to the top was trembling. Some of the R.Ms. were splendid, but on the whole it was an impossible state of affairs. Carson had nerve however. I sent him all over the place, prosecuting, getting convictions. We worked together.

Experience was the only way to find out how the Crimes Act should be used. Lord Salisbury wrote on October 20th:

The only course is to go on "pegging away." You will soon by experience learn the precise limit of your powers,—and then within those limits you will be able, without ever, or often, incurring a defeat, to inflict an intolerable amount of annoyance.

Chamberlain was with me yesterday. He told me that 2 or 3 Conservative land-owners had told him they did not think you would make anything of attacks on the League,—and that your campaign should be fought against the offences we have brought under summary jurisdiction.... I only give it to you for what it is worth. Joe is much given to self-justification....

SALISBURY.

Mistakes no doubt there were. It is questionable for instance whether the imposition upon arrested Members of Parliament of all the ordinary prison regulations was worth the storms it raised. When Mr. William O'Brien and Mr. Mandeville were sent to gaol for their speeches at Mitchelstown they refused to clean their cells, or wear prison dress. Their violent resistance to the last of these rules made it necessary to relax it on account of their health.[1] Before this was done, however, the interest of the general public became focused on "O'Brien's trowsers," which were subjects for tragic or farcical treatment, according to the political views of the various newspapers, but in neither aspect did the discussion of them assist the work of Irish Government. The prison treatment of the leading agitators was one of the most persistent of the minor questions with which Balfour continued to be harried.

An Englishman was sentenced to two months' imprisonment that autumn for trying to address a proclaimed meeting. "I was delighted to see you had run Wilfred Blunt in," wrote Lord Salisbury. The arrest created some sensation. Mr. Blunt was a man of gifts and charm who spent half his year in the Egyptian desert, dressed in the flowing robes of a sheikh, and the other half on his estate of Crabbet Park in Sussex. Poet, traveller, breeder of Arab horses, he had strong views about British policy in Egypt and Ireland at this time, and in both places was ever eager to proclaim "my country, always wrong." Socially he moved somewhat in the same world as Balfour, and in the summer of 1887 they had been staying together at a country house. While Mr. Blunt was in Galway Jail, he made a statement to the effect that in conversation Balfour had declared his intentions of imprisoning six leading Nationalists, in the expectation that they would die. When the Press first asked Balfour for his comments on this story, he telegraphed: "Ridiculous lie. I do

---

[1] Mr. Mandeville's death, which occurred later in prison, had nothing to do with this episode.

not believe Blunt ever made the assertion." Mr. Blunt, however, on emergence from prison wrote to *The Times* upholding his statement, and finally Balfour had to devote part of a speech in St. James's Hall to denying the assertions.

I do not allude to the grotesque weakness of the plan that Mr. Blunt attributes to me, but I should like to say that I should profoundly regret the permanent absence of any of the distinguished men who lead the Parnellite Party.... I do not know how it comes about, but if you sit opposite a man every day, and you are engaged in fighting him, you cannot help getting a liking for him whether he deserves it or not....

Balfour was too good a Parliamentarian not to appreciate the gifts of the Irish Parliamentary Party. But there were other people in Ireland whose lack of political sagacity was a sore trial, and among them were many Irish landlords. In November 1887 he wrote to Colonel King-Harman, his Parliamentary Under-Secretary, and a personality in the Kildare Street Club:

In my judgment, where the Plan of Campaign has been fairly fought it has been invariably beaten, and the cost has been so heavy as to afford very little encouragement to the tenants in other parts of Ireland to indulge in the same expensive luxury. But, undoubtedly, if the Plan is allowed to win, it will become a most formidable engine for destroying the whole of the landlord's interest in his property. Under the circumstances it is surely a piece of most elementary wisdom for the landlords to combine together to help owners in the test cases where the Plan is being attempted. They require of course some money. But, as a mere speculation, I do not believe Irish landlords could invest their money better.

(Reference follows to a case where funds had been allowed to come to an end, and the owner had been advised by other owners to settle.)

Of course, as a Government we cannot interfere. It drives me to despair to see the game so ill-played by the landlords, who will not apparently energetically combine for any other purpose than to abuse the Government.

In spite of handicaps, he continued the strong-hand policy, only in one instance carrying it a little further that winter than the Prime Minister thought wise. Mr. Parnell had to study the thermometer of Gladstonian sympathy with law-breaking. Balfour was under the same necessity in respect of English Unionist sensitiveness to methods of law-enforcement. In November it became obvious that the Irish Nationalist Press meant to defy the penalties against newspapers which reported proclaimed meetings, and Balfour tried the experiment of prosecuting shopkeepers who, after due warning, sold the offending prints. After a few weeks he received a private letter of expostulation from a responsible quarter. He sent it to Lord Salisbury, who answered:

FOREIGN OFFICE.
Dec. 24th, 1887.

MY DEAR ARTHUR,

I am inclined to agree as to English opinion; that is, I think you will find it tough enough work defending the prosecution of newspapers and newsvendors—especially the latter; and if anything unlucky happens, the difficulty will be much aggravated. I am speaking of course of the effect of this policy on English prejudice. I am not discussing its utility for Irish government, of which I am a very inadequate judge.

My reasons are: (1) The general prejudice about the press; (2) the fact that these newsvendors will be represented as small struggling people; (3) that what they are punished for is part of their ordinary trade action, which has suddenly become illegal, and was certainly never illegal before; (4) it will be said that they are certainly free from the deliberate design of breaking the law—possibly even from the consciousness of it. They break the law by the way,—but their object is simply to earn their living by an act not *malum in se*. Much of the sympathy felt for smugglers will therefore be felt for them.

I agree that there are traces of this opinion spreading, and we cannot tell how far it is going. These thoughts were not suggested to me by this letter. It is odd that as I was walking to the Office yesterday morning I was debating with myself whether I should write to you as to the misgivings I was beginning to feel—and in the evening I received this letter from you.

But if you resolve to change your tactics in any degree on account of my opinions, do it as unobtrusively as possible—simply abstaining from this or that prosecution without giving any reason. Do not avow a change of policy—even to your pillow, for pillows chatter in Ireland. . . .

ever yours affly.,

SALISBURY.

Balfour was not at the moment prepared to give in, although as a matter of fact no newsvendors were prosecuted after February 1888. He wrote to Lord Salisbury in reply:

DUBLIN.
27.12.87.

My DEAR UNCLE ROBERT,

Thanks much for your letter. I had a suspicion that the current of public opinion was beginning to run in the direction you indicate.

Certain facts not very present to Englishmen, but very pertinent to our Irish case, must not be lost sight of.

(1) The publication of proceedings of suppressed branches is undoubtedly made for the purpose of promoting those branches; and *does* promote them.

(2) The newspapers that publish, avowedly and by their own admission, do so in order to defy the law.

(3) We have carefully abstained from proceeding against even the most violent *articles* or *expressions of opinion*.

(4) We have worked our prosecutions so as in no way to attack anyone who did not knowingly and deliberately offend. We have gone against no newsvendor who promised not to offend: and those whom we attacked can be shown, I believe, in the most conclusive manner to have broken the law with the object of breaking it.

(5) I think it will be a very serious matter to allow the newspapers to win. This is very seldom good policy—least of all in Ireland.

(6) The general public regard the press prosecutions as a separate department (so to speak) of our policy. This is not so. It is an element, and, I fear, in some shape or another, a *necessary* element in the policy of suppressing the League in Clare and Kerry. It must be judged therefore not by itself, but in connection with the general question of dealing with the League.

Of course these observations in no sense imply that the greatest caution is not necessary in steering our course through these dangerous shoals. I only desire briefly to suggest some of the considerations which it is necessary to keep in view in coming to a decision on the subject.

I shall probably have to bore you again about all this. I really almost wish Parliament were sitting so as to give me a chance of laying *my* case before the country. However when it is sitting I dare say I shall change my tune....

yours,

A. J. B.

This letter closes the correspondence of 1887. The writer of it was a promising young man when the year began, the strongest Minister in the House of Commons when it ended. If the account of the next three years deals less with "Coercion" and its defence in Parliament than does the story of the first nine gruelling months,

Supplement Gratis with

"UNITED IRELAND."

Saturday, January 14th, 1888.

HOW BALFOUR MAKES WAR ON THE NATIONAL PRESS.

the reason is not that crime has faded from the picture. Nevertheless the foreground clears for the constructive effort. Meetings were still proclaimed, Members of Parliament arrested, the Plan of Campaign carried on. Terrorism and murder were not stamped out. But the Chief Secretary was able now to turn his mind to less barren problems.

Chapter VII

THE IRISH OFFICE

1888–1891

Parliamentary performance. Mr. William O'Brien. Balfour and the Law Officers. The Parnell Commission. The Vatican and Irish crime. Balfour's scheme for a Catholic University. Balfour's battering-ram. Irish Landlords. Constructive legislation. Congested Districts Board. Potato Famine. Balfour's tour in the West. Land Purchase Bill. Parnell's divorce and its political consequences.

THE Parliamentary Session opened on February 9th, 1888, and Balfour remained in Dublin well on into January. He wrote thence to Lady Frances Balfour:

If I could only persuade you that health is the pre-requisite condition to all happiness, all usefulness, and almost all excellence....
I am taking much care of myself, golf or real tennis 12–2, Castle 2–7. The work that does not get done in the 5 hours remains undone;—for I positively decline to take anything home. My tennis is really surprisingly good considering my age and infirmities. Golf moderate. We have foursomes: Col. Hill and Fisher v. self and G. Wyndham. The ground is bad. The only topic connected with Irish administration in which Dublin at present takes any interest is *My Ball*.

yours affecly.,

A. J. B.

Entertaining was expected of the occupier of Chief Secretary's Lodge. Balfour often invited one or two colleagues to informal dinners, and to these sometimes came also bright spirits of Dublin society. The set dinner-parties were not always so sparkling. Some of the Dublin ladies achieved the almost impossible feat of non-plussing their host. No one could surpass him in the art of conversational return, no matter who sent him the ball, or what kind of a ball it was. But his first service was never the strongest point of his brilliant social game, especially if it had to be directed at a stranger. Miss Balfour used to coach him hurriedly about personalities as the guests were arriving, but there came an evening when he sat between the wives of a distinguished astronomer and of a light of the Dublin Bar, and addressing the latter said: "I believe your husband is very interested in the stars?" To which the answer came promptly and indignantly: "Indeed, Mr. Balfour, he is not!"

One problem that had to be settled before the House met was whether Mr. William O'Brien should be re-arrested on a charge preferred against him as editor of offending newspapers. Balfour consulted Lord Salisbury, who wrote:

> I am clear that a second prosecution of O'Brien would do more harm than good. . . . I write not knowing the result of the Cunninghame Graham trial,[1] but in its progress it gives me the impression that, the scare being over, the English public are getting good-natured again. . . . Your very success will have an embarrassing effect; the public is no longer compelled by fears to concede what it naturally dislikes.
>
> I think as to Blunt [2] the impression among the new electors is good. The great heart of the people always chuckles when a gentleman gets into the clutches of the law.

The Queen's Speech promised development Bills, and a Land Purchase Bill for Ireland, and announced a decrease in agrarian crime. Mr. Gladstone demanded the statistics, and Balfour, producing them, remarked that his conclusions were not based merely on figures, but on testimony from all over the country. Last year he had rested his case for the Crimes Bill largely on Judges' Charges. He could quote another of these now:

> Moonlighting is fast becoming a matter of history in the dark and blood-red history of Kerry, and boycotting is becoming less general and less effective, because people are beginning to see that the strong arm of the law can protect those who stand up firmly against any such system.

Balfour's speech was listened to by the same Parliamentary connoisseur who had discerned quality in his early efforts. Sir Henry Lucy wrote:

[1] Mr. Cunninghame Graham and Mr. John Burns had been committed for trial in connection with disturbances at a meeting that the Unemployed attempted to hold in Trafalgar Square.

[2] See above, Chapter VI, p. 103.

Vastly improved since Fourth Party days. He now addresses the House with the consciousness of the responsibility and importance of his position.... He is undoubtedly the favourite Minister of the day.[1]

This was still more true before the end of the Debate on the Address, which ran for seven nights. Mr. William O'Brien entered the House of Commons straight from Tullamore Jail at the end of his Mitchelstown sentence, and delivered his soul of a passionate philippic against the Chief Secretary and all his works. Even on ordinary occasions Mr. O'Brien's voice was apt to rise to a shriek as his speeches proceeded, and before he finished them he would be drenched in perspiration. These symptoms of feeling were greatly stimulated by the mere sight of Balfour gracefully prone on the Treasury Bench, listening with his usual mild attentive smile. Balfour treated Mr. O'Brien's speech as stage thunder from first to last, and inferior thunder at that. "His jaded palate," he said, "was no longer tickled by anything so lacking in flavour." In Mr. O'Brien's own newspapers he had been accustomed to read that he had "a lust for slaughter with a eunuchised imagination," and that he had "a strange pleasure in mere purposeless human suffering, which imparted a delicious excitement to his languid life." This "excitement" Mr. O'Brien continued to provide.

On March 28th Balfour wrote to Lord Salisbury:

Mr. William O'Brien has been guilty of taking part in an unlawful assembly at Youghal and is at present doing a good deal of mischief in that part of the country.

Two questions arise upon this.

The first is whether he should be prosecuted for his action at Youghal. The second is whether, supposing the question is answered in the negative, and he (Mr. O'Brien) should lay himself upon some other occasion clearly open to prosecution, it is expedient on general grounds of policy to take proceedings against him.

On the first of these points I have informed the Under-Secretary that until I get the full Report from the Attorney-General I can give no opinion; but that as regards the second point I hold that there is no objection, on the grounds of public policy, to take proceedings, provided the case be a clear one, not merely in its legal aspect, but also from the point of view likely to be adopted by the lay mind. As there will be a row over this I shall be glad to know if you have any objection to these instructions.

28.3.88   A. J. B.

[1] Sir H. Lucy, *Diary of the Salisbury Parliament*, 1886-1892, pp. 14, 26.

This letter touches the question of ministerial intervention in regard to prosecution for political offences, and other matters within the responsibility of the Law Officers of the Crown. Balfour's correspondence with the Attorney-General for Ireland indicates the limits within which they discussed decisions ultimately falling into their respective spheres. Here is a typical interchange:

Law Room,
Dublin Castle.
April 3rd, 1888.

My dear Chief Secretary,

In my opinion some strong action must be taken with reference to the meetings announced for Sunday next. The intention clearly is to defy the Government—to endeavour to show that the League is still flourishing where it has been suppressed. ... Now the promoters and speakers are sure to commit themselves. Their acts and language will be an incitement to unlawful assembly. If the meetings are allowed to take place the promoters should be prosecuted, and should, in my opinion, be treated as the English delegates were when they came over to incite to meetings of the League, and got a month. Of course we could not say what the Magistrates would do, but they would be likely to follow the precedent of the English delegates.

Now you see that O'Brien is announced to speak at Loughrea. ... You might wish perhaps to proclaim the meeting, but I would allow them all to go on and give the fellows every one of them the benefit of a prosecution. ... It is in my opinion easier for us to prosecute, for we can formulate our own charges, than to be defendants in action for assault and to be raising as defence the sole question of unlawful assembly. If men are allowed to speak there will be more evidence against them and they will probably render themselves liable to be prosecuted for a variety of offences. However that is the legal view. I speak for the law, and Irish opinion. You understand of course far better than I do the feeling of the House of Commons and English public opinion, but, whatever the latter may be, we must deal drastically by Proclamation or prosecutions, with the meetings of Sunday next.

very sincerely yours,
Peter O'Brien.

Irish Office, *S.W.*
April 5th, 1888.

My dear Attorney-General,

I have not had much time to think over the question of the meeting next Sunday for the matter is pressing and must be dealt with without delay. In coming at such decision as I could, I have resolved to proclaim all the illegal meetings where there is sufficient force to enforce the proclamation. . . . My feeling is this: if we allow the meetings to be held, and content ourselves with prosecuting afterwards, we may no doubt deter those wandering agitators from repeating the offence. On the other hand, all the mischief that a meeting is capable of doing . . . will have been done. . . . And to allow the meetings to go on would produce . . . an impression of weakness . . . which could not but be fruitful of further mischief. . . .

I am fully alive to the inconvenience, and even the danger, which may attach to civil proceedings brought against us before political juries. I would do much to avoid this. . . . But I am disposed to think we must run the risk. I hope you do not dissent from these views, which I entertain, I admit, wtih considerable diffidence in face of the contrary opinion which I gather you are disposed, on the whole, to adopt.

I have received no memorandum with regard to the prosecution of William O'Brien, so I suppose you have for the present abandoned the idea.

yours very sincerely,
ARTHUR JAMES BALFOUR.

Once legal proceedings were decided upon, nothing interfered with the processes of law. These, sometimes, turned out to be politically disadvantageous. This risk increased the difficulty of the decisions which had to be taken almost daily by the Chief Secretary and the Chief Law Officer, and if they had not worked in closest co-operation, disasters would have multiplied. One of the peculiarities of the situation was the double front on which Balfour had to manœuvre. In Ireland and at Westminster he met the same adversaries, and in both places they had the power of initiative in attack.

That summer the Cabinet had to make as difficult a decision in regard to Irish policy as any which occurred during Balfour's Chief-Secretaryship—namely, the granting of the "Parnell Commission."

On July 2nd, 1888, a libel action had been opened against *The Times* by a former member of the Irish Parliamentary Party, Mr. O'Donnell, with reference to a series of articles called "Parnellism and Crime," published in March and April 1887. In one of these articles appeared the facsimile of a letter, dated May 18th, 1882, alleged to have been signed by Mr. Parnell, in which he apologised for having publicly condemned the murder of Lord Frederick Cavendish, and the Under-Secretary, Mr. Bourke. Mr. Parnell, in the

House of Commons, had declared this letter a forgery on the day
it appeared, but he did not take legal proceedings against *The
Times* for publishing it. In November 1887, however, Mr. O'Donnell, conceiving himself also accused in the *Times* articles, brought
a libel suit. At an early stage he withdrew from the jury all the
alleged libels except two, in which he was specifically named. On
these two *The Times* won the case, and also pleaded that all the
statements published had been true. In the course of the trial
the Attorney-General, Sir Richard Webster, acting as Counsel for
The Times, had stated the facts he proposed to give in evidence,
if the question of the truth or falsehood of all the articles came
before the jury.

Thereupon Mr. Parnell in the House of Commons asked for a
Select Committee to enquire into the authenticity of the *Times*
letters, especially the one in which he was represented as approving
of murder. The Government refused his request for a Select Committee, offering instead to appoint a Statutory Commission, with
terms of reference covering a much wider field than Mr. Parnell
had desired: to enquire namely into all the charges made against
certain Members of Parliament and others during the recent libel
action. The effect of this enquiry would be to disclose the full history of the activities of the National League, and of its promoters,
a very different thing from a mere investigation into the genuineness of certain letters.

Nothing could less have suited Mr. Parnell, but he could hardly,
in view of the nature of the accusation against him, refuse to accept.
The Commission began its sittings in the middle of October 1888,
and published its Report in February 1890. Public interest increased
up to February 1889, when the letter about the Phœnix Park mur-
ders was proved to be a forgery, and the forger, Piggott, broke
down in the witness-box, fled the country, and committed suicide.
Up to that point the history of this great State Trial—for such it
virtually was—is well remembered. The enquiry however did not
cease with the sensational episode which had the effect of diverting
public attention from the facts about political crime in Ireland. The
discovery of the forgeries was a godsend to Mr. Parnell, for it ob-
scured the larger indictments contained in the *Times* articles.
Knowing, as of course he did, that the letters were not his, Mr.
Parnell was entirely right, from his point of view, in struggling to
make the whole issue turn on them. The Government were equally

right in insisting upon the wider enquiry, although before the
forgeries were proved, the wisdom of their course was less obvious.
There were responsible Unionists with knowledge of Ireland, who
believed Mr. Parnell capable of having written the letters. The fact
that he had never instituted an action for libel against *The Times*
on his own account was undoubtedly a strong argument for this
belief, and one for which the only explanation still seems to lie in
the character of Mr. Parnell himself. To this day the inner work-
ings of that frigid and passionate nature remain unanalysed. To
many even of his nearest friends he was an awe-inspiring enigma—
a man "with eyes of red flint" as one of them said. To his opponents
he was utterly unknown. It is unlikely however that those with the
coolest judgment believed he had written the letters. Balfour made
a speech at Tunbridge Wells on August 7th, 1888, the day before
the Commission was granted, when he said:

I have never relied upon the accusations advanced by *The Times;*
I have always found sufficient material for my political controversies in
the contemporary facts of Irish history. I have never had to go back
beyond the year 1885 to prove that the Irish leaders desired to obtain
what they call the freedom of their country by illegal and anarchic
means. . . . The case that I have made . . . against the Gladstone-Parnell-
ite Party will not be one whit weakened if every single word in the
pamphlet "Parnellism and crime" were proved to be a baseless accusation.

Balfour, from the moment of Mr. Parnell's demand for a Select
Committee, had taken the stand which he remained convinced had
been right. Talking about it in 1928 he said:

I wasn't going to have an enquiry unless it was capable of bringing
out the *whole* truth, not only a bit of it. We framed the Commission so
that it could do that—and, as the event proved, we did it the right way.
The Commission did bring out the whole truth. If you read the preliminary Debates in the light of the findings you will see that we were perfectly justified—and—don't you see?—it was an opportunity of putting
the whole truth about Ireland before the people in England, those Non-
Conformists and others, who boggled at Parnell the adulterer and shut
their eyes to the whole question of crime in Ireland that was being
fomented by the Organisations.

These remarks stand here exactly as they were noted. Mr. Parnell's
divorce and his consequent abandonment by the Gladstonians had

not in fact taken place when the Commission reported in February
1890. For a time after the exposure of Piggott, Mr. Parnell became
the hero in Liberal circles up and down the country. The National
Liberal Club made him a life member. Edinburgh gave him its freedom. He was invited to stay at Hawarden. When he next entered
the House of Commons after the forgeries were proved, Mr. Gladstone's followers rose as one man, while Sir William Harcourt and
Mr. Gladstone himself stood in their places and bowed to him. But
Mr. Parnell took no notice whatever of this homage.[1]

The impression left by the Enquiry was on the whole damaging
to the Government. Balfour wrote to Sir West Ridgeway on
March 1st:

When I observe the absurd demoralisation, or rather discouragement,
of our own side in the House, I feel more in charity with the demoralisation on the other side of the Channel. My private impression is that the
worst is past, and past without permanent damage. Of course a great
deal depends on the future course of the Parnell Commission, but we
have the consolation of knowing that whether *The Times* can conclusively prove their case or not, they are undoubtedly in the right. It is
clear that the Opposition think this is an opportunity for trying to im-
plicate the Government in *The Times* catastrophe, and every effort will
be made to show that we have given *The Times* illegitimate assistance.
As however our record is quite clean in this matter my impression is
that the more violent the attacks on us, and on the Attorney-General,
the better for the cause.

From Dublin, "Peter the Packer" himself wrote to Balfour:

The Report is very satisfactory in several respects, especially as regards the finding that the respondents were guilty of entering into an
agrarian conspiracy with the object of driving the landlords, as being
the English garrison, out of Ireland. This completely disposes of the
everlasting pretence that the Parnellites had conducted their agrarian
agitation with a view merely to the relief of an oppressed tenantry.

At the Vatican the Commission's Report roused great interest.
Successive British Governments had tried to grapple with the difficulties of ensuring an accurate presentment in Rome of the facts of
the Nationalist agitation, without offending any susceptibilities.

[1] Sir Edward Clarke, *The Story of My Life*, p. 275.

Direct official relations between our Foreign Office and the Vatican would not have been tolerated at this period by British Protestant opinion. Mr. Gladstone's Government had however made a link of communication through Sir George Errington, an English Member of Parliament and a Roman Catholic, who carried credentials to Rome as being an independent, impartial observer of Irish affairs. This arrangement was open to certain objections from the Catholic point of view, some of which are contained in a private Memorandum sent to Balfour by Captain Ross of Bladensburg, one of the most active of the Roman Catholic Unionists who exerted their influence with the Vatican. He wrote, on March 18th, 1887:

Any repetition of the so-called "Errington Mission" would fail. It was too much of a real mission, and yet devoid of the characteristics of a proper diplomatic mission. . . . Ireland was to be pacified by the action of the Pope, and yet the Pope was to receive information which was not duly authenticated, and if he acted upon it he might have jeopardised his influence; the Pope was in fact to treat with a person who was publicly repudiated at home, and thereby the dignity of the Holy See would be lowered. The Errington Mission has complicated the question; it has made it difficult for the Government to initiate any step in the Roman direction, and it has made it difficult for the Pope to receive anything but an open Mission.

Lord Salisbury's Government were careful not to create embarrassments for themselves, or for the Pope. The attitude of the priesthood in Ireland was too important a part of their problem. The best way was to trust the tact and discretion of influential English Roman Catholics. At the petition of some of these, a Commissary Apostolic, Monsignor Persico, was sent over to Ireland in the summer of 1887. He was there for some months, and near the end of his stay an Irish Protestant Unionist, Professor S. H. Butcher, met him in a country house, and described his impressions in a private letter:

Sept. 13th, 1887.

I think facts which rather amaze him [Mgr. Persico] are beginning to penetrate the ecclesiastical barrier within which they are attempting to keep him. . . . I think he spoke his real sentiments upon the main questions. There was evident sincerity in the way in which not once, but several times, he declared that the land question is at the root of all others,—that it *can* be solved if reasonable men will give their minds to it, and that *no pretext for Home Rule will then be left*. I gathered more from his private secretary than from himself that he is horrified at the political part played by the priests. As for the Plan of Campaign he threw up his hands over it himself, and expressed a hope in modest and guarded language, but still a good hope, that his visit would lead to some results.... He observed with much emphasis: "One thing I see and know better than I ever did before,—there is no country in the world where the Catholic Church has such freedom as it has in Ireland. This must be said for English statesmanship."

The Irish bishops were the product of a free country in more senses than one. They were Nationalists almost to a man, and the Italian prelates may naturally have hesitated before advising the Pope to risk direct exertion of his authority over them.

Much however was hoped from the issue of a Papal utterance, but there were many setbacks before it came. However in April 1888, a Rescript at length appeared, condemning boycotting as "against the principle of justice and charity," and the Plan of Campaign as unlawful. The Irish bishops were directed to teach these pronouncements to their people "prudently, but efficiently."

Mr. William O'Brien published an eye-witness's account of how the Decree was received in one episcopal residence, that of Dr. Duggan, Bishop of Clonfert:[1]

One evening while the fun round the dinner table was at its top sparkle, a postman's knock resounded at the hall-door outside, and a letter with a foreign superscription was placed in the Bishop's hand. ...He craved the company's leave while he adjusted his ancient spectacles, examined the outside of the envelope as though it were some curious insect, took a pinch of snuff before he tore it open and absorbed another and a vaster pinch of snuff as he settled himself to translate its contents, which were in Latin. His guests felt that something portentous had happened. They preserved a respectful silence while he slowly, with repeated aid from his snuff-box, mastered the exquisite Latinity of Leo the Thirteenth, preserving all the while an altogether untranslatable countenance himself. He at last broke the silence, embracing the company around the table with a circular glance over the top rim of his spectacles. "Ha, ha, my lads, listen to this!" was what he said, and proceeded to read to us his English version of the Vatican Rescript formally condemning Boycotting and the Plan of Campaign. There ensued a period of pained silence. "Well, my lord," the traverser at last remarked, "I daresay it is time for us outlaws to clear out of the house where you have made us all so happy." The Bishop took another

[1] W. O'Brien, *Evening Memories,* p. 349.

pinch of snuff, still with the visage of a Sphinx; then, throwing his eye upon his man-of-all-work, who was beginning to wonder what was to happen to the dinner, "Mike," he said with a solemnity worthy of the Day of General Judgment, "Mike, kill another pig!" Not another word, but if I am not mistaken it was one of the great answers of history.

Dr. Duggan no doubt represented the most intransigent type among the bishops, but he was not singular in his attitude. It was shared by many besides Dr. Croke, Archbishop of Cashel. The Archbishop of Dublin, Dr. Walsh, more prudent in his manifestations, because an abler man, did all he could to neutralise the effect of the Rescript. Very few obeyed it whole-heartedly, Dr. O'Dwyer, Bishop of Limerick, being almost alone in giving it a hearty welcome. Its influence on the parish priests depended very much upon their superiors. Even in the worst parts of Ireland some of them had always discouraged crime, though others used their almost limitless power to instigate it. Between 1887 and 1890 there were twenty-three prosecutions of priests under the Crimes Act, fifteen taking place after the date of the Rescript, and these represented a very small proportion even of the reported cases where priests actively took part in conspiracy.

The Government watched anxiously for results from the Pope's intervention. Publicly these came to very little. Mr. Parnell spoke of "a document from a distant country," and his lieutenants received it with more open indignation than the bishops could show. Some of these professed to agree with the Rescript in theory, but wrote to Rome that the conditions were abnormal, their people the victims of a cruel Government, and that the Rescript could not therefore be promptly made effective. Strong hints continued to reach Balfour that while the Vatican remained without a British Representative the difficulties of exerting influence in Ireland were immense.

The question of Irish education, especially higher education, also came up. Balfour had already reached the conviction that it was right as well as expedient for the State to provide the Roman Catholic majority with acceptable opportunities for University training. The conditions prevailing in the existing Irish Universities could not be so described, and he now made his first effort to meet the need by proposals for a Roman Catholic College, to be built and maintained by the State. In August, almost on the last day of the Session he outlined his proposals in the House. Mr. Parnell pursued his usual course of approving anything he thought good for Ireland, but most of his followers foamed at the mouth at the mere thought of what one of them called "Mr. Balfour's bribing University." Moreover a storm of protest arose in Ulster, and among Protestant Associations all over the country.

Balfour wrote to the Prime Minister:

NORTH BERWICK.

MY DEAR UNCLE ROBERT,   17.9.89.

It will be interesting to watch the movement of public opinion about the proposed Catholic College—not University, as everybody seems to assume.

We shall have trouble, and my impression is that the trouble will come rather from the no-popery middle class of England than from the Organisers in Ireland. But I may be wrong;—I have at present little to go upon but the correspondence I receive on the subject.

It is curious that the row, if row there is, should have been deferred so long, for I said nothing in the House which I had not before said on more than one occasion on the platform; though for some reason or other Protestant sensibilities have never before taken alarm. However it is satisfactory that, at a period so long before any Bill could be introduced, we have a means of gauging public opinion on the subject, and of forming some sort of judgment as to what can or cannot be done in the direction of satisfying the demand for Higher R. Catholic Education in Ireland.

If, as seems not impossible, the feeling aroused by my proposal is so strong that we have to abandon it, we shall be bound in honour to inform the English Catholics and the Pope of the fact as soon as possible, unless indeed the influence of Rome in enforcing its own decrees is so feebly exercised as to absolve us entirely from any feeling of obligation towards them. The whole question will have to be discussed at an early Cabinet, and we must endeavour to form some idea of what the value in votes is of the opposition which is being got up. I should like to see if putting the case fairly before our people would soothe their outraged feelings—but I will say nothing in public till we meet.

Coupled with all this, the attitude of the Roman Catholic authorities was a death-blow to the scheme for the time being. Cardinal Rampolla took exception to several points on which it was impossible to meet his views, especially on the question of endowment of the Theological Chair. Balfour wrote on November 30th, 1889, to Colonel Ross of Bladensburg:

I do not deny I am much concerned at the views expressed ... by Cardinal Rampolla. What I am anxious to do, had it been possible to carry feeling with us in England and Scotland, was to provide out of public funds for the cost of building and endowing a College, the discipline of which should be on principles agreeable to Catholics in Ireland, and in which the whole cost of secular learning should be borne by the State. The difficulties of carrying out such a scheme would have proved at any rate, enormous, possibly insuperable, but there is no use in proposing it even as a matter for discussion under the conditions which Cardinal Rampolla has proposed, and I shall be compelled to say at Glasgow that our plans could only be carried into effect if three conditions were fulfilled, i.e.—that they could be made generally acceptable to English public opinion; that their proposal in the House of Commons would not be perverted by Irish representatives into an occasion for attempting to inflict some political blow upon the Government; and that they were generally acceptable to those for whom they were designed.

The Glasgow speech, made a few days later, was entirely devoted to the subject of higher education in Ireland. The country was much perturbed. Mr. Gladstone had made it a Party question. Balfour was more than willing to explain his views.

My object [he said] is not to bribe the Irish people, ... not to conciliate the Irish hierarchy, who are moved by principles I do not accept. My object is a simpler one—to afford Irish Roman Catholics some of that education which we in Scotland enjoy in so full a measure.... I desire to see them taught philology, philosophy, history, science, medicine, and I fail to see how, in instructing them in these great branches of knowledge I am likely to advance the interests of any particular church, and least of all the church to which they belong.

There the matter had to be left, though Balfour never dropped his hopes of establishing a Catholic University education in Ireland. Some other undertakings of the year 1889 did better. On October 31st, 1889 (the Crimes Act having been in operation for rather over two years), he could write to Lord Salisbury:

I think we may safely *unproclaim* the greater part of Ireland. I am investigating the pros and cons from the Irish point of view. Have you any observations to make on it from the English point of view? ... If we do it now it may of course be alleged that we have done it because of recent bye-elections. If we wait till Jan. 1st (in some respects a more natural date), it may be said we do it in order to meet Parliament. On the other hand, if we wait till the period when no Nationalist can tell a lie about it we shall wait for ever!

The Prime Minister answered:

I should be inclined to vote for Jan. 1st. It is the least splashy of the two alternatives, which is a great advantage. I am very glad you are able to do it,—as the step will be an answer to many lies.

Some forms of crime were decreasing, but on the other hand, the Plan of Campaign was more formidably organised than ever. Evictions were now often preceded by sieges, for the defaulting tenants fortified and defended their houses. Crowds assembled to applaud them, while the local priest went to and fro between them and the Magistrate suggesting terms, and the unedifying scenes went on for hours, because the military force, though usually present, was there only to overawe the crowd, and the duty of protecting the servers of the writ lay with the police, who had no equipment for storming fortified buildings.

Balfour determined to alter all this. On January 4th, 1889, he sent a long telegram to a Resident Magistrate in Donegal, in which he said:

The conciliatory spirit you have shown is fully approved, but ... from to-morrow a more vigorous and continuous procedure must be adopted. ... You should warn all concerned that if resistance involves serious danger to your men your duty will at once require you to use the military force on the spot. ...

Four days later he wrote to Lord Salisbury:

The Donegal evictions ... would, I believe, never have been finished if I had not sent a telegram of which I enclose a copy. The threat of firing, and the threat of firing alone, caused the surrender of the more fortified houses. This is a new departure, and one of our best officials literally got white with terror when he was shown the text of the document. I think it possible, though not probable, that one day or other there will be firing at one of their Plan of Campaign evictions. But if proper appliances are supplied to the police, and if it is well understood we mean business, the chances are very small of such a calamity. ... By "proper appliances" I mean a suitable battering-ram, ... and possibly a fire-engine. If there is anything in the proposed arrangement you dislike please let me know.

This letter heralds the appearance of the battering-ram of which much was heard from the Opposition Benches later on. In April, Balfour was writing to Sir West Ridgeway:

Conybeare [Liberal Member for Camborne] has sent me the enclosed telegram about the battering-ram. I do not much care whether he sees it or not, but I confess I am utterly puzzled about what has been done with regard to this interesting machine. I have always been of opinion, as you know, that it ought to be supplied by the landlords.... Is it to appear on the Estimates? ... Our great difficulty here is not so much that the Irish officials do the wrong thing, as that they do it in the wrong way, in a way (that is) which greatly facilitates the only thing we have to fear: i.e. misrepresentation on the platform.

Balfour's new attack on the Plan of Campaign did not end with the battering-ram. Among his papers of this date is a list, jotted in his own hand, of the names of a dozen or so of the biggest territorial magnates among the Government's English supporters, and the draft of a letter to one of them:

Most private.

MY DEAR DUKE,

It is of the first importance in fighting the social revolution in Ireland that the Plan of Campaign should not be allowed to win on any of what are known as the "Test Estates." Unfortunately those who are conducting the resistance to the Plan are necessarily at the mercy of the various landlords concerned. And if they give in, it is useless, indeed, impossible, to carry on the battle any further. When the owner of a heavily encumbered estate has been kept out of his rents for two or three years he is very apt to become pliable under the stress of sheer want: and yet on the strength of his resolution may depend some of the most important of the national issues now in question.

We are, I am afraid, on the eve of a surrender by one of those landlords. There is, I believe, no way of averting what amounts to a great public disaster, but by buying the estate.

The question arises: can we find a dozen people who are prepared to run the risk of guaranteeing a purchaser against loss, or (which is the same thing) who are prepared themselves to share in purchasing the property? ... It is of the first importance that whatever is done should be done quickly.

The sequel to this is in the report of Parliamentary Questions of March 12th, 14th, 18th, when Balfour blandly denied all "official knowledge" of the purchase of the Ponsonby estate by a syndicate.

Soon afterwards his development programme began to take shape. On May 31st he introduced Drainage Bills for the Bann, the Barrow, the Shannon, and the Suck, and a Bill for a Light Railway serving the poorest and remotest parts of the Congested Districts on the West Coast. Balfour wanted all these Bills to be discussed together, but the Speaker upheld the objection of the Irishmen, who intended to get the railway, and to obstruct the passage of the other schemes. A Treasury Grant of £380,000 was provided for the drainage, the management to be in the hands of the occupiers of land in the areas, under the Board of Works. Landlords would exercise no control, and get no direct advantage, for no rents might be augmented on account of improved value of the drained land. There were the usual sneers about bribery of the Irish people, but it was not very easy to attack this legislation convincingly. One Nationalist found courage to praise it freely. The member for North Mayo, Mr. Crilly, told the House that four million salted mackerel had gone to the United States the year before, by means of the only existing Light Railway, representing £17,000 to Irish fishermen and curers. If one item of export to one country amounted to this, he, for one, would vote for the Railway Bill.

Balfour became more and more absorbed in his constructive legislation. Even before the Parliamentary work was over at the end of August two big schemes were simmering—a Land Purchase Bill, and a plan for permanently relieving poverty in the west. He wrote to his Under-Secretary in May:

No doubt the Congested Districts supply us with the most insoluble part of the Irish difficulty. In other parts it would probably be enough to restore obedience to the law, and to facilitate the acquisition of the freehold of the tenancies,—in the Congested Districts something more is required and what that something more should be is a most perplexing question. Railways no doubt will produce some benefit, but the chief advantage . . . is providing employment in the districts through which they are constructed, and thus tiding over . . . before any more permanently beneficial scheme can come into the question. You say they promote emigration. I have often been told so, but . . . we know that the whole male population is in the habit of annually going to Scotland or other parts of Ireland to earn a living, and therefore it is hard to see why a railway should produce any material alteration in their customary mode of living.

The fixity of tenure given by Mr. Gladstone's Land Bill of 1881 was certainly a doubtful benefit to the inhabitants on the coast and in parts of the interior of Connaught, for it stereotyped numbers of holdings utterly incapable of supporting the tenants. The problem here was one of life, not of rents. Conditions varied, but in some

districts the cash value of the produce of the "farm," together with
the receipts of the family from every source, was not more than
£15 in the year.[1] The cabins and holdings were scattered among
rocks, bogs, and mountains, through huge and magnificent wastes.
"Congestion" meant that the soil was not capable of supporting the
people who were rooted upon it. The definition of the term was
taken to be a Poor Law Division in certain counties, where the total
rateable value, divided by the number of the population, came to
less than thirty shillings per head.

Balfour always considered the machinery he set up as some of
the best—if not *the* best—work he did for Ireland. It was certainly
the most lasting of the tangible heritages of his administration. His
Crimes Act died with the repeal of the Union (to be succeeded by
another, and far more drastic, law). His Congested District Board
survived the birth of the Free State, and was only dissolved by Mr.
Cosgrave's Government in 1923.

The legislation of 1890 was a frank and striking departure from
the Victorian tradition of *laissez-faire*. Balfour based it on acceptance of the principle of State responsibility for poverty-stricken
areas, and then proceeded to free his organisation as far as he possibly could from State interference. He got his money from part of
the surplus of the funds of the late Established Church of Ireland,
which yielded over £41,000 a year. There was a further capital
sum of £84,000 from two Fishery Loan Funds. Nothing in the
finance was controlled by the Treasury or Parliament except salaries
and administrative expenses. The "Board" consisted of the Chief
Secretary and six permanent members, and three temporary (for
fishery, agriculture, or special matters), all nominated by the Lord-
Lieutenant or the Crown. The Chief Secretary had, except at Board
meetings, only the status of an ordinary member; he possessed
neither controlling power nor Parliamentary responsibility.

The official mind was rather slow to grasp these innovations,
which were characteristic of their author's unprejudiced approach
to new problems. He had ceased to be Chief Secretary before the
Board got into full working order, and there exists a Memorandum
of January 1892, to his successor, interpreting his intentions. It runs:

The Congested Districts Board is not in the ordinary sense a Government Department, nor is it subordinate either to the Chief Secre-

[1] See *History of the Congested Districts Board,* by W. L. Micks. The
figures refer to the year 1891.

tary's Office nor to the Ministry of the day.... Applications to the Treasury for expenditure out of the Vote must pass through the Castle. With this exception all correspondence ... with Government Departments may be conducted independently. It will probably however be advisable to keep the Chief Secretary, as Chairman, personally informed of all such transactions ... though it is purely a matter for arrangement between the Chief Secretary and the Board.

When the Board first met in November 1891, a Memorandum by Balfour was in their hands, suggesting a preliminary survey of the different congested areas, to discover their varying wants and the possible remedies, and to "provide a baseline by which to calculate the exact amount of progress we are making."

The result was a set of Reports, which give a historical picture of life in the poorest agricultural parts of the British Isles of that date. During the year this survey took to make, the Board started improving the live stock of the peasants, and the implements of the fishermen. It refused, at any rate in Balfour's time, to undertake ownership or management of any of the small industries which were presently started, though it made grants to some private undertakings big enough to be classed as factories. After the women had got some training through home-weaving, etc., manufacturers began to explore the possibilities. In 1897 Messrs. Morton, of Ayrshire, opened one factory, and later three more, employing in all about 800 workers in 1914, making "Donegal carpets," some of which "jumped" the United States tariff walls, and went to the White House in Washington. Apart from seed supply loans, etc., the Board spent only £100,000 in rapidly decreasing annual amounts on direct relief works between 1894 and 1908, when this kind of expenditure ceased altogether.

This success was due to the sound lines on which the Board was started, and to the men Balfour chose to start it. It is not invidious to name in particular men like Mr. Frederick Wrench [1] and Mr. Horace Plunkett.[2] Mr. Wrench was already a Land Commissioner in 1890. The co-operative movement, which Ireland owed so largely to Mr. Plunkett, was then beginning. Balfour probably heard for the first time of him, and his work, in 1889 in a letter from a friend to which he answered: "if others of his [Mr. Plunkett's] class would imitate his example, more could be done to knit classes together than

[1] Afterwards Sir Frederick Wrench.
[2] Afterwards Sir Horace Plunkett.

is possible by any amount of legislation, or any strength of administration."

Balfour's lot in almost every office he ever held was to stimulate, and to be stimulated by, remarkable and devoted colleagues. Not many survivors of his Irish days are alive now, but they were the first among a number who could testify to the delight of working with his critical, receptive mind.

The Bill for the Congested Districts was introduced in March 1890. A potato famine was foreseen in that year. Balfour absorbed himself in the details of preventive measures against a crisis. Although he knew little of farming, he always brought to the discussions of the scientific side of agriculture the zest he had for scientific discussion of everything, especially when there was something to be done about it. That autumn rows of little bags were laid out on the terrace steps at Whittingehame, some, I think, containing varieties of sound seed potatoes, some certainly holding rotten samples from Ireland, for one of my childhood's memories is of his putting a potato into my hand, where it squashed into a black and nasty-smelling mess. On August 27th he wrote to Lord Salisbury from Whittingehame:

The continued wet weather makes it quite certain that we shall have to meet a more or less severe crisis in the West. . . . My impression is that it will be the worst since '47. Of course we meet it under much more favourable circumstances. The population dependent on potatoes is much smaller, the oat crop is said to be good. I hope the people are getting fair wages in their annual migration to England. . . . Still, I anticipate difficulty. . . . I have telegraphed to Wrench to buy with all possible secrecy and despatch large quantities of potatoes. The crop is evidently going to be a short one both in England and Scotland. Seed potatoes will most certainly have to be provided for the Irish;—I hope at cost price, but whether given, lent, or sold, they will have to be provided: and it would be folly to wait till we had to buy them at famine price. I have not consulted the Treasury on this transaction. Jackson, representing the Treasury, has gone to Ireland with full instructions from me in respect of Railway and Public Works. . . . If there is any hitch I shall have to go to Ireland to see if I can help him. He is an excellent man to work with. I wish I could say the same of some of his subordinates at the Board of Works. They are all old women. . . .

yours affecly.,

A. J. B.

RIDING THE PIG
(August 1st, 1891)

He was back at Chief Secretary's Lodge in October 1890 and started on a week's tour of Mayo and Galway to visit congested areas and look at the proposed route for the light railway. A few days later he went to Donegal. Miss Balfour, Sir West Ridgeway, and Mr. George Wyndham went with him, and they travelled in two jaunting cars, with a covered carriage for servants and luggage. Pressmen followed, but no detectives—a sign of changed times since 1887. The people crowded round them in every little centre. Balfour discussed local needs with the priests and others, addressed the people, got down often from the car on the bogland roads to talk to peasants in their little fields. It was not the kind of journey he much enjoyed, and its discomforts were increased by an injury to his thumb caused by a window dropping on it in one of the inns. But the whole thing was a great success. Only once, at Dungloe, was there an "incident." Mr. Swift McNeill, the Member, appeared suddenly in the hotel where Balfour was receiving a deputation about a contract for knitting stockings for the British Army, and spoke thus:

You will understand that I am not addressing you now as a Cabinet Minister, or as the chief agent for the coercion, but in your new capacity as a professional humanitarian.

He went on to discuss some evictions at Gweedore, and begged Balfour there to examine the battering-ram and some cottages demolished by it, and referred to the abhorrence of the people for his regime. "What I have done I have done," said Balfour in his reply, "and if I had to do it again I would do it again in the way I have done it." The deputation eventually induced Mr. Swift McNeill to go away, denounced his interruption, and returned to business.

In his autumn holiday of 1889 Balfour began to work out his Land Purchase Bill in the way he liked to do with his own Bills. He wrote to Lord Salisbury on September 17th, 1889:

You will be glad to hear that I have drafted a Land Bill and have sent it with an explanatory Memorandum to be printed as I know you will never tolerate it in my handwriting.

As a piece of drafting I think it is *monstrous;* but it will sufficiently explain my ideas. I shall have it sent on to Ireland to be criticised by departmental experts, as soon as it is ready. Goschen ought also to see it; but he is in Ireland, and if I send it him there, he is sure to leave it about, and it will appear in the *Freeman's Journal* next day!

And to Sir West Ridgeway a fortnight later:

I send you the fruits of my September holiday in the shape of a sketch Land Bill. As a piece of drafting I should think it will make Lane's hair stand on end. . . . As you know I should like myself to have gone in for more heroic measures, but I clearly see that is impossible. A compulsory measure would be accepted neither by the House of Commons, nor the House of Lords, nor by the landlords.

The Bill, which Balfour introduced on March 24th, 1890, was the outcome of months of hard work, traces of which survive in a mass of correspondence with the Chancellor of the Exchequer, with Irish landlords (very acrid critics some of them), and with experts on the intricacies of a land system which Balfour described in his Second Reading speech as "essentially and radically rotten." He continued:

You cannot remain where you are; you cannot go back, you must go forward, and the only way is by attempting as far as your means allow, to substitute some rational system of tenure.

This Bill marked the first great step towards removing the truest of Irish grievances against the English. On the principle of voluntary sale and voluntary purchase, to which the Conservatives held, the process that turned the peasantry into the owners of the land was not to be begun and ended in the lifetime of one Parliament, even by a strong Government in prosperous times. British Government credit was pledged by Balfour's Bill for some £33,000,000 as guarantee for the required loans. Balfour always looked on this Land Purchase Act as the beginning of the new Ireland. In 1928 I asked him: "What is left now of your Irish policy?" "Everything, everything!" he answered. "What was the Ireland the Free State took over? It was the Ireland that we made, though the Liberals went back on our policy. . . . They could have done nothing—nothing with Ireland but for our work."

Mr. Gladstone opposed the Bill. Mr. Parnell felt constrained to vote with him, though not whole-heartedly. Obstruction prevented the passage of the measure that summer, and it was accordingly held over to the autumn Session which opened on November 25th,

1890. On the 27th Balfour reintroduced the Bill, with certain changes in its finance and machinery. But this time only twenty-five Irishmen walked behind Parnell into the Government Lobby. The united front of Irish Nationalism was already broken,—split asunder at sight of a letter from Mr. Gladstone. On the floor of the Chamber the phalanx that for ten years had compelled British Parliaments to almost perpetual discussion of its affairs was shrivelling into impotence. The position and prospects of the Unionist Party were thus changed in the twinkling of an eye. All this because a decree of divorce between Captain and Mrs. O'Shea had been pronounced on November 14th with Mr. Parnell as co-respondent.

I remember Balfour, in later years, skimming a study of Parnell dealing at some length with the personal side of the event which led to Mr. Gladstone's repudiation of him, and his abandonment by the bulk of the Irish Party. Balfour remarked that the book seemed to be all about the uninteresting part of Parnell's life. He expressed utter incredulity when I reminded him of how he himself had once been offered an opportunity of exploiting the private affairs of his great Irish opponent. But the following letters were among his papers, and convinced him of a fact which had clearly never dwelt for a moment in his mind.

Private.

124 VICTORIA ST., S.W.
Dec. 26, 1889.

DEAR MR. BALFOUR,

Owing to delay in the delivery of a letter informing me that the legal formalities had been complied with, it is only now that I find myself in a position to write you the letter which I expected to send on the 24th inst.

Although the matter is a private one I think it well to inform you that the day before yesterday I presented a petition for divorce, and that Mr. C. S. Parnell is the co-respondent in the action.

As the Unholy Alliance will doubtless misrepresent the matter in every mood and tense, I should be very glad if you could spare time to read the enclosed. Dr. O'Dwyer is not only a very great personal friend, but also one of my bishops.

I have telegraphed to Chamberlain who is acquainted with the facts and who owing to a previous experience he and I had of Cardinal Manning, will not be astonished at the attitude His Eminence has adopted, no doubt in concert with Sir Charles Russell. I hope I am doing right in explaining matters to you; if not, excuse me on the plea of good intention. yours truly,

W. H. O'SHEA.

Private.

DUBLIN CASTLE.
27.12.89.

DEAR CAPTAIN O'SHEA,

I have safely received your letter of the 26th inst., and I return herewith the letters of the Bishop of Limerick and Mr. Chamberlain.

It would be impertinent in me, a comparative stranger, to comment on the distressing family matters to which your communication refers. It deals with a subject necessarily painful, and of which the painfulness must, I fear, necessarily be increased by the publicity which would seem to be now forced upon you. I sincerely trust that no aggravation of inevitable suffering may be brought about by the unwarrantable introduction of political and party feeling into private affairs, from which, in my opinion, they should be wholly dissociated.

With much sympathy for the position in which you are placed,

Believe me,

ARTHUR JAMES BALFOUR.

Captain O'Shea could hardly have chosen any confidant in the Conservative Party who was less likely to interest himself in such confidences politically.

Balfour wrote to Sir West Ridgeway the day of the reintroduction of the Land Bill.

IRISH OFFICE,
27 Nov. 1890.

MY DEAR RIDGEWAY,

I think you would like to hear a little gossip from here as a change from your labours in connexion with relief of distress. I have very little to say which has not already appeared in the papers. Gladstone's action in pronouncing against Parnell was, I am told, prompted by the report of the feeling at the Sheffield Conference brought home by Morley and Harcourt. He thereupon, against his own judgment, wrote a letter which appeared in the paper next day. He is naturally furious at the Irish Parliamentary Party having been asked to give an opinion on Parnell in ignorance of the letter.[1] It serves him perfectly right—he should have

[1] From Mr. Gladstone saying that he could no longer lead the Liberal Party if Mr. Parnell remained leader of the Irish Nationalist Party. See Morley's *Life of Gladstone,* Vol. III, Chap. V.

remembered Lord Carnarvon,[1] and have formed a more accurate estimate of our friend.

The division last night was a most curious and significant one. Parnell ostentatiously voted for the Government, and carried with him some
twenty-four of his own followers (mostly extremists) and was deserted
by the rest of his Party. My own belief is that Parnell's back is now up,
that he will stick to his guns as long as he can, and nothing but *force
majeure* will turn him out. I do not see where this *force majeure* is to
come from, unless he has lost far more influence in Ireland than I believe
to be the case.

How all this is to end I do not know, and I do not much care. It is
extraordinarily amusing while it lasts, and, at all events, it enables us to
get through our business in a reasonable time. *Now* the rapidity with
which Parliament does its work is almost embarrassing, and we do not
know how to spend our evenings after five o'clock. Loving deputations
of priests come to me every day, and altogether the situation is so novel
that I feel quite out of my element. Unless the Gladstonian Parliamentary Party shows powers of reorganisation of a very remarkable
kind, the Session will be over sooner than was anticipated, and I shall
turn up in Ireland before the 20th Decr.

yours very sincerely,

ARTHUR JAMES BALFOUR.

The year 1891 was Balfour's last at the Irish Office. In the course
of it he saw his Land Bill through Parliament, and his Congested
Districts Board set up. He saw the Crimes Act fade into the background, for in June he was able to suspend its operation in nearly
every part of Ireland. In August he announced the next item of the
constructive programme, thereby rather fluttering the Conservative
Party, for the measure was one for Irish Local Government.

But before the next year came Balfour had handed over the Chief
Secretaryship to Mr. Jackson[2] in order to take the leadership of the
House of Commons in succession to Mr. W. H. Smith, who died on
October 6th. Balfour wrote to Mr. Goschen on October 27th, from
Dublin:

I don't like leaving Ireland. It is odd, but nevertheless true, that quite
apart from the interest attaching to Irish administration, there have
grown up ties with the grim old Castle, and this beastly town, which it

[1] The reference is to a statement by Mr. Parnell concerning a confidential interview with Lord Carnarvon. See *Life of Robert Marquis of
Salisbury*, by Lady G. Cecil, Vol. III, 157 *et seq*.

[2] Afterwards Lord Allerton.

is painful to sever; I feel as if I had had a good time which has for ever come to an end; and the thought is not agreeable.... There are other reasons for regret ... about which I will only say that I have never before so clearly understood how much more important in the eyes of ordinary men are *nominal* differences• than real ones; how indifferent they are to substantial agreement if only the catch-words are not identical.

Soon after writing this, Balfour faced, almost for the last time, the passage of St. George's Channel, which he was wont to call "not the least invincible of Irish difficulties."

Chapter VIII

PRIVATE LIFE IN THE NINETIES

The children of the Family. Picnics. Routine of home life. Balfour's reading. Tastes. Golf. Bicycling. Social life. The Souls. Balfour as a friend.

WHILE Balfour was at the Irish Office he was in the habit of spending some months of the autumn recess at Chief Secretary's Lodge in Dublin, and family life at Whittingehame was correspondingly interrupted. When it was resumed in 1891 its circle was enlarging through the rise of a new generation. Both Balfour's surviving brothers now had families, for Gerald Balfour had married Lady Betty Lytton [1] in 1887. The nurseries and schoolrooms at Whittingehame were populated by an increasing tribe of his children, and the children of Eustace and Lady Frances Balfour. These two families of Balfour's nephews and nieces eventually numbered eleven, eight of them girls.[2] They and their parents lived at Whittingehame for some six months of every year, and the children looked upon it as their home, and upon its owner as the giver of all delights.

He had a charming way with children he knew well. His genuine interest and ready attention were there for them as for their elders, the moment they were capable of demanding it. All in turn became aware at a very early age that the best had not been got out of any day until "Nunky" had made his comments on the recital of its doings. Picnics on the seashore were much favoured by young and old, and the rising generation used to listen anxiously when one of these expeditions was proposed, to hear whether he was coming. Most often he came. A procession of waggonettes and pony carts would be brought to the front door, and the children watched like lynxes the manœuvres of their elders to entice him into this or that carriage. At the first certain indication the vehicle would fill like

---

[1] Daughter of the 2nd Earl of Lytton.
[2] See Family Table at end of this volume.

magic. Victory was to the nimble of mind and body, but all such family dramas were conducted with outward calm. It was an axiom that "Nunky" would be "bored" by rivalries or quarrellings.

Arrived at the picnic place, he strolled about, surrounded by an ecstatic giggling bodyguard of nieces, while the kettle was boiling. I remember him also lying on a rug on the beach at Tyninghame and writing his *Foundations of Belief* until summoned to tea. There was another picnic when the bunch of keys, including the key to his Cabinet boxes, fell out of his pocket into the sand, and its loss remained undiscovered for more days than his biographer cares to reveal. That, however, is a later story, for two of the nieces, who were babies in the nineties, rode down to the sea and found the missing objects.

At Whittingehame children pervaded all the house, but they early imbibed the respect for good conversation which prevented them from interrupting their elders unduly. Nobody, however, hesitated about saying anything on any subject, provided that, in their own opinion, they had something to say. This impression had to be very erroneous before it provoked even a mild look of the dreaded "boredom" from the head of the family. Such a look was deemed a greater catastrophe than the gentle deadly little blasts of sarcasm which occasionally found a deserved victim, for these, at any rate, amused everybody else. The greatest excitement was to try to fall in serious argument with the mightiest of wrestlers.

The compression of a number of strong personalities and of several family units into one house made existence at Whittingehame a whirlpool of everything in life. He was its calm centre. Nobody invaded his sitting-room except by invitation, or on their own request. Every rule, however, is made to be broken, and he was once rescued during the particularly sacred hour between tea and dinner from an invasion of a young instalment of nieces, who, having cooked for him a sparrow rolled in clay according to a Red Indian recipe, had presented it on a platter, and were seated round in hopes of seeing him eat it.

The routine of Balfour's day at Whittingehame was more or less this. He always breakfasted in bed, and seldom came out of his own rooms before luncheon, by which time he had dictated his letters. At luncheon the family vied with each other to tell him what was in the newspapers. In the afternoons before the days of motors, there might be a bicycle ride, or an expedition to play golf at North

BALFOUR ON THE LINKS

Berwick or elsewhere. Alternately garden golf on the terraced lawn round the house, though this was rather abandoned after he built a hard lawn-tennis court. Then tea—a leisurely meal—and he disappeared from the library which was the general sitting-room. After dinner, unless there was good music available, he usually played a rubber of pretty bad Bridge. At eleven o'clock the family separated, and Balfour in his own room would read for an hour or two.

Nothing ever interfered with his reading. He always had several books on hand at once. The latest work on science might be found propped up on the mantelpiece of his bedroom to vary the process of dressing, and Lady Frances once declared that she suspected him of "making a raft of his sponge" to support a French novel while he took his bath. It was seldom that some work by Edgar Wallace or P. G. Wodehouse was absent from his bedside after these authors rose to fame, and the table by his arm-chair was always heaped with books of history, or Memoirs. It would be difficult to define the limits of his reading. Its range could astonish even his oldest friends, as for instance when, staying with Lord and Lady Desborough at Taplow Court on the eve of a General Election, he carried off to his bedroom a manual on chess, a game which since his boyhood he was never seen to play. Serious fiction was perhaps the only class of book upon which he was cautious of embarking. He never began a new novel until he was assured that it ended well. If no such assurance was forthcoming, he fell back upon Scott, Jane Austen, Kipling, and Stevenson.

He chose "The Pleasures of Reading" for the subject of his Rectorial Address to St. Andrews University in 1887, and there gave his personal answer to that most personal of questions—what to read and how to read it. Mr. Frederic Harrison had lately given forth some portentous warnings against "gorging and enfeebling" the intellect by over-indulgence in carelessly chosen literature. Balfour suggested that the analogy between the human mind and the human stomach might be pressed too far. He had never himself met the person whose natural gifts had been overloaded with learning. No doubt many learned people were dull, but not because they were learned. "True dullness is seldom acquired. It is a natural grace, the manifestations of which, however modified by education, remain in substance the same." People should not be afraid to read what they enjoyed. Idle curiosity, so-called, was a thing to be encouraged. Here follows a passage which might well mislead posterity into supposing Balfour a newspaper addict, ingeniously defending his favourite vice. The exhaustive study of the morning and evening papers was "only a somewhat unprofitable exercise of that disinterested love of knowledge that moves men to penetrate the Polar snows, or to explore the secrets of the remotest heavens.... It *can* be turned, and it *should* be turned into a curiosity for which nothing ... can be wholly alien or uninteresting."

Such being his views, Balfour was naturally a lavish book-buyer. The library at Whittingehame is a large room, well stocked before his day with standard works of every kind. Soon it overflowed, and other rooms were lined with shelves. His own sitting-room was packed from floor to ceiling, mainly with books on philosophy and theology, and its sofas were heaped with flotsam and jetsam of current publications. The books at Whittingehame had an alert look about them, as if expecting to be pulled out at any moment. They were, in fact, often temporarily lost, for the ever-growing library was too large to be kept in order by the family's spasmodic efforts at arrangement, continually begun, but never ended. If Balfour was found wandering down the corridor at unwonted hours he was most likely in search of some book, and his relations would rush to proffer conflicting evidence about the present position of the missing volume.

"Read everything you find interesting and nothing that you don't," was nearly the sum-total of his advice to the younger generation with regard to literature. It sounded easy, yet to try to keep up with him along any of his primrose paths to knowledge, was to discover how deceptive was that apparently leisurely pace.

Life at Whittingehame was very easy-going, but not without its framework of rules. We did not play cards on Sundays, nor, until quite the latter years, lawn-tennis, and then only after consultation with Dr. Robertson, Minister of the parish from the days of Balfour's own youth. Balfour went regularly on Sunday mornings to the parish church, which is on the other side of the deep glen separating Whittingehame House from the garden, as is so often the case in Scotland. After Church the family used to walk home, discussing the sermon, arguing about the tunes of the Psalms and Paraphrases. The garden and all the flowering shrubs inside it were Miss Balfour's affair. Outside Balfour directed the planting, but there was a certain amount of debatable ground, and debated it frequently was. Indoors he left everything to her, even down to the management of the wine cellar, though this did not imply a lack of interest in vintages on his part. From his grandfather's day Whittingehame had a great stock of fine old wines to which he added, and the family treated them with due respect.

In the matter of food Balfour was on the whole easy to please, though he expected good cooking, and was critical of bad. But he had no violent aversions, except for tapioca pudding. Plenty of cream was apt to be his criterion for dishes, just as velvet was his criterion for women's dress. His nieces soon discovered that he would probably admire a velvet dress, no matter what its age or cut. He was not apparently very observant of such matters, though upon this you could never rely. Praise or criticism might emerge at any moment. He had strong views about comfort for his own clothes, especially shoes, where he liked experimenting with all sorts of patent soles that gripped well on the turf of golf-links. He never smoked, and for a good many years upheld Miss Balfour's laws against smoking in the library, though in his own room anybody could do what they pleased. He was not very punctual, nor was unpunctuality ever criticised, but he always insisted on waiting to go in to dinner until even the youngest was present. There was in fact a slight, unemphasised, but perceptible regulation of family life, a flavour of the breeding of an older generation. After cocktails came into fashion we never had them at Whittingehame. He once told me he liked, but disapproved of them, and I said: "Do you mean that you would refuse one if I offered it you in my house?"

"I think I should drink half," he said, laughing, "so as to mark *my* feelings without hurting *yours.*"

For one month of every holiday season between 1891 and 1914 he gave himself up entirely to golf. In his Autobiography he wrote:

I spent each September at North Berwick, at the Bass Rock Hotel, or in later years at Bradbury's, in rooms which looked down on the 17th green and the first tee, framed in a landscape embracing the little harbour, the Isle of May, and other islands which skirt the Firth of Forth, and the stately profile of the Bass Rock. Even now I never drive down the hill past Bradbury's without thinking of it as in some respects, a second home. When at North Berwick I lived a solitary but well-filled life, playing two rounds of golf or more each day, and in the evenings carrying on my official work, and such philosophic and literary undertakings as I happened to be engaged on. Each Friday after my morning's round I drove to Whittingehame in the best substitute that could then be found for a modern motor-car, a brougham with a pair of horses, and spent the week-end with my family and guests. On Monday I drove back to North Berwick in time for the afternoon's round, and the happy experiences of the week before were repeated, never to satiety.[1]

North Berwick was undoubtedly his favourite golf-course, supreme even among the noble series that fringe his beloved Firth of Forth. To see him on a fine clear day striding bareheaded over those links was to see an obviously perfectly happy man, provided always that he was on his game. Even if he were not, the sweetness of his temper was never ruffled, but he became a little depressed. Playing his best no extraneous circumstance ever apparently spoiled that eager concentration of delight, except perhaps on one or two occasions during the South African War. His great golfing days were over before the worse war came.

There was one series of foursomes in particular to which he looked forward and back, during the years when they were played, with a fervour almost impossible to exaggerate. They were always referred to as "The Great Match." In these the late Mr. Walter de Zoete and the late Mr. John Penn played against Balfour and Mr. John Laidlay. Every autumn and Christmas holidays between 1894 and 1908, when the death of Mr. Penn broke up the partnership, the Great Match was played several times. Mr. Laidlay was the strongest, Balfour the weakest of the four, but in these matches particularly his power of concentration was always at full stretch, and he was usually at the top of his form. Mr. Laidlay has told me that in all those years he never once heard Balfour say a word of reproach to his partner. If he made a very bad shot himself he would turn away and gaze over to the coast of Fife for a moment, and then come back smiling.

Driving, he had a long easy swing and could hit a fairly long ball, not too high, with a considerable run on it. The stroke that troubled him most was his brassy through the green, and he always took great pains over it and his stance. His putting was pretty good, especially so at critical moments. The shot that gave him the most pleasure however, when he brought it off, was with his iron. His handicap was never lower than 8, which he received in 1903. In

[1] *Chapters of Autobiography*, pp. 229, 230.

PARTNERS IN "THE GREAT MATCH"

Mr. J. Laidlay   A. J. B.   Mr. John Penn   Mr. W. de Zoete

1905 and 1906 it was 12, and in the latter of these years he won the Dalrymple Cup at North Berwick, with a score of 89.[1]

The social revolution caused by the invention of the safety bicycle was instantly reflected in the family life at Whittingehame. It brought even a greater addition to Balfour's enjoyment of existence than did the motor car later on. His delight in mechanical advance was only equalled by his incapacity to manipulate any sort of machine. He never dreamed of trying to drive a motor car, but he did learn to ride a bicycle, as was once evidenced by his appearance on the Treasury Bench with his arm in a sling, and his foot in a slipper. This incident is not chronicled in his correspondence, but a letter to Lady Elcho[2] relates a happier experience.

HOUSE OF COMMONS,
March 20th, 1895.

MY DEAR LADY ELCHO,

You will be amused to hear that I went for my first bicycle expedition through the streets of London on Sunday afternoon. I chose Sunday of course because the traffic was small, and I hoped that I might escape being run over by hansom or omnibus, even though my skill should be somewhat in default. I got on pretty well; in fact the streets were so empty that I found no difficulty at all except on one occasion when a hansom immediately in front of me turned the wrong way in order to get on to its stand. The driver apologised, which is a rare exercise of politeness on the part of his kind. I won't tell you where I went, for you would not know the names of the streets!

The real joy of a bicycle to him was the independence it gave in the matter of locomotion. He early gave up riding, and was never an enthusiastic walker except on a golf-links, or for the purpose of going through his own woods and plantations with his forester. Through bicycling he learned, as he said, to know his own county for the first time. Roads, gradients, ordnance maps, began to play a part in conversation which some of the family thought excessive. "People come here," said his ever candid sister-in-law, Lady Frances, "having perhaps heard of you as an agreeable talker, and all they carry away is a description of the two roads to East Linton!"

[1] I am much indebted to Mr. John Laidlay for the notes on which this passage is founded.

[2] Mary, daughter of the Hon. Percy Wyndham, wife of Lord Elcho, afterwards Earl of Wemyss and March.

His bicycle was sometimes a means to solitude as well as to independence:

BLENHEIM PALACE.
Nov. 23rd, 1896.

MY DEAR LADY ELCHO,

There is here a big party in a big house in a big park beside a big lake. To begin with (as our Toast lists have it) "the Prince of Wales and the rest of the Royal Family"—or if not quite that, at least a quorum, namely himself, his wife, two daughters and a son-in-law. Then there are two sets of George Curzons,[1] the Londonderrys, Grenfells,[2] Gosfords, H. Chaplin,[3] etc., etc. We all came down by special train—rather cross most of us—were received with illuminations, guards of honour, cheering and other follies, went through agonies about our luggage, but finally settled down placidly enough.

To-day the men shot and the women dawdled. As I detest both occupations equally I stayed in my room till one o'clock and then went exploring on my bike, joining everybody at luncheon. Then, after the inevitable photograph I again betook myself to my faithful machine, and here I am writing to you. So far you perceive the duties of society are weighing lightly upon me!

Last week was a very heavy one—especially Thursday, when I had to open a bazaar in Edinburgh and attend a banquet at Sheffield within six hours of each other. I flew past Gosford[4] in my special about 12.15 and wondered what you were doing, whether you are well, and whether you were enjoying one of the most exquisitely lovely days I ever saw.

Now I must go down to tea and leave this scrawl. I am oppressed at this moment with many cares, the lightest of them being the total impossibility of devising a generally acceptable Education Bill. I have expended treasures of ingenuity on this most thankless task.

yrs.,
A. J. B.

It is a difficult task to portray Balfour as he appeared in the social world where for sixty years he enjoyed a popularity which had little to do with his prestige and position in public life. It may have been partly his own unaffected pleasure in amusing company which caused every company to become more amusing when he joined it.

[1] Hon. G. N. and Mrs. Curzon, afterwards Lord and Lady Curzon of Kedleston, and Viscount and Viscountess Curzon, afterwards Lord and Lady Howe.
[2] Afterwards Lord and Lady Desborough.
[3] Afterwards Viscount Chaplin.
[4] Lord Wemyss' house in East Lothian.

He never "talked down" to anybody, but his touch in conversation was so light-handed, that he could, as it were, turn the heaviest pudding of talk into a *soufflé*. No topic came amiss as raw material for such transformation, nor was he in any way put out if the topics of his choosing were a little above the heads of his audience. The end of the following letter shows how this did occasionally happen.

10 DOWNING ST.,
Dec. 4th, 1896.

MY DEAR LADY ELCHO,

... Yesterday I had an interesting experience. It appears that Herbert Spencer expressed to J. Morley a desire to make my acquaintance. This, considering all things, I could not regard as otherwise than a high compliment, so off we set together in a hansom to call on the old philosopher (he is 76 and has just finished the endless volumes of his so-called Synthetic Philosophy) in St. John's Wood. He had put off his journey to Brighton for a day in order to see me, and we found him lying nearly at full length, with his feet on a chair, and, by his own account, in very poor health. Controversy, it appears, immediately brings on serious palpitations; we avoided therefore all subjects of difference and he talked interestingly of his early life as an engineer, of my brother Frank, of the new edition of his Biology, and how he is employing five young men of science to bring it up to date, and so forth. He looks like a cross between a village school-master and a farmer.

I dined in the evening with the Duchess of Manchester. I mentioned incidentally that I had seen H. S. She had never heard of him. I said he was a philosopher. She asked if I cared for Philosophy. This gave me pleasure. yrs.,

A. J. B.

A discerning woman advised another who was about to meet Balfour for the first time to talk to him about her preoccupation with the illness of her kitchen-maid's mother. She had a great success. There was another young lady who prepared to meet him by studying the newspaper, and began with clasped hands: "Oh! Mr. Balfour! Russia!" That conversation languished, but its end came gently. Balfour never consciously snubbed innocent offenders. But he would use his formidable powers to crush certain forms of conversation. A man told a dirty story after the women had left the dinner-table at a country house party. Balfour was not a prude, but on this occasion two Eton boys were present. He became white with anger, and said in a voice of ice: "Who did you say was the hero of this singularly disgusting tale?" The teller of the unhappy anecdote shrivelled into silence.

The years of which I am writing stood midway between the time when feminine society looked a little awe-struck upon the wonderfully clever young man who smiled at them so serenely through his pince-nez, and the later times when the débutante daughters of his lifelong friends talked to him with the freedom that he hailed with delight in the rising generation. The nineties were the years when the formality of the Victorian period was being irradiated by an ease, a gaiety, an intelligent inclusiveness largely due, as far as London society was concerned, to the influence of the particular group that has come to be known as "the Souls"—a nickname slightly irritating to many who belonged to it, and particularly so to Balfour. The mere idea of shutting himself up within a clique was abhorrent to him, and when in 1929 Lady Oxford urged him to put into his Autobiography some description of the gay days when that now scattered circle was still unbroken, he made little effort to respond. Perhaps he was wise. Another member of the "Souls" writing once of the "laughter and delight" of those far-away days, described their joys as "imponderable as gossamer and dew."

It was in the companionship of the men and women who once were the "Souls" that the undercurrents of Balfour's real affections and feelings ran nearest to the surface of his social enjoyments. It was for the most part among them that the lasting friendships of his life were formed, and to their testimony his biographer turns for help in shattering a legend which to his family seemed ridiculous beyond measure—the legend namely of his cold-heartedness and lack of sympathy with grief. People who might have known better have from time to time helped to spread this myth, little guessing perhaps when they did so, how much light they were shedding upon their own characters, and on the genuineness of their own appeals for sympathy. He had an uncanny power of detecting any false ring in such matters. Much secret amusement was caused by the complaints of a lady, who had poured out to him a rather hysterical story of a rather sham tragedy, and had only been rewarded by the exclamation: "Lor!"

Against that shall be put the experience of another friend who went to him in deepest grief.

He never got tired of being sorry for people, and gave the most vital help, because his consolation was never of the kind that is a mere sop to unhappiness. It was when those who loved him were in anguish that the great power of his faith was revealed. The depth and tenderness of his realisation and understanding, the incentive of his belief in courage. He gave fully, nobly and generously of himself, if he gave at all,—with a truth that seems only possible for those who are reserved by nature. There never can have been such a friend.

Chapter IX

LEADING THE COMMONS

1891–1895

Pros and cons of Balfour becoming Leader. Criticisms. Speech on democracy and the future. Balfour and the newspapers. Mr. Gladstone takes office. Balfour visits Belfast. Second Home Rule Bill. Balfour's views on oratory. Balfour visits Hawarden. Balfour's first encounter with Mr. Lloyd George.

By coincidence the great administrative period of Balfour's life ended, as it had begun, suddenly, and through accidents unconnected with the beginning or end of Lord Salisbury's Government. The Prime Minister recalled him from Ireland reluctantly after Mr. W. H. Smith's death, and mainly because the Party insisted on him for Leader in the Commons. Lord Salisbury wrote to the Queen:

15th Oct. 1891.

The choice of a successor to Mr. Smith involves very serious difficulties. Sir M. Hicks-Beach has expressed his wish not to succeed to the leadership which he held before. The choice therefore lies between Mr. Goschen and Mr. Balfour. Mr. Goschen's age and reputation commend him greatly, and it would be inconvenient to take Mr. Balfour from Ireland at this moment. But against these considerations must be set the almost unanimous view of the members who support the Government in the House of Commons. So far as Lord Salisbury can judge, he fears he would run great risk of breaking up the Party, he certainly would dishearten it very seriously if he were to recommend Mr. Goschen. Lord Salisbury . . . as at present advised thinks circumstances are concurring to make Mr. Balfour an inevitable choice, though the objections to it from many points of view are considerable.[1]

Some of these objections had been discussed between uncle and nephew three years earlier, as soon as the state of Mr. Smith's health had shown that the Conservatives might be forced to choose a new

[1] See *Queen Victoria's Letters*, Vol. II, p. 76.

leader before the end of that Parliament. In 1888 Balfour was seriously balancing the pros and cons of coalition with the Liberal Unionists. Perhaps he felt the result of his thoughts too inconclusive to be useful, for the following draft letter to Lord Salisbury was apparently never sent.

4 CARLTON GARDENS,
23.11.88.

My DEAR UNCLE ROBERT,

My uneasiness about Smith's health ... induces me to put down the following stray thoughts, with most of which however you are probably familiar.

If Smith goes, there are as far as I can see only two men now on the Bench who can possibly succeed him—Goschen and myself. There are many grave objections to the latter. But there is one which is insuperable. Goschen will certainly object, and be right in objecting, to serve under one who was not in Parliament when he first became a Cabinet Minister. But he could hardly lead the Conservative Party in the House of C. unless he consented to call himself a Conservative and join the Carlton.

Even if, however, he consented to swallow the name, after having digested the principles, of the Tory Party, there are objections to him. His fussiness drives Smith mad. It would, I hope, produce a less drastic effect on his other colleagues, but it would be trying. He cannot stay on the Bench, through mere fidgetiness, for ten minutes consecutively; during those ten minutes his perpetual comments on what is going on quite drown the text, so that when one gets up to reply it is Goschen one feels inclined to reply to, as he is the only person one has heard! These however are small matters, and he is so able, loyal, good-tempered and good-natured, so obviously honest and so incapable of intrigue that, *faute de mieux,* he would, I believe, do very well both by his colleagues and the Party.

But is nothing better to be had? This brings me at once to the whole question of coalition. Shall we gain or not gain by having Hartington as leader, and James (say) as Home Sec.? Against it I put the considerations:—(1) We shall lose Bury certainly; Rossendale possibly.[1] An inauspicious inauguration of a new regime! (2) It might embarrass your arrangement of Cabinet offices; and it would certainly cause much bother with the smaller appointments, some of which you would have to give to the L.U's.

(3) You would introduce into the Cabinet two Counsellors, one of whom always recommends standing still, and the other of whom always

[1] Pending bye-elections.

recommends running away. A forward movement under such leaders is difficult. (4) The Conservative Party, led by a Cavendish, and a Cavendish leading the Conservative Party, would both find themselves oddly placed!

(5) Chamberlain could not and would not join. It is possible that our Party could not and would not have him. But if he is deserted by Hartington and his followers he would probably rapidly drift back into the bosom of the True Liberal Church, and we should lose the value of his support. I rate this more highly than perhaps you do. But it means the Birmingham seats *certainly*, other doubtful seats in the Midlands *probably*, and one of the most useful speakers and debaters in the House. It is true that he will hardly leave us while Gladstone lives, and that after Gladstone dies he would probably leave us anyhow. Nevertheless I am convinced that Joe as leader (though in the second place) of eighty Liberal Unionists—and Joe as leader of half a dozen Radical Unionists, would be very different people indeed. (6) Hartington's presence in the H. of Commons depends on the life of a person whose life is probably as fragile as Smith's health. If therefore his acceptance of the lead in the Commons is the solution of our difficulties it can be a very temporary one at best.

On the other side it is possible that the fusion of Parties might (as Randolph would say) "influence the popular imagination" and gain votes.... It would provide us with a leader who could certainly command the highest admiration of his followers. And above all it would save us from the difficulties on which we have more than once nearly made shipwreck, the difficulties, I mean, arising from having a separate and irresponsible council of war directing the movements of one wing of the allied army. The difficulty is not likely to diminish. It will become formidable again so soon as ambitious legislation is attempted. And therefore it is important, I think, to keep the policy of coalition at least in view, when we are considering the question of possible vacancies in the Cabinet—say in the Home Office.

My cold is responsible for the leisure which has produced this portentous epistle!   yours aff.,
                                                                    A. J. B.

This picture of personalities shows the obstacles to a combination of the anti-Home Rule parties even at a time when Lord Hartington was still available as Liberal Unionist leader in the House of Commons. When Mr. Smith's death made a decision necessary this was no longer the case, for Lord Hartington's father, the Duke of Devonshire, was then dying.

There was no desire for coalition in the ranks of the allied parties, and Balfour, now First Lord of the Treasury, took up his leadership of the House by unanimous demand. "I do not think it wholly for your comfort or advantage," Lord Salisbury wrote to him on October 16th, 1891. "It will make you a target for very jealous and exacting criticism. But I do not think you can avoid or refuse it as matters stand."

Balfour answered next day from Whittingehame:

You will have got my telegram accepting the leadership in the H. of C. The prospect is not exactly exhilarating:—a (temporarily) waning cause and a dying Parliament:—but even if I were disposed, which I think I may say I am not, to look at the question from a personal point of view, I am too much of a fatalist to trouble myself about possibilities when the matter seems so clearly marked out....

The Parliament of 1886 met for its last Session in February 1892, and was prorogued in July. In those six months Balfour had a new technique to learn, and an old technique to forget. His previous Parliamentary practice, especially in the existing House, had been in acrimonious debate, and oftenest single-handed. The conduct of Irish business had afforded him little exercise in the arts of conciliation. His very presence was to the Irish Party like a red rag to a bull. He sat now in the place of a man whose strength had not lain in his fighting power, but in his common sense and his quality of *bon bourgeois*. Mr. Smith had won the respect of the House by his own respect for the claims of its business upon his time and attention. From the beginning of Questions till the rising of the House he was in his place, or available at a moment's notice. He dined off a chop in his room, not even absenting himself long enough to go to his own house in Grosvenor Square. This assiduity was not counted as anything extraordinary. Mr. Disraeli and Mr. Gladstone had taken the same view of their duty to the House, even when they were combining the Premiership with the Parliamentary leadership, and in days when there was no "twelve o'clock rule." The presence of the Leader of the House within the precincts of the House, even if not actually on the Bench, was taken so much for granted that Balfour's first appearance in evening dress after the Dinner Hour caused almost a sensation.[1]

The Conservative Party, in the opening weeks of the Session, were inclined to be critical of their gladiator in his new rôle. In particular,

[1] Sir Henry Lucy, *Diary of a Salisbury Parliament*, p. 491.

the nonchalant manner, which had been so piquant when applied to the Irish, lost some of its popular appeal when it reappeared applied to the ordinary course of public business. The Session had run three weeks when Sir Henry Lucy thought it worth while to enter in his Diary that Balfour "lounging in" was hailed with ironical Irish cheers.

Time was when this demonstration would have been overpowered by a thunderous cheer from the Ministerialists. To-night they made no response. It was perhaps a trifling thing, not meriting the increasing attention growling round it in the Commons. But small errors of conduct are sometimes more fatal to success in high places than are breaches of the Decalogue.[1]

Balfour may or may not have been aware of a slight chill in the air. All his life he walked through the hot and cold belts traversed by a politician's path too serenely to make it safe to dogmatise about the extent to which he noticed them, or was affected by them. He was economical of effort in his House of Commons work as in everything. Many years later, during a debate on some important subject, he entered the Chamber and stood near the Speaker's Chair for a moment or two. "Blank is attacking us—and making a good speech," said the Whip, sitting alone near the end of the Bench. "Yes," said Balfour listening intently, and presently added, "Unnecessarily so." This comment was made in a post-war Parliament, but it might have belonged to any period.

Balfour's handling of an Irish Local Government Bill, which he introduced early in the Session, brought out a side of him which his Party had not yet seen, because never till now had he introduced any legislation about which he was himself slightly apathetic. Yet before leaving the Irish Office Balfour had in fact given considerable thought to the main lines of the Bill, especially to the question, crucial in Ireland, of securing fair representation for religious minorities. The upshot of his labours he now presented to the House:

The mode of Minority election we have put in the Bill is not, in my opinion, the best ... but I do think it is easily worked and understood, and there are very great advantages in doing a stupid thing which has been done before, instead of doing a wise thing that has never been done before.

[1] *Diary of a Salisbury Parliament*, p. 459.

"THE COMING OF ARTHUR"

SHADE OF PAM: "H'm! A little young for the part,—don't you think?"
SHADE OF DIZZY: "Well, yes! *We* had to wait for it a good many years!—But I think he'll do!!"

(February 20th, 1892)

The point was one which appealed to himself, but it evoked scant enthusiasm in his audience. The moderation of his claim for the Bill reached its climax when he placed it lower in importance than all his other legislation, including the Crimes Act.

"It is the first time," said Mr. John Morley, "that any Minister, in any country, has prefaced the introduction of a Bill for extending Local Government with an avowed preference for a Coercion Act." This was a fair debating point, and Balfour had laid himself open to a good deal of criticism. He was said to have been playing up to Conservative prejudices; but the incident was perhaps more due to a streak of insensitiveness to the mentality of his audience. Only for this reason has it seemed worth description, for the Bill, thus presented in a pan of cold water, never got beyond its Second Reading. Local Government was not conferred upon Ireland until the Conservatives were again in office after 1895.

In the spring and summer of 1892, Parliament suffered increasingly from the paralysis of old age. Interest shifted to the platforms, and to Home Rule once more, a Liberal victory being foreseen. The Irish Nationalist Party was split into Parnellite and anti-Parnellite factions, and for this and other reasons the Gladstonians were not as eager as they once had been for the fray. Ulster however was in ferment, and the Conservative Party were determined to hold their opponents down on the trail of Irish policy.

Before the campaign really opened in the month of June, Balfour made an uncontroversial speech at a Press Fund Dinner. He chose a subject on which he could always speak with enthusiasm—the future. Some men have the gift of illuminating the past,—the headlights of his mind seemed to throw their beam ten or twenty years on, and to be directed by an unappeasable curiosity.

He talked of the changes the next twenty years would bring into the political thought of the nation—of the overwhelming demand for social betterment which he foresaw to be coming, not as a direct consequence of the extended franchise, but coinciding, possibly in dangerous fashion, with the increased power of democracy. For the demand itself he had nothing but sympathy.

We all of us see—the blindest of us must see—that a change has come over the character of political controversy, political speculation, and political aspiration during the last generation, which some people describe as Socialism, but ... which ought more properly to be described as a desire for the amelioration of the lot of the great classes of the community.... It is an interesting question to see how far the democratic constitution now firmly established in these islands is going to deal successfully with the social problems with which we are brought face to face.... Let it be noted that never yet since the increase of the Franchise ... have we seen the Government carried on by any Administration that is in a small majority.... I am sure that at some time—some Government will have to take office in a democratic Parliament acquainted by long practice with the most modern developments of Parliamentary tactics, in a small majority, and I confess I look forward to that experiment with interest and curiosity. I should look forward to it with more alarm than I do, if I had not the example before me that the English Press presents of a common sense of the responsibility of Englishmen....

There follows a eulogy of the Press, not merely demanded by the occasion. His habit of not reading the papers did not at all diminish his respect for good journalism. It was a trait which for some reason took the imagination of the public and has in consequence been rather exaggerated. Certainly after he had a private secretary he heard all news of importance in the daily papers, and was always ready to look for himself at anything specially interesting or amusing. During the Great War he read the newspapers as avidly as anybody. It is true that he generally skipped the leading articles, and some good judges of the statesman's art thought him wrong. Mr. Chamberlain wrote to him in December 1894:

You do not read the newspapers, and I must say that the longer I live the less time I am inclined to give to the lucubrations and partisan writing in which I find very little that is new or suggestive.

But may not this disregard of the Press be carried too far? After all there is no other way of finding out the trend of public opinion, and the knowledge which is always necessary to a politician.

It is very well to know what is right,—but it is also well to know what is possible—and where, among many roads to choose from, the line of least resistance is to be found....

The speech delivered at the Press Fund Dinner of 1892 may have arrested little attention in the ding-dong of Party oratory. Nevertheless, it is an example of the side of his political thinking which justified the instinct that had moved the Party to insist on putting him next in succession to the Conservative leadership. But the Twentieth Century was still years below the horizon. Balfour had little time to speculate about it, during the next few weeks.

East Manchester polled on July 6th. Balfour held the seat with a majority of 398, as compared with 644 in 1886. The drop was partly due to his opposition to the eight hours' day in coal-mines, and partly to the amount of time he spent during the campaign outside his constituency. The Liberals had in fact hoped to get him out, and enormous crowds waited late into the night in and about Fleet Street till the Manchester figures were announced.

The lime-lighted spot in this second Home Rule Election was Protestant Ulster. On June 17th 12,000 delegates had attended a great Convention at Belfast. The numbers present, the solemnity of the proceedings and the singing of "God is our Refuge and Strength," the moderation of the speeches and the restraint in the wording of the Resolution, produced a great impression. In Midlothian Balfour declared that Mr. Gladstone's solution for Irish difficulties would only add one more—the "gigantic difficulty" of Ulster. He warned his Scottish audience that the Protestant North would resist, as they themselves would resist, a domination they abhorred. The speech was delivered in Mr. Gladstone's own constituency, on the eve of the poll. Mr. Gladstone held Midlothian next day, but only by 690, a drop of over 3,000 votes. Nearly everywhere the Liberal figures had similarly decreased. The English constituencies, as distinct from Scotland and Wales, had returned Unionists in a majority of 71. With a majority of only 40 in the House of Commons the Gladstonian Party was again at the mercy of the Irish vote.

Lord Salisbury decided to await defeat in Parliament before resignation, and a question therefore arose as to the character of the Queen's Speech, and even of whether there should be a Queen's Speech at all. This turned out to be a constitutional necessity, as the following letter from Balfour shows.

10 Downing St.
July 24, 1892.

My dear Uncle Robert,

I saw Joe yesterday; but before I come to that, I had better tell you of a conversation I had on Friday night with Harcourt and Morley. I met them at a large banquet given by Natty.[1] After the ladies had gone, to everyone's astonishment they rushed up and sat themselves down, one on one side of me and the other on the other. Much of the conversation was casual chaff with which I need not bother you. But after

---

[1] Lord Rothschild.

a while Harcourt asked me if there was any truth in the rumour (which I suppose he had heard from Randolph) that we did not mean to have a Queen's Speech. I replied that we had not yet had a Cabinet, and that therefore nothing was settled: but that I personally saw one very grave objection to having a Queen's Speech, namely that they might play us the same trick as in '86, and ride off upon some insignificant Amendment. Harcourt replied that of course he could say nothing definitely till he saw Mr. G., but that his opinion and feelings ran very strongly in favour of constitutional precedent; that there was no precedent for *not* having a Queen's Speech, that he rather thought (though he had not looked into the matter) that the form of words used by the Sovereign in directing that a Speaker shall be elected, commits her to a subsequent speech; and that he thought there would be no difficulty in supplying us with a formal and explicit assurance that the precedent set by Peel in '41 would be followed in the Amendment to the Address that would be proposed by Mr. G.

I asked Mallet to investigate the point raised by Harcourt. I enclose his minute. From this it seems plain that if we dispense with a Queen's Speech, we shall have also to modify the invariable form of words used by the Chancellor on behalf of the Sovereign when the Commons are directed to choose a Speaker.

A Queen's Speech being found necessary, the demand for a programme came from a powerful quarter. Balfour's letter to Lord Salisbury goes on to recount how he had told Mr. Chamberlain that "Hartington thought that there would be damaging unreality in enumerating measures which everyone knew we should not survive to propose, much less to pass."

On this the old antipathy between Radical and Whig flamed up. Balfour gives Mr. Chamberlain's reply within quotation marks.

"This raises a most important issue. Hartington is impossible. I cannot embark my political fortunes in his boat. . . . The country will not have Whiggism. I have nothing to complain of in the Conservative Party. Very much the contrary. Of course we differ on many points. I expect to be refused three times out of four when I advocate a particular course. I hope to succeed the fourth time. There is no disagreement that may make co-operation difficult. I think they (the Conservatives) are wrong not to disestablish the Welsh Church on condition of keeping its endowments, for such a policy would not injure the Welsh Church and would make Wales Conservative from one end to the other. But I know they cannot give this, and I am ready to go on voting for Disestablishment as long as such a vote is inoperative, and to stay away as soon as it becomes dangerous. The movement for 'social legislation' is in the air; it is our business to guide it. This policy is as much (or more) in harmony with Conservative traditions than Liberal ones. We, the Unionist Party, *can* do it, which the other side *cannot*. I am strongly in favour of a programme and a Queen's Speech.... It will be extremely difficult for me to maintain my position in the Midlands without a substantive policy on which to take my stand...."

Having thus "Boswellized" Mr. Chamberlain, Balfour sums up his own impressions:

He [Chamberlain] is especially irritated by Hartington's Whiggism—by which I understand him to mean a readiness to give up everything and to accept everything if sufficient "squeezing" is resorted to; but never to do anything except under torture.

The final point in the letter was this:

He [Chamberlain] would rather like, if he saw his way, to unite with us, and sit with us, under the common denomination of a National Party....
You know already that speaking generally I am not in disagreement with Joe's views.

Lord Salisbury however in this case thought a non-committal policy the better part of wisdom. He answered:

Confidential.

HATFIELD.
July 26th, 1892.

MY DEAR ARTHUR,

I think Harcourt means to trick you; but if you don't mind to risk that, I do not very much care. That is to say—the difference to my mind between a formal Queen's Speech and no Queen's Speech at all is not a very serious matter.

But the proposal for a programme Speech *is* a very serious matter. It implies that we have Bills ready—at least in outline—to sustain our programme—which we have not. It must deal with subjects on which people are very sensitive on both sides; and though we may use phrases which will please Joe, we must in so doing alarm a good many people who have always been with us.

I fear these social questions are destined to break up our Party; but why incur the danger before the necessity has arrived,—and while the Party may still be useful to avert Home Rule?

Of course this danger may be averted or mitigated by a wishy washy Speech; but surely that course would combine all the disadvantages.

yours ever aff.,

SALISBURY.

The new Parliament met on August 4th. The Queen's Speech said absolutely nothing, and Mr. Gladstone skilfully contrived to get through the Debate on the Address, without disclosing the Liberal policy on Home Rule or any other subject. The Government was defeated by 40 on August 11th, and Mr. Gladstone set about the formation of his last Administration. Parliament separated, not to meet again until February 1893. Balfour went to Whittingehame, and in September to North Berwick, for the first uninterrupted holiday since he had taken the Irish Office five years before. His thoughts reverted to metaphysics, and his second book, *Foundations of Belief,* was begun that autumn.

The holiday was only once interrupted, by a speech made to the local Volunteers at Tranent in his own county. Here again his mind turned to the coming years, and this unpremeditated speech was really a bit of thinking aloud. Perhaps the history of the Committee of Imperial Defence, founded ten years after, might properly be begun by extracts from this address to E Company of the 7th Battalion of the Royal Scots in an East Lothian mining village.

I do not think that the House of Commons provides a very good machinery for either criticising or constructing a great naval or military policy....

And again there are difficulties in connection with Ministerial management of affairs of national defence.... And if, when the time comes,—it should be found that either through laxity of Parliamentary criticism, or through the opportunism of governments, or through the apathy of the public, the machinery of national defence ... has been allowed to rust in our armoury, then indeed will come too late to each one of us the reflection that we have not done our duty ... the first duty that devolves upon a citizen.

After Christmas, Balfour went with his sister to Pau, before the meeting of Parliament on January 31st. The Unionist opposition took their seats in a cheerful and truculent mood, encouraged by stories of Liberal dissensions over the provisions of a Home Rule Bill. Liberal Unionists and Conservatives cheered each other's leaders with new heartiness, and Balfour had a great reception.

Two months later he went to Ulster. Lord Salisbury had accepted an invitation to attend a Demonstration in Belfast, but he fell ill, and his place was taken by Balfour. The Orangemen flocked into the city in their thousands. Miss Balfour wrote a description of the scene.

... Every house was decorated with flags; every window was full of spectators, and the streets were packed with men, women and even children, so that it seemed impossible that carriages would ever get through them. . . .

After waiting some time we saw at the far end of Donegall Place, through the vibrating hot air above the crowd, the first carriages of the procession, and immediately the crowd below turned round, so that instead of the sea of faces, nothing was visible except myriads of round felt hats. . . . The carriages came up at foot's pace, and as they approached, the roar of the cheers and the waving of handkerchiefs and hats increased more and more. . . . The pressure must have been terrific, shouts of men and screams of women coming up at every moment, till one became so possessed with fear that some horrible accident would take place that one could hardly give attention to the oncoming procession. At last the Mayor's carriage got up, followed by Lord Londonderry's, also with four horses and outriders. In the first Arthur was standing up, bare-headed and smiling and bowing, while the crowd surged round shouting and making frantic efforts to shake his hand. As he got out and made his way into the building the people pressed in and round the carriage, climbing up over sides and seats.

As Arthur appeared on the stand the cheering broke out louder than ever. Again all faces were turned towards us. The sun was behind us full on the faces of the crowd; but where the shadow of the stand fell every face was clearly seen, the hats far back on the heads, the eyes wide open. Outside this shadow the hats were drawn down over the eyes, and the faces were screwed up with eyelids squeezed together and mouths open, so that the effect of the two parts of the crowd was curiously different. . . . Some wildly excited so that I thought they were drunk, tho' I afterwards found that they were quite sober as far as alcohol was concerned.

We remained for several hours in the stand, Arthur getting so tired with standing that they at last provided him with a high office stool against which he leant. The procession took some hours to go by, each lodge or other body having its huge appropriate banner and usually a band, the music of which was scarcely heard. When the Scotch contingent went past with a company of pipers, the cheering was so great that it was impossible to hear a sound of the pipes.

I afterwards saw a Doctor who had attended a man who had his leg rather badly injured by the wheel of the carriage Arthur was in going over it in the crowd. The Doctor said the man stoutly declared he didn't care,—he'd be run over again only to shake hands with Balfour.

In the evening Balfour spoke in the Ulster Hall. He said:

I shall go back to my work in the House of Commons strengthened by the conviction I have obtained to-day of what Ulster is, and what Ulster means. And depend upon it, that if the British people can only have that brought home to their minds, not all the forces arrayed against you can prevail against righteousness and justice in the end.

Two days later, on April 6th, Mr. Gladstone entered on his last Parliamentary fight, with a great speech on the Second Reading of the Second Home Rule Bill. The Debate lasted twelve nights, closing on April 21st with a majority for the Government of forty-three. Before the Committee stage opened Balfour announced from a Primrose League platform that the Unionist policy would be one of unrelenting opposition: "to discuss in detail one absurdity after another as they arise, and to show how absolutely impossible it is to frame a Bill on any lines that shall at once give Home Rule to Ireland and maintain the very elements and foundations of the British Constitution."

The Unionist Opposition carried out this programme in all its laborious fullness. The strain told on tempers as the weeks wore on, "scenes" multiplied, but the attendance on both sides of the House was extraordinary during this remarkable Session. Night after night the Division Lists show six hundred members and more, dividing on quite minor Amendments.

Balfour held the work well in hand, and no voice was raised in criticism of his leadership now. At the end of June Mr. Gladstone was constrained by his followers to agree to closuring by compartments. Very naturally he tried to parallel his action with the application of the closure by which Balfour's Crimes Act had been got through in 1887. Balfour retorted that the Crimes Act, right or wrong, had been urgent, whereas what mattered a week here or there in considering the ultimate form of the Constitution of Great Britain? It happened that at 10 o'clock on July 6th he was speaking again when the guillotine fell on the Bill for the first time. He sat down at the first stroke of Big Ben, and the excited House fell to dividing, to the accompaniment of furious cries of "Gag" from the

Unionists. Thereafter the House of Commons registered its decisions on the future of Ireland oftener in terms of physical than of intellectual exercise.

After forty-seven nights the Bill emerged from Committee on July 27th. On September 1st it passed out of the House of Commons with a majority of 34 and went up to the Lords. The Peers proceeded to its destruction without indecent haste. They devoted four days to disposing of a matter which had occupied the House of Commons for over eighty sittings. On September 8th their Lordships divided, but to the onlookers it seemed that there was no division. Sir Henry Lucy wrote:

Watching the multitude it seemed as if all were going into one Lobby. In ordinary times the Whips stand by the wicket and "tell" members as they pass through on their return. Although undesigned there was not lacking something of dramatic effect in Lord Salisbury's proposition that this usual course should be departed from. Better let them pour through into the outer hall and there be counted. So . . . the peers, spreading out the full breadth of the floor, pressed slowly onwards. With them went the Bishops, their white lawn looking like flecks of foam on the eddying current. . . .

The Division over, noble Lords returned to the Chamber and "stood round on the Woolsack an almost impenetrable mass." Through the throng struggled one holding a piece of paper. Amid the hush the voice of the Lord Chancellor sounded with clarion clearness:

For the Second Reading 41, against 419.[1]

Gladstonian Home Rule was dead.

For the time being, interest in politics collapsed, Parliament had been in almost continuous session since February, but Estimates had been blocked by the Irish Debates, and the House did not rise till September 22nd. Till then the Opposition Leader could not flee from London, as the bulk of his Party did, but he began his holiday after his own fashion nevertheless. On the day after the scene in the House of Lords his sister, Lady Rayleigh, wrote in her Diary:

Sept. 9th, 1893.

I walked down to the House with Arthur this morning—the manuscript of the begun book of philosophy under his arm. In Committee of

[1] Sir Henry Lucy, *Diary of a Home Rule Parliament,* p. 255.

Supply he thinks it necessary to be "about the place," but hopes for a good deal of time for going on with the book. He remarked that his mind did not naturally turn to politics. He never thought about them in bed, which was the test. He regarded them with a calm interest, but as for getting excited over them as some people did, he could not do it.

There was Goschen; he got quite worried if anything went wrong, and as for Chamberlain, he thought of nothing else....

Arthur asked me what the newspapers said about last night's Debate. "I can't tell you; you have none in your house."

Arthur admitted that he had not looked at a paper for weeks—knew he ought to—Buckle of *The Times* often scolded him for it.

In actual fact, and apart from the technical interest of the professional politician in conducting an attack upon an intricate Bill, the Session must have been tedious to a mind which always found to-morrow more interesting than yesterday. The arguments against Mr. Gladstone's Bill had been used so often that they sounded, as Sir William Harcourt said, like an old hurdy-gurdy grinding out old old tunes. The temptation to trust the Peers to defeat the Bill must at times have been strong. Now they had done it—and what next? The political horizon was blank, and Balfour turned with pleasure to his metaphysics.

The Autumn Session was Mr. Gladstone's last in harness. On December 29th, Balfour offered him on behalf of the Unionist Party the congratulations of the House of Commons on his eighty-fourth birthday. A letter written a few days before to Lady Frances ends with a tribute to Goliath. It begins with some opinions of speech-making in general, drawn forth by his sister-in-law's criticisms of his own lack of power of "oratory."

It is quite true that preparation is useful for public speaking,—is indeed *necessary* for all the best public speaking which is not pure debating. It is also quite true that I do not prepare enough, and that many of my speeches suffer.

But preparation such as ——— gave to his speech is wholly destructive to oratory as I conceive it. Every sentence, indeed every word, *was,* and what is worse, *appeared* to be, the result of careful premeditation. Directly this becomes clear, then good-bye to all intercourse between speaker and audience; what ought to have been a speech becomes a recitation, and is little better than reading aloud.

There are only two men living whom I would cross the street to hear,

and that not too often. Both, though great artists in their way, are undoubtedly very limited in range. One is Joe, the other is Asquith. . . .

.   .   .   .   .   .

PS. I omitted your father [1] from the list of speakers. His style has
more amplitude than I quite like; but take him all round, he is the best
of the lot. Mr. G. I count not among the living, though he can still
perform some tricks of Parliamentary *leger-de-main* which no-one else
can even attempt.

Once before Mr. Gladstone's death in 1897 Balfour was given an
opportunity to renew the friendly private relations which had been
interrupted by twelve years of political antagonism. Much water
had indeed run under the bridges since the visit to Balfour's shooting lodge in 1879, when in 1896 Balfour was invited to stay at
Hawarden. He described the visit in a letter to Lady Elcho:

I ran up from the station on my "bike"—an uninteresting incident
in itself, but amusing in that it shocked the Old Man. He thought it
unbefitting a First Lord of the Treasury. . . . He is, and always was, in
everything except essentials, a tremendous Tory, and is peculiarly sensitive in the matter of dignities. . . . He showed me a volume of his
Journal, a little flat book containing a space of about two years. . . . He
kept it without break from the time he was fourteen, till his eyes were
attacked by cataract. An extraordinary feat! . . .
Have I anything else to tell you? I think not—unless you are interested by chance in the question of foreign competition. Herbert [2] told
us that on the Board of the Manchester, Sheffield and Lincoln Railway
they had been recently considering offers of *steel rails*. The cheapest
tender was by the great German firm of Krupp,—and this for a line
running through the very centre of our steel industry. Mr. G. admitted
that this seemed a serious case, but said that as a rule he rejoiced to
hear of instances of foreign competition. "Nothing less," said he, "will
rouse the British producers. John Bull is a wonderful fellow when he *is*
roused, but he cares nothing for perfection in itself; he has no stirrings
after the ideal, . . . and he can never be made to do anything better
than he is compelled to do by the necessities of the case." So much for
Mr. G. on his countrymen. I am not sure that he is right. [3]

The year 1894, in which Balfour for the last time crossed swords
with Mr. Gladstone, was the year of his first notable encounter

[1] The eighth Duke of Argyll.
[2] Herbert Gladstone, afterwards Viscount Gladstone.
[3] *Chapters of Autobiography,* pp. 81-82.

with Mr. Lloyd George. The occasion was a Debate on a Bill for
disestablishing the Church in Wales, and in the process of demon-
strating the national spirit of the Welsh, Mr. Lloyd George was a
little slap-dash about his history. "What about the Act of Union
between Wales and England?" he said in the course of his speech.
"What was the date of it?" enquired Sir Richard Webster. Mr.
Lloyd George answered that it was passed in the reign of Henry
VIII, and he would give the Hon. Member the date later on. "It
was an Act of Union between the Principality or Dominion of
Wales and the Kingdom of England. Was not that a recognition
of separate nationality?" The speech flowed on. When Balfour rose
to answer it the Statute in question was in his hand.

"I asked a friend to procure it from the Library," he observed,
"and the House will perhaps be interested in a few words from its
preamble. This is the Statute apparently, which indicates the special
character of Wales as a nationality, and is the foundation of her
freedom. It begins thus:

"Albeit ... Wales justly and rightly is, and ever hath been incorporated, annexed, united, and subject to and under the Imperial Crown
of the realm, ... and also because that the people of the said Dominion
have, and do daily, use a speech nothing like, or consonant to, the natural mother tongue used within this realm, and because some rude and
ignorant people have made distinction and diversity between the King's
subjects of this realm and of Wales, ... His Highness desires utterly to
extirpate all and singular of the sinister usages and customs differing
from the same and to bring the said subjects ... to an amicable concord
and unity.

"I really think," Balfour went on, closing the book, "the Hon.
Gentleman should have looked carefully at this Charter of Welsh
liberties before he led us to think that there were, I will not say
rude, but still ignorant, persons who did make a diversity between
the King's subjects of this realm and his subjects of the said Dominion or Principality."

The Liberal Government was very near its end. A week later it
fell, after defeat in a snap division on a motion concerned with the
reserve of cordite for the Army. The General Election of July 1895
returned the Unionists with a majority of 133, and the three years
of "ploughing the sands" were over. *Foundations of Belief* was
through the press. Six months earlier Balfour had written to Mr.
R. B. Haldane (then Liberal Member for Haddingtonshire):

I am now wearily struggling with the dregs of my book, which is to be sent forth. It will, I am sure, be equally repulsive when finished, to the philosopher, the theologian, and the man of the world. You at all events—as the first and the last, will, I am sure, not like it. But you have a broad tolerance, even for your opponents! I am going to denounce you at Haddington on Friday if I am well enough. At present I am laid up with a cold, which brings home very clearly to my mind the insoluble character of the problem of evil.

Chapter X

AMERICA AND BI-METALLISM

Jameson Raid. Venezuelan Question. Balfour on Arbitration. Balfour and Anglo-American friendship. Balfour as a bi-metallist. An unsent letter on Silver. Refusal of the Indian Government to adopt a double standard. Balfour counters their arguments. Balfour's suggested reply to United States' proposals.

In the Government of 1895–1900 Balfour was again First Lord of the Treasury, a post free from departmental routine. His work as Leader of the House, with the Prime Minister in the Lords, was however exceedingly heavy, especially in the first spate of domestic legislation with which the Unionist Party celebrated its accession to power.

Both sections of the Liberal Unionists were at last represented in full force in the Cabinet, the Duke of Devonshire being Lord President of the Council and Mr. Chamberlain Colonial Secretary. The General Election was no sooner over than Balfour received his first letter from him in his capacity of Cabinet colleague.

HIGHBURY,
BIRMINGHAM.
July 23rd, 1895.

MY DEAR BALFOUR,

First let me congratulate you on your increased majority in Manchester. . . . You seem to have done an immense amount of work, and must be awfully tired. I finished last night, and it was about time. I felt as if I could not make another speech to save my life. . . . I am anxious to be exactly on the same lines as yourself, and I believe there will be no difficulty, but it would be of great advantage to have a quiet talk with you. . . . Just at first we shall have it all our own way, and much depends therefore on the order of procedure which we give to our work. I see the possibility of great things—in administration as well as in legislation, and when the inevitable reaction comes I should like to feel that we have not lived—and suffered—in vain.

yours very truly,
J. CHAMBERLAIN.

Before Parliament met, which was not until February 1896, the energies of the Colonial Secretary were fully absorbed by the affairs of his own Office. The New Year opened with a South African crisis, precipitated by the Raid into the Transvaal of Dr. Jameson and six hundred followers. They crossed the frontier on January 1st. Next day they surrendered at Krugersdorp, after thirty-six hours' fighting, to an overwhelmingly strong Boer force. On January 3rd the German Emperor sent his telegram of congratulation to President Kruger, which practically recognised the independence of the Transvaal from British suzerainty.

Feeling in Britain became violently excited. The grievances of the Uitlanders was enough understood to create a good deal of active sympathy for Dr. Jameson. Balfour's own first impressions are recorded by Lady Frances Balfour, in letters to a relative absent from the family party at Whittingehame.

Arthur shocked Alice [Miss Balfour] by saying he should probably have joined Jameson had he lived there, ... that Jameson's character was the only attractive feature in the matter, tho' "he ought to be hung" all the same.... Then he went through rebellions in history which those outside have endeavoured to bring to a head and failed.—Monmouth's rebellion—the rebellion of '15—of '45, and all the Irish ones. I think his spirits have gone up with the evidence of how well Jameson fought.

The letter then alludes to Balfour's evident preoccupation with his forthcoming big speech at Manchester. The date of it was January 15th, 1896, and as it happened to be the first utterance by a Cabinet Minister since the crisis developed, every word had to be carefully weighed. It was perhaps the only time that Balfour's notes for a speech were written days beforehand. They are annotated "Approved by Lord Salisbury, January 11th." In respect of the Transvaal they run:

(1) Without attempting to excuse the inexcusable, it is plain that difficulties *must* arise with a State whose inhabitants are so arbitrarily divided between those who pay and those who govern. We must hope that the Boers, who have behaved with generosity, will see this in *their* interests as well as ours.

(2) A controversy has arisen between those who say that the Queen *is*, and those who say she is *not*, suzerain of the Transvaal. We need not dispute about words. The Transvaal is independent as regards *internal*, but not *external* relations. Those are under our control. Our rights are not denied by any foreign Power, and we intend to maintain them.

The speech kept pretty closely to these notes, and cries of "German sausage" from the audience failed to draw forth any direct allusions to the Kaiser's telegram. Balfour passed to another matter of grave international concern, which had lately startled the British public almost as much as events in the Transvaal. Just before Christmas 1895 our relations with the United States had suddenly become violently strained through President Cleveland's Message to Congress, asserting the right of the United States, by virtue of the Monroe Doctrine, to intervene in a long-standing dispute between Great Britain and Venezuela about the boundary of British Guiana. The President recommended the setting up of a United States Commission to settle the question and declared that it would be the duty of the United States to defend the right of Venezuela to the territory as defined by that Commission.

Ministers themselves were taken by surprise. Lord Salisbury had received in August the first despatch from Washington suggesting arbitration. His reply, which contained a refusal of unrestricted arbitration, had required to be carefully prepared. It was sent off in November, but had not actually been received when the President's Message was sent out to the world. The British public, ignorant that a question even existed which held possibility of trouble, suddenly heard America talking of the possibility of war. Thus Balfour's first important speech on foreign affairs as a Minister was largely devoted to a subject which occupied him increasingly in later life—the subject of Anglo-American relations.

The idea of war with the United States [he said] carries with it some of the unnatural horror of a civil war. War with any nation is a contingency to be avoided at almost all costs,—except the cost of dishonour. . . . We may be taxed with being idealists and dreamers in this matter. I look forward with confidence to the time when our ideals will have become real. . . . The time will come, the time must come, when someone, some statesman of authority, more fortunate even than President Monroe, will lay down the doctrine that between English-speaking peoples war is impossible.

In 1896 these sentiments were not platitudes. Most people who had considered the subject probably held them, but the feeling of kinship with the United States was not a strong political factor on either side of the Atlantic before the Spanish-American War, which was still two years ahead. From this time onwards Balfour exerted his influence to promote Anglo-American understanding in every possible way. The Manchester speech produced a long letter from Senator Lodge, who was already a power in the Republican Party, and reputed in England to be very belligerent over the Venezuelan affair. Balfour had made his acquaintance a year or two before, through his own friendship with Mr. Henry White, then First Secretary to the American Embassy, and his wife. After reading Balfour's speech Senator Lodge wrote:

It is just what I should expect from you, generous, fair and high-minded.

Perhaps in view of the misrepresentations which have been sent to London about myself it may not be out of place for me to say that I feel as you do about a war between the two great English-speaking peoples, and should regard it as a terrible calamity to civilisation. . . .

You speak with surprise about the outburst of hostile feeling in the United States towards England which followed the President's Message. I trust you will pardon me if I trespass on your time long enough to explain it, as it is a matter of great importance. In the first place you . . . have kept yourselves in a state of ignorance about the United States. Until very lately your newspapers gave it less space than to Belgium and Holland. Surely this was not wise. Such information as you got in the newspapers was generally wrong, and even now you are badly served.

But the causes of hostile feeling lie deeper and go far back. There is no nation on earth which England could so easily make her fast friend as the United States. . . . Yet from 1776 England's policy has been one of almost studied unfriendliness. I know we have always had friends among English public men from the time of Chatham to the days of Bright, and still later of yourself. But these have been individuals. The people of England during our war were our friends.

But the Ministries have always spoken and acted, as they represent the Government, against us.

After enumerating examples, including the Behring Sea Arbitration of 1893 and the beginnings of the Alaskan Boundary question, Senator Lodge goes on:

Last and deepest of all present causes is the money question. The times have been very bad, and there is much suffering. The Silver question is widely believed to be at the bottom of it all. The Bimetallists know that England alone stands in the way of an agreement. The Free Silver men ... believe that England not only prevents international Bimetallism, but that her influence is largely responsible for the resistance of the North and East to Free Silver. I am not concerned to discuss the correctness ... of their feelings. All I desire to point out is that they exist. When the President took a stand which the country thought right in Venezuela, the materials were ready and the explosion followed....

I do not believe there is the least danger of war, or that there ever has been. On the contrary I think we shall come out of this difficulty with a better understanding than ever.... So far as Venezuela is concerned, all we ask is arbitration, which seems to us not unreasonable....

The United States politicians, concerned mainly to uphold the Monroe Doctrine, looked on the Venezuelan question itself merely as one of a frontier line. Lord Salisbury saw much deeper aspects. The territory claimed by Venezuela amounted to about two-thirds of British Guiana, on which British subjects had been settled—some of them for generations. The Venezuelan claim rested on early documents fixing the frontier between the Dutch and Spanish colonies, and it was conceivable that an arbitral award based on those documents might ignore the titles of the population subsequently acquired. Therefore Lord Salisbury steadfastly refused to allow the case to go to unrestricted arbitration. Not till the United States agreed to certain provisos safeguarding long-standing rights, did he consent to sign an Arbitration agreement. The real difference between the Governments was on the limits, not on the principle, of arbitration. When the scope was so defined as to secure the settlers' rights, Lord Salisbury's point was gained. His handling of the dispute with the United States, and its successful result from the British point of view, has probably had a good deal to do with the unwillingness displayed by successive Conservative Governments in this country to give general pledges for submitting disputes to arbitration. Balfour's own opinions were certainly permanently influenced by his experience of the injustices that might have arisen if the use of methods of diplomacy had been ruled out in advance in the Venezuela case.

These negotiations were overlapped by others on the subject of a general Treaty of Arbitration, proposed by the United States Congress, but rejected finally by the Senate in 1897 after a draft had been agreed upon by the Governments of Great Britain and the United States. Much labour had been expended on it, and the breakdown caused great disappointment, especially in Washington. The American Secretary of State indeed called its rejection "a calamity not merely of national, but world-wide proportions."[1] The work as a matter of fact was not all wasted, for this abortive Treaty advanced the study of International Arbitration a further stage. Balfour contributed at least one constructive suggestion for bridging the gap between the British reluctance to give vague and general pledges, and the American enthusiasm for the arbitral method of settling disputes. He wrote to Lord Salisbury on March 3rd, 1896:

I have always had a certain leaning myself to a form of arbitration by which every possible case of difference would be dealt with, or at least reported on, though only the smaller class of cases be dealt with finally.

Without pressing that a plan on these lines should be substituted for the one contained in the proposed Treaty with America, would it not be well to provide that matters such as those mentioned in paragraph 5, should, whenever it is thought desirable, be referred to this limited and imperfect form of arbitration? In the Treaty as it stands no room is left for this intermediate course, which, under certain circumstances, might I think prove very convenient. A. J. B.

One incident connected with the rejection of the Arbitration Treaty shows Balfour's eagerness to spread among his colleagues understanding of the United States. Mr. White showed him a letter from Mr. Olney, the American Secretary of State, explaining the defeat of the Treaty. Balfour asked permission to circulate the document to the British Cabinet.[2] Dated May 14th, 1897, it contains an early analysis of the balance of forces in the United States Constitution, the effects of which our own generation has had further opportunities of studying.

The Senate [wrote Mr. Olney] is now engaged in asserting itself as *the* power in the national government. It is steadily encroaching, on the one hand on the executive branch of the Government, and on the other on the House of Representatives.... This aggressive attitude of the Senate ... is largely responsible for the treatment it has given to the

[1] Mowat, *Life of Lord Pauncefote*, p. 171.
[2] Nevins, *Life of Henry White*, p. 125.

Arbitration Treaty. After long and troublesome discussion, a perfected Treaty was laid before the Senate by the executive branch of Government, exercising therein an undoubted constitutional function. The Senate immediately assumed a hostile attitude. The Treaty, in getting itself made by the sole act of the executive without leave of the Senate, had committed the unpardonable sin. It must be either altogether defeated, or so altered as to bear a Senate stamp—and this must be the means both of humiliating the executive, and of showing to the world the greatness of the Senate.

The letter goes on to adduce the currency question as a second reason for the defeat of the Treaty, owing to the irritation of the Silver party against Great Britain as the great supporter of the gold standard.[1] This information found a particularly attentive listener in Balfour.

For more than a year he had been watching with eager sympathy the movement in the United States towards an international agreement for employing silver as well as gold as standard value for currency. He was himself a bi-metallist of long-standing. Currency questions had interested him from youth up, and the fluctuation of the rupee had been the topic of his maiden speech in the House of Commons in 1878. He had been appointed, while still a private Member, to sit on the Royal Commission on Currency which reported in 1888. In the Minority Report of that Commission he had made his first responsible declaration of belief in the advantages which would flow from a return to the double standard. International agreement was the proviso, and it was from the United States that he always thought the proposal ought to come. His private correspondence in the early nineties is full of encouragement to his bi-metallist friends to meet and stimulate the movement in America. The most interesting of these letters was written a year after the General Election of 1895 brought him again into office, and for that very reason it was never seen by the American correspondent to whom it was addressed, for Balfour showed it in draft to the Prime Minister, the Chancellor of the Exchequer and the Secretary of State for India, the colleagues whose work would be most affected by any results which might follow. All three Ministers were unanimous against sending the letter. The Chancellor, Sir Michael Hicks-Beach, wrote that it would be objectionable and dangerous for anyone in Balfour's position to communicate views on a leading issue of the

[1] There is a summary of this letter in the *Life of Henry White*, p. 125.

forthcoming Presidential Election. The Secretary for India, Lord George Hamilton, was equally horrified, and Lord Salisbury wrote:

The Americans have not got our system of Cabinets; I doubt if they understand the difference between what a Minister does as a private individual and what he does as a Minister. I think the position of the First Lord of the Treasury will be a good deal misunderstood if he sends this letter.

The letter [1] was mainly a statement of what Balfour thought Great Britain might and could do for rehabilitation of silver, short of the adoption of a double standard for herself, of which he saw no immediate prospect. India was at that moment "being subjected to one of the most curious currency experiments ever devised in the history of the world." The Indian standard of value was neither free gold, nor linked gold and silver. It was "silver artificially appreciated by Mint restrictions, so that the rupee had a value in excess of the silver it contained,—an arbitrary system calculated to aggravate the silver difficulty from which the world was then suffering, but never likely to be abandoned so long as a return to free silver would subject the Indian Government to fluctuations of exchange from which it had suffered stress before." But if an international arrangement were to be made, the Indian Government might, by once more opening their Mints to silver, restore one of the chief silver markets of the world. This would probably be the chief contribution of the British Empire to international bi-metallism. Would it be enough to justify the other great commercial countries in adopting the system? Speaking simply as a bi-metallist, Balfour thought it would. By the immense development of her banking arrangements England had diminished the strain on gold, which her vast trade transactions would otherwise have produced. Opening the Indian Mints and increasing the silver reserve of the Bank of England would add enormously to the demand for silver. Great Britain would thus be making a great contribution to international bi-metallism. If she did not do more, "it would be a matter of regret chiefly for Great Britain herself."

This unsent letter was drafted in July 1896. When the Presidential Election soon after replaced President Cleveland by President McKinley, 35 Senators and 127 Members of the House of Representa-

[1] It was published in full after Balfour's death in the Silver Supplement of the *Financial News* of December 14th, 1931.

tives declared themselves ready for the free coinage of silver. The hopes of the international bi-metallists in England rose, for in the spring of 1895 official envoys from the United States visited Paris, and when they came on to London, the French Ambassador was instructed to support their proposals. Balfour did his utmost that summer to impress his Cabinet colleagues with his own convictions. He had however little hope that Great Britain would adopt the double standard. The mass of City opinion was strongly mono-metallist, and the Chancellor of the Exchequer had pledged the Government, after the General Election of 1895, not to depart from the gold standard. But there was no pledge in respect of India, and the proposals of the United States envoys were referred by the Cabinet to the Indian Government for an opinion, which, being adverse, turned the scale. The last favourable opportunity for an international agreement on currency reform that occurred during Balfour's lifetime passed. The arguments of the Government of India filled him with scorn. His first reaction was a brief Memorandum addressed I do not know to whom. The draft is dated October 2nd, 1897.

10 DOWNING STREET, S.W.

In my opinion the reasons given for rejecting the American proposals are of a kind with which it would be impossible for the Government to associate themselves.

The whole contention rests upon the principle that a rise in prices due to a fall in the value of the currency is an immense benefit to the country in which it takes place, and in particular, to the export trade of that country. They therefore deprecate any arrangement which would raise the value of the rupee above ¼, *not* because such an arrangement would be impossible to carry out or difficult to maintain, but simply and nakedly because it is better for Indian trade to have a cheap currency than a dear one.

In the economic principles which underlie these arguments there is, I believe, a nucleus of truth. But, driven to the extent to which the Government of India drive them, they are simply the arguments in Indian garb familiar to us in the North, of the Silverites and "soft money" men of the Western States.

It may be true—I think to a certain extent it is true—that a depreciating currency is more stimulating to commerce and manufacturers than an appreciating one, and that of two conditions of things—both of which are bad—the first is therefore the best. It may also be true that a fall in the gold price as compared with the silver price of Indian products may, until a readjustment is effected, stimulate Indian export trade. But consequences of this sort, which may be tolerated or welcomed when they are due to variations in the value of honest money, cannot safely be urged in defence of so artificial a system of forced coinage as that which prevails in India.

Moreover if a fall in the value of the rupee is good for the Indian public, and indirectly good for the Indian Government, what possible justification can there be for the attempt artificially to raise the value of the rupee to ¼ or any other arbitrary point by closing the Mints? Let it be noted that the legitimate inference is that if America and the Latin Union were, without any assistance from India, to establish bimetallism, it would be the duty of the Indian Government, by the issue of paper or otherwise to keep the value of the rupee down to ¼, just as it is at present their duty to keep it up to that level by restricting the coinage.

Finally would it be possible to face the farmers of England and the cotton spinners of Lancashire with a statement that the Finance Minister of India refuses to revert to a natural and unforced currency, because such a course would remove an artificial bounty upon the exports of wheat and the manufacture of cotton?   A. J. B.

Between the writing of this, and the following Memorandum to the Cabinet, Balfour must have given up hope of vanquishing the Government of India; for the document is an example of rear-guard action. Accepting defeat as a bi-metallist, he tries to minimise its consequences as a diplomatist.

Confidential.

October 12th, 1897.

As I gather that my own views on the answer which should be returned to the United States Government are not in perfect accord with those either of the Secretary of State for India or of the Chancellor of the Exchequer, it may be convenient that I should concisely state them before the meeting of the Cabinet next Saturday.

The question has to be considered from two points of view—the *diplomatic* and the *financial*. From the diplomatic point of view, it seems to me of the first importance that if the negotiations started at Washington are to fail, the blame for their failure should not rest at our doors. Such a result would probably injure our international relations with the United States; but it would certainly injure us with great bodies of opinion among the manufacturing and agricultural classes at home; and it would lay us open to severe comment after the public statement of policy which we have made in the House of Commons and elsewhere.

Let me add that some well-informed persons are cynical enough to doubt whether the Governments of the United States and India are absolutely sincere in the negotiations which they are conducting,—whether, in short, they have not been moved by the necessity of doing something to please their bi-metallic friends without any strong wish that that "something" shall issue in practical reform. If so, it is manifest that they would hail with unbounded satisfaction the chance of throwing all the odium upon England. This is a satisfaction which I am anxious to deny them at any reasonable cost.

Turn now from the diplomatic to the financial aspect of the question. I cannot personally profess any contentment at the prospect, which seems so agreeable to the Indian Government, of permitting that country to remain permanently under the absurd system initiated in 1893. This system is, I observe, decorated with the title of a "gold standard currency" by the Indian Council. It is nothing of the kind, and I foresee that its maintenance will be a source of recurring perplexities, and, when its real operation becomes known, of well-founded discontent among the natives. I am, however, not going to over-load these notes either with arguments against the existing Indian Mint Regulations, nor against the despatch in which they are embodied.

This last contains, in my opinion, only two arguments which deserve consideration:—

(a) That founded on the suddenness of the jump from the old to the new value of the rupee;

(b) That founded on the possible instability of any international arrangement, and the serious injury which any break-down of that arrangement would inflict on Indian financial interests.

Both these dangers would, I think, be avoided by the exercise of a little ingenuity and good-will on the part of the American and French Governments, and I should frame my despatch to them with the whole object of leaving the responsibility for failure on their shoulders, if they fail to find a satisfactory solution of these two particular difficulties. If these difficulties *were* solved, I should over-ride the Indian Government on all other points.

The following, therefore, are the heads of the sort of despatch I should be inclined to write:—

(1) Recite United States proposals.

(2) Recapitulate desire expressed by this and previous English Administrations to mitigate as far as possible the evils resulting from the present relations of silver and gold.

(3) Recall the fact that while no expectation had ever been held out that the people of this country would consent to a change in the currency to which they had been so long accustomed, the Government,

following on the steps of their predecessors, had publicly expressed the opinion that an adequate contribution towards the rehabilitation of silver would be made by the British Empire if free coinage for silver were maintained in India, and by furthering in some particulars its use in this country.

(4) Then go on somewhat as follows: When the suggestions were made, no difficulty was anticipated in carrying them into effect. On consulting the Indian Government, however, they find a course which, before the Mints were closed, would have been welcome, is now met with decided hostility.

(5) Into the arguments adduced by the Indian Government it is not necessary to enter at length; but there are two with which Her Majesty's Government have strong sympathy.

(6) It is urged, in the first place, that the change in the value of the rupee produced by the adoption of the 15 to 1 ratio would be so sudden as to cause a violent dislocation of trade, with all its attendant evils. Inasmuch as under the proposals which are now being dealt with, no part of Her Majesty's dominions would come under a bi-metallic arrangement, Her Majesty's Government do not think it any part of their duty to offer advice as to the ratio which the United States of America and France may see fit to adopt. But, whatever that ratio may be, Her Majesty's Government cannot think there would be any difficulty in making the approach to it a gradual, though not necessarily a lengthy process, and thus avoiding—at least in their acutest form—the evils which the Indian Government anticipate.

(7) As regards the permanence of the new arrangement, the Indian Government point out that they can hardly be expected to give up the system which they have been endeavouring for years to bring to perfection, unless they have substantial security that the new system to be substituted for it is likely to be stable. Her Majesty's Government have no desire to throw any doubt upon the power of the United States and the Latin Union together to maintain a par of exchange between gold and silver at the proposed ratio. But, though this may be possible or even probable, it cannot be described as certain and the consequences of failure have therefore to be faced. If such a failure to maintain the par of exchange were not followed by the closing of the Mints in bi-metallic countries to silver, the result would probably be that gold would be driven out, and that in practice those countries would become mono-metallic on a silver basis.

Whatever other consequences might ensue on this condition of things, it does not seem to Her Majesty's Government probable that as long as the American and French Mints remain open, the gold price of silver would fall to anything near its present level, or that any results would follow of a character so serious as to justify the termination of the present artificial system of currency.

Matters would be different, however, if, as the result of the failure to keep up a bi-metallic par of exchange, the countries which had attempted it were to revert in some form or other to gold mono-metallism. In that event the position of silver would be worse than before, and the Indian Government would be put in the position of seeing all the results of their previous efforts destroyed, and of having laboriously to recommence, under circumstances of the greatest difficulty, the artificial enhancement of the value of the rupee. Her Majesty's Government therefore feel that they cannot press the Indian Government to retrace the steps taken in 1893 unless they can offer them some security that the new system to be adopted is one likely to be permanent, not merely if the international arrangement secures the bi-metallic ratio, but even in the event of its failing to do so.   A. J. B.

October 12, 1897.

Never an advocate of lost causes, Balfour made this Memorandum his last word. After the Great War he foresaw the time when a double standard would again be a topic of living controversy, but when he was writing his Autobiography in 1928 and 1929 he would not restate his opinions, unchanged though they were. "Who would read anything on such a subject?" he said.

Chapter XI

A FAILURE AND A PRELUDE
THE EDUCATION BILL OF 1896

Board Schools and Voluntary Schools under the Act of 1870. "Cow-per-Temple" teaching. The Bill of 1896 gives State aid and denom-inational teaching. Annoyance of Church Party and Dissenters. Balfour accepts an Amendment. The Bill withdrawn. Lord Rose-bery condoles. Passage of Irish Land Bill. The end of the Session of 1896.

EXCEPT for the negotiations with the United States, Balfour took little part in international politics during the first two years of Lord Salisbury's third Government. In the Session of 1896 he had little time for anything outside his own work of conducting Government business in the House of Commons. Home Rule in this Parliament was, as Balfour described it, the "Sleeping Beauty," and the Union-ists eagerly turned to the social legislation which the Irish contro-versy had blocked for so long. A portentous programme of domestic Bills was promised in the Queen's Speech, and actually brought in. Many were passed, including two out of the three major measures, which dealt with Irish Land, Agricultural Derating, and Education. The Education Bill however perished ignominiously, and under cir-cumstances which caused much of the blame to be put on Balfour's handling of it. Confidence in his Parliamentary skill underwent a steep temporary decline. That however is not the reason why the fate of the Education Bill of 1896 deserves even a short chapter in the long story of his life; it is because this failure was the prelude to the Education Act of 1902—associated always with Balfour's name, the Act that laid the foundation on which the system of National Edu-cation in this country has since been built. The Conservative Party paid a heavy price for it at the polls. Possibly but for the experience of 1896 the price of unpopularity might have been paid without the purpose being achieved.

When Lord Salisbury took office in 1895 the system of Elementary Education was as Mr. Gladstone's Government had left it a quarter of a century before. In 1870 the "Forster Act" had set up the Board Schools, paid for and managed by the local rate-payers, to supplement the gaps left by the Voluntary Schools, managed by the Church of England and other religious denominations, and paid for from their funds, with some help from State grants. About half the children in England and Wales were at that time attending Voluntary Schools, which were as deeply interwoven with the traditions and sentiment of the English people as was the Church that supported most of them, whose living membership they renewed from generation to generation. But they could not increase fast enough, or otherwise meet the needs of the growing population of the towns.

The Bill of 1870 had attempted to provide a link between the two types of schools, by permitting the locally elected School Boards which controlled the rate-supported schools, to help the denominational schools financially, provided that these conformed to the conditions laid down for the Board Schools in respect of efficiency, State inspection, and conformity to the "Conscience Clause," which provided that no child should be either required, or forbidden, by the School Board, to attend any particular place of religious worship or instruction. All possibility of connection between the two kinds of school was however given up when Mr. Gladstone accepted an Amendment moved by a Nonconformist supporter, Mr. Cowper-Temple, which introduced a vitally important Clause, afterwards known by its author's name. The purport was to exclude from rate-built schools every catechism or formulary distinctive of a denominational creed, and to sever altogether the relation between the School Boards and the Voluntary Schools, leaving the latter to look solely to the central grants for outside help.

Interminable arguments raged over the definition of what constituted the "simple Bible teaching" to which Board School religious instruction was confined. The Cowper-Temple Clause fixed a gulf in the eyes alike of Dissenters and of Churchmen, between "Board" and "Voluntary" Schools. For twenty-five years these existed side by side, the Board Schools dominating in the towns, especially in the poorer areas, the Voluntary Schools in country villages.

In the nineties agricultural depression increased, and the decline of rents and tithes hit the squires, the parsons, the farmers, and the little towns. Thus the Church schools sank deeper into financial straits, and were increasingly unable to keep their buildings and teaching up to standard. The Board Schools had their own difficulties in the many places where rates were too heavy. Apart from all these troubles, the Secondary Education of the country was suffering from overlapping, competing authorities, and a lack of co-ordination with the primary schools. The English educational system had become "chaotic, ineffectual, utterly behind the age, the laughing-stock of every advanced nation in Europe and America." [1]

In 1896 no real survey had yet been made of the chaos, and the difficulties of reducing it to order were underestimated. It was imagined that this could be done simultaneously with the rescue of the Voluntary Schools from ruin, which was, in the eyes of the Conservatives, the really urgent thing. The core of the Bill of 1896 therefore was State aid for the Voluntary Schools. At the same time it was proposed to set up a local education authority over all National Schools, in the shape of an Education Committee of each County Council, the members to be appointed at the County Council's discretion. This new authority would administer all State grants, including those to Voluntary Schools. And then came one condition of such grants, namely that in every Elementary School, separate, denominational, religious instruction should be given to children whose parents desired it.

Thus was the Cowper-Temple arrangement, dear to the Dissenters, to be blown away. At the same time the hackles of the Church Party were raised by the introduction of popular control into the management of their schools. Still, in spite of the growling groups behind and before the Ministerial Bench, the Bill received a Second Reading by a majority of 267, more than a hundred over the normal ministerial majority. It was swollen by the Irish, voting for denominational education, under orders from their bishops, to the rage of their English Nonconformist friends. Soon after this initial success Balfour pinned the Government credit to the Bill. But the Church Party on the Government side were gathering for action, and the moment the Bill entered Committee they began to smother it in Amendments. One suggested that municipal boroughs should appoint their own Educational Committees. This interfered with the principle which made County Committees the unit of decentralisation under the Bill, and the Minister in charge, Sir John Gorst, held out through a long debate, during much of which Balfour was not present. But

[1] See Balfour at Manchester, October 1902.

after listening to part of it, he suddenly rose, and, to the surprise of his colleagues, accepted the Amendment, as regards boroughs of over 20,000 inhabitants. The concession, wise or unwise, was the death of the Bill. It opened the flood-gates of local passions, and the turmoil grew. With over twelve hundred Amendments on the Paper, the Government were forced to cut their losses, and withdraw the Bill. Lord Salisbury was annoyed, and the Queen greatly incensed at this treatment of one of the measures promised in his Speech.[1] Such an outcry arose against Balfour that it drew forth an expression of sympathy from an unusual quarter. Lord Rosebery and he, though bound together by lifelong acquaintanceship and community of intellectual interest in many things, were in others as the poles asunder, and their genuine respect and affection for one another flourished without the aid of much personal intercourse. The following letter was certainly appreciated, though Balfour was less affected by the passing shadow on his Parliamentary reputation than his sensitive friend imagined:

> 38, BERKELEY SQUARE, W.
> *June 24th*, 1896.

MY DEAR BALFOUR,

You are experiencing the fickleness of fortune, and the hollowness of all political things, and I cannot help writing one line to say that I am sure you are not surprised or discouraged. I am confident that all will come right for you, for the present trouble only arises from the anxiety to find a scape-goat which shall carry all the sins and errors of all the Party into the wilderness. You will remain calm and courageous, and the world will come back to you quickly enough.

You will not misunderstand this letter from a political opponent but a very old friend, who thinks with the profoundest sympathy of that bed between two windows in Downing Street!

> Yours sincerely,
>
> R.

Tactically Balfour's intervention in the management of a Bill which was not his own may be counted as one of his few Parliamentary mistakes. But the instinct that prompted him on this occasion may have been right. At all events the principle of the Amendment which he accepted with apparently so little reflection, reappeared in his own Education Act of 1902.

[1] See *Queen Victoria's Letters*, Third Series, Vol. II, p. 54.

As the Session went on, criticism died down. Balfour's brother Gerald, now Chief Secretary for Ireland, was piloting a difficult Land Bill which also had the misfortune to offend friends as much as foes. Balfour reported one lively scene in the letter to the Queen which, as Leader, it was his daily duty to write:

24.7.96.

Mr. Balfour with his humble duty to Your Majesty begs humbly to inform Your Majesty that the House sat yesterday till 5 o'clock in the morning. The Irish Land Bill was (so far as the Committee stage is concerned) completed; and the whole of the proceedings were amicable and businesslike. There was indeed one episode of rather sharp controversy between Mr. Carson and Mr. Balfour. Mr. Carson has always taken a very exaggerated view of the possible injuries to Irish landlords which the Irish Bill may possibly produce; he is a man of great ability, and has a somewhat bitter tongue. He made a speech to which Mr. Balfour thought it necessary to make a strong reply. But no permanent breach has or will result; which is a source of great gratification to Mr. Balfour, as he has a great admiration and regard for Mr. Carson, who served under him as Solicitor-General for Ireland through many difficult times.

The rapid passage of this large and complicated measure through the House is satisfactory; and though extravagant fears have been entertained by certain persons as to the effects of the measure on the interests of Irish landlords, the representatives of that class behaved on the whole very well, as did the Nationalists on the other side.

He did not renew these praises in respect of the Unionist Peers, who revolted against the Government when the Bill reached their House. It was an anxious finale to the exhausting Session, but at last the Irish Land Bill came back to the Commons in an acceptable form. The House passed it and rose. On August 16th Balfour could write to Lady Elcho from Lord Rayleigh's house:

TERLING PLACE,
ESSEX.
August 16th, 1896.

I now feel as if there never *had* been a Session—the very memory of it seems fading away....

I biked about 20 miles on the way here yesterday, and to-morrow I go to the Bell Inn, Sandwich, for golf, where I hope to have a goodish time....

I have been so hard worked for the last month or two that now I hardly know what to take up in the way of reading, or writing. I have absolutely no book going except an exceedingly bad detective story. But when I have pulled myself together and have accustomed myself to the novel sensation of not trying to do three things at once, I shall plunge again into philosophy.

A. J. B.

This was the end of a heavy six months. In spite of the *contretemps* of the Education Bill, Balfour's skill in management of business on the floor of the House was established at its close. His authority over his followers there was less unquestioned, and in spite of the devotion, admiration and enthusiasm that his personality evoked, authority was the weak side of his Party leadership till its end in 1911. His influence may have been too seldom consciously exerted through contacts with the rank and file. Yet from the first he was, in the opinion of them all, the obvious successor to Lord Salisbury.

Mr. Chamberlain was the only other man of his calibre in the Cabinet, and it was his dynamic presence that put Balfour's position in the Unionist Party beyond all doubt; as much in the minds of the Liberal Unionists (beginning with Mr. Chamberlain himself) who were willing to serve under Balfour, as in the minds of the Conservatives, who were not willing to serve under Mr. Chamberlain.

Whatever smaller-minded people may have imagined, neither rivalry nor jealousy entered at any time into the relations between these two. Their minds, their tastes, their philosophies of life, were too diverse perhaps for sympathy. Liking and affection are more appropriate words to use in attempting to describe their relationship. Liking and affection—but above these, an unwavering respect for each other's point of view, formed a bond which no strain ever snapped.

In Balfour's case the respect was no less real for being tinged with the sardonic element that often coloured his observation of people pursuing lines which were not his own. While Lord Salisbury lived, he had a confidant for this side of himself, without fear of misunderstanding.

10 DOWNING STREET.
April 10th, 1897.

MY DEAR UNCLE ROBERT,

...You have, I suppose, by this time heard from Joe about his renewed proposal for an addition to our South American garrison. His favourite mode of dealing with the South African sore is the free application of irritants; and though it does not easily commend itself to me, this method may possibly be the best. In any case, however, I cannot think it wise to allow him to goad on the Boers by his speeches, and refuse him the means of repelling Boer attacks, when, as responsible Minister, he earnestly and persistently presses for them. My own view is that a Boer attack is exceedingly improbable, and that it will only take place if the Boers come to the conclusion that we are fixed in the determination to attack them, and that what must come had better come soon. The production of the Harris telegrams before the S. African Committee (which seems now to be inevitable) may foster this frame of mind, and it is a nice point whether the sending out of 3,000 men may prove to be sedative or a stimulant.

It was decided to send the reinforcements, and Balfour wrote to the Queen:

29.4.97.

... To-day the Chancellor of the Exchequer made his Financial statement. It was an admirable speech, very well received, and disclosing a most satisfactory condition of Public Finance. ... Two hundred thousand pounds will be required to transport a brigade of artillery and a regiment of infantry to S. Africa. The last item produced a short but violent controversy between Sir William Harcourt and Mr. Chamberlain; the former vehemently making, and the latter rebutting the charge of embarking on a policy of provocation towards the Transvaal. The incident may produce unfortunate consequences, not here indeed, but abroad and in S. Africa.

Chapter XII

DEPUTY FOREIGN MINISTER

1895–1899

The Far East 1898. Mr. Chamberlain's efforts for an Anglo-German Alliance, 1898. The Spanish-American War. Manchuria. The Portuguese Colonies. Balfour on Lord Kitchener.

IN Lord Salisbury's last Government Balfour occupied a special position as regards foreign affairs, by reason of the confidence which the Prime Minister placed in him. This went far beyond the normal co-operation between Party leaders in the Lords and Commons, and by 1898 had reached a point which enabled Lord Salisbury sometimes to leave affairs at the Foreign Office in the First Lord of the Treasury's hands for weeks together, when his own health required him to go abroad for rest or a cure. Otherwise he could hardly have carried for so long the double burden of the Foreign Office and the Premiership. But the very completeness with which responsibility was from time to time transferred makes it difficult to describe or measure Balfour's influence in some of these great international affairs. It might be exercised at the beginning, middle, or end of an episode, and his personal handling might cease as abruptly as it started. His adaptability to these conditions sprang from a harmony between Lord Salisbury and himself which rested on deeper foundations than mere intellectual agreement.

Balfour took to diplomatic work with the same natural aptitude that he had displayed when confronted in Ireland with administrative problems. He used to say, in tones the reverse of complaining, that whenever Lord Salisbury left him in charge of the Foreign Office he found himself dealing with a crisis. This was a period when nerves were set on edge, and confidence disturbed by the foreign policy of Germany. There were few questions arising in any quarter of the globe in which William II and his Government did not deem it their right, and indeed their duty, to interfere. The European competition for colonial acquisitions in Africa had been proceeding for more than ten years. Owing largely to Lord Salisbury's firm conciliatory diplomacy, the partition of huge tracts had been peacefully carried out by agreement between the Powers before the date at which the thread of this narrative mingles with foreign policy. But in 1898 there were still some African questions outstanding, apart from the conquest of the Soudan, and the increasing tension between the Boer Republics and the British Government.

It was however in connection with the Far East that the first crisis arose in Balfour's experience as acting Foreign Minister in 1898. The Chinese Empire lay helpless after its defeat by Japan in 1895. The Continental Powers, with Germany and Russia in the van, had rushed in with demands for concessions, leases of ports and territories, and trade privileges of every sort. It seemed as if the only defence for China against ultimate partition were the jealousies and quarrels of those who would partition her.

The integrity of China was a cardinal point of British policy, but so long as that was preserved, Lord Salisbury was prepared to acquiesce in a great deal for the sake of maintaining the concert of Europe and the peace of the world. With these two objects as the goal of his Far Eastern policy, he aimed at creating spheres of influence in China by friendly agreement between the Powers. In November 1897, Germany had seized the pretext of the murder of two German missionaries in China to send a naval squadron into Kiao-chau Bay. British ships thereupon entered Port Arthur, but were withdrawn in deference to the feelings of the Russians, who themselves then sent a naval force to the same place. This happened in January 1898—the month in which Lord Salisbury made his first effort, through our Ambassador in St. Petersburg, to come to an understanding with Russia, with regard not only to China, but to Turkey, the other moribund Empire, whose decay was a danger to Europe. The basis of an agreement was to be "no partition of territory, but only a partition of preponderance." [1]

This first tentative step towards putting an end to the isolation of Britain came to nothing, owing partly to rivalries over the question of a British loan to China, which was being discussed at the same time. The Chinese Government, under pressure from Russia, eventually declined the proposed loan. In compensation for this (though

[1] See Gooch and Temperley, *British Documents on the Origins of the War*, Vol. I, p. 8.

not ostensibly so) the British Government obtained a promise from the Chinese not to alienate the Yangtze provinces to any other Power, and also the assurance that, while the volume of British trade kept above that of any other country, an Englishman should remain at the head of the Maritime Customs.[1] When these points had been gained, neither the understanding with Russia, nor the Loan mattered so much to Great Britain as they had done in January.

In the meantime however the impression the abortive loan negotiations left was that Great Britain was losing grip in the Far East. At least one of Lord Salisbury's Cabinet colleagues shared the fears which were agitating that large portion of the community interested in our trade with China. Parliament met on February 8th, 1898, and on February 3rd Mr. Chamberlain wrote to Balfour:

Secret

HIGHBURY,
BIRMINGHAM.
Feb. 3. 98.

MY DEAR BALFOUR,

I wish that you read all the papers just now. If you did, you would, I think, agree with me that grave trouble is impending upon the Govt. if we do not adopt a more decided attitude in regard to China.

What are the facts? We have a permanent interest in the trade, and have gained much credit both at home and in America by insisting that while we do not intend to oppose the occupation by Germany and Russia, we are determined that their ports shall be Treaty Ports,[2] or subject to treaty regulations, and that our influence shall be maintained.

The Germans appear to have accepted our terms, although we have not got, as we ought to get, a definite assurance that Kiao Chau will be a Treaty Port. But the Russians have done us at every point.

They have induced us to let our ships leave Port Arthur, while they have reciprocated our friendly attitude by opposing our loan proposals. They have forced us to withdraw our proposal to make Talien Wan a Free Port.

They are placing Russian officers in control of railways, &c., to the exclusion of English.

They are ousting us from influence in Corea.

They pretend that their occupation is temporary and not in restraint of our trade. We all believe that this is false, and that they will

[1] See Memorandum by Mr. Tilley, *British Documents,* Vol. I, p. 2.
[2] *Ibid.*

transform the occupation into a permanent one, and will exclude us altogether from the Liao Tung peninsula.

We pretend to rely on our treaty rights; but if they declare an annexation these rights disappear, and in any case they will know how to make the position intolerable for our merchants. All this is known to our friends and to our enemies. If matters remain as they are, our prestige will be gone and our trade will follow. I would not give a year's life to the Government under such conditions.

The question is, what can we do, and it is most difficult of course for any of us outsiders to frame a policy. If only Lord Salisbury sees the peril and is prepared to meet it I would rather leave to him the methods than rush in with what may be impossible suggestions. But, as the matter now appears to me, I should propose:

1. To approach the United Sates officially, and to ask an immediate reply from them to the question—Will you stand in with us in our Chinese policy?

2. To approach Germany at the same time with the same definite questions.

3. Our Chinese policy to be a declaration that any port occupied by a foreign nation shall be, *ipso facto,* a Treaty Port open to all on precisely similar conditions.

That this applies to Talien Wan, Port Arthur and Kiao Chau, and to any other further acquisition of land or ports by any European nation, or by the Japanese.

Further that they should join with us in putting pressure on the Chinese—loan or no loan—to open Nanking and the other Ports suggested by us and to give freedom of internal navigation.

That if Russia refuses these terms, we should summon her fleet to leave Port Arthur and make her go if necessary.

I dare say this line is much too strong for the Cabinet, but if we do not do something and that quickly we shall have a bad quarter of an hour when Parliament meets.

yours very truly,
J. CHAMBERLAIN.

The approach to the United States advocated by Mr. Chamberlain was made on March 8th, with Balfour's approval.[1] At the moment however the United States was thinking chiefly of the approaching war with Spain. The answer to the British proposal for a joint policy on the "Open Door" in China was chilly and indifferent, and Great Britain could count on no support from Washington when the Russians occupied Port Arthur on March 16th.

[1] See *Life of Henry White,* by A. Nevins, p. 162.

The counter-move to the Russian entry into Port Arthur (which in due course was leased to them by the Chinese) was the acceptance by the British Government of a lease of Wei-hai-wei. The offer of this had been refused by Lord Salisbury as lately as February 25th, on the ground that British policy was to discourage alienation of Chinese territory, and that it was therefore premature to discuss leasing Wei-hai-wei, unless the action of other Powers altered the position.

This Russia had now done, but Ministers still hesitated to change the policy they had emphatically announced. Lord Salisbury had gone to the Riviera early in March, and Balfour was presiding in the Cabinet as well as in the Foreign Office, when the occupation of Port Arthur took place.

On March 26th he telegraphed to the Queen:

Cabinet met yesterday and deliberated for more than three hours and a half till 7 p.m. The discussion was entirely confined to the policy to be pursued in the Far East; her Majesty's Ministers held the opinion, in which Mr. Balfour knows that Lord Salisbury concurs, that it was not worth while to promote a war with Russia in order to keep her out of Port Arthur: her influence at Pekin depends principally on her land position, and though the position at Port Arthur may augment it, the difference is not sufficient to justify hostilities. It was, however, thought desirable that Great Britain should maintain her position in the Gulf of Pechili, and in the neighbourhood of Pekin, by closing with the Chinese offer of the reversion of Wei-hai-wei.[1]

Balfour's conversion to this policy was apparently due to Mr. George Curzon, who was then Under-Secretary for Foreign Affairs. As soon as he was convinced himself he invited the junior Minister to attend a Cabinet in order to convince his colleagues.[2]

Policy being settled, the next thing was to soothe feelings in Berlin. On April 2nd Balfour telegraphed to the British Ambassador, Sir Frank Lascelles, to inform the German Government that Great Britain had asked for the lease of Wei-hai-wei.

...Point out to them that this step is forced on us by action of Russia. Its sole object is to maintain balance of power in Gulf of Pechili, menaced by Russian occupation of Port Arthur. We believe this policy is in conformity with German views.

[1] *Letters of Queen Victoria,* 3rd Series, Vol. III, p. 238.
[2] See Ronaldshay, *Life of Lord Curzon,* Vol. I, p. 285.

We do not anticipate that it will give any umbrage to German interests in Shantung, since Wei-hai-wei cannot be made a commercial port, and it could never be worth while to connect it by railway with the peninsula. A formal understanding on this subject would be given if desired.

We could not of course occupy till Japanese have left the port, and it is a matter of indifference to us when this event occurs.

A. J. B.[1]

The negotiations with Germany were delicate. She had signed her own Agreement with China for Kiao-chau on March 6th, but questions arose about prior rights to railway concessions in the hinterland. On April 14th Balfour wrote to Mr. Curzon:

...I do not see my way quite clearly about our arrangements with Germany in Shantung. It requires careful steering, because, on the one hand, it seems very desirable to mark out spheres in which we shall not interfere with each other's concessions, and yet very difficult to do this without either giving them too *big* a sphere or ourselves too *small* a one.

While Balfour was discussing these matters at the Foreign Office with Count Hatzfeldt, the German Ambassador, in the normal way of business, Mr. Chamberlain was engaged, on his own account, though with Balfour's knowledge, in a personal negotiation intended to pave the way for an Anglo-German alliance. Count Hatzfeldt was a willing co-operator, and the beginning of the conversations was engineered by Baron von Eckardstein, a member of the German Embassy in London. The prospects of an agreement seemed good, but hopes were wrecked in the middle of April 1898, by influences in the German Foreign Office.[2]

Balfour's correspondence with Lord Salisbury supplies a few missing links in the history of this diplomatic episode, and in particular the answer to the question of the real attitude of the Prime Minister and his nephew towards the incursions of the Colonial Secretary into foreign policy. Count Hatzfeldt thought that when the negotiations halted he perceived in Balfour a spice of that malicious kind of pleasure called by the Germans *Schadenfreude,* for which no other

---

[1] *British Documents,* Vol. I, p. 31.
[2] *British Documents,* and the *Grosse Politik red Europäischen Machte,* with the translated selections from it in *German Diplomatic Documents* (E. T. S. Dugdale), Vol. III, p. 21, et seq.

language than their own provides an adequate word. The German Ambassador wrote to the Chancellor in Berlin on April 7th, 1898:

... On April 5th I had other business reasons for calling on Mr. Balfour, and he took occasion to mention my conversation with Mr. Chamberlain, which the latter had evidently reported to him. When I described the considerations forbidding us at present to enter into so sudden and far-reaching a proposal as that formulated by Mr. Chamberlain, I found Mr. Balfour somewhat unexpectedly ready to admit the weight of our arguments. He confessed that it could not be foreseen with certainty how Parliament would accept a treaty of alliance with the Triple Alliance, for which public opinion had been so little prepared. He did not deny that the leader of German policy would be undertaking an immense responsibility if, in view of this parliamentary uncertainty, he was ready to conclude a treaty, which, if rejected by Parliament, would almost inevitably result in an attack by France combined with Russia against Germany. Another remark added by Mr. Balfour that Mr. Chamberlain sometimes wished to advance too quickly gave me the impression that this *personal* ill-success of Mr. Chamberlain's in this matter was not altogether unwelcome to him. ... [1]

It is interesting to contrast this with letters then passing between the Foreign Secretary and his deputy.

Private.

LA BASTIDE,
BEAULIEU.
April 9. 98.

MY DEAR ARTHUR,
I told you I would write to you when I thought I was up to work again. I think that epoch has arrived, for everything that can be conveniently sent out. If any matters arise which require immediate decision I must ask you kindly to decide them. ...

I am exceedingly indebted for the trouble you have taken over my work and for the admirable manner in which you have done it. I am afraid that for some weeks the strain must have been severe. But I could not help myself in throwing it on you.

Jim [2] gave me your message about Hatzfeldt and Chamberlain. The one object of the German Emperor since he has been on the throne has been to get us into a war with France. I never can make up my mind whether this is part of Chamberlain's object or not. The indica-

[1] *German Diplomatic Documents*, Vol. III, pp. 24-25.
[2] Lord Cranborne.

tions differ from month to month. As to France's future conduct, these elections will tell us a little more. But France certainly acts as if she meant to drive us into a German alliance: which I look to with some dismay, for Germany will blackmail us heavily.

Ever yours affly.,

SALISBURY.

April 14th, 1898.

MY DEAR UNCLE ROBERT,

If I had your morals with regard to correspondence I should have answered you two days ago,—but somehow golf and F.O. combined have prevented me from doing more than keep abreast of necessary work, and where letter-writing is concerned I find the spirit tolerably willing, but the flesh invariably weak.

As regards F.O. work do you think that in future it might be found possible for me or some other colleague to take it over for (say) a month each year when nothing very particular is going on? It is not the severity of the work which I at all fear for you; it is its unrelieved continuity. Some real holiday is really desirable.

Since I saw Jim there has been a further development in the matter about which I asked him to speak to you. The general outline of their amateur negotiation is perhaps worth putting on record. Among the minor actors in it are Harry Chaplin, Alfred Rothschild, and Eckardstein,—the principal roles being filled by Hatzfeldt and Chamberlain—a very motley "cast"! The drama opened by a suggestion that much might be done if there was a friendly, private, and quite unofficial conversation between Hatzfeldt and myself on strictly neutral territory. It was at the moment when things were approaching their hottest in connection with Port Arthur: and as I thought that some good and no harm could come of it, I accepted—Alfred Rothschild accordingly abandoned his dining-room to us and provided a sumptuous "déjeuner," between the courses of which there was an infinity of talk, out of the nebulous friendliness of which I really gathered very little except that the Germans did not at all like Joe's methods of procedure in Africa, and felt aggrieved at our protest about Shantung Railways. This took place on Friday the 25th—the day on which, at an afternoon Cabinet, the Government took their courage in both hands and (Joe dissenting) agreed on the Wei-hai-wei policy. The next incident was that Joe informed me that he had been asked to meet Hatzfeldt under like conditions. I raised no objection and (again I believe at Alfred's) another unofficial and informal conversation took place. Joe is very impulsive: and the Cabinet discussion of the preceding days had forced on his attention our isolated and occasionally therefore difficult diplomatic position. He certainly went far in the expression of his own personal leaning towards a German alliance; he combatted the notion that our form of Parliamentary government rendered such an alliance precarious (a notion which apparently haunts the German mind), and I believe even threw out a vague suggestion as to the form which an arrangement between the two countries might take. Hatzfeldt, who had thus spent the morning unofficially with Joe, came to see me officially in the afternoon. Not a word did he say of his previous interview—a reticence which rather amused me, who had just had an account of what passed from the mouth of the other interlocutor! In the meanwhile the results of the interview had been wired to Berlin and received an immediate response. As far as I can remember it, v. Bülow in his telegraphic reply (paraphrased to Joe at a second interview) dwelt again on the Parliamentary difficulty,—but also expressed with happy frankness the German view of England's position in the European system.[1] They hold (it seems) that we are more than a match for France, but not more than a match for Russia and France combined. The issue of such a contest would be doubtful. They could not afford to see us succumb,—not because they loved us, but because they know that they would be the next victims,—and so on. The whole tenor of the conversation (as represented by Chamberlain to me) being in favour of a closer union between the countries. This is how the matter stood when Jim left for Beaulieu on Monday 4th. On Tuesday the 5th, just before I made my statement, Joe informed me that Hatzfeldt had expressed a desire for a third interview, but it seemed difficult to arrange, as he (Joe) was going that evening into the country. I then told him that Hatzfeldt was coming to see me by appointment that afternoon at 5 (in the H. of C.), and that I would give up my room to him and Joe when my business was finished. Conceive my amusement when H. altogether repudiated any wish for such a meeting. He said that if J. wanted it he was of course ready, but that he had nothing to say. This sudden change was not due to any diplomatic reticence as to his unofficial communications with one of my colleagues, for by this time he was aware that I knew everything that had passed. It was undoubtedly due to some change of weather in Berlin. For he went on to discuss the difficulties in the way of an Anglo-German alliance. The old parliamentary objection was trotted out again with amplifications. Where could Germany be, if, after a treaty was concluded, it was repudiated by the H. of C.? Germany would then be left helpless between Russia and France, whose enmity would have been incurred by her seeking our alliance, but not rendered innocuous by her obtaining it. She was not so happily placed as England. She had no "silver streak." Moreover, the condition of public

[1] *German Diplomatic Documents,* Vol. II, p. 23.

opinion in Germany, and, so far as he could judge, in England also, was unfavourable to such a step. It might indeed have to be taken; it might even have to be taken soon. But for the present—and so on. In the meantime, what he, H., advocated was those small concessions between the two nations which Joe (he said) was so reluctant to make, but which, if made, would soften international prejudices, and prepare the way for stricter and more formal union! ! I was much entertained by this conclusion, but took care to express no dissent from it, as, although I am inclined to favour an Anglo-German agreement, it must, if possible, be made at the worst on equal terms. Of this loving couple I should wish to be the one that lent the cheek, not that imprinted the kiss. This, I take it, is not the German view; and they prefer, I imagine, reserving their offers until they are sure of being well paid for them.

I reserve discussion of the policy, however, till we meet. This letter, even as it stands, will exhaust your stock of patience, as it has already exhausted my stock of industry. I thought it, however, necessary that a curious episode, of which no record will be found in the F.O., should not vanish without leaving a trace;—and I thought I ought to add that H. Chaplin informs me, by letter received yesterday, that behind Hatzfeldt's back, Eckardstein (you know that fat fellow who married Maple's daughter?) is still engaged (by his own account successfully) in persuading his Emperor of the transcendent value of the English alliance, and the opportuneness of the present moment for concluding it!

I return to London on Monday; and foresee no Parliamentary work which will make it difficult to take any amount of F.O. work until you return.

Love to all.

Your aff. Nephew,
A. J. B.

This letter was written from Clouds, Mr. Percy Wyndham's house in Wiltshire. Two days later, before the Easter recess was over, Balfour dealt from there with another international question of importance. The long-threatened declaration of war by the United States against Spain was on the eve of being sent forth. Great Britain was suddenly required to take a line about a Joint Note which it was proposed that the six Great European Powers should address to the United States Government, proffering mediation. The idea originated at a meeting of the Ambassadors of those Powers in the British Embassy at Washington, and was transmitted by our Ambassador, Sir Julian Pauncefote.

When the papers reached Balfour from the Foreign Office, there was no time to consult Lord Salisbury; but he followed his instinct to avoid anything that might rouse resentment against Britain in war-fevered America.

He acted at once, and informed Mr. Chamberlain.

> CLOUDS,
> SALISBURY.
> *April 16th, 1898.*

MY DEAR CHAMBERLAIN,

The Messenger yesterday brought me the enclosed note from Sanderson,[1] together with the various documents to which it referred. I sent him in reply the telegram which I have just repeated to you, and wrote him a letter in the following terms:[2]

Spain and the U.S.A.

"I confess to be in great perplexity. The Representatives of the Powers at Washington and the Austrian Ambassador in London appear to wish us to give the United States a lecture on international morality. If Pauncefote had not associated himself with this policy I confess I should have rejected it at once; but he knows our views, he is on the spot, and he is a man of solid judgment. It seems a strong order to reject his advice. Will you telegraph to him in this sense:

"We are ready to join in any representation agreed on by the other Powers in favour of peace. We are also ready to make it quite clear that we have formed no judgment adverse to Spain, as is assumed apparently by Congress, and to express the hope that the declaration of an armistice by Spain may afford an opportunity for a peaceful settlement. But it seems very doubtful whether we ought to commit ourselves to a judgment adverse to the U. S., and whether in the interests of peace anything will be gained by doing so.

"You might ask, if you thought proper, for any observations which his local knowledge might furnish upon this view."

The whole thing had to be done in a quarter of an hour or 20 minutes, and it was just possible that I ought to have been even more peremptory than I have been in my resistance to the course pressed upon me.... But when your own Ambassador on the spot and all the Great Powers are in agreement, one does not feel disposed to be too rough in one's antagonism.

> yours sincerely,
> ARTHUR JAMES BALFOUR.

[1] Sir Thomas (afterwards Lord) Sanderson, then Permanent Secretary to the Foreign Office.

[2] The original letter to Sir Thomas Sanderson here quoted is not to be found in the Foreign Office Archives.

Mr. Chamberlain telegraphed back on the same day:

Am convinced message will do no good and will be bitterly resented. Americans insist Spain should leave Cuba. Nothing less will satisfy them. Spain will rather fight. Message practically takes part with Spain at critical juncture, and will be so understood both in America and this country.

CHAMBERLAIN.

Next day he wrote:

Your instinct was much better than Pauncefote's "experience and judgment," and I am afraid our interference will do harm. The American position may be right or wrong, but it is a very clear one,—and to ask them in the name of the "Concert of Europe" (*absit omen!*) to alter it will probably be regarded by them as offensive.

Hitherto public opinion in the States has gratefully recognised that we have been more sympathetic than the other Great Powers,—now I fear we shall be held to have thrown in our lot with them. As they never help us, nor are grateful for any assistance we give them, the less we have to do with them the better!

However, what is done is done—and I only hope that I am mistaken as to its effect.

The result of the Note by the Powers, modified on the line of Balfour's draft, was not so unfortunate as Mr. Chamberlain feared. How disastrous the original proposal might have proved, may be gathered from a letter written by Lord Salisbury to Queen Victoria on April 22nd, 1898.

Lord Salisbury with his humble duty respectfully submits that he believes the Powers are sorrowfully agreed that at this stage nothing can be done to arrest the war. Even the very temperate and guarded Note which was addressed by the Powers to the U.S. Government was very much resented by a large portion of the community as an undue interference, and had no other effect than to harden the war feeling. But of course your Majesty's Government will most gladly do anything which will bring hostilities to a conclusion....[1]

The war, declared on April 22nd, was over by August. After two crushing defeats the Spanish fleet withdrew from American waters. The Philippines, Cuba and the other West Indian possessions, passed

[1] *Letters of Queen Victoria*, Series III, Vol. III, p. 244.

to the United States. Therewith set in a profound change in world politics, and the rising of a new world force. A new consciousness of strength, new commercial interests, new ambitions, and the new mentality following on all these, began to alter the attitude of Americans towards European and Asiatic affairs.

Balfour's next spell of responsibility at the Foreign Office ran from the 10th to the 30th of August, 1898. These three weeks were again fraught with big affairs. Before they were over the Anglo-German Convention regarding the Portuguese Colonies in Africa was concluded and signed, and the foundations were laid for an Agreement with Russia, putting an end to disputes which were rendering our Far Eastern diplomacy very troublesome. Balfour wrote a Cabinet Memorandum on British policy with regard to Manchuria after he had studied the question at close quarters for five days. In it he summed up the courses open to British diplomacy.

(1) We may accept the position as far as Russia is concerned, and content ourselves as against China with insisting that adequate compensation shall be given, and some new security found for the Banks' advance which Russia will not allow to be made on the Railway.

(2) We may come to some arrangement with Russia.

(3) We may inform Russia that we cannot tolerate this violation of our rights, and if she refuses us satisfaction, send the fleet to Talien Wan, withdraw our Ambassador, and (should it prove necessary) declare war.

(4) We may adopt some violent, but still, less dramatic method of procedure, such as informing China that we insist on the Railway being made; that if she refuses we shall help ourselves to some of her territory, and possibly that we shall make the line ourselves,—if need be ... landing Marines to protect operations.

Of these four alternatives Balfour's Memorandum declares that "the first, viz. acquiescence, is on every ground inadmissible." For the second "there is much to be said." The third

is the simplest of all. It would produce either a war, or a diplomatic humiliation for Russia, and the public in their present temper would probably regard either result with equal satisfaction. Of the first ... I need only say that ... *we* should be fighting because we want Manchuria and the Yangtze to be a common field for English and Russian concessionaires. *They* would be fighting because they preferred dividing the field into two portions.... A small matter about which to set the world on fire....

A striking diplomatic triumph for this country... would be of enormous importance at the present moment when we are really fighting a battle for prestige rather than material gain, yet its utility would be temporary. I mean it would not greatly affect the distant and final destinies of China, or even of Manchuria. The forces moulding these destinies cannot indeed be accurately estimated, but we may surely say that among them are not to be estimated the number of steel rails we export, or the number of lines that are managed by English engineers.

Balfour goes on to state arguments against the fourth alternative, the chief of which is that "we want no more fragments of China for ourselves."

The Memorandum concludes:

If my colleagues think that course 2 affords the basis of a solution, I am prepared to work on these lines. If, on the other hand, they prefer 3 or 4, I must call a Cabinet and have its authority before taking steps which may have momentous and unforeseen consequences.

Nothing illustrates better Lord Salisbury's confidence in Balfour's handling of extremely difficult affairs than the change over of control when the negotiations were in progress with Germany which ended with the conclusion of a Convention regarding the Portuguese Colonies in Africa. Germany had become highly agitated in June when the Portuguese Government sent the Marquis de Soveral to London to negotiate with the British Government for a loan to improve the desperate state of Portugal's finances. The security was her African colonies, including Lourenço Marques, in Delagoa Bay, through which the Transvaal had its access to the sea, and Angola, which adjoined German South-West Africa and contained Tiger Bay, a valuable harbour. Over Delagoa Bay England already had a right of pre-emption. Germany was absolutely determined that in the event of a loan, the lien on these possessions should not be the monopoly of Great Britain, and although Lord Salisbury at first refused to discuss with the German Ambassador financial dealings which, he said, concerned only ourselves and Portugal, he always admitted that if Portugal were compelled to sell her Colonies their fate would have to be discussed between her African neighbours. It was not his intention that the Portuguese Empire should break up if it could possibly be saved, and therefore when, on continued pressure from Germany, he consented in July to begin negotiations for a secret Convention over territorial partitions in Africa, the attitude of the British Foreign Office was different from that of the Germans, who were only eager to get as much as possible of the anticipated spoil. Lord Salisbury's chief aims were to avoid antagonising Germany, or offending the susceptibilities of Portugal. When Balfour took over the bargaining on August 10th, an explanatory Memorandum was put before him by Mr. Bertie, the Assistant Under-Secretary, which began:

Germany is pressing us to come to an immediate agreement with her about Portugal in Southern Africa—east and west,—and she makes the usual more or less covert threats that if we do not do so she will join Russia or France, or both of them, to our detriment all the world over.[1]

For the next ten days Balfour was engaged in cutting down the extravagant German demands. Berlin was in a hurry. Count Hatzfeldt had written on August 8th:

Although the delay caused by handing over further negotiations to Mr. Balfour is undesirable, yet I think we must consent to it. The last time he represented Lord Salisbury Mr. Balfour was honest and forthcoming towards us; when we come to discuss the matter with him it will probably soon be evident whether a quicker conclusion is to be expected in this way.[2]

On the 12th Count Hatzfeldt was warned from Berlin that news from Lisbon showed France also to be coquetting with the idea of lending Portugal money, "a clear sign that England and Germany ought to lose no time." [3] Nevertheless Germany remained stiff in her demands, the crux at this stage being the island of Timor, part of which belonged to the Dutch, and part to the Portuguese. There was some difference of opinion as to what Lord Salisbury had promised under this head. On the 19th Count Hatzfeldt was instructed to "make it clear orally, direct to Mr. Balfour or through Mr. Bertie, that an arrangement without Timor is unacceptable to us, and that

[1] See *British Documents*, Vol. I, p. 60.
[2] See *German Diplomatic Documents*, Vol. III, p. 37.
[3] *Ibid.*

we shall only continue to negotiate on the understanding that the promise made to us by Lord Salisbury...remains untouched."[1] In the meantime Mr. Chamberlain had been writing to Balfour (August 16th): "I agree with Lord Salisbury as to Timor, which ought to be left out of the present Agreement." In answer to this letter, which contained other comments and criticisms by the Colonial Secretary on the Agreement now in first draft, Balfour wrote a Minute.

10 Downing St.
Aug. 17, 1898.

Mr. Chamberlain.

My Draft Agreement was undoubtedly intended (i) to prevent either Power from advancing any money to Portugal on the security of her African possessions without the other Power having a right to share and (ii) to prevent either Power foreclosing on its security without the other Power simultaneously obtaining a similar privilege. This is what the Government want, and they want it, as I understand, for the following reasons:

What they originally wished for was a *joint* loan. If there had been default on a joint loan, evidently both the Powers granting the loan would have had a right to foreclose upon its own share of the security. We insist, for Treasury and other reasons, that the loans should be separate though simultaneous, and the Germans then ask that the consequences of the double loan should be assimilated to those which would have followed from a joint loan.

What they are afraid of are consequences such as the following (1) Portugal might content herself with borrowing only upon our half of the security. In that case, if we foreclosed, we should obtain territorial control over Delagoa Bay, leaving Germany out in the cold.

Again this might happen: Portugal might contract a simultaneous loan with Germany and England. Portugal might have sufficient means for paying the interest on both; she might, on England's suggestion, go on paying the German interest, making default on the interest due to England. In this case also England would foreclose, would obtain Delagoa Bay, etc., while Germany would be left with nothing but the barren privileges of her interest and Sinking Fund.

Now I understand that one of the difficulties which the German Government feel about the whole arrangement is that it deals a final and conclusive blow to their S. African aspirations.

[1] See *German Diplomatic Documents*, Vol. III, p. 38.

Transvaal.

On this Germany feels strongly, and they can only be consoled if they get some obvious advantages in return. That advantage they seek in a provision which will prevent England ever obtaining Delagoa Bay unless Germany simultaneously obtains control over Tiger Bay and the rest of her ear-marked securities. They would, therefore, I suspect strongly object to any arrangement which rendered it possible for England to get what England wants while Germany did not get what Germany wants.—Probably they would break off negotiations and wait for a time when England, being in difficulties elsewhere, would become more malleable with regard to South Africa; or, they might try and do what they are always threatening, namely, to come to some agreement with France about Portuguese finances.

Perhaps you will let me know your views. I send this by Messenger.

I have just put Hatzfeldt off till to-morrow, saying that you and I had still to consider some outstanding points.

To this Mr. Chamberlain replied:

> COLONIAL OFFICE.
> *Aug.* 17, 1898.

MY DEAR BALFOUR,

As far as I know there is no difference of principle between us, but we are undoubtedly treading on rather dangerous ground.

We both want (1) control of Delagoa Bay and Railway, (2) good relations, and, if possible an alliance or understanding with Germany.

We have got at present a pre-emption right over Delagoa Bay and the surrounding territory.

As regards (1) do we get more than this by the proposed agreement with Germany? I am afraid not, unless Portugal consents in return for a loan to hand over real control *at once* to us.

We must take especial care that by the proposed agreement we do not derogate from our existing pre-emption right, and that we do not make the exercise of this right (which is now dependent on Portugal and ourselves alone) conditional on the assent of Germany, or on her getting some other advantage which she has not got at present.

If you are clear that the wording of your declaration does not in any way weaken our existing position, I should be satisfied to go on; providing that we can secure our second object, viz. a better understanding with Germany.

But the tone of Hatzfeldt's communications is not very reassuring on this head. He speaks as an injured man who is being fleeced by usurers. This is not my view. In return for a permission from Germany to do a thing which we have a perfect right to do—namely, to pre-empt

Delagoa Bay, he gets our assistance to gain similar opportunities in North Mozambique, in Tiger Bay, and on the Congo—where he has now no rights or claims at all.

Unless he recognises that the advantage is very much on his side, I should say it was not worth going on, because we shall have given up a great deal and shall have no gratitude or better feeling in return.

I should be inclined to tell him our view plainly and to ask him whether it would not be more satisfactory to widen the scope of the negotiations, and to settle Neutral Zone, Zanzibar and China at the same time.

If he says No—then I would agree that it would be a pity to allow all the gains to be wasted, but I would insist on confining the discussion to your lines (the two declarations), and I would not yield another inch.

You will have in dealing with these to see:

(1) That our right to pre-empt Delagoa Bay, if Portugal wishes to sell, is untouched by this new agreement and is independent of the loan, of a possible default, and of German consent;

(2) That Germany agrees to give us a Chinde on the Congo, if ever she inherits this strip of North Angola from Portugal.

Balfour persisted in a more conciliatory policy than Mr. Chamberlain advocated. He did let fall to Count Hatzfeldt some criticisms of German intransigence, which were resented with the usual touchiness of the Berlin Foreign Office. On August 19th Baron von Richthofen wrote to Count Hatzfeldt:

... Say that Mr. Balfour's statement—which has no doubt been inspired from without—that we do nothing but threaten and neither concede nor promise anything, is incomprehensible at the moment when we are letting England have South Africa and are ready to fulfil *our* promises. In our eyes the Agreement was the starting point of a joint colonial policy. Our demands are the minimum for leaving the Boers to themselves. Failing this recompense we should be unable to justify the Agreement in the eyes of our own public opinion, and should be forced to strike out another course and to broaden the question by introducing other elements.[1]

Count Hatzfeldt, whose notions of diplomacy were less crude, telegraphed back the following day:

Timor is settled, and I am convinced that we owe it to Mr. Balfour alone, for he urgently desires a conclusion. I beg therefore that as few

[1] *German Diplomatic Documents,* Vol. III, p. 38.

difficulties as possible be made for him regarding his draft, and that a secret note in explanation be agreed to in the manner I recommended.

After this the negotiations ran better. Balfour had consented to the inclusion of Timor among the securities for the loan, and he sent Lord Salisbury the drafts for the financial Convention and the Secret Agreement to oppose the intervention of any third Power in respect of Portuguese territories. Lord Salisbury answered on August 28th:

I am afraid the German negotiations must have given you a great deal of trouble. If the Germans take to being punctilious they are quite intolerable. The result seems to me quite satisfactory. . . .

On August 30th Balfour reported once more:

I have signed the Anglo-German Convention—for good or ill.

"I only hope," wrote Lord Salisbury in reply, "that it will not come into use for a long time." In point of fact it never did. Portugal improved the state of her finances without having recourse to an external loan, and the support of Lord Salisbury was felt behind her resistance to the pressure put upon her to borrow in Paris and else-where. Germany was disappointed that the Conventions did not bear the fruit she desired. From one point of view however they fulfilled their primary purpose. For years past Lord Salisbury's policy had been to remove causes of rivalry between the Powers one by one, especially in respect of the African continent. When he returned to the Foreign Office in September he found that the course had been steadily held in his absence.

The story of Balfour's first responsibilities at the Foreign Office is, by the nature of the case, somewhat disconnected, and it does not enter upon the great crisis in Anglo-French relations, which occurred in the autumn of 1898, when Captain Marchand, at the head of a French expedition, reached the Upper Nile from the south, and planted his country's flag at Fashoda. Lord Kitchener, fresh from his victory over the Khalifa at Omdurman, hastened up, and after hoisting the Egyptian flag beside the other, left the further settle-ment of the matter for diplomacy. For six weeks, war with France seemed very near, and Lord Salisbury passed some anxious moments before the Agreement was negotiated which crowned his career as

Foreign Minister, and led on to the Entente that it later fell to Balfour and Lord Lansdowne to conclude.

In 1898 Balfour came into contact for the first time with Lord Kitchener.

BALMORAL CASTLE.
Nov. 2nd 1898.

MY DEAR LADY ELCHO,

I intended to write to you yesterday, but the Sirdar [i.e., Lord Kitchener], who is better with the sword than the pen, begged me to assist him with the speech which he has to deliver to-morrow night at the Banquet to be given in his honour. I did my best to clothe his ideas, or some of them, in suitable language, but whether he will reproduce it when the time comes, and whether, if he does, it will harmonize with the portions of his harangue in which my valuable assistance has not been vouchsafed, remains to be seen.

I had much interesting talk with him at Hatfield, and here, yet do not find it easy to form any very confident estimate of his capacity. He possesses, without doubt, boundless courage and resolution; how far he could adapt himself to wholly different, and perhaps larger problems than those with which he has been dealing, I do not feel confident. He seems to have a profound contempt for every soldier except himself; which, though not an amiable trait, does not make me think less of his brains.

I find the Queen in the best of health and spirits, though somewhat perturbed over our relations with France. She has the utmost horror of war, on the simple but sufficient ground that you cannot have war without a great many people being killed. No better reason can be given for this laudable sentiment, but she expresses it with singular naïveté.

The international position about which you ask me appears to be this: *We* say that England cannot discuss frontier questions while the French are at Fashoda where they have not the slightest right to be; the French say that they have a perfect right to be at Fashoda; but inasmuch as it does not prove to be all their fancy painted it, perhaps they will leave it. This is fairly satisfactory as far as it goes, but we are far from being out of the wood.

yours,
A. J. B.

PS. By the way I have *long* inclined to Dreyfus' innocence on the broad ground that all the Military Attachés (who have the best means of knowing) hold that view.

Chapter XIII

CHURCH AND STATE

Anti-Ritualism. The Bishops fail to enforce obedience. Balfour appeals to the Archbishop. Balfour's gloomy forebodings for the Church of England. The "Wee Free" case. Balfour's Scottish Churches Bill. "Clause V." Balfour's view of organised religion.

In the history of this country the year 1899 is chiefly associated with the outbreak of the South African War. For the next two years and more the South African situation dominated politics. A few weeks after hostilities ceased, Balfour took Lord Salisbury's place at the head of the Government, in July 1902. The four years of his Premiership were years in which some of the great economic and military problems of the new century began to disclose themselves.

An entirely different question however, which recurred in different guises during this time, is both too important and too illuminating of Balfour's point of view to be passed over. It concerned age-long controversies touching the relations between Church and State. Balfour, the Scotsman, had to deal with this first of all in England.

In the year 1898 the anti-ritual agitation of Mr. John Kensit had roused so much feeling that the Episcopate felt compelled to deal with it by submitting a Bill to Parliament for reform of the Ecclesiastical Courts. But the faith of the Low Church section of the public in the power of the bishops to enforce the law, and in their will to enforce discipline, was not strong. A special attack was launched on the use of their Veto under the Public Worship Regulation Act, which some bishops were accused of having deliberately employed to stop prosecutions of ritualistic clergy. Sir William Harcourt—an Erastian undiluted—wrote letters to *The Times* claiming the abolition of the Veto, and the unrestricted right of Parliament not merely to lay down, but to interpret the ecclesiastical law. Balfour's annual series of speeches in his constituency, delivered shortly before the opening of Parliament, had to be much concerned with the whole question. A deputation from the "Manchester Protestant 'Thousand" and the "Protestant League" on January 31st gave him the opportunity to put his own views at some length. Dealing with the ritual part of the controversy, he observed that he did not "meet with those practices" himself, nor encounter many people who did, but he accepted "as an unhappy fact" that in certain churches things were done contrary to the law of the Church of England.

The amount of importance which he attached to these practices in themselves was shown in the final words with which he received the deputation's vote of thanks.

We may or may not differ as to what we may think is in conformity with Protestantism, but that England is always destined to be a Protestant country I regard as incontrovertible, and when I hear of a conspiracy against Protestantism I don't know whether it exists or not; I treat it personally with no more regard than I should a conspiracy against the law of gravitation.

Throughout the Sessions of 1899 and 1900 the "Crisis in the Church" continued unabated, the bishops being unable to bring the weight of united authority to enforcement of conformity to the law. Whenever the controversy was debated in the House of Commons, as it frequently was, Balfour held to the line of "trust the bishops" and pleaded for a minimum of interference with them. "Parliament," he had said in Manchester, "has no doubt to be called in to deal with questions of religion, but anybody who knows the House of Commons will agree that the less it is called in the better." His papers testify to a considerable amount of consultation with his Cecil cousins, especially with Lord Cranborne. The Cecil family, as a whole, were High Church people of the moderate school and deeply interested in the internal politics of the Church. Balfour's personal point of view about observances and dogmas of religion differed widely from theirs, but in determination to uphold the dignity and authority of the Church as by law established they were entirely at one. A letter to an old friend defines his opinions.

Private.

10 DOWNING STREET.
Feb. 16, 1899.

MY DEAR GEORGE TALBOT,

...I am quite aware that, as you say, there exist behind all this surface controversy grave differences of opinion on the subject of the

ARTHUR JAMES BALFOUR

Courts appointed to deal with matters ecclesiastical, and many search-
ings of heart as to the relations which ought to exist between Church
and State. You allude to the Presbyterian Free Church, and the parallel
is instructive. The Presbyterian Church of Scotland has, I fear, for ever
been maimed by the metaphysical scruples entertained on this subject by
the seceding clergy and laity. I think it quite possible that a similar disruption is in store for the Church of England. If it comes about, however,
it will certainly not be because the Ministers of the Crown for the time
being mistook the gravity of the crisis, or were indifferent to it.

I am not only not an Erastian, but I have a strong dislike to
Erastianism. If it were possible (and perhaps it may be possible) to give
the English Church the full autonomy possessed by the Scottish Church,
I should like to do it. Nevertheless, in all these discussions as to the
relations between Church and State, I think the disputants are very
apt unnecessarily to turn cases of expediency into cases of conscience, to
lose all sense of proportion, and to insist on forms while abandoning
substance. Throughout the whole history of the Christian Church, from
the time of the great Councils downwards, the State *has* interfered in
matters of doctrine and ritual, and the interference has not been less
because in most, if not all, of the cases the final decision was formally
given to Ecclesiastics.—Moreover, it is not possible absolutely to divide
by a clear and consistent line the province of the State from the province
of the Church where both co-exist in the same community; at least it
is impossible so long as the Church is the owner of property. I am
aware, however, that this line of thought does not in the least appeal
to the clergy of whom you speak, and it is therefore useless perhaps
to dwell upon it....

Believe me,

yours very sincerely,

A. J. B.

The support and advice he might reasonably have looked for from
the bishops was not spontaneously forthcoming, as the following letter shows. It was written confidentially, and without Balfour's
knowledge to Dr. Davidson (then Bishop of Winchester) by one
of Balfour's private secretaries, Mr. Parry.[1]

15*th Dec.*, 1900.

MY DEAR BISHOP,

...I want to remind you of what I may call the H. of C. history
of the so-called Church crisis. It began with the protracted debates on

[1] Afterwards Sir Sydney Parry. He had known Dr. Davidson all his
life, and had great trust in his discretion. Hence the frank tone of this
personal letter.

the Benefices Bill in the Session of 1898. It revived next Session in Samuel Smith's Amendment to the Address on 9 Feb. 1899. It crystallised in the debate on Gedge's Motion of the 11th April, when the House, by 200 votes to 14, definitely censured the lawlessness of certain members of the Church, and recommended the Crown to refuse preferment to any clergyman who would not obey the Bishops and Prayerbook and the Law as declared by the existing Courts.

It was of course against these Courts that the "lawless" part had directed its objections. To meet these objections the two Archbishops opened their Enquiry at Lambeth on the 6th May. On the 10th the Church Discipline Bill came up for 2nd Reading, and the Government then declared its policy in a motion which was unanimously adopted by the House, to the effect that:

"This House, while not prepared to accept a measure which creates new offences and ignores the authority of the Bishops in maintaining the discipline of the Church, is of opinion that if the efforts now being made by the Archbishops and Bishops to secure the due obedience of the Clergy are not speedily effectual, further legislation will be required to maintain the observance of the existing laws of Church and Realm."

The Archbishops' decisions condemning Processional Lights and the ceremonial use of Incense were pronounced in July, 1899; that condemning Reservation was not delivered till May, 1900. On all 3 points the Archbishops practically confirmed the decisions of the existing Courts.

Meanwhile the H. of C., though still restless, remained quiet partly because it recognised the reasonableness of waiting to see whether the "lawless" clergy would yield to the Bishops what they had refused to the Courts, and partly because its attention was occupied by the War.

I would now beg you to . . . consider what has been, all along, the attitude of Mr. Balfour as Leader of the House. I can assure you that it is not too much to say that, but for his restraining power over both sides of the House, and but for that unique magnetism and attractiveness which he exercises over everyone with whom he comes in contact, the Bishops' sympathisers in the Commons would have been in a pronounced minority. Few people seem to realise the immense weight which any appeal to the "Law and Order" argument carries with it in the Lower House. They do not give Mr. Balfour a tithe of the credit he deserves for his steady and successful efforts to induce the great "Law and Order" party in the House, against its own convictions, to trust the Bishops and give them time.

Meanwhile, what advice or encouragement, or even acknowledgment has he received from the Primate or the Bishops generally? I was new to my work under him when he had to pilot the Benefices Bill through a hostile House; and I well remember my astonishment at finding how, during the whole campaign, the Archbishop [1] never consulted with him, never advised him, never even recognised his existence until the Bill was through. Indeed I remember hearing Mr. Balfour himself express his surprise that the Archbishop never offered his counsel upon the difficult questions of policy involved in the preparation and discussion of the Bill. Similarly with the Church Discipline Bill and other later attacks. On each occasion my Chief fought the same uphill battle for the Established Church and its leaders, and on each occasion its first officer left him severely alone. On a minor and (comparatively speaking) insignificant matter, the proposed amalgamation of the Ecclesiastical Commission with Queen Anne's Bounty, his Grace of Canterbury is ready enough to volunteer advice, even if not to answer criticism; but when the reputation of the Bishops and the very constitution of the Church has been at stake, he has passed by like the Levite on the other side. Few statesmen, I think, would have been as loyal as Mr. Balfour; none as patient....

Mr. Balfour, though completely ignored by the Episcopate, and though he has stretched the loyalty of his followers almost to breaking point, has so far succeeded single-handed, as I think you will agree that no one else could have succeeded, in inducing a reluctant House to wait and trust the Bishops—on what grounds? That the existing machinery has not been proved to be inadequate; that the recalcitrant clergy will probably be induced to obey their spiritual masters even though they defy the temporal courts; *but* that, if they do not obey, the Bishops will put the necessary machinery into motion, and that, if it is then shown to be inadequate, it will then, and not till then, be time to talk of Reform.

The House *has* trusted the Bishops; it *has* given them time; and now their Lordships (for, as I said, the collective Bench must share the responsibility for the Bishop of London's action) without a word of warning to Mr. Balfour, throw him over completely, and announce that though the recalcitrants defy the Archbishops' ruling as much as they defy the Courts, the Bishops refuse to prosecute! They appealed to "Law and Order" in the civil government to defend them against the Kensitite iconoclasts and brawlers; they ignore it in their own domain.

This is at once flung in Mr. Balfour's teeth. He is being challenged on all sides to make good his words and take up Reform, whether the Bishops like it or not.... He has been forced to arrange to receive a most influential deputation from Liverpool before the House meets in February. He will have to make a formal declaration of the Government's policy; and then, when the House meets there will be a general attack....

[1] Dr. Temple.

I believe Mr. Balfour intends to tell the Primate that His Grace must really provide him with *some* "brief" in the matter; but what I want *you* to understand is that the Archbishop's policy of ignoring both the strained attitude of the great "Law and Order" party whether inside or outside the House, and also the strenuous and self-denying efforts of the most loyal champion the Established Church possesses, is disheartening and dangerous to the highest degree. . . .

No one denies that the resources of Parliament are equal to the task of enforcing "Law and Order" in the Church by means of the lay arm; but I know that there are statesmen (and I have some reason for thinking that Mr. Balfour may be numbered among them) who hold the view that this result will probably be attended by the severance of the tie which unites Church and State at the present moment. . . .

yours very sincerely,

F. S. P.

On the same day Balfour wrote to the Primate:

Private.

10 DOWNING ST.

Dec. 15, 1900.

MY DEAR ARCHBISHOP,

During the Session now closing the House has consented to abstain from any discussions not relating to the business of War. When it re-assembles two months hence we shall not enjoy the same immunity, and I am therefore most anxious to be armed at all points against the time when I shall have to take part in the inevitable battle over ritualistic excesses.

So far, the main burden of dealing with the political and legislative sides of these ecclesiastical controversies has by a Parliamentary accident fallen upon me, and I have done my very best to moderate the passions of the contending parties, and to discourage rash projects of legislation. The task has not been easy, and it is not likely to become easier so long as there is any ground for saying that practices which the Courts and the Archbishops have both pronounced to be illegal are continuing unchecked.

What we have to reckon with is a theological prejudice in its extreme form not perhaps very widely spread, but supported by a very simple and plausible argument which directly appeals to the conscience and intellect of "the man in the street." "There is a law: it has been declared by competent authorities: let it be obeyed. If the existing means of enforcing obedience are insufficient, let new means be devised. But in any case do not tolerate avowed and open illegality."

Such is the view which nine laymen out of ten will declare to be sound common sense if the point is put to them. On more than one occasion I have endeavoured to point out why I do not think the matter quite so simple as this way of putting it would seem to imply. But I cannot flatter myself that in these efforts I have obtained the smallest success, and I am afraid that the great majority of the House of Commons are still of opinion that the simple formula, "Enforce the law or alter it" is the last word which wisdom has to say on the subject.

This is a very dangerous position of affairs, and I see no really satisfactory method of meeting the cry for legislative action except that of showing that the existing machinery for enforcing the law is sufficient, not only in theory but in practice. It may be that the efforts which I know the Episcopal Bench have been making to check these extreme practices have been crowned with complete, or nearly complete success, and, if so, I look forward without misgiving to the future. But it would greatly strengthen my hands if you could cause me to be supplied with facts adequate to support this happy view, should it in your judgment be the correct one. . . .

I would very earnestly beg Your Grace to consider how difficult will be the position of those who are anxious to walk warily in dealing legislatively with these critical questions if the failure of the existing system should prove to be flagrant and undeniable.

I need only add that I am well aware of the difficulties with which the Bishops have had to contend. They are naturally and properly desirous of influencing rather than coercing their Clergy, and the cases in which the congregations are even more extreme than their ministers present problems of peculiar perplexity. Nevertheless there is another side to the question which cannot be ignored: and it is this other side which I have ventured in this letter to impress upon Your Grace.

The Archbishop of Canterbury replied:

> OLD PALACE,
> CANTERBURY.
> 17 *Dec.*, 1900.

MY DEAR MR. BALFOUR,

I have just received your letter on the possibility or even probability of what we shall have to face in Parliament next Session concerning the Church.

The letter states clearly and forcibly what most of the Bishops have been already anticipating.

The Bishops of both Provinces meet at Lambeth on the 15th of January. Do you think it will be sufficient if we then consider the matter and lay before you the results of our discussions immediately after? or do you think that that will be too late?

The discussions will be obviously much more likely to be useful if all have some weeks' notice of the matter to be discussed, and the 15th of January will not be wasted, as I shall at once call the attention of the whole Episcopate to the matter.   I am, &c.,

F. CANTUAR.

This correspondence led to the Bishop of Winchester, Dr. Davidson, visiting Whittingehame early in January 1901. Before the next year was out he was himself Archbishop of Canterbury, and Balfour Prime Minister. The confidence which dated from this meeting was therefore of immense value, and bore fruit later in a matter of the utmost importance—namely the preparation of the Education Act of 1902. The question of Ecclesiastical Discipline did not however prove amenable to solution.

In 1903 Balfour let himself go on the subject to one of his oldest friends, Dr. Talbot (then Bishop of Rochester, and, later, of Winchester).

Confidential.

EASTBOURNE.

Feb. 6, 1903.

... I confess to entertaining the gloomiest apprehensions as to the future of the Church of England. I can hardly think of anything else. A so-called "Protestant" faction, ignorant, fanatical, reckless, but every day organising themselves politically with increased efficiency. A ritualistic party, as ignorant, as fanatical and as reckless, the sincerity of whose attachment to historic Anglicanism I find it quite impossible to believe. A High Church Party, determined to support men of whose practices they heartily disapprove. A laity, divided from the clergy by an ever deepening gulf, and exercised by religious problems which the clergy cannot help them to solve. An Episcopate—but I will not pursue the subject; my sheet of paper is finished and I should weep for very soreness of spirit if I went on! ...

I will write again.

Ever your affectionate though much tried friend,

ARTHUR JAMES BALFOUR.

In the year 1904, Balfour's Government appointed a Royal Commission to enquire into Ecclesiastical Discipline. Before it reported he had ceased to be Prime Minister, and the narrative of his life is not again concerned with the relations between Church and State in England, until near the end, when he saw, and disapproved, the action of the House of Commons in rejecting the New Prayer Book in 1927. This was entirely of a piece with the principles on which he acted in another matter which disclosed the fundamental Scottishness of his character. He regarded himself always as a member of the Church of England, as well as of the Established Church of his native land; but there is no doubt which of them he understood as from within, and which as from without. It was an abiding source of pleasure to him that his Government had the opportunity of reaffirming by legislation the autonomy of the Church of Scotland in matters of doctrine. It was a no less happy thing for the Church that a Scottish Prime Minister, personally interested in the subject, was in power when the opportunity offered.

It arose out of a situation which had to be set right by Parliamentary action. A decision of the House of Lords in 1905 deprived the United Free Church of Scotland of some two millions of Trust money, in favour of a very small minority of Free Church Members, who claimed that the Free Church had abandoned certain theological principles which were an essential part of her constitution. The case had really turned on the point of whether a Trust for a Church was a Trust to promulgate a rigid doctrine, or whether it might be a Trust for an organisation free to mould its own doctrine and its own constitution. The refusal of the Law Lords by a majority, to accept the second interpretation, stripped from the United Free Church the whole of her property. The United Free Church represented at that time about a fourth of the whole Church Membership of Scotland, and public opinion revolted at the situation which had been created. There was no opposition in principle to the provisions of Balfour's Scottish Churches Bill which gave to the Free Church the relief necessary to enable her to retain the bulk of her property. It was another thing however when to the same Bill a fifth clause was added, dealing not with the Free, but with the Established Church of Scotland, empowering her, without recourse to Parliament, to alter the form of subscription to the Confession of Faith laid by the Act of 1690.

By an impulse hard to explain on the part of a Scotsman, the leader of the Opposition, Sir Henry Campbell-Bannerman, took the point of view of English Nonconformists, and objected to liberating an Established Church from State control in matters of faith and doctrine. He described Clause V as an "undesirable alien" (the phrase was highly topical at the moment owing to the controversies over the Aliens Act), and demanded that it should be introduced, if at all, in a separate Bill. On that ground Balfour fought him, well knowing that a dying Government could never force a second controversial Bill on this subject through a dying Parliament. Clause V, he declared, was no intruder. It was relevant to the general interest of Presbyterianism in Scotland. All the Scottish Presbyterian Churches had the same origin. Their reunion was something to be looked forward to. The decision of the House of Lords, from which relief had just been given to the Free Church, had made many people feel that the Established Church was left handicapped, and a barrier raised against unity. "I shall always be found," said Balfour, "on the side of freedom and the side of unity."

Sir Henry Campbell-Bannerman was no match for the combination of knowledge and enthusiasm of the champions of Clause V on the Government Bench, where the Prime Minister was brilliantly seconded by the Lord-Advocate, Mr. Scott-Dickson, and the Attorney-General, Sir Robert Finlay. Balfour took Clause V through Committee himself, meeting only one notable opponent in Mr. James Bryce, who fought to exclude Professors of Theology in the Universities from the authority of the Ecclesiastical Assemblies. Balfour countered this powerful speech by admitting sympathy for the unfettered freedom of theological teaching, but he deprecated raising the big question of University Tests on this Bill. It was passed into law on July 20th, 1905.

"Freedom and Unity."—The lesser loyalties necessary stepping-stones to the greater,—the Church Universal built, not out of one block, but of many. Balfour held these concepts as firmly in the sphere of organised religion as in the sphere of organised international life.

One race, many nations, a universal Church, many ecclesiastical organisations—those are the facts we have got to take and make the best of. . . . I have no hope that these divisions among us will be healed by being abolished. Nay, I say that if Christianity is going to be what we all think it ought to be, and will be—the world religion—if it is really going to attack successfully those great populations in the Far East, . . . it must be by the help of teachers of their own race, who are going to lead them, and in leading them, will probably add something to the apparent divisions of the Christian world, although they will add, I trust, greatly to that universal Church to which every one of us, whatever his ecclesiastical allegiance, belongs. . . . Therefore I have to face the fact, and I do face it, that Christendom is and must remain ecclesiastically divided, ... and that what we have to do is to see beyond the separate organisation to which we all belong, that greater whole of which we are all Members.[1]

Yet Balfour lived to see the reunion of the Presbyterian Churches of his native country, which came to pass in 1929 by the voluntary act of the Churches themselves. This was one of the public events of the last year of his life which gave him real happiness; a happiness increased by the reflection that it was his legislation of 1905 which had set the Established Church of Scotland free to find her own basis of theological agreement with her sister Churches.

[1] Speech at City Temple, June 19th, 1906.

Chapter XIV

SECOND IN COMMAND

1899–1902

*Opening of South African War. Balfour's conversation with the
German Emperor. The "Black Week." Balfour and Lord Lansdowne suggest change in the Supreme Command. Balfour's private criticism of General Buller. Balfour suggests leasing Delagoa
Bay. Balfour's unpopular speeches. Dissolution of Parliament.
Balfour's first motor-car. General Election of 1900. Lord Salisbury
leaves the Foreign Office. "Hotel Cecil." Peace signed in June
1902. Lord Salisbury resigns the Premiership.*

THE South African War began in the autumn of the year 1899. The
summer was one of critical negotiations and deepening anxiety for
the Government, although Parliament was not preoccupied with
South African affairs, and the outbreak of war, when it came, was
a shock to the nation. Balfour, whose time was full with his House
of Commons work, made no public utterances on the dispute with
the Boer Republics until a platform speech at the end of July, when
there were still hopes of a peaceful settlement. He made his views
perfectly clear about our responsibilities towards the English-speaking population of the Transvaal, whose treatment by the Boers was
the crux of the quarrel. What his private opinions may have been
about the diplomatic handling of affairs at this stage it is impossible
to say. Considerable freedom had been accorded to Mr. Chamberlain
by the Cabinet as regards South African policy, nor was Lord
Salisbury ever quick to interfere with the judgment of those to
whom he had entrusted responsibility in matters great or small.
In the summer of 1899 his physical strength was beginning to ebb.
Moreover Lady Salisbury had fallen into a long illness, which before
the end of the year proved fatal. In fact the Prime Minister was at
the death-bed of his wife when, in the middle of November, the

British Expeditionary Force began to arrive in strength at Cape Town.

Their appearance put an end to the first period of the extreme anxiety which attended the early stages of this war, for when the Boer Ultimatum demanding the withdrawal of all British forces had hastened our declaration of war on October 11th, the military situation was very dangerous. At one moment it had almost seemed as if the British flag might disappear from South Africa while reinforcements for our troops on the spot were still in the transports. The fifteen thousand men who were defending Natal, including all the available cavalry, were hemmed in round Ladysmith. The garrisons at Kimberley and Mafeking were beleaguered, and Cape Colony seething with disaffection. This was the position when General Sir Redvers Buller landed at Cape Town in October. The Field Force under his command consisted of a Cavalry Division of nearly 6,000 men, an Army Corps of about 32,000 with some 9,000 for lines of communication, making 47,000 in all, with 11,000 horses, 14,000 mules and 114 guns. By the middle of November all these were safely disembarked at Cape Town. Ministers breathed more freely, and there were few Englishmen who doubted that the war would be over in the four months for which the House of Commons had been asked to vote an Estimate of £8,000,000.

Balfour took Lord Salisbury's place at a banquet at Windsor, where the German Emperor had just arrived on a visit to the Queen. The advance of the British forces to repel the invasion of Cape Colony and to relieve Kimberley and Ladysmith was just begun when, on November 22nd, Balfour put on record for the benefit of Lord Lansdowne, the Minister for War, some of the views which the Kaiser had imparted to him "with extraordinary verve and on a large variety of topics."

We spoke about the war in South Africa. He was full of the warmest admiration for the way the mobilisation and transport had been effected, said it was a feat unique in the history of the world, far surpassing in magnitude and difficulty the nearest parallel to it, namely the Japanese landing (of 1894) in the Lao-tung Peninsula.

When I turned him from the question of mobilisation and transport of our troops to that of their strategy and tactics in the field, he was, naturally enough, less favourable in his comments.—"Whenever war occurs in any part of the world," he said, "we in Germany sit down, and we make a plan." I ventured to ask him what plan they had made on this particular occasion. He answered: "According to our plan Sir George White would have fallen slowly back, striking out at the Boers whenever a favourable opportunity occurred, until he reached the neighbourhood of Maritzburg. This would in the meantime have been fortified, and by the time White reached it a large force from England could have been concentrated behind it. White would have withdrawn a little to his own right, and when the force from England attacked the Boers in front he would have fallen upon their left flank. This," said the Emperor, "would have been our scheme. But we quite understood that it was the remonstrance of the Civil Governor that prevented anything of the kind being adopted." I asked him about the Boer long-range guns, and he told me that the German military authorities have for some time come to the conclusion that mobile siege guns should be part of the field equipment of any army. "This," he said, "is a reversion to the state of things in the time of Frederick the Great." In his days, in addition to the two field guns that accompanied every regiment, there were guns of position employed in set battles to defend the chief tactical position. There were many difficulties attending the modern adaptation of the ancient practice, but both the French and the Germans were working at them.

I turned him upon Asia Minor and the Euphrates Valley, which induced him to give me at length the twice-told tale of his interview with Rhodes.[1] He seemed very keen on these commercial and industrial enterprises, and I said that, speaking for myself, I saw them with the greatest pleasure, as I did all the expansion of German commercial enterprise. "The Russians," he said, "won't like it, but when I have my schemes complete, I will see them damned before I let them into Asia Minor"—a most wholesome frame of mind.

He was in full cry about the merits of the Turk—the Turkish peasant, I mean, not the Turkish Pasha—when the interview was interrupted by a message from the Queen.

I ought, by the way, to have mentioned that he spoke with satisfaction of the (1898) Anglo-German Agreement as settling the relations of the two countries in S. Africa "for all time." "They (i.e. France and Russia) do not even know what is in it. Sometimes I lift the lid of the box just a little (imitating a half-opened box with his hands) and let them have a peep; then I shut it down again. They do not like it."—with a loud laugh.

A. J. B.

At the time this Memorandum was written, sections of the Continental Press, including the German, were scurrilously anti-

---

[1] Cf. *German Diplomatic Documents*, Vol. III, p. 49.

British in tone. Balfour's indifference to such attacks comes out in this private document:

Part of his [i.e. the Emperor's] conversation I find was similar in tenor to that which he had with Sir A. Bigge and Mr. Bertie. This has already been reported, and I will not repeat it here; merely observing that he, like Count von Bülow, seemed very unnecessarily apologetic about the German press, on the iniquities of which they dwelt at some length.

Only a few days after this conversation that crescendo of evil tidings from South Africa began which culminated in the disasters at Stormberg, Magersfontein and Colenso; the "Black Week" of December 1899. At this crisis Balfour stepped willingly to the fore, his first thought being to save the Prime Minister every unnecessary worry at a time of private grief. He described some of his experiences in conversation in after years, leaving upon his hearers an impression of the primitive conditions and amateurish confusion which seem to have prevailed about the circulation of news even to Ministers.

Every night [he said] I used to go down to the War Office (it was in Pall Mall then) between eleven and twelve at night, and walk up all the stairs, for there weren't any lifts, and get the Clerk in Charge to show me the late telegrams. And there never was any news except defeats.

In the midst of this gloomy December week, which he called "one of the most disagreeable recollections of my life," he kept one private engagement, to dine with Mr. St. Loe Strachey to meet a South African, Sir Percy Fitzpatrick, whose book, *The Transvaal from Within,* was then selling faster than the printers could turn it out. Sir Percy had been in England since August, but in five months had not talked with any member of the Government. Balfour read his book and wished to meet its writer. Mr. Strachey, a friend of both, warned Sir Percy to hold himself ready at the shortest notice, for Balfour would send word of his first free moment. It fell on the evening of December 15th, the day on which Sir Redvers Buller was known to be advancing upon Colenso on the way to Ladysmith. Balfour came to dinner, and was summoned from his host's fireside to hear the news of the disaster of the Tugela River. Sir Percy Fitzpatrick has described his demeanour before and after this blow [1] in a graphic narrative which can be only epitomised here. Balfour entered the room apologising for the short notice, and adding: "Even now I have had to tell them where I am, . . . as they are expecting important news at any moment from Buller."

The conversation developed exactly as would have been predicted by anyone who had ever watched Balfour when he was really anxious to extract information. The method was new to Sir Percy. He writes:

He asked questions on all subjects, and led me on as he liked. Once or twice it struck me that he was not quite "as innocent as a child," or he could not have put the questions, which, while seemingly impulsive or almost irrelevant, invariably uncovered something of interest or significance.

Nevertheless certain remarks impressed Fitzpatrick as a "revelation of complete misunderstanding of the position" and a "woeful misconception of the facts and factors." Finally the talk turned from the general and political situation to the probabilities of what Sir Redvers Buller might that day have done. "You are quite sure then," asked Balfour, "that Buller will not make a frontal attack on Colenso?" " 'Never,' Sir Percy replied, 'never! That net is cast in the sight of the bird. He knows!' Balfour at once seemed really anxious and alarmed; . . . his manner was quite changed and he seemed to become more and more uneasy."

Presently there was a summons. Balfour left the room. He was absent a quarter of an hour.

He returned to tell them that the main blow of the campaign had been delivered. Buller had made the frontal attack. He had failed. Balfour imparted this information, writes Sir Percy:

with the extreme gentleness and slow choice of words that in no way detracted from the clearness and courage of one who softens the blow of bad news without concealing truth. Through the gentleness and consequent politeness there shone something of which men had more than a glimpse in Ireland. . . . The serene unshakable faith in his people, the lofty inspiring calm of a leader, the firmness, the nerve, the finest tempered courage.[2]

From Mr. Strachey's house Balfour went straight to Lord Lansdowne, then Secretary for War, and that night they took the gravest

[1] Sir Percy Fitzpatrick, *South African Memories,* p. 144.
[2] *Ibid.*

decision that can confront Ministers in the crisis of a war—the decision to change the supreme command. The suggestion to send out Lord Roberts to supersede Sir Redvers Buller emanated from Lord Lansdowne,[1] and was agreed to by Balfour. Balfour went to see Lord Salisbury next morning and overcame his objections, which were on the score of Lord Roberts' age. "However, he consented when I pressed him" (so said Balfour describing these events at a later date) "but he said he must associate a younger man with him. He wanted Kitchener. I was perfectly willing of course; we knew nothing but good of K. in those days."

Balfour's recollection here bears out Lord Salisbury's own statement to the Queen,[2] that it was Lord Salisbury who insisted on Lord Kitchener going out with Lord Roberts. The decisions thus taken were confirmed by the Defence Committee of the Cabinet on the same day, but held up for twenty-four hours until Lord Roberts should reach London from his command in Ireland, and a telegram be received from Lord Kitchener who was then in Egypt. By an oversight, which shows how far Lord Salisbury must have been at the moment from taking his proper place at the head of affairs, neither the Queen nor Lord Wolseley was told of the intended changes until they were accomplished [3]—a circumstance which gave rise to a state of feeling thus described by Balfour:

10 DOWNING STREET.
Dec. 19*th*, 1899.

MY DEAR UNCLE ROBERT,
When I arrived at Windsor yesterday I found Bigge full of grievances as to the recent treatment of the Queen by her Ministers. According to him she complained

(1) that no account of the Defence Committee's proceedings had been sent her on Saturday;
(2) that she had not been consulted before the telegram ordering Buller to relieve Ladysmith was sent;
(3) that Roberts had been appointed without giving her an opportunity of expressing an opinion, and
(4) that the Commander-in-Chief had not been consulted with regard to this important military decision.

[1] Cf. *Life of Lord Lansdowne,* by Lord Newton, p. 165.
[2] Cf. *Queen Victoria's Letters,* Third Series, Vol. III, p. 445.
[3] *Ibid.,* 446.

I told Bigge as regards (1) that Roberts was really asked to command in South Africa not on Saturday, but on Sunday afternoon, when Kitchener's favourable reply had been received; this being in your opinion an indispensable part of the arrangement.

As regards (2) I said that this represented a theory of constitutional government which I could not accept. The Queen's advisers must be permitted to issue important military orders without her previous sanction.

As regards (3) I had absolutely no excuse to offer. I cannot understand why Lansdowne did not send by Special Messenger and by special train a submission to the Queen on Sunday afternoon. He contented himself with telling Bigge (who was in London) the whole story, and asking him to convey it to Her Majesty.

As regards (4) I told him that it was impossible to consult the Commander-in-Chief upon such an appointment, as his well-known jealousy of Roberts made his advice on such a subject perfectly worthless.

The Queen's own complaints in her interview with me were a very pale reflection of Bigge's forecast, and except on the subject of Roberts' appointment, where I think she is perfectly right, I found no great difficulty in smoothing matters down. Indeed, she was wonderfully good-humoured and wonderfully cheerful. With a very wise self-control she insists not only upon being serene herself, but on everybody round her keeping their serenity also. "I will have no melancholy in this house," is her formula—and not a bad one either in moments of anxiety....

The War Office are working away with great unanimity and energy, and with, I hope and believe, a total absence of red tape, to get a body of volunteers who can both shoot and ride. My private conviction is that before the end of this war we shall have too many unmounted infantry battalions in South Africa—we cannot possibly have too many mounted ones.

I gather Buller has ordered four-fifths of Warren's Division to go to Natal, but has not asked for Warren himself.—Upon my word when I think over the whole course of Buller's proceedings, I feel that the case against him could be made so strong that it is hard to justify retaining him in command of even a portion of our army. He seems quite capable of forming a good plan but quite incapable of sticking to it. He came to the conclusion when he first arrived at the Cape, without the least justification, that there was an immediate risk of Ladysmith falling, and it was, I presume, on this ground that he gave up the scheme of marching straight on the Orange Free State, which was his first, and by far his best, thought. No other reason at least for the change was ever given.

Having thus scattered his troops all about South Africa in three separate Divisions, none of them equal to striking a decisive blow, he forms an excellent scheme for relieving Ladysmith, which he abandons with the same facility and with the same absence of reasons as he had abandoned his broad plan of campaign. The attack on Colenso, which ought never to have been undertaken, and which he had himself said was impracticable, having failed, he deliberately counsels the abandonment of White to his fate, and the adoption of a purely defensive scheme of operations, to be protracted over the next three months. But when the Home Government indignantly repudiate this suggestion, he tells them that the more courageous policy thus forced upon him was exactly what he wanted, and that his only doubt arose from his ignorance of the weight which the Government attached to financial considerations at Kimberley! ! ! considerations which, so far as my knowledge goes, have never once been mentioned by him or to him on any previous occasion.

Methuen having been repulsed, he sends him a peremptory telegram saying that he must either fight again or retire—a very rash direction to be given by one who is 700 miles away from the operations he was directing. The object of this order was no doubt to prevent Methuen being cut off from his base, as White has been cut off. But now, if I understand him rightly, he has exactly reversed his policy in this, as in other matters, and has ordered Methuen to fill up his supplies and to hang on where he is under any circumstances.

Having told us a week ago, before Methuen's repulse, that he had no confidence in Methuen, he sends a most insolent telegram to the Commander-in-Chief, complaining of Methuen's supersession, and apparently stating that he had given orders on the subject inconsistent with those which came from home.

I think it is a most melancholy story, and I can only account for it by the theory that for the last ten years Buller has allowed himself to go downhill, and, for the moment at least, is not the man he once was. My hope is that the decisions we have recently come to will prove a "spur" to him, and not a discouragement, that he will pull himself together, and that he will effect at last something worthy of his reputation.

yr. aff.,

A. J. B.

The next question after that of the Command was that of reinforcements for South Africa and especially of reinforcements of the Mounted Infantry which the military authorities at last admitted to be direly needed. The Reserves were called up, the Seventh Division with artillery sent overseas, twelve battalions of Militia allowed to volunteer for service abroad, and a strong mounted force formed from the Yeomanry regiments.

Funds for this "Imperial Yeomanry" were partly provided through the War Office, and partly by private subscription in the counties. The Appeal to the Lord-Lieutenants was made through a letter signed by Balfour himself and addressed to Lord Haddington in his own county of East Lothian. He wrote to Lady Elcho on December 23rd:

I had intended, as you know, to go home last week, and was actually engaged to speak at Glasgow on Monday. But I hung on in London till I could hear the result of Buller's attempt, hoping that if this was a victory I might enjoy my Xmas with a good conscience in Scotland; but when it proved to be a repulse, I felt I had no choice but to stay.

This day week was thoroughly unpleasant! I was sent for by Lansdowne on Friday night late to have the bad news communicated to me; and on Saturday a still worse telegram (not connected with any battle, and not communicated to the public) completed the tale of woe. Since then I have not left London even for an afternoon's golf; I have seen during the day no one but soldiers and officials, and have dined in the evening with no one but colleagues and Jim Cranborne. Nor do I see any immediate end to this state of things. If I am to be of any use it is by being on the spot ready to help if anything turns up, so that I shall not dare to go away even for Xmas Day. . . .

I had a long interview with Roberts on Sunday last, the day of his appointment. His serenity is admirable. He had travelled all night; he was called upon at a moment's notice to carry out a most difficult job; his only son was thought to be dying, and was in fact dead; yet he showed neither depression nor misgivings nor over-confidence. He indulged in no unnecessary criticisms on others, and made no boasts about himself. One thing he said to Lansdowne (not to me) which moves me strangely. L. said to him that our only doubt in appointing him had arisen from his age. "You need have no misgivings," said R., "about my physical vigour; for years I have led a most active and abstemious life, waiting for this day." Don't you like it?   yours,
                                                  A. J. B.

Besides the military side of the situation, a proposal of Balfour's was discussed during the Christmas Cabinet meetings, relating to matters which Lord Salisbury was not content to leave to any judgment but his own. There was reason to believe that contraband of war was reaching the Boer Republics through the port of Lourenço Marques in Delagoa Bay, a Portuguese possession, where it arrived in ships flying neutral flags. The search and stoppage by

British cruisers of three German vessels in January 1900 produced a crisis in Anglo-German relations at a very awkward moment. That however was a transitory result of an incident which had a direct effect upon the German Naval Programme of the year 1900. Only a fortnight before the incident occurred Balfour had been prepared to go great lengths to get complete control of Delagoa Bay. On December 24th, 1899, he wrote a Memorandum for the Cabinet, proposing to take a lease of the Portuguese colony for the period of the war.

I suggest [he wrote] the following diplomatic scheme as offering the best chance of a satisfactory solution, promising that before anything is said to Portugal our whole hand should be shown to Germany. Before concluding any arrangement, we are in any case, bound by treaty to consult Germany. It is clearly our interest to go a step further, and consult Germany before opening negotiations.

The plan to which I suggest that we should ask Germany's consent is that of leasing Delagoa Bay *by the week* for a period not in any case longer than the war, and as much shorter as we choose to make it. The rent should be on the most liberal scale; I should not myself shrink from £100,000 a week if we could not get what we want for less. For this Portugal would surrender practically nothing. No Portuguese officials need be dismissed, no interference in general administration need be attempted except such as was in our opinion, absolutely requisite either for the defence of Portuguese possessions or the stoppage of supplies to the Boers. We should, of course, engage to maintain the integrity of the Colony, and to repay any damages which the Boers might succeed in inflicting on it. I am informed that this engagement would present no material difficulties, and that a force of 2000 (possibly Indian) troops would be sufficient. The whole wealth of the Colony is concentrated at Lourenço Marques and some coast villages, and these would be easy to protect.

It will be noticed that this plan is not one which the Germans will be greatly tempted to copy in their own "sphere." It may be safely said that the occupation of no Portuguese possession is worth paying for at the rate of £100 a week (let alone £100,000) if that occupation is to carry with it no privileges but that of stopping all trade with the hinterland, and defending the Colony against external aggression. . . .

Lord Salisbury disapproved of the project, seeing difficulties in obtaining the approval of the House of Commons, the consent of Portugal, and the acquiescence of France and Germany, all of which were necessary to carry it through. Unless the proposal were certain of success he was against even making it, on the ground that it would become common property at once and be interpreted as showing that the British Cabinet thought the prospects for success of the British military efforts to be almost desperate.

So nothing was done. It is possible that the action suggested by Balfour might have had the effect on foreign opinion which Lord Salisbury feared. There is a significant phrase in a telegram from the German Ambassador in London to his Government at this period. He had sent word that some proposal for getting control of Delagoa Bay was likely to be put forward, and Lisbon was warned that any agreement made without consultation with Berlin would be considered an unfriendly act. Count Hatzfeldt then cabled: "Agree absolutely with instruction to Lisbon. I think we must go slowly and get the British to meet us half-way. They are not yet reduced enough to think of giving up Zanzibar." [1]

The military position had not in fact improved at all when the year 1899 closed. Lord Roberts had not yet arrived at Cape Town, and the fate of the besieged force in Ladysmith hung in the balance, and with it the fate of Natal. In these circumstances of intense anxiety Balfour paid his yearly visit to his constituency, and delivered three speeches on January 8th and 9th, 1900. Owing to the fact that Christmas had followed almost immediately upon the "Black Week," no Minister had as yet spoken in public since the series of disasters had begun. The British people, bewildered and mortified to a degree only possible for a generation which had never been involved in a serious war on any scale, eagerly awaited explanations. What they wanted to hear it is hard to say. It is certain that what they heard was not what they wanted. Rarely can a great political leader, in the heyday of his strength and power, have been met with such violent blasts of criticism from every quarter as the Manchester speeches evoked. Indignation was not confined to the Opposition newspapers. *The Times* had a censorious article on the morning after the first speech, and the attacks went on through Balfour's private letter-bag, and were renewed when the House of Commons met at the end of January. Nothing sets in better perspective the gulf that separates our own times from those of the Boer War than the almost hysterical reactions of the national mind to unwonted misfortunes. At the same time the three speeches illustrate Balfour's weak point as a political leader, namely the un-

[1] *German Diplomatic Documents,* Vol. III, p. 117.

certainty of his instinct for gauging the popular mind, or persuading it to follow his own.

In the first speech, delivered on January 8th, he answered the current criticisms of South African policy and the preparations for war. He declared that diplomatically our hands had been tied for years past by the Jameson Raid, "that most unfortunate and ill-omened enterprise," and it had been this also which had prevented protests against the accumulation of arms by the Transvaal Republics. As to the probabilities of war as measured in the summer, everybody was on an equality—"the man in the street knew as much as the man in the Cabinet"—and if the Government held the view that peace could still be secured—"if we...made that mistake, we made it in common with the great mass not only of public opinion in this country, but of that portion of public opinion which knew most about South African affairs." Then— after sketching the evil effects which might have followed from asking Parliament in the summer for vast supplementary Estimates to provide immediate transport to South Africa—he proceeded to say that "when the nation and the community lags behind the necessities of the case, there may be occasions when rapidity of action is denied the Executive Government."

This passage was one of those fastened upon next day by *The Times*. "That is a most serious statement, and if it represents the settled opinion of the Leader of the House, it is to be hoped he will indicate in what way so dangerous a flaw in our system of government ought to be made good."

The speech contained a phrase—twice repeated—which proved exceedingly infelicitous, and was long resented. Admitting that we did under-rate the military efficiency of the Boers, Balfour said he still thought that the 25,000 men put into South Africa before the Field Force was sent out, were, or might have been, sufficient, had it not been for the "unhappy entanglement of Ladysmith." This way of referring to the position in Natal caused much offence. The most serious criticism however was against his vindication of the Cabinet and the War Office. "I don't feel the need," he said, "so far as my colleagues and I are concerned, of any apology whatever, and if I have appeared to take too argumentative a turn, it is as the best, shortest, and clearest way of putting before you all the leading points in our policy which it is necessary to bear in mind before that policy is judged of as a whole." He then passed on to a technical discussion of guns, the sacrifices of range that had been made to achieve mobility, defending the use of shrapnel as against shell,—points which had become the subject of much outcry since the casualties of the December battles. He finished by alluding to three things which he had abstained from stressing: criticism of the generals in the field,—appeal to the nation to persevere in the contest, because such an appeal would be an insult,—and lastly prophecy, because it might be that "we still have to go through a period of great darkness and great difficulty before the light of success shines assuredly before our eyes."

The speeches made on the following day added volume to the opening chorus of disapproval, and since Balfour realised when he made them that he was pursuing an unpopular line, they are the most interesting from the point of view of the psychology, both of the speaker and of the public.

It is quite true [he said] that we expected much greater success and more rapid success than, as a matter of fact, has crowned our efforts. It is not true that we have suffered in this war strange and exceptional reverses. There have been no great reverses in this war. Those who talk of great reverses have not made themselves acquainted with the inevitable—or almost inevitable—incidents of a protracted campaign.

To this *The Times* rejoined:

The tone of acquiescence in which he seems to regard our mishaps and reverses as though they were consequences of some malign destiny is a little irritating to a people who are not fatalists.... "We had," he said, "no great reverses in this war," though our casualties in three months reach a total of seven thousand.[1]

The criticism of the final speech does not depend on a sense of scale:

Mr. Balfour's successive speeches at Manchester, by completely ignoring the fiduciary relation in which the Government stand to the country, afford the strongest possible confirmation of Lord Charles Beresford's statement that so far as the Services are concerned, no such thing as Ministerial responsibility exists.... The course of the war is a clear proof that somebody is to blame. Fault must be somewhere between the Generals, the system, and the Cabinet.... The Cabinet choose the Generals and control the War Office, or allow the War Office to control

[1] *The Times,* January 10th, 1900.

them. There is need of apology on the part of the Cabinet for serious errors, both in policy and warlike preparation.[1]

Balfour knew perfectly well that the people were demanding a scapegoat. A letter to a friend shows what lay beneath the so-called "flippancy" of his refusal to provide a victim.

10 DOWNING ST.
Jan. 24th, 1900.

I am really obliged to you for your letter because I know that it is dictated by no other sentiment than that of warm personal friendship to myself and devotion to the Party. I must frankly admit that I am a good deal puzzled at it. You make four charges against the speeches delivered by me at Manchester:

i. that they were "flippant";
ii. that I denied that there was any cause to complain of the War Office management even in detail;
iii. that I fail to recognise the gravity of the situation;
iv. that I failed to assert that the Government were determined to spare no effort to bring the War to a successful conclusion.

Now, honestly, these charges perplex me beyond words. (i) I cannot imagine what is meant by the allegation of "flippancy." I know that this war has never been out of my thoughts for one moment for the last two months, that I sacrificed my whole holiday to assisting to the best of my ability those colleagues of mine in whose special departments the conduct of the war rests, and that the time of anxiety I have been going through is far greater than anything of which I have had experience, even in the worst periods of our Irish troubles. Perhaps you would be kind enough to point out in my speeches what phrase or phrases are inconsistent with this attitude of mind.

(ii) So far from not recognising that mistakes have been committed, the whole key of my speech was the statement that the Government had under-rated the military strength of the Boers. It is perfectly true that I do not think the Government were to blame for this, as they were supported by unanimous expert opinion upon the subject. But this I did not say in my speech, contenting myself with the general admission.

(iii) I not only think blunders have been committed, but I think they have been of the most serious kind, imperilling the whole progress of the war. But I do not think these blunders are due to War Office mal-administration, and, until I see reason to think so, nothing will

[1] *The Times,* January 11th, 1900.

induce me to say so. The chief blunders have been made, in my private opinion, by our Generals in the field; but I do not of course think it desirable to make any such statement in public.

I have said in these speeches not all that I thought, but nothing that I did not think. I cannot give my full opinions without blaming gallant men whom I do not wish to blame; but I entirely decline to make a scapegoat of people who I do *not* think deserve any such fate. Far rather would I leave public life for ever. . . .

When Parliament met at the end of January, Sir Henry Campbell-Bannerman had succeeded in drafting an Amendment to the Address capable of rallying the Liberal Imperialists into the same lobby with the "pro-Boer" Liberals, by extending the criticism of the Government's South African policy back to 1895. Balfour gave the Opposition their say for a full week, steadily resisting the pressure put upon him to closure a Debate which was doing little to strengthen the prestige of the country in the still critical stage of the South African campaign, and only attempting at the end to drive a wedge between their factions. Alluding to speeches made by Mr. Asquith and Sir Edward Grey, the Liberal Imperialist leaders, he declared them so good that on an ordinary occasion he would say: "Give me your speech, and vote as you like," but that now "every abstraction from the Government lobby of the votes of the men who agree with the Government on the main policy is really a weakening of the forces of their country in the field."

As the months passed, divisions of opinion in the Liberal camp became such that their leader, Sir Henry Campbell-Bannerman, "could do nothing but mark time, . . . and not infrequently had the annoyance of seeing his colleagues on the Front Bench decline his lead into the Division Lobby." [1]

Balfour's defence of the Government in his speech on the Address did not depart from the line taken by the Manchester speeches, and was equally little liked. His mind was however absorbed in matters that interested him more than criticism of himself—he was writing to Lord Lansdowne strings of questions,—thus, on February 1st, 1900:

Is the War Office doing anything to encourage extra exertions at the present time in the way of drill or shooting? Are we in a position to supply the Yeomanry with magazine carbines? I will try to come over

[1] Cf. *Life of Sir Henry Campbell-Bannerman,* Vol. I, p. 276.

to the W.O. this afternoon, but now that the House has met I am reduced from the position of a useful public servant to that of an auditor
and critic of parliamentary wish-wash.

Lord Roberts had landed at the Cape on January 10th, and by the
middle of February was across the Modder River and invading the
Free State. By February 15th Kimberley was relieved, and the Boer
army under General Cronje had surrendered. Therewith ended the
acute phase of the Boer War.

It was not a period to which Balfour looked back with satisfaction. Yet the experience it brought became of incalculable benefit.
I have quoted in an earlier chapter a speech [1] delivered, to a handful
of local volunteers in his own county, showing how his random
thoughts were gathering round problems of Defence at a time when
the strength and power of Britain seemed most absolute. During
the South African War the weaknesses of the British Constitution
as a fighting machine were pointed, and thenceforth formed the
subject of concentrated thought in his mind. From the confusions,
overlappings and deficiencies of information that handicapped
the Executive Government during the Boer War sprang the train
of ideas which presently took shape in the constitution of the
Committee of Imperial Defence, and the examination, and re-
examination, of our military practice and philosophy, which was
a feature of the ensuing years.

The final Session of the Parliament which was dissolved in September 1900 was fretful. The Government had no intention of
embarking on the Peace settlement—whenever that should come—
with a dying Parliament behind them, and they were known to be
contemplating a General Election. But the hopes of an early end
to the war melted with the summer, and the Liberals, whose open
disagreements on the one topic of the day prevented them from
looking forward with any optimism to a political campaign, loudly
advertised the unanimity of their feelings of disgust at the un-
scrupulousness of the Ministry in seizing Party advantage out of
national peril. Meantime the "pro-Boer" faction sniped the Government on every point connected with the conduct of the war.

The crisis of the war over, Balfour's London life had returned
more or less to its accustomed ways. He wrote to Lady Elcho on
Thursday, July 19th:

[1] See p. 154.

I have been very busy and very frivolous since you left. I suppose
you will now require some account of my doings—if I can only remember them! I already find I can't! What did I do on Friday besides
Cabinet and House of Commons? Where did I dine? or did I dine?
There is no hint in my pocket-book, so I think I must have stuck to
the House.

Sat. was Eton and Harrow match, forever embittered from the fact
that I quite gratuitously and out of sheer disgust at Eton's collapse in
its second innings fled the ground, and thereby lost the most exciting
finish of modern times....

Sunday I spent at Panshanger,[1] the Chesterfields,[2] Etty,[3] Jenny
Churchill, and her young man,[4] Ly Windsor, Duchess of Sutherland,
the Vincents,[5] de Vescis,[6] Evan,[7] etc. An excellent party, all in the best
of spirits. We played bridge after dinner in the open air, criticising the
moon between the deals!

On Monday, motor-car to London. It had a mild break-down about
every three miles—and finally, when we arrived within striking distance of home, we betook ourselves to hansoms, leaving the little French
chauffeur in tears of mortification.

I dined last night with the Asquiths, and as the fortunes of debate
would have it, A. and I had rather a sharp passage in the House after
dinner. Asquith was the challenger; but I felt a mild awkwardness in
replying to a man in the strength of his own champagne! I did it all
the same, and with considerable vigour.

Tuesday, dinner with Charty.[8] All that happened on this occasion
worthy of record happened after I left for the House, when Barbara [9]
acted a couple of French pieces, and I am told acted well.

Wed. The House lasted until 6.30. I had to be away for an hour in
the middle memorialising Mr. Gladstone.

yrs.,
A. J. B.

In Balfour's private correspondence of the year 1900 the triumphs,
or (more often) the break-downs of the motor-car are a constant

[1] The residence of Earl and Countess Cowper.
[2] The Earl and Countess of Chesterfield.
[3] Lady Desborough.
[4] Lady Randolph Churchill, and her second husband Captain J. Corn-
wallis-West.
[5] Afterwards Lord and Lady d'Abernon.
[6] Viscount and Viscountess de Vesci.
[7] The Hon. Evan Charteris, afterwards Sir Evan Charteris.
[8] Lady Ribblesdale.
[9] The Hon. Barbara Lister, afterwards Lady Wilson.

theme. He had acquired the first of his own series, a little De Dion, whose four occupants sat facing each other round the steering handle, exposed to wind and weather, but fortunately able to spring out at a moment's notice to apply to the hind wheel a block of wood designed to prevent the car from running backwards down the formidable hills that are met with on every road round Whittingehame. This fantastic little vehicle was the pride and anxiety of its owner. Where its credit was concerned his insensitiveness to public opinion was much diminished. Almost the only occasion on which I can recall feeling alarmed at the prospect of telling him anything was on return from a garden party where the De Dion had stopped through lack of petrol twenty yards from the front door, in sight of all the guests. My apprehensions were justified. The light of interest was instantly quenched from his eye, and merely remarking, "Unnecessarily silly," he left the room.

When the General Election of 1900 had resettled the Unionists in office, Lord Salisbury travelled to Balmoral to discuss the personnel of his last administration with the Queen. Balfour went from Whittingehame to meet him in Edinburgh as he passed through. The keeping of important appointments by automobile was still a rash proceeding, but Balfour set forth thus to traverse twenty-six miles on a dark windy October evening. Every few minutes the head-lamps blew out (they were only bits of candle), and the unfavourable comments of the passers-by caused him to fear lest his meeting with the Prime Minister might be frustrated by the police. Therefore in Musselburgh he bought a large stable lantern and drove into Edinburgh waving it about from his seat beside the chauffeur.

The Parliament of 1900—within whose span fell also the whole period of Balfour's Premiership—showed a Unionist majority of 134. At the dissolution of its predecessor the figure had been 130, but the gain in votes throughout the country was over ninety thousand, and the change of opinion was particularly marked in Scotland. For the first time since the Reform Bill of 1832 the Liberals were in a minority north of Tweed. In Wales, on the other hand, Unionism suffered a definite decline in seats, as in votes. A territorial base was forming there for a leader of the coming time.

Balfour's majority in East Manchester was increased from seven hundred to over two thousand. After his own poll, he toured the country. It was an ill-tempered Election, according to the standards

A. J. B. STARTING FOR A MOTOR RIDE

of those days. Mr. Chamberlain had struck a note, which was hotly resented by the Liberal-Imperialist section of the Opposition,—that "every seat lost to the Government was a seat gained by the Boers." Balfour reminded the Opposition leaders that, apart from the varieties of view held by their English and Scottish supporters on the righteousness of the Boer cause, a full third of their backing in the House of Commons if they got into power would come from the Irish Nationalist Party, eighty men "avowedly and openly pro-Boer." To call a Party thus composed "pro-Boer," by comparison with the Unionists was "perfectly fair, perfectly true, perfectly just." He was not in love with this kind of controversy. But one could not deal with a Party that was "half-oil, half-water." [1]

The campaign over, Mr. Chamberlain wrote:

HIGHBURY.
Oct. 21st, 1900.

MY DEAR ARTHUR,

I want in the first place to thank you for the kind things you said in my defence during the recent Election. I am grateful to you and other friends for the confident loyalty of your friendship. The attacks made upon me . . . exceed anything I have ever known. They are all on private character, and hardly at all on public policy or actions,—and yet the only leader on the other side who repudiated them was Sir E. Grey. Campbell-Bannerman, Harcourt, Asquith and Fowler all silent— while allowing the insinuations to be distributed by the Radical Association at 5/- per thousand. Enough of this. . . . I am leaving on Friday for a trip to Gibraltar and Malta; . . . there are several points I should like to mention before I go. . . .

Should not a strong Commission be appointed to enquire into the conduct of the war? If you leave it till Parliament meets you will be forced into a demand for a Parliamentary Committee—the worst tribunal in the world where Party interests are at stake.

The rest of the letter is occupied with the personnel of the new Government, a subject on which Balfour had the day before heard the views of the leader of the Whig wing, the Duke of Devonshire. His private papers of this time show that the wishes of those who were, and also of some who thought themselves to be, key men in respect of the allocation of offices were laid very freely before him.

His own first preoccupation was with Lord Salisbury's own

[1] Speech at Kilmarnock, October 6th, 1900.

position. The doubling of the parts of Prime Minister and Foreign Secretary was now too much for him, in the opinion of his family and his doctors; but the Queen needed some persuasion before she would consent to let the charge of the Foreign Office pass from his hands. Balfour wrote a long letter to his colleague, Mr. Akers Douglas, who had gone to Balmoral to prepare the ground,[1] and received a reply by return of post.

> BALMORAL CASTLE.
> *Oct. 19th*, 1900.

Your letter came just at the right moment—was exactly what was wanted—and I think has quite settled the matter. The Queen has always been convinced that Lord S. ought not to go on with this F.O. work,—she was for the moment a bit upset and unsettled ... but told me yesterday she knew we were right, and would support our view. Her only difficulty now is that she fears Lord S. may himself suggest that he should stay at the F.O., and she shrinks from the task of telling him *she* thinks he ought to go.

This difficulty was spared the aged Queen. Lord Salisbury acquiesced in the verdict of those about him, and Lord Lansdowne took the Foreign Office in his last Government.

The Cabinet had twenty members and was criticised for its size, and also for the number of the Prime Minister's relatives it contained. In the "Hotel Cecil," there were in fact two of Lord Salisbury's nephews, Balfour and his brother Gerald (who left the Irish Office for the Board of Trade), and Lord Salisbury's son-in-law, Lord Selborne who had held the post of Under-Secretary for the Colonies, and became First Lord of the Admiralty. Besides these Ministers in the Cabinet, the Prime Minister's eldest son, Lord Cranborne, was given his first office as Under-Secretary for Foreign Affairs, an appointment which did something to reconcile the Queen to the change at the head of that Department.[2] This last appointment increased by one the participation of the family as compared with the former Administration, as Lord Salisbury pointed out to Balfour in a letter written on the eve of discussion of the motion by a disgruntled Conservative member on the subject.

[1] See *Queen Victoria's Letters,* Third Series, Vol. III, p. 606.
[2] *Ibid.*

Dec. 9th, 1900.

My dear Arthur,

Touching Bartley's motion—please note that exactly the same number of "relations," minus Jim [1] were in the Government in July 1895, as there are now. The arrangement has therefore been before the country during two General Elections without provoking any adverse comment. ...No doubt one or two have been promoted. But they cannot be treated as a class apart who can be employed but not promoted, like Second Division clerks.

"Bartley's motion" was an Amendment to the Address expressing regret at the appointment of so many of the Prime Minister's own family to office, as being calculated to diminish the responsibilities of Ministers to Parliament, and gravely to impair the efficiency of the public services. It was perhaps easier to draft the criticism than to present it thus for the attention of the Leader of the House. Mr. Bartley did not grasp his nettle very firmly, and showed himself aware of the probable consequences. Balfour got up as soon as the Amendment had been formally seconded, and the House could almost see him gently testing the point and suppleness of his rapier. For many of the new members this was a first demonstration of his style.

My honourable friend [he said] appeared to be absorbed during the latter part of his speech with a feeling of glowing satisfaction at the courage he was displaying in carrying out a difficult and dangerous public duty. He seemed to think that some terrible Nemesis would fall upon him, and that he was acting a very heroic and patriotic part in throwing himself undaunted into the breach. I do not quite understand my honourable friend's point of view in this matter. I have been in the House now for twenty-six years, and I do not think there is any Parliamentary task more easy than, amid the cheers of your opponents, to make a personal attack on your friends. ...

I listened with great attention to my honourable friend, and though I discovered that he had a very strong aversion to the number of persons in the Cabinet connected with the Prime Minister, I did not exactly understand the line of argument by which he attempted to prove that it was inimical to the public service.

The honourable gentleman said that the Cabinet is an overgrown Cabinet. If this is so, the proportion of this unhappy and persecuted family has the smaller influence for evil. But, he said, the Cabinet is so

[1] Lord Cranborne.

overgrown that there must be a sub-Cabinet, and that is composed of the Prime Minister's near relations. . . . I could not help smiling to myself when I remembered how inconsistent that view is with the other theory, . . . that this Cabinet sits simply to register the decree of one too powerful Minister, and that too powerful Minister is not the Premier backed up by his family, but my hon. friend the Secretary for the Colonies. . . . These are two quite opposite views—not only opposite but inconsistent, . . . both equally the creation of an uninformed imagination.

Then he weighted the irony:

This I must and can say: If the country did anything at the last Election, it entrusted the present Prime Minister with the task of forming an Administration. It did so with a knowledge of him reaching back to the year 1885 when he formed his first Administration, of which, I almost regret to say, I was a member, so inveterate are the faults of Lord Salisbury, so early had his unhappy leaning towards his relations shown itself. But if the country has had before it the knowledge of the manner in which Lord Salisbury has exercised his high trust, a trust which no one can share with him, . . . and if the decision of the country means anything, it means that they repose not only in his integrity, which no man doubts, but in his ability to carry out the most responsible, difficult, . . . heart-breaking and thankless task that could be imposed upon any subject of Her Majesty.

At the turn of the century Balfour was as usual at Whittingehame with all his family. On that New Year's Eve he insisted that the nursery party should be wakened up to join the elders before midnight struck. Accordingly a procession of little figures in pig-tails and scarlet dressing-gowns was mobilised, and with his niece Alison on his knee, he dispensed to her and to all, the mulled claret which was part of the annual ceremonial. Then we opened the front door and let the Twentieth Century in.

The Queen died on January 22nd. Balfour's memorial speech in the House of Commons contained these words:

In my judgment the importance of the Crown in our Constitution is not a diminishing, but an increasing, factor. It increases, and must increase, with the development of those free, self-governing communities, those new commonwealths beyond the sea, who are constitutionally linked to us through the person of the Sovereign, the living symbol of Imperial unity.

(Above) THE LIME AVENUE AT WHITTINGEHAME
(Below) WHITTINGEHAME HOUSE

Twenty-five years later, at the Imperial Conference of 1926, he saw his prophecy realised. His views on this matter conspicuously justify one of the things he said a short time before his death: "When I look back, I think that my opinions have hardly ever changed at all about anything."

On June 1st, 1902—a Sunday—the news reached London that the negotiations which had been in progress for two months with the Boer leaders had at last ended in the Peace signed at Vereeniging. Balfour announced the terms to the House of Commons the next day—terms that gave complete and decisive recognition to British sovereignty over the territory of the Boer Republics, and were entirely free of conditions humiliating to the defeated. There was no debate, only a swelling murmur of approval and vast relief from both rows of benches.

On July 10th, 1902, Lord Salisbury laid down his office. It had been known for so long that he intended to do so after the conclusion of peace that the quiet withdrawal, when it came, made little sensation, though it was deeply felt. To his successor in office the day of Lord Salisbury's retirement assuredly seemed an end, not a beginning. Thirty years of a great companionship in arms was broken now, and for the younger man the wrench was great. It was not Balfour's way to speak directly of matters that moved his feelings, but these betrayed themselves; and often when speaking of the past, he would date not in terms of his own career, but say "that was before (or after) uncle Robert went."

Preserved among Balfour's papers is one of July 7th, 1902; it is a notice of a Parliamentary Question, of trivial importance, but requiring the Prime Minister's opinion. Below the answer is traced a little shakily the large "S," and below the familiar initial is minuted in the handwriting of the Private Secretary, "for the last time of asking I fear." Even at this distance of time it is impossible to look unmoved upon this piece of paper—at any rate for one who can remember Salisbury and Balfour together, and the impression of profound affection, confidence and harmony which that vision recalls.

Chapter XV

THE EDUCATION ACT OF 1902

The drafting of the Bill. Balfour and Morant. Cabinet tries to avoid rate aid for Voluntary Schools. Lord Salisbury and Mr. Chamberlain against rate aid. Balfour insists. Balfour explains his policy in Manchester. The "Kenyon-Slaney" Amendment puts control of religious teaching in hands of whole body of School Managers. Wrath of Church Party. Balfour's reply to Dr. Clifford. Passive resistance to the Act.

THE political history of the Act, which became the foundation of the Education system in England and Wales, extends over some four years, and the actual passing of the Bill through Parliament is only one episode of a long campaign. Balfour's name will always be associated with this great piece of legislation. His was throughout the determining mind in framing its policy and subsequently in the tactics that carried it through the House of Commons.

The story begins in 1901, and falls into three periods of struggle—in Cabinet, in Parliament, and in the constituencies—ending with the General Election of 1906.

Fresh proofs of the necessity for a Bill had been given by the judgment of the Court of Appeal on the Cockerton case, which denied to the School Boards the power of using rates for any purpose beyond the strictly limited requirements of Elementary Education. Determined that the fiasco of the Bill of 1896 should not be repeated, Balfour gave his whole mind to the subject as soon as his September golfing holiday of 1901 was over. During October and November discussions were held at Whittingehame with people concerned, and by the time that the Cabinet, in December, began to estimate the obstacles to acceptable legislation along any lines, Balfour had more or less made up his mind as to how the difficulties should be faced. He was still only First Lord of the Treasury, and so without any particular *locus standi* in the Board of Education, which was, as in 1896, administered by the Duke of Devonshire and Sir John Gorst, in their capacities of President and Parliamentary Secretary of the Board. The Duke's interest in education did not lead him in the direction of constructive proposals, and Sir John had not proved himself the most reliable of guides through the pitfalls besetting the question.

There happened, however, to be a man in the Education Office whose technical grasp of the subject was equalled by his courage, vision, and enthusiasm; qualities which, in conjunction, produce the great Civil Servant. Mr. Robert Morant [1] was one such, and his collaboration with Balfour proved exceedingly fruitful.

The effect on the course of politics of the relationship between Ministers and permanent officials would make an interesting study. Even when, as with Balfour, personal contacts are normally harmonious, the chemical compound of personalities does not always produce a maximum of efficiency. In the case of Mr. Morant however the result was very striking. Balfour never inspired a deeper devotion in a subordinate, and the zeal of another never had more influence upon himself.

Unless you are going to take the helm in Education next Session and before the Session, nothing will be done successfully.

So wrote Mr. Morant in September 1901, and in the following month came to Whittingehame. I recall the two walking about the place, deep in conversation. Morant was a giant, with a large pale face, and glowing eyes, set in deep hollows. Beside him Balfour, tall as he was, looked small in frame.

Other visitors came to Whittingehame that autumn on the same business, among them the Bishop of Winchester, Dr. Davidson (a year later to become Archbishop of Canterbury). A family discussion took place on the day of his arrival upon the propriety of sending the motor-car to meet him at the station. Balfour's ideas of motor transport had expanded since the incidents related in the last chapter. The little De Dion was no more, and the car now in use was less unsuited to the dignity of a prelate, being in fact a large Napier saloon, nicknamed "Black Maria." Younger members of the family were urgent that she should meet the distinguished visitor at the station, but a serious consultation between Balfour

---

[1] See above Chapter XI, p. 176.

and his sister ended in the decision that courtesy demanded the brougham and pair. Unfortunately the intended effect was marred by the carriage, with the Bishop inside, meeting one of Balfour's nieces in difficulties with her pony, whereupon the coachman descended from the box, requesting the Bishop to stand at the horses' heads while he adjusted the child's broken stirrup.

The Cabinet set up a Committee in December, instructing it to frame a Bill, which, among other drastic alterations of the existing system, abolished the compromise on which religious instruction in Board Schools had hitherto been given. This (in the jargon from which it is impossible to escape in alluding to these controversies) was known as "Cowper-Temple" teaching.[1]

The intention of the Cabinet at this stage was to give State aid, and not rate aid, to the Voluntary Schools. At the same time they strove to bring these Schools under the County Authority which was to replace the old School Boards. Mr. Morant perceived the confused thinking, and wrote to Balfour:

BOARD OF EDUCATION.
7.xii.01.

... May we try to get the Committee to put the Bill on one side, and go through the points that are of vital importance, and formulate their views, and their reasons, on each? This would clear the issues that *have* to be decided before any Bill, however drafted, can be passed. Thus—

Is the new County Borough Authority to be the Authority for all education in the Borough? Yes.

Is it to set the standard of efficiency of the Town Schools? Yes, for if not, it is not *the* Authority.

But if it may not finance the non-Board Schools, it cannot bring *them* up to proper efficiency. Obviously, and therefore it *must* be able to finance those Schools when necessary.

But will there not be a turmoil at every Town Council election as to whether or not the rates are to go to such and such a denominational School? Yes, if there be an option.... This means compulsory rate maintenance of all existing Schools. But that means my rates may go to teaching Mariolatry! No. The religious instruction must be paid for by the Managers, if it is denominational....

But what about the religious instruction in Board Schools? Is the colour of that to be settled by the Local Authority? No, for if so there would be a fight every year.... It will be best for the sake of peace ... not to repeal Cowper-Temple; preserve the *status quo*.

[1] See above Chapter XI, p. 176.

The Committee of the Cabinet soon reached the same conclusions as Mr. Morant. On its behalf Balfour addressed a Memorandum to the full Cabinet, describing the results to be expected from a Bill drawn on the original plan:

The Radicals would oppose it because its effect would be to abolish School Boards and to repeal the Cowper-Temple Clause. The friends of Denominational Schools would oppose it, since it would wreck their last hopes of saving these Schools from ruin. The teachers would be hostile, as they desire a Bill which would place increased means at the disposal of the school managers.

Thus the logic of facts began to compel the reluctant Government to accept the principle of rate aid for Church, and other Voluntary Schools. Not however without resistance, from two powerful quarters. Balfour found himself in direct disagreement with Lord Salisbury, who argued against rate aid on the ground that voluntary subscriptions for the schools would run dry, and that it would be impossible to ask ratepayers, who were already paying for the Board Schools, to assume the additional burden. Lord Salisbury summed up by advocating recourse to the rates only in exceptional cases and at the entire discretion of the local authority, and making no attempt at the moment to unify the whole system of primary and secondary education or to abolish the School Boards. A copy of his Memorandum is annotated in the margin with Balfour's contrary arguments—perhaps the only extant documentary evidence of such grave conflict between their opinions.

The other opponent was Mr. Chamberlain. Every tradition of the Nonconformist townsman revolted against the policy now proposed, and every instinct of the great Party manager (an instinct undimmed in this instance by any enthusiasm for the cause) foretold how the enemy would use the opportunity. Possibly the breaking down of Mr. Chamberlain's resistance is the greatest tribute to the necessity of the Bill. Mr. Morant appears to have been the chief instrument. He sent Balfour the record of a conversational duel, wherein the arguments of the expert gradually silenced the arguments of the politician, and the acquiescence of the Liberal-Unionist leader was finally wrung out.[1]

How far it was from being consent can be illustrated by a letter

[1] See *Life of Robert Morant* by Dr. B. Allen, p. 167 *et seq.*

written nine months later, to the Duke of Devonshire by Mr. Chamberlain:

> The political future seems to me—an optimist by profession—most gloomy. I told you that your Education Bill would destroy your own Party. It has done so. Our best friends are leaving us by scores and hundreds, and they will not come back. I do not think that the Tories like the situation, but I suppose they will follow the flag. The Liberal-Unionists will not.

Mr. Chamberlain's conversation with Mr. Morant took place in December 1901. Three more months of Cabinet struggle were required before the Bill was finally in shape. Balfour worked during his Christmas holiday on draft clauses in which he strove to gild the pill of rate aid. It was probably in connection with this effort that he used to quote with amusement the letter of the Government draftsman acknowledging the receipt of the clauses: "You have written a very good popular account of the Bill." Balfour, when telling this story added: "But a good deal more of that popular account remained in the Bill than the Drafting Office quite approved of."

The Bill was introduced on March 24th, 1902. It did not finally leave the House of Commons till December 18th. In the meantime Balfour had become Prime Minister, and in his reconstructed Government Lord Londonderry and Sir William Anson had replaced the Duke of Devonshire and Sir John Gorst at the Board of Education. These changes made no difference to Balfour's personal conduct of the Bill.

The interest of the battles he fought on the floor of the House, and in the country, centres round the religious side of the controversy, although that was only a part, and, seen in perspective, not the largest part, of a measure which reorganised the finance and control of secular teaching. The steady support of the educationists, including the great body of the teachers, was on the whole behind the Government throughout.

Balfour defined his position as half-way between the militant advocates of denominational teaching and the no less militant anti-denominationalists. Both these types of partisan were equally far from enlisting his sympathies, a fact that probably contributed not a little to his firm resistance of the cross-fire to which he was subjected from the extreme Church Party on his own side. "I do not stand here," he said, "to plead for any particular form of denominational teaching. I do stand here to say that it is our duty as far as we can, to see that every parent gets the kind of denominational teaching that he desires."

On the Second Reading the Liberal Opposition, united as they had not been for years, opened by an attack on the abolition of School Boards, and the transfer of control from these directly elected bodies to the Education Committees of the County Councils. "Liberal Imperialists" and "Little Englanders" agreed in denunciation of this "denial of the People's rights." On Monday, June 2nd, the Bill went into Committee, and Parliament rose in August before the Committee stage was half over. By that time the House of Commons had struck out, by a free vote, the option left to the Local Authority in respect of the taking over of Voluntary Schools, which the Cabinet had left in the Bill in hopes of appeasing the fears of Mr. Chamberlain and the Liberal Unionists. Thereupon the main Parliamentary battle was joined on the question of the amount of control to be exercised over religious instruction by the School Managers. The struggle turned upon the proportion of denominational representatives in the total number of the Managers. This was undecided when the House rose. The holidays brought an intensification of the attacks on the Bill, to the cry of "The Church on the Rates." Just before Parliament reassembled in October, Balfour spoke in Manchester. This was his first important platform speech as Prime Minister, his first also since the conclusion of peace with the Boer Republics. Yet he addressed a huge and eager audience for an hour and a half on no other topic than the Education Bill. Such was the interest felt by the English people in this subject in the year 1902—the year in which the curtain had finally fallen on the nineteenth century, but had not yet been rung up for the prologue to the melodrama of the twentieth.

The Prime Minister's Manchester speech stripped his education policy of the technicalities and misrepresentations that had bewildered thousands of minds, a feat the difficulty of which can only be appreciated by those who have waded through the polemics of the time. Balfour's final appeal unveiled his inmost feelings about the Bill:

I tell you that there are at stake issues greater than the fortune of any political party; there is at stake the education of your children for a generation, and . . . if we—I mean the majority of the House of Commons—hesitate to do our duty, and to carry through this great reform, . . . we shall receive the contempt of the parents and the children living and to be born, and that contempt we shall most justly earn.

Many Unionists came back after the recess dismayed by the feeling in their constituencies. Great pressure was put on Balfour to concede something to Nonconformist opinion in the matter of popular control of the religious teaching and especially of appointment of teachers in the Voluntary Schools. This feeling found expression in the Amendment to the Bill which became famous under the name of its author, Colonel Kenyon-Slaney. By it religious instruction was placed under the authority of the whole body of the Managers of any given school, thereby putting an end to what had often been the exclusive direction of the parson of the parish. This Amendment, which Balfour left to a free vote, was accepted by a large majority, and thereupon the extreme "Church Party" arose in their wrath. Balfour was unperturbed, though at this point even Mr. Morant showed signs of failing nerve. He wrote to one of Balfour's secretaries:

I confess to feeling not a little perturbed as to the fate of the Bill. This question of giving to all the six Managers the control of the religious instruction, and altering all the Trust Deeds so as to take it away from the parson who now has it is most horribly dangerous. . . . Also I fear we shall get into awful quagmires if we begin to set up lay tribunals in every parish to decide what is Church of England teaching.

It seemed for a moment as if the great Albert Hall Demonstration in favour of the Bill arranged by London churchmen to take place in November might turn into a meeting of protest. But this catastrophe was prevented by the common sense of the leaders who most disliked the Kenyon-Slaney clause. Lord Hugh Cecil,[1] who had gained in these debates his reputation as a great Parliamentary orator, told the Albert Hall audience that they would be foolish indeed if they threw the Bill away. Nevertheless Lord Hugh never relaxed his efforts to expunge from the Bill the slur on the clergy which he held to be implied in the Kenyon-Slaney clause. He made his final protest on the last day that the Bill was before the House of Commons, and the debate was enlivened by Balfour's rejoinder

[1] Youngest son of the 3rd Marquis of Salisbury.

to his relative, who had accused him of not having made clear in the early stages that the principle of control by Managers was part of the Government plan. Balfour quoted a passage from his own Second Reading speech which was perfectly unambiguous on the point, and proceeded:

I may lack lucidity of expression on many occasions, but on this occasion I surely did, if only by accident, blunder into a phrase which was absolutely precise, and which I do not think even a theologian can explain away.

He went on with a solemn warning to the extreme Church Party against "driving deeper the wedge which unhappily is separating certain classes of ecclesiastical opinion from the great body of religious opinion in this country, in which I see the greatest danger looming in the future to the cause of religion as a whole, and more especially to the cause, the welfare, and the prosperity of the Church of England." [1]

These were the final words addressed to the malcontents of his own Party in the House of Commons. Next day, December 18th, his reply to a Pamphlet by Dr. Clifford, the militant Nonconformist divine, was published under the title of *Letter on the Criticisms of an Opponent*. It filled all connoisseurs of polemical literature with enthusiasm, and the Conservative Party with glee. Balfour in fact never wrote a more scathing piece of prose. It is, unfortunately, as unsuited for quotation as the exuberant rhetoric to which it was a reply, though for entirely opposite reasons. One passage must serve as an example of the whole. It is a commentary on Dr. Clifford's doctrine of the type of religious teaching proper to be given by the State.

Dr. Clifford would, it is true, admit the teaching of the Bible, but only if it be used as an instrument of "purely literary and ethical" education, and because the study of it may enable us the better to understand "Shakespeare, Milton, Wordsworth and Burns," and is therefore "necessary for a full secular education." It is apparently to be treated as a collection of elegant extracts and edifying maxims. The Sixth Commandment may be taught, for, taken by itself, this is merely a moral pronouncement. The First Commandment, on the other hand, must be treated only as "literature"; for manifestly it has a theological implication. Of the two precepts which contain "all the Law and the Prophets,"

[1] See Hansard, December 17th, 1902.

the second may be taught, but not the first. The Lord's Prayer may be used as an introduction to Burns, but not as the outpouring of the spirit of man to his Maker. According to Dr. Clifford, Parliament would be going beyond its functions in teaching, at the cost of the public funds, that man *has* a Maker.

If the cry of "The Church on the Rates" could have been killed with a pen, the pen that wrote the reply to Dr. Clifford would have been capable of killing it. But the passing of the Education Act was only the first stage in the struggle. By the end of 1903, a year after the Bill had become law, more than seven thousand summonses had been issued against persons who "passively resisted" payment of the Education Rate in England, and distraint sales of their goods had taken place in over three hundred cases. These figures were trebled in 1904. They were however confined to a few counties. In the greater part of England the Act was working, and working well. Nevertheless in September 1904, the Government were obliged to pass a Default Bill.

In Wales the County Councils themselves were the "passive resisters." The movement there was organised by a leader of genius, towards a more ambitious goal than "simple Bible teaching" for Welsh children. With Disestablishment of the Welsh Church in view Mr. Lloyd George set out to wreck the working of the Act which protected the Church Schools. Mr. Morant described the "plan of campaign" to Balfour in a letter dated September 19th, 1904.

Put briefly the plan of campaign is this: The moment we use the Default Bill to pay any money direct to a Voluntary School, the County Council (at least in that one County) will cease wholly the administration of the Education Acts in respect of all Council Schools, as well as of all Voluntary Schools. The notion is that thus we here [i.e. in the Board of Education in London] will have a heavy administrative task in administering all the Voluntary Schools and that the people generally will be furious with what they will be told is the Government's fault, in their children having to be taught higgledy-piggledy in Chapels, which, under the "plan," will be opened everywhere to take the place of the closed Board Schools. Looking a considerable distance ahead, I am myself inclined to think that the Church would be wise to arrange, between now and Christmas, a concordat in Wales. It seems to me extremely desirable to know whether the Government, on the other hand, definitely prefer, with all the risks, to smash the proposed plan of campaign; for if so we ought immediately to be taking ... very definite

ARTHUR JAMES BALFOUR
1903

steps, and to be prepared to play a stiff, scientifically prepared game. . . . This would need firm handling, . . . and your very definite moral support, to keep the play up to the mark, incessantly.

The phrase "plan of campaign" may have stirred memories in the Prime Minister, though it was some fifteen years since he had last heard it, in another context, in the Ireland of which Parnell had been called the "Uncrowned King." He promptly answered Mr. Morant's letter.

NORTH BERWICK.
Sept. 21st, 1904.

DEAR MORANT,

We are apparently in for ticklish times over education. If you cared to come to Whittingehame for Sunday week, or later, I hope to be back then from Balmoral. In the meantime, my first instinct in reference to the problems you put before me is that no compromise which the Voluntary Schools are likely to get out of Lloyd George and Dr. Clifford is likely to do them much good, and that Lloyd George and his Party are likely to do themselves much harm by carrying out their plan of campaign.

I gather that your view is that if the Government go out before this plan of campaign is broken down, through want of funds or other causes, the Church in Wales will be seriously damaged, and Lloyd George will have secured a great political victory. I am by no means sure things would so turn out. I believe public opinion would resent the Welsh action, and that the new Government would attack the education problem under considerable difficulties if one of its Cabinet Ministers had spent the autumn in urging his countrymen to break the law, and using the Welsh children as "counters" in the political game.

If the Department has enough money to run the Voluntary Schools in any Welsh County which refuses to do its duty, why should it trouble itself about the School Boards which are being neglected by the Local Authority—not even on the pretence of conscience, but as a shameless "move" in the Party battle? It is true that indignation might be excited by the consequent injury to the cause of education, but the indignation would surely in the main be directed against the true authors of the evil.

Yours sincerely
ARTHUR JAMES BALFOUR.

The Welsh County Councils went as far as they could towards making the Act unworkable without actually bringing the Default

Act into operation, but the opposition was too much inspired by politics to die down while Balfour's Government held office. As late as May 1905, the Local Authorities of Merionethshire refused the necessary sums to enable certain Voluntary Schools to carry on, and the Board of Education used its power to withhold the equivalent amount of State grant to the county. The Government resisted a motion to adjourn the House on this action of the Board, and their majority of 98 was larger than they were accustomed to in this final year of their declining power.

Early in December Balfour resigned, and Sir Henry Campbell-Bannerman took office. Repeal of the Education Act was part of the Liberal programme, and Balfour, speaking at the Queen's Hall at the opening of the General Election campaign of January 1906, warned the new Government that they would find it had been easier to obstruct and denounce his legislation than to find a better working solution of its problems. And so in fact it proved.

Chapter XVI

CHAMBERLAIN LEAVES THE GOVERNMENT

Balfour's Cabinet. Opening of Fiscal discussions. Decision to retain Corn Tax. The Chancellor of the Exchequer changes his mind. Balfour's dilemma. Mr. Chamberlain's Birmingham speech. Divisions begin in the Party. The "Cabinet of Final Decision." Balfour's Fiscal Policy. Balfour's tactics. Ministerial resignations. Mr. Austen Chamberlain becomes Chancellor of the Exchequer. Balfour's Sheffield speech. The Duke of Devonshire's resignation.

THE making of a whole Cabinet was an experience which never befell Balfour in the course of his leadership. Prime Minister only once, he made the smallest possible number of changes in the personnel of the Government which he took over from Lord Salisbury. Before its course was run he had indeed to refill an unusual number of vacancies caused by ministerial resignations, but these dispositions of office were made under circumstances too peculiar to afford much material for judgment of his skill in fitting the right men into the right places.

His most important appointment at the outset was not fortunate in its consequences. The choice of a new Chancellor of the Exchequer was forced upon him by the retirement of Sir Michael Hicks-Beach, who maintained a resolve to quit office for good at the same time as his old leader. Balfour was very loath to let him go, feeling his Administration weakened by the withdrawal of the Minister who had "justly earned a greater financial reputation than any Chancellor since Mr. G."[1] It was not only on personal grounds that Balfour deplored the departure from his Council table of the rugged and independent spirit of "Black Michael." He held the resignation of a Chancellor of the Exchequer to be, under almost any

[1] See letter from Balfour to Sir M. Hicks-Beach in the *Life of Sir Michael Hicks-Beach,* by Lady Victoria Hicks-Beach, Vol. II, p. 173.

circumstances, a blow to confidence which a Prime Minister should make many sacrifices to avoid.

The new Chancellor was Mr. Ritchie, who had adequately filled the post of Home Secretary under Lord Salisbury. The Cabinet was deficient in men trained to business or finance, and Mr. Ritchie's appointment was probably the best that could then be made. He carried weight in the country and had industrial experience. But there is no office in the Government, except that of Foreign Secretary, whose holder more requires to be on easy and intimate terms with the Prime Minister than does the Chancellor of the Exchequer. In this case it turned out to be particularly unlucky that Balfour had few points of intellectual or social contact with Mr. Ritchie. The Chancellor's mind was something of a closed book to him, as no doubt his was to the Chancellor. From this some of the coming troubles arose. Mr. Ritchie was a dogmatic Free Trader. But the question of a change in our fiscal policy had not taken practical form when he went to the Treasury in July 1902, although it was arising at that very time in the Imperial Conference, then sitting in London. It is true that Mr. Chamberlain, in a speech at Birmingham in May, had uttered a challenge to the "out-worn shibboleths" which had governed our economic policy for two generations. But this planting of the Protection standard had brought forth no serious protest from the Free Trade purists in the Government, and Balfour had no reason to suppose that danger to the unity of his team would develop from it.

Apart from Sir Michael Hicks-Beach, only two of Lord Salisbury's Ministry were omitted from Balfour's Cabinet. Lord Cadogan retired from the Vice-Royalty of Ireland, and his successor, Lord Dudley, was not a Cabinet Minister. This made room for Mr. George Wyndham, who already held the Irish Secretaryship, but till now without Cabinet rank. Another new entrant was Mr. Austen Chamberlain, who left the Financial Secretaryship of the Treasury to become Postmaster-General. Lord James of Hereford, aged seventy, was not invited to resume his office as Chancellor of the Duchy of Lancaster. This did not prevent him from engaging actively behind the scenes as a militant Free Trader, in the councils of those of his former colleagues who shared his opinions.

Among prominent figures in the Government, Lord Lansdowne, the Foreign Secretary, takes first place; with the exception of Balfour's brother Gerald (who retained in his Cabinet the Presidency of the Board of Trade), no colleague stood closer to the Prime Minister's confidence.

Balfour, talking to me about Lord Lansdowne in 1929, said:

"I shouldn't call him very clever. He was—I don't quite know how to put it—better than competent."

Myself. "Sort of typical 'governing classes' kind of ability, do you mean?"

A. J. B. "Yes, that's what I do mean, I think. Lansdowne had the mentality of the great Whigs—remember he was descended from a great line of them. But one must qualify even that a little, he wasn't quite an Englishman. His mother was French—she was a Flahault. I always felt a sort of Continental quality of mind in Lansdowne. I was always very fond of him. I was his fag at Eton, you know."

Mr. Brodrick, Secretary for War, and Lord Selborne, First Lord of the Admiralty, were Ministers of a somewhat younger generation, with whom Balfour was on affectionate and intimate terms. Mr. Akers Douglas, the Home Secretary, was one of those colleagues whom all Prime Ministers cherish, steady, wise, vastly experienced as an ex-Chief Whip; he was a stand-by throughout.

Then there was the group of orthodox Free Traders, shortly to be bracketed together by their views and action. Mr. Ritchie has already been mentioned. Lord George Hamilton, Secretary of State for India, was his disciple in fiscal principles. Lord Balfour of Burleigh, Secretary for Scotland, in whom his countrymen reposed great confidence, was a man not to be moved from any position either by changing circumstances or the opinions of others. The other monumental personality in the Cabinet was the great Whig leader, the Duke of Devonshire, Lord President of the Council. For all Englishmen, whether of his following or not, the Duke was a national figure, a pledge to his countrymen of uprightness and stability.

The Cabinet was thus not lacking in heavy metal. Its dynamic force was chiefly concentrated in a single individual.

Mr. Chamberlain had retained the office of Colonial Secretary, which the new era, and his own genius, had transformed into one of the most important in the State. He held it by his own desire. No other post would have been possible for him, except conceivably the Premiership itself. That idea had indeed been mooted, and contemporary evidence shows how he himself was prompt to reject it. The following Memorandum was written by Mr. J. S. Sanders,

Balfour's Private Secretary, after a conversation which took place some four months before Lord Salisbury's retirement.

10 DOWNING STREET.

About 5.30 to-day—Tuesday, Feb. 25—Mr. Chamberlain asked me to come into his room (H. of Commons). He said he had been much concerned by statements in the *St. James's Gazette* and other papers, the net effect of which was that he had claims to be the next Prime Minister. He went on to say that these statements were not confined to mere newspaper gossip, but that he had been approached—not by Liberal Unionists—but by Tories—"your people," some of them, who had expressed their wish that he should succeed Lord Salisbury.

Mr. Chamberlain then went on further to say in most emphatic tones that I was to understand that he was *"not a candidate"* for that office. "I have my own work to do and it is not done yet, and I am quite content to stay where I am. It is true that I once said that I meant to be the next Prime Minister in succession to Mr. Gladstone, but circumstances have entirely changed and I frankly recognise that such is the case. I say again what I have said before, I shall be quite willing to serve under Balfour—but mark, I would not serve under anyone."

All this was said with great earnestness and almost passionate emphasis, and the impression he made on me was that he was talking *through me* not only to A. J. B. but to other persons who might be interested in the political drama.

Our conversation ended with Mr. Chamberlain begging me to remember that he had always been most deeply touched by A. J. B.'s splendid and unselfish loyalty towards himself, and that every member of his family shared his feeling.

It was an interesting conversation—Mr. Chamberlain being to all appearances determined to commit himself.

J. S. SANDERS.

25 *Feb.*, 1902.

The "political drama" soon developed. Balfour had not been Prime Minister for five months when the question arose which within a year was to break up his Cabinet and disintegrate his Party.

The Tariff crisis of 1903 is often represented as beginning with the explosion of a bomb flung by Mr. Chamberlain in his famous declaration in favour of Imperial Preference, made at Birmingham in May of that year. The real origins are best described in Balfour's own words, in a letter to the Duke of Devonshire of August 1903.

The question of "fiscal reform," which has now burst into so violent a flame, is not new; it has feebly smouldered for many years. . . .

The question might however have continued to slumber until some economic catastrophe roused public opinion, had it not been for the Colonial Conferences of 1897 and 1902, for the overt action of Canada in giving a preference to this country, and for the diplomatic controversy which thereupon ensued with Germany.

I do not myself believe that it would have been possible after these events—emphasised as their economic aspect has been by the West Indian problem and the Sugar Convention—to have prevented the subject coming within the sphere of practical politics in the immediate future.

The Imperial Conference Resolutions of July 1902 bear out Balfour's views. The last of them, put forward by the Prime Ministers of the Colonies, "respectfully urges on His Majesty's Government the expediency of granting in the United Kingdom preferential treatment for the products and manufactures of the Colonies, either by exemption from, or reduction of, duties now or hereafter imposed." The British response to this advance could not be long delayed. Its nature would have had to be settled in any case before the Budget policy of 1903 was framed, and the fate of the existing shilling tax upon corn decided. The connection between this trifling duty, imposed for revenue purposes during the South African War, and Imperial policy, had been emphasised by the Canadian Prime Minister, who had welcomed the tax as "placing Canada in a position to make offers which she could not make in 1897."

Nevertheless, but for the Colonial Secretary's projected visit to South Africa, the questions raised by the Resolutions might not have been brought before the Cabinet till the spring. It is hard to say whether, in that case, they would have lost some of their explosive force, so unaccountable was the timing of their reactions upon some of Balfour's colleagues. Mr. Chamberlain, who was sailing at the end of November, 1902, and remaining away till March, naturally wanted a decision on this point of policy before he left. He wanted it—and the following letters from the Prime Minister to King Edward VII set beyond doubt the fact that he got it, in the sense that he so ardently desired. These letters, published by gracious permission, are the only authoritative record of what passed in Cabinet, for no minutes of Cabinet meetings were kept in those days. The story has been told in print in the Memoirs and Biographies of several Ministers, but never, as yet, from the point of view of the leader of the Government.

Oct. 21st, 1902.

Mr. Balfour with his humble duty to your Majesty begs respectfully to say that at Cabinet to-day three questions were discussed—all of first-rate importance....

The third subject was the most important of all, and Mr. Balfour only permitted its discussion on the distinct understanding that no premature decision was to be taken upon it. It is suggested that while retaining the shilling duty on corn as regards *foreign* importation, our Colonies should be allowed to import it free. There is a very great deal to be said in favour of this proposal. But it raises very big questions indeed—colonial and fiscal,—and the Government which embarks upon it provokes a big fight. On the whole Mr. Balfour leans towards it; but it behoves us to walk warily.

After this nearly a month elapsed, during which Ministers formulated their opinions for and against retention of the corn tax; for on the 19th of November Balfour wrote again:

10 DOWNING ST.

Mr. Balfour with his humble duty begs respectfully to inform your Majesty that only two subjects were discussed in Cabinet to-day.

(1) ...

(2) The advisability of giving to the Colonies a preferential abatement of the Corn Tax....

In respect of the second question, the discussion was long and elaborate; but no argument was advanced on either side with which your Majesty is not already familiar. The Cabinet finally resolved that, as at present advised, they would maintain the Corn-Tax, but that a preferential remission of it should be made in favour of the British Empire.

The Prime Minister must have composed this letter with a sense of relief. He may or may not have overheard the jocular observation of the Duke of Devonshire as the Cabinet broke up, that it was time for some of them to resign their membership of the Cobden Club, but he certainly assumed that his colleagues realised that a decision had been taken, and had not failed to apprehend its importance. Nevertheless, it appears from statements made by the Free Traders at various periods after their resignations in 1903, that they left this fateful Cabinet under the impression that the question was still open.[1]

Technically no doubt the responsibility for any misunderstanding must lie with the Prime Minister, whose own peculiar difficulties were later on to be so much enhanced by it. Balfour always maintained that Mr. Chamberlain had good ground for complaint when he returned to England in March 1903, and found the Chancellor of the Exchequer not only opposing the use of the corn duty for preferential purposes, but determined to repeal the duty itself. The hardening of Mr. Ritchie's Cobdenite orthodoxy had proceeded throughout the winter in the recesses of the Treasury, without the Prime Minister becoming aware of what was going on. He was only enlightened early in March, in the course of a conversation with Mr. Ritchie himself on the subject of the Budget which was soon to be laid before the Cabinet. The Chancellor in fact pressed for a Budget Cabinet immediately; but Balfour, gravely disquieted, insisted on waiting until Mr. Chamberlain could be present if the question of the corn tax was to be reopened. The Colonial Secretary was due back in England on March 14th. Balfour met Mr. Austen Chamberlain at a Levee shortly after the conversation with Mr. Ritchie, drew him aside, and asked him whether it would be possible to communicate with his father, who was already on the high seas. Balfour desired that he should be prepared for the situation which must be met immediately after his return. Mr. Austen Chamberlain accordingly wrote a letter which caught the Colonial Secretary at Madeira, and gave him the first intimation that there was a movement among his colleagues to reverse the policy which he and Balfour had believed to have been settled in the autumn.[2]

Deliberately or not, the Chancellor of the Exchequer had sprung a mine under the feet of the Prime Minister. The challenge to Mr. Chamberlain's policy involved in the repeal of the corn tax in the very week of his return from the Empire journey, was bound to precipitate a struggle inside the Government on a question which, in itself of small importance, had been erected into the symbol of a fundamental principle. The decision on the Budget must lead to

[1] See Bernard Holland, *Life of the Duke of Devonshire*, Vol. II, p. 28. Lady Frances Balfour, *Life of Lord Balfour of Burleigh*, p. 120; *Recollections of Lord George Hamilton*.

[2] I am indebted to Sir Austen Chamberlain for permission to quote from a Memorandum kept by him of these events.

a pitched battle. It was hardly to be hoped that the Cabinet crisis, now inevitable, could be prevented from spreading into the ranks of the Party.

Balfour played for time. To do so involved capitulation to the Chancellor of the Exchequer, at any rate for the moment. The alternative would no doubt have been Mr. Ritchie's resignation. It is impossible to say whether at this juncture he would have been accompanied by all or any of the Ministers who left with him six months later. Anyhow Balfour considered dispensing with his services immediately and rejected the idea. Apart from the awkwardness of losing his Chancellor of the Exchequer on the very eve of the Budget, he felt that he could not afford to make another change at the Treasury so soon after the departure of Sir Michael Hicks-Beach.[1] The arguments must certainly have seemed cogent, for Mr. Chamberlain himself on his return acquiesced in the necessity of submitting to Mr. Ritchie's ultimatum.

There is no record in the Royal Archives of the Cabinet Meeting of March 15th, 1903. Probably Balfour reported verbally to the King. In the absence of any contemporary statement from him, the most authoritative recollection is Mr. Chamberlain's:

The difficulty of carrying out my policy arose only from the fact that the Chancellor of the Exchequer was opposed to it, and that there was no time to fight the question out there and then before the Budget had to be introduced. Accordingly the Cabinet, while allowing Mr. Ritchie to have his way with the Budget, decided to use the summer in further investigation of the questions that had been raised. No decision adverse to them had been taken, and there was no occasion for me to resign.[2]

Thus for the moment the Prime Minister's tactics were successful in preserving, at any rate outwardly, the unity which he considered it his principal duty to guard. A conversation with me, many years later, throws some light on the extent to which, at this stage, his responsibilities as leader of the Party overshadowed his personal views on the corn-tax controversy. The talk arose out of the following letter from Sir Austen Chamberlain to myself, which I read aloud to Balfour:

[1] My authority for this statement is Balfour's brother, Gerald, who urged upon the Prime Minister that Mr. Ritchie should be allowed to resign, and was met with these objections.

[2] B. H. Holland, *Life of the Duke of Devonshire*, Vol. II, p. 300.

Nov. 11th, 1929.

DEAR MRS. DUGDALE,

I have been thinking over your question about A. J. B.'s attitude towards Tariff Reform. . . . He never had any sympathy with the Manchester Free Trade school, either in their economic contentions, or in the political corollaries of them (compare his Essay on Morley's *Life of Cobden*).[1] When my father broached his scheme A. J. B. found no objection in principle to *any* of his proposals, but he was as little inclined to treat Tariff Reform as a dogma as he was so to regard Free Trade.

On the domestic, or purely protectionist, issue his attitude was more like that now adopted by the Safe-guarders than by the old-fashioned Protectionists. Protection was not a dogma, but an expedient, and its expediency was to be judged according to the need of the particular cases. If between him and my father there was any difference on this point, it was that my father felt that it was easier both to carry and to administer the whole than the part.

On the Empire side all A. J. B.'s sympathies were with my father, but he probably had grave doubts as to the possibility of winning the country's acceptance of the new policy, and he was determined as far as in him lay, that the Party should be kept together. I recall an incident . . . just after the publication of Parker's *Life of Peel,* I think in 1899, when I remarked to A. J. B. that I had been immensely impressed by it. He seemed to me to be the last great Prime Minister. "Now that is very curious," said A. J. B. "St. John[2] has just been saying the same thing. Why?" I replied that he was the last Prime Minister to have surveyed the whole field of politics at the moment of the formation of his Government, and to have set each of his principal colleagues the task to which he wished them to devote themselves, so that the activities of the Government were a corporate whole, instead of the disconnected activities of a series of able men. . . . A. J. B.'s reply was brief and emphatic: "He smashed his Party, and no man has a right to destroy the property of which he is a trustee."

The reading of Sir Austen Chamberlain's letter had got thus far when Balfour interrupted it:

"I never can hear Peel praised with patience. He twice split his Party; I don't like to go so far as to say he betrayed it, though really it's a very strong order, when a man leads a Party as he did, twice to

---

[1] *Nineteenth Century,* Jan. 1882. Also in *Essays and Addresses,* by the Rt. Hon. A. J. Balfour. David Douglas, Edinburgh, 1893.

[2] The Hon. St. John Brodrick, afterwards Lord Midleton.

throw over its strongest convictions, twice to break it, twice to get office in consequence. And it isn't as if the questions on which he betrayed it were complicated."

Myself. "You think Catholic Emancipation and the Corn Laws were simple questions?"

A. J. B. "I think so. I mean by that that no new factor came into them after Peel took office."

Myself. "And would you say that the history of Joe's Tariff proposals in your Cabinet was quite different?"

A. J. B. "There is no analogy at all. Joe's was a *new* doctrine. Joe was becoming an Imperialist, and he saw that Imperialism was impossible on the bare naked Free Trade basis,—or at any rate that it would lose half its strength."

Myself. "And you agreed with that?"

A. J. B. "Yes, I did—I should say I did certainly. Austen in this letter is considering my position, not so much his father's. He hasn't mentioned a very strong factor in the situation, that Joe was ill-used by the Cabinet. We had discussed the principle of taxing food-stuffs before he left the country, and he certainly had a right to suppose that the bulk of the Cabinet were in favour of a shilling duty on corn, or some analogous small tax. That was my impression, and I was perfectly horrified at what happened. I did not regard it as a betrayal, for we were not committed; but if I had been asked whether he had encouraged it—well—I wish I could look back at the Minutes."

Myself. "There were no Minutes in those days."

A. J. B. "I suppose not. I wonder what I said in my letters to the King."

The time which Balfour had gained brought him little except embarrassments. The first arose out of the arguments selected by the Chancellor of the Exchequer in his Budget speech on April 23rd, to justify the remission of the Corn Duty.

Corn [Mr. Ritchie said] is in a greater degree a necessity of life than any other article. It is a raw material; it is the food of our people, the food of our horses and our cattle, and it has certain disadvantages,— that it is inelastic, and, what is worse, it is a tax that lends itself very readily to misrepresentation. I do not think it can remain permanently an integral portion of our fiscal system unless there is some radical change in our economic circumstances, or unless it is connected with some boon much desired by the working classes.

Balfour's view of this speech is given in one of his letters to the Duke of Devonshire, written from Hatfield on August 29th, 1903.

In defending the surrender of the shilling duty on corn, he [Mr. Ritchie] used arguments absolutely inconsistent with those used by Beach, myself, and others, when the duty was originally imposed. This procedure was so gratuitous that it can only be explained by the fact that he was already completely under the control of Mowatt and E. Hamilton [1] and that he was resolved to make it as difficult as possible for any one else ever to resort to a tax on corn again.

After the Budget Debate the "fat was in the fire," and any faint hope there may ever have been of discussing Imperial Preference without Party feeling, vanished. Sir William Harcourt taunted the Government for running away, while he congratulated them on removing the "infamous" tax. The section of the Conservatives who were already convinced Protectionists protested bitterly through their spokesman in the House of Commons, Mr. Henry Chaplin. On May 12th the Prime Minister wrote to the King:

Mr. Balfour with his humble duty to Your Majesty begs respectfully to say that Cabinet was almost entirely occupied with a discussion of the present position of the corn tax. The difficulties attending the remission of the tax seem almost as great as those attending its imposition! But there can be no doubt that in spite of the agitation against the repeal, the weight of general opinion is in favour of it: and that the smallest symptom that any change of front is intended would produce a protest compared with which Mr. Chaplin's would sink into insignificance. The real difficulty lies not in determining the policy to be pursued with regard to this year's Budget, but in determining the precise form in which a refusal to make any change should be couched. Mr. Balfour suggested to the Cabinet that he should answer Mr. Chaplin's deputation on Friday next in such terms as would indicate the possibility of reviving the tax, *if it were associated with some great change in our fiscal system*. Such an announcement may cause some disquiet in certain circles: but in view of possible eventualities, such as the necessity of retaliating on foreign countries, or of the expediency of a closer fiscal union with our Colonies, it seems desirable to make it. The Cabinet unanimously assented.

Three days later Balfour received the Deputation, and made the case for repeal of the corn tax. Unable heartily to defend the course which had been taken, he fell back on the subtlety of argument that was always his easiest refuge. His own regrets at the removal of the tax can be discovered between the lines, but when the speech ap-

[1] Treasury Officials.

peared in the newspapers, another, much more plainly worded, stood beside it. On the very day that the Prime Minister was talking of a change in our fiscal system as a remote possibility, the Colonial Secretary was demanding a new definition of Free Trade, which should no longer deprive us of power to favor our friends or retaliate against our rivals.

Mr. Chamberlain's famous Birmingham speech of May 15th has been represented as a contradiction of the policy of the Government of which he was still a member. Balfour did not hold that view, for he wrote, in the letter to the Duke of Devonshire dated August 27th:

Then came the Cabinet, at which I asked permission to make some guarded reference to "Fiscal Reform" in answer to the Deputation. ...Chamberlain, if you remember, took the occasion to observe that *he* proposed to say at Birmingham much the same as what *I* proposed to say at the Deputation, *only in a less definite manner!* The famous Birmingham speech embodied his practical endeavour to carry out this undertaking.

Chamberlain always declares (and I am quite sure he believes) that the excitement this speech caused came upon him as a complete surprise; and it is quite true that he gave expression in it to no sentiments which he had not before uttered on public platforms, and that it contained an exposition of no new doctrines. For my part I am ready to admit that no one would have had much reason to complain had his utterances stopped there.

It would have been futile to expect that they could. The Birmingham speech became the focus for much besides wrath and alarm. Other emotions evoked by it have been described by Mr. Amery, one of the rising generation, whose torch was lit on that day.

The Birmingham speech was a challenge to free thought as direct and provocative as the theses which Luther nailed to the church door at Wittenberg. To many of the younger generation, passionately Imperialist by conviction, beginning to be intellectually sceptical about Free Trade, the speech was a sudden crystallisation of all their ideals in an imperious call to action.

My mind went back to that morning when, the speech just read, I walked up and down my room in uncontrollable excitement. The door flung open, and in rushed Leo Maxse. For a moment we danced round hand-in-hand before we could even unloose our tongues. Within an hour I was busy telephoning to friends and getting together the nucleus of what a week or two later became the Tariff Reform League.... [1]

But the militant supporters of Imperial Preference were a minority, even within the Conservative Party. Moreover, following upon the Birmingham speech, Mr. Chamberlain made two in the House of Commons, far from helpful to his cause or his Chief. In a Debate on Old Age Pensions he allowed Mr. Lloyd George to goad him into declaring that he could not see how funds could be forthcoming for this great item of his old programme except through a change in our fiscal system.[2] Again, before the House adjourned for Whitsuntide, he made a speech on preferential tariffs, thoroughly alarming to the bulk of the Party.[3] Balfour wrote:

Neither of these speeches was the least necessary. The first was a distinct violation of an arrangement come to with me, while the second was a quite gratuitous challenge both to his colleagues and the world after what I had myself said in the course of the same debate at an earlier hour. It is these two utterances which have caused most of the soreness and suspicion which have been so unhappily aroused in connection with this subject, and for neither of them was there, in my opinion, justification or excuse.[4]

Nevertheless the Colonial Secretary was making great sacrifices behind the scenes to preserve Cabinet unity. He agreed, at a Meeting held on June 9th, before the opening of Debate on the Second Reading of the Finance Bill, to a statement which the Chancellor of the Exchequer read to the House of Commons.

So far as the Members of the Government who have spoken on this matter are concerned, all that has been said has been that the question of preferential treatment for the Colonies should be discussed and inquired into.

"It is a heavy blow for him [Mr. Chamberlain]," wrote Sir Michael Hicks-Beach after this, "but he will stay on in the Cabinet

---

[1] The Rt. Hon. L. S. Amery in the *Sunday Times* of February 7th, 1932.
[2] See Hansard, May 19th.
[3] *Ibid.,* May 28th.
[4] Letter to the Duke of Devonshire of August 27th, 1903, quoted above.

and has promised to held his tongue on the subject for the rest of the Session." [1]

Sir Michael himself contributed a speech to that same Debate which hastened the cleavage of the Unionist Party. His opinion carried more weight than that of any man outside the Government, or of almost any man within it, and the House of Commons was crowded to hear the verdict of the ex-Chancellor who had imposed the corn tax in 1902, upon its repeal by his successor. He ridiculed the objections to the tax itself, but in its political aspect he approved its removal. The duty had come to be regarded not as protective in itself, but as heralding a return to a system of Protection and of Colonial Preference on corn.... Tariff Reform had "united the Party opposite, divided for the last eight years, into a happy family. It was dividing our Party;... if persisted in it will destroy the Unionist Party as an instrument for good."

"Sir Michael's speech delighted the Free Trade Unionists, and he was fêted at a House of Commons dinner by Lord Hugh Cecil and the group known as the "Hugh-ligans." Sir Michael wrote that he was trying to stop anything like the start of a Free Trade organisation on the Unionist side; "if Joe is quiet I don't want to make any move to disturb him." [2] These good resolutions, however, were not long-lived. Before the end of June he was hard at work canvassing in the House of Commons for the "Free Food League."

On July 1st this body came into being at a meeting in the Grand Committee Room of the House of Commons, attended by fifty-four Unionists. Merely counting heads this denoted a serious schism even in a Party whose majority was still over six score. Moreover the meeting included some of the best fighting strength of the Party, for example, Lord Hugh Cecil, Major Seely, and Mr. Winston Churchill. The Prime Minister incurred much outspoken censure from some of these rising politicians by refusing them Parliamentary facilities for an abstract discussion on fiscal policy.

The holiday after this wearing Session was unusually short. Balfour went straight to North Berwick, and there wrote to Lady Elcho a letter which illustrates his power of casting off worry.

---

[1] See letter from Sir M. Hicks-Beach to his wife. *Life of Sir Michael Hicks-Beach*, p. 192.
[2] *Ibid.*

August 9th, 1903.

MY DEAR LADY ELCHO,

I am having a delicious time. I cannot quite understand why I am so happy here. I think it is the solitude, and consequent peace, of my existence. And yet this does not quite explain it. In London I prefer dining in company to dining alone. At North Berwick it is felicity to reflect that after the excellent Mr. Short [1] has finished the day's correspondence about 5.30 I shall not see another soul but the waiter till I go to bed at mid-night! Explain that if you can!

I have just finished correcting the proofs of the "Notes on Insular F.T." to be published next week. The changes are small, but they have cost me a good deal of trouble. Why is it so easy (given the ideas) to make a speech, and so difficult to write an essay? This is conundrum No. 2.

One of my colleagues (by the way) who is *not* going to leave me, frankly admits that he can make neither head nor tail of it! !

I am restricting my golf at present to *one* round a day. It requires some self-control, but it is worth it. It is better for my health: it is better for my work: and, not least, it is better for my golf. I am playing a fair game: and so far have won all my matches.

I am looking forward with much interest to Monday. At one time I thought I should keep Devonshire. I had a long and most friendly talk with him last Monday week. Now however I think I shall lose him, and with him, of course, all the waverers.

As I understand D's position he does not disagree with *me:* but thinks that Joe will push us all into a further and less tenable position. Why not wait and see?

The weather is cold and showery, but the cloud effects are extraordinarily beautiful, and it is not bad for golf, and I hope not *very* bad for the harvest.

yours,

A. J. B.

This letter, and one written a day or two later to the King, show that Balfour had by now made up his mind that a Cabinet split must come.

14.8.03.

Mr. Balfour with his humble duty to Your Majesty begs respectfully to say....

There was some little disagreement at the end of Tuesday's Cabinet as to whether a *final* decision should be come to at Thursday's Cabinet

---

[1] For many years Balfour's personal secretary.

on the subject of "Fiscal Reform." Mr. Balfour however subsequently laid it down that a final decision was *not* required until the Cabinet again meets to consider the subject on September the 12th. It was subject to this ruling that the discussion took place on Thursday. It was not very satisfactory. Mr. Balfour does not feel justified in entertaining any confident hope that he will retain the co-operation of all his colleagues for the scheme which he himself favours. But if (as he does not doubt) Mr. Chamberlain shows a readiness to accept Mr. Balfour's scheme and to modify some of the plans which he has from time to time put forward rather hastily, Mr. Balfour is of opinion that the majority of the Cabinet will cordially support him in the moderate, yet important, suggestions which he, Mr. Balfour, is prepared to recommend.

There cannot be anything in the nature of a Cabinet crisis till the middle of September at the earliest; and whenever that happens, Mr. Balfour is confident that he can carry on the work which Your Majesty has entrusted to him. In any case he will do his best to steer between the opposite dangers of making proposals so far-reaching in their character that the people of this country could not be expected to acquiesce in them—and, on the other hand, of ignoring in a spirit of blind optimism the danger signals which indicate approaching perils to our foreign and to our colonial trade.

The date fixed for the Cabinet of "final decision" was Monday, September 14th. In the meantime a truce was supposed to be observed in the constituencies between the Conservative Free Trade and Tariff organisations, whose branches began to cover the country and were producing propaganda galore. The situation was becoming intolerable to the rank and file. No one knew where he stood, or his friends from his foes. In the paralysis of the Unionist Party the Opposition revelled.

We are on the eve of a gigantic political landslide [wrote Mr. Winston Churchill to the Duke of Devonshire on September 1st]. I don't think Balfour and those about him realise at all how far the degeneration of the forces of Unionism has proceeded, and how tremendous the counter-current is going to be.[1]

Balfour was under no illusions. Before the recess, he had circulated the Cabinet Memorandum which was afterwards published under the title of "Notes on Insular Free Trade." It embodied his own views of the changes that might be made in the fiscal system without disrupting the main body of the Unionists. It became the official

[1] See Bernard Holland, *Life of the Duke of Devonshire*, Vol. II, p. 320.

programme of the Party after the Prime Minister's Sheffield speech of October 1st, 1903. In the meantime he explained it to the King in a letter which shows him quite aware that the policy of "retaliation," to which he now pinned himself, would be too much for the Free Traders, and not enough for the Protectionists.

15.9.03.

Mr. Balfour with his humble duty to Your Majesty begs respectfully to give an account of the present Cabinet position.

Mr. Balfour can perhaps most easily make clear a very complicated position if he begins by describing his own views on fiscal reform—views to which he proposes to give full expression at Sheffield on October 1st, and the economic bases of which are set forth in a pamphlet which he begs respectfully to send with this letter.

The root principle for which Mr. Balfour pleads is liberty of fiscal negotiation. Hitherto it has been impossible for us to negotiate effectively with other Governments in respect of commercial treaties because we have neither anything to give which they wish to receive nor anything to take away which they are afraid to lose. Our negotiations are therefore barren; and we have been obliged to look on helplessly while in all the most advanced countries a tariff barrier is being built up against our manufactures which is an ever-growing obstacle to our legitimate trade development. Mr. Balfour does not contemplate that at this stage the evil can be removed; but if there are means of mitigating it, those means should be tried; and they cannot be tried if the canons of taxation at present in force are not respected. In Mr. Balfour's opinion the change he contemplates would promote, not hinder, "free trade."

There are however, two quite different shapes in which this "freedom to negotiate" may be employed—one against foreign Governments, the other in favour of our own Colonies. In dealing with foreign Governments we may threaten—and if need be employ—"retaliation." In dealing with our own Colonies we can only offer "preference." The second is perhaps the most important; if, that is, a really good bargain could be struck between the Mother Country and her children. But it is also far the most difficult. It is difficult because a bargain is always difficult; it is especially difficult because it is hard to see how *any* bargain could be contrived which the Colonies would accept, and which would not involve some taxation of food in this country.

In Mr. Balfour's opinion there are ways in which such taxation might be imposed, which would in no degree add to the cost of living of the working classes. But he is also of opinion that in the present state of public feeling, no such plan could get a fair hearing; to make it part of the Government programme would be to break up the Party, and to endanger the other half of the policy—that which authorises retaliation—for which the country is better prepared. Mr. Balfour therefore, as at present advised, intends to say that, though Colonial Preference is eminently desirable in the interests both of British commerce and Imperial unity, it has not yet come within the sphere of practical politics.

Mr. Balfour believes that the policy thus indicated is the right one for any statesman to recommend who is responsible to Your Majesty for carrying on the Government. He believes that the great majority of the Unionist Party—Conservative or Liberal—will accept it. But he cannot conceal from himself, and he ought not to conceal from Your Majesty, that in all probability several members of the Government will feel unable to accept it, because it goes too far, or because it does not go far enough. Mr. Balfour will write further to Your Majesty on this point when he has more definite information. But he may perhaps say at once (1) that the course he advises will cause *less* disruption than any other, (2) that he believes it to be *right in itself,* and (3) that he entertains no doubt of being able to make proposals for filling up vacant places which will enable Your Majesty's Government to be carried on with credit so long as it retains the confidence of Parliament.

This letter of September 15th refers to ministerial resignations as if these were more probable than certain. As regards the Free Traders this was still technically accurate, since neither Mr. Ritchie, Lord George Hamilton nor Lord Balfour of Burleigh had as yet sent the Prime Minister their letters formally announcing their withdrawal. Balfour however had the strongest reason for knowing that these Ministers were about to leave his Cabinet, for it was his own fixed intention that they should. He had arrived at the conclusion that his fiscal policy could not command the loyal co-operation of the Cobdenite Ministers, and he was determined to put an end to dissension, at least inside his own Cabinet. As regards the Duke of Devonshire, his feelings were different. He fought hard to keep him, and the Duke's departure was actually staved off for a little while. Balfour knew when he excluded Preference from his programme that Mr. Chamberlain's resignation would follow, but he had made up his mind to shed the extremists on both wings, believing that thus the minimum of disruption would ensue. It is significant that he puts that motive first when explaining his policy to the King.

He had matured his plans during the month before the Cabinet of September 14th. Some ex-Ministers have implied that they were jockeyed into resigning by a deliberate withholding of the information that Mr. Chamberlain was also leaving the Government. The recollections of other colleagues contradict this notion, which however hardly depends upon outside testimony for its refutation. The Prime Minister was not compelled to resort to cheating members of his Cabinet in order to get rid of them. He had before him at the Cabinet Meeting, Memoranda by the Chancellor of the Exchequer and Lord Balfour of Burleigh, stating their objections to the fiscal policy which he was now proposing. The fact that Mr. Chamberlain, for opposite reasons, was also unable to accept it did not appear to Balfour to affect the vital issue thus raised. The Free Trade Ministers apparently considered that it did. To Mr. Ritchie and his followers Mr. Chamberlain was the great obstacle across the path back to orthodoxy. But they did not realise that the Prime Minister was not going in that direction, and when he focussed the discussion in Cabinet upon future policy, leaving to individual Ministers the responsibility of making their position clear, the Free Traders, taken aback by his initial readiness to dispense with their services, failed to take in the import of the declaration which Mr. Chamberlain made at a later stage of the meeting.

Their misunderstanding produced from the Prime Minister a Paper, circulated to his colleagues on September 22nd:

There seems to have been some misapprehension among some of my colleagues as to what occurred in and out of Cabinet in the early part of last week in connection with fiscal reform.

It has been implied, for instance, in some statements that I have seen, that I came to Monday's Cabinet knowing that Mr. Chamberlain was determined to resign, but resolved to keep the circumstance from the knowledge of my colleagues. The true facts are as follows:

I received Mr. Chamberlain's letter of the 9th by the last post on Thursday the 10th: I made no reply to it, hoping to have an interview with him on Sunday.

He did not, however, leave Birmingham till Monday morning; and I did not see him till an hour before Cabinet on that day (the 14th).

We talked over his letter; he reiterated his view, afterwards expressed to Cabinet, that if preferential duties were dropped, there were reasons personal to himself, which made it impossible for him to stay; and I said to him, what I said to Cabinet within the next hour, that I was becoming more and more convinced that public opinion was not ripe for a tax on food, and that any attempt at the present time to impose one would endanger that portion of fiscal reform against which there was no such widespread prejudice.

Whether, however, a duty on food-stuffs should be attempted seemed to me then—and seems to me still—a subsidiary point, important indeed, but in no way fundamental.

I was not therefore of opinion that either Mr. Chamberlain's attitude or mine towards a food tax was relevant to the question of principle; nor could I suppose that any discussion on it would affect the opinion of those Members of the Cabinet who were not prepared heartily to accept a change of fiscal policy at all.

Over and over again, in the early part of Monday's Cabinet, I therefore called the debate back from all minor issues to this, which I conceive to be the main point; and I never doubted then, and I do not gather that there is any reason for doubting now, that, on this point, Mr. Ritchie, Lord George Hamilton, and Lord Balfour of Burleigh took, and take, a different view from myself and the majority of the Cabinet.

I may add that I repeated to the Duke of Devonshire, who came to see me before dinner on Monday, my belief that a tax on food was not yet within the region of practical politics, and that, if this were so, I was confident that Mr. Chamberlain would resign.

The fiscal discussion has now been going on in an acute form since the middle of May. Never once, so far as I am aware, did any hesitating Minister of the Cabinet suggest to me that his objection to tariff reform would be completely met if no attempt were made to put a tax on food.

Let me add that it was only with much reluctance that I was compelled by opinion inside as well as outside the Cabinet, to withdraw "Tariff Reform" (so far as the Government are concerned) from the category of "open questions."

As soon as it was so withdrawn, it became evident that no Cabinet could regard itself, or would be regarded by the public, as being collectively in favour of fiscal change which both lost the services of Mr. Chamberlain and retained those whose distrust and dislike of it had been publicly expressed, or were matter of common knowledge. If, therefore, the Cabinet is both to be, and to seem to be, in favour of the policy I myself favour, the losses which it has sustained, deplorable as they are, would seem to have been inevitable.

A. J. B.

September 22, 1903.

Balfour here refers to a conversation with Mr. Chamberlain an hour before the Cabinet Meeting. Mr. Gerald Balfour was the only other person present during an interview in which Balfour undoubtedly carried out the first, and the most important, part of his plan for "minimum disruption." He met Mr. Chamberlain by

RICKETY

B—L—F—R (CABINET MAKER): "There! It looks lovely!—I only hope it'll hold together!"

(October 7th, 1903)

appointment at Mr. Gerald Balfour's flat in Whitehall Court. He acquiesced without argument in the determination of the Colonial Secretary to resign; but he urged Mr. Chamberlain to use his influence to induce Mr. Austen Chamberlain to remain a Member of the Government, and he revealed his intention of recommending Mr. Austen Chamberlain as successor to Mr. Ritchie at the Treasury, when that post became vacant, as it soon would. Mr. Chamberlain agreed. An impression was left on Mr. Gerald Balfour's mind that something had happened likely to save the Party from the complete cleavage otherwise inevitable. A great weight seemed lifted from Balfour's mind after the suggestion about Mr. Austen Chamberlain had been made and accepted. Nor is this surprising. The continued co-operation in the Government of the son, who entirely shared his father's fiscal creed, was a token that there was in truth no cleavage on the matter of principle. As Balfour himself put it, in his reply (dated September 16th) to Mr. Chamberlain's letter of September 9th:

there could be no more conclusive evidence that in your judgment, as in mine, the exclusion of taxation of food from the Party programme is, in existing circumstances, the course best fitted practically to further the cause of fiscal reform.[1]

But Balfour and Chamberlain had been bred to Party politics. They knew too well the strength of the forces that would tend to drive them apart. Therefore, the link to be forged through Mr. Austen Chamberlain was welcome on every personal and public ground.

The proceedings in Cabinet began with discussion of the Prime Minister's Memorandum, as well as the arguments against it put by Mr. Ritchie and Lord Balfour of Burleigh. Balfour at once made it clear that the holders of these opinions could not remain members of his Government. The Duke of Devonshire wrote in a private letter: "I never heard anything more summary and decisive than the dismissal of the two Ministers."[2]

Later during the meeting Mr. Chamberlain said that while agreeing that Balfour's fiscal policy was the right one for the Government to follow, it involved his own resignation. This was the statement that failed to permeate some minds. The Free Traders met in conclave, making the Duke of Devonshire their go-between with

[1] See *The Times* of September 2nd, 1933, where both letters are published in full.
[2] *Life of the Duke of Devonshire*, Vol. II, p. 340.

Balfour. Balfour's correspondence with the Duke shows [1] how strenuously and patiently Balfour strove to expound his own fiscal principles, and persuade the Duke that the "liberty of negotiation" involved in the policy of "Retaliation" was the only hope of maintaining or extending Free Trade. "If, like the Cobden Club, we preach a doctrine of Free Trade which takes account of nothing but the *immediate* interests of the consumer,... depend upon it Free Trade, thus made unnecessarily repulsive, will be repudiated by the nation in the first great commercial stress which occurs."

It is doubtful whether the Duke ever fully understood the economics of Balfour's policy. He certainly complained that he could not follow the arguments of the "Notes on Insular Free Trade." This struck Balfour as so humorous, that he never alluded to it without laughing. On one of these occasions (it was in 1926) he said to me: "The Duke never read it, you know. I remember hearing he had confessed to somebody that he tried, but couldn't understand it. Dear Devonshire! Of course he couldn't. He told me once he had been content to leave his financial conscience in the hands of Mr. Gladstone. But it was all a muddle. He got himself into such a position, that he had to behave badly to somebody—and there it was! But it never made the slightest difference to my love for him." The Duke had in fact allowed himself to undertake special obligations to the other Free Traders, which the Prime Minister had felt compelled to comment upon. Balfour wrote on August 29th:

There was one passage in your letter which a little disturbed me,—that in which you describe yourself as under some special obligation to consult the views of Ritchie, Hamilton and B. of B. I quite understand that each and all of us are under obligations of this kind to the Cabinet *as a whole*: but surely not to any fraction of it. This is having a Cabinet within a Cabinet with a vengeance!

If the Duke had made a mistake he bore the penalty himself. He had withdrawn his resignation after a talk with Balfour on the 16th of September, when he had at last been convinced of the reality of Mr. Chamberlain's departure, and had heard why the Prime Minister would not allow the other Free Traders to reconsider their resignations on this ground.[2] After this the Duke's mind was in a

---

[1] *Life of the Duke of Devonshire*, Vol. II, Chapter xxvii.
[2] See letter from the Duke to Mr. Ritchie, *Ibid.*, Vol. II, p. 347.

torment. His continued presence in the Government did not satisfy his keen sense of honour and loyalty,[1] and the ex-Ministers were not concerned to soothe his scruples. He was "vastly relieved," when Balfour proclaimed the fiscal policy of the Party at Sheffield on October 1st, to find some expressions in the speech on which he might base a resignation which this time was final. Balfour received the Duke's telegram in Edinburgh, where he had stopped for breakfast after a night journey on his way home from Sheffield. He drafted a long answer immediately, in which some acerbity betrays itself for the first time in this correspondence. "I felt so cross," he told me once, "that I wrote to him from the New Club before I had even had my bath." But he loved and respected the Duke too much to feel personally irritated for long, and he sent a second letter regretting any strong expressions in the first.[2]

Balfour went to Whittingehame after this for a few more days of the holiday which had been cut in pieces by the crisis. His return was jubilantly greeted by the assembled family, eager to discuss the latest developments, but, as always, observant of his conversational mood. One chair at the long dinner-table was vacant owing to the unexpected absence of one of the party. "Where is Frances?" he asked—and on being told, observed: "Oh, I was afraid she had resigned too!" When the shouts of laughter had died down he went on: "I certainly seem to have resignations on the brain at present!"

The loss of five Ministers was trying enough. Balfour had however calculated that he must pay a heavy price for a fiscal programme capable of rallying the bulk of the Party. The question was whether he had got that. The morrow of the Sheffield speech was too soon to feel confident, although Balfour may have overrated the appeal that his Retaliation policy would make to the ordinary man's mind. Education of public opinion on fiscal questions had hardly begun, as both Balfour and Mr. Chamberlain knew. It had moreover begun badly, in the midst of political sensation and party passion. Out of this Balfour was doing his best to lift it, but in so doing he deliberately rejected the aid of Imperialist sentiment at the same time that he repudiated the old slogans of Free Trade. The chief difference between him and Mr. Chamberlain at this stage was Mr. Chamberlain's scepticism as to the possibility of carrying through an educational campaign on Balfour's programme. Their estimates

[1] *Life of the Duke of Devonshire*, p. 351.
[2] For the letters see *Ibid.*, Vol. II, pp. 363-365.

on this point diverged more as time went on and Mr. Chamberlain became surrounded with the enthusiasm evoked by his own fire of conviction. Balfour, surveying the whole field, never, while he was responsible, thought opinion sufficiently mobilised for an advance by the Party from the position taken up in 1903. He therefore gave no lead, and in consequence, was often afterwards declared to be no leader. This criticism can hardly be endorsed without reserve by a generation which knows by experience, what Balfour knew by instinct, that the fiscal conversion of the majority of people in this country would only be accomplished through economic catastrophe.

The second phase of the Tariff controversy opened with the Shef-field speech of October 1903. But the history of Balfour's Government is not entirely summed up in the temperature chart of "fiscalitis."

Chapter XVII

DEFENCE AND FOREIGN POLICY

1904–1905

Creation of Committee of Imperial Defence. The Anglo-French Entente. Russo-Japanese War. Renewal of Anglo-Japanese Alliance.

THE reform of the Army, and the creation of the Committee of Imperial Defence, go far to outweigh many disappointments in the domestic policy of the four chequered years of Balfour's government. It is impossible now to think of the period between 1902 and 1914 except as one more and more heavily charged with catastrophe. The test of statesmanship in those years must in the first place be the measure of foresight. Contemporary opinion here loses much of its significance and importance, for its standards of value differ too widely from our own. The Party, or a section of it, found Balfour wanting in certain attributes of leadership. Grant them right. Other qualities were to set him in an altogether different category from that of Party leaders. The development of his political genius was greatly stimulated by the unfolding of the problems with which it was best fitted to deal. When the transition from the nineteenth to the twentieth century was completed after the Great War, the times had come abreast of his mind. The second period of his career placed him beyond dispute in the front rank of British statesmen. That place would hardly have been accorded him at the close of his Premiership. Nevertheless in some of his work as Prime Minister the foundations were laid. The first example, in time and importance, is in the early history of the Committee of Imperial Defence.

The Boer War had revealed the weaknesses of Cabinet government for co-ordinating war-time effort. The discovery was a shock to Balfour, coming as it did at a time when the ultimate responsibility for the safety of these Islands and the Empire was about to fall upon his shoulders. The technique of administration was a subject which his mind gripped readily. He now evolved the idea of an organisation, to form the missing link between the military and civilian authorities. The story may be begun with a bit of his own conversation in 1927.

I've told you before what a state the War Office was in when I became Prime Minister. It was the Cinderella of Departments, and I found this eternal and most important question of our safety against invasion was a subject of bitter controversy between the Services. There was no co-ordination, no co-operation between the people in charge of land and sea war, and defence.

You know Uncle Robert never paid any attention to these things— his mind didn't work on those questions, they didn't bite on it. It appeared to me we ought to get at the facts. After all, the safety of these Islands is a pretty heavy responsibility for Ministers. ...

It was obvious a civilian Cabinet could form no judgment, and I had the idea, which was really original. I don't say that out of conceit,— I mean simply that the Defence Committee had no precedent. It started, and it has worked admirably from the very start. We began on the particular subject—the defence of these Islands. ...

The new features of the Committee of Imperial Defence were these:

In the first place it was purely consultative, and had no power to enforce its findings. Thus it roused no jealousy, and required no statutory sanction for its own existence.

This [wrote Balfour in a Cabinet Memorandum of 1904] is a great advantage, when we remember how inflexible any machinery created by Act of Parliament is apt to be. No fixed constitution for the Committee need be framed, the persons composing it need not be formally enumerated, nor is any elaborate definition of their duties and powers required. As a consequence it becomes far easier to make the Committee a truly Imperial body, in which the Colonies as well as the Mother Country may find an appropriate machinery for considering together the greatest of their common interests—the interests of Imperial Defence.

The adaptability was carried to a point which at first startled some of Balfour's own advisers. The organisation which was henceforth to be a permanent part of the Constitution had nevertheless only one permanent Member. Balfour's Memorandum summed up his plan:

The Defence Committee, as I conceive it, would be an advisory body summoned by the Prime Minister of the day to aid him in the consideration of the wider problems of Imperial Defence. A permanent staff would be provided to give it assistance and continuity. Only the persons summoned would have the right to attend. In the vast majority of cases, perhaps in all, the Navy and the Army would be represented by their Parliamentary heads and by their expert advisers. Other persons would be summoned as the particular occasion required. But nothing in the constitution of the Committee would fetter the Prime Minister's discretion in the choice of its Members. He would be compelled neither to add unnecessarily to its numbers, nor to exclude from its deliberations persons specially qualified to assist them.

At each meeting all Members would be on an equality. Though in practice some of them would be summoned almost as of course, yet they would be there because they *were* summoned, and not as of right. There would, therefore, be no distinction of dignity between one Member and another; the Committee would be small enough to be effective; and its constitution would vary with the varying problems it was required to consider. This flexibility would be impossible if the Committee had a statutory right to give orders or determine policy; it is only attainable so long as the Committee restricts itself to advice.

The value of this advice will depend, of course, upon the reasonings by which it is supported, and upon the authority of the persons giving it. A permanent record of both will be kept in the archives of the Department, and will be communicated to the Sovereign.

These ideas were all realised eventually, though the Committee did not spring full-grown from the head of Zeus. A weighty Memorandum had been submitted to Balfour in November 1902, signed jointly by the First Lord of the Admiralty and the Secretary for War,[1] urging that the existing Defence Committee of the Cabinet should be abolished, and a body set up which could consider with authority the "most difficult and important problems of all, viz.: those which were neither purely naval, nor purely military, nor purely naval and military combined, but which may be described as naval, military and political."

Balfour pushed the suggestion of the two Service Ministers forward with all his might, and the Committee of Imperial Defence held its first meeting on December 18th, 1902. The Duke of Devonshire, who had presided over the defunct Defence Committee, took the chair. Balfour's ideas about the Prime Minister's special position

[1] Lord Selborne and Mr. Brodrick.

had not yet been formulated, and he attended as an ordinary Member. Lord Selborne, Lord Walter Kerr, and Prince Louis of Battenberg represented the Admiralty, and on the Military side were Mr. Brodrick, Lord Roberts (then Commander-in-Chief), and General Sir William Nicholson, Director of Military Intelligence. This was the personnel of the Committee until the Duke of Devonshire left the Government in the autumn of 1903, and Balfour succeeded him in the chair. Then the *ex officio* status of Members was altered, and Balfour realised his vision of Dominion representatives sitting in full equality with British Ministers to discuss problems of Empire Defence. This happened for the first time on December 11th, when the Canadian Minister of Militia, Sir Frederick Borden, then visiting London, was summoned to attend a meeting.

In March 1904 the Committee of Imperial Defence was definitely made "the corner-stone of the needed edifice of reform." The quotation is from the Report on War Office Reconstitution, signed by Lord Esher, Sir John Fisher,[1] and Sir George Clarke.[2]

They put in the forefront of the recommendations which led up to the making of the Army Council and the General Staff, the need for providing the Cabinet with the means for shaping national policy with regard to war. Without that, no measures of War Office reform would touch the root of the matter. Nothing could have better vindicated Balfour's persistent refusal to criticise the War Office for South African blundering than the Report of the "Esher Committee." Adopting all his ideas about the Defence Committee, they insisted on strengthening the permanent element. Their Report pointed out that "there have been in the past, and there will be in the future, Prime Ministers to whom the great questions of Imperial Defence do not appeal.... It is not safe to trust matters of national security to the chance of a favourable combination of personal characteristics." Therefore they recommended a permanent Secretariat. From this dates the revival (although in a different form) of the eighteenth-century practice of keeping Minutes of Cabinet proceedings.

Sir George Clarke himself was the first to fill the post of Secretary to the Defence Committee; he was succeeded in 1907 by Sir Charles Ottley and in 1912 by Colonel Hankey.[3]

[1] Afterwards Lord Fisher.
[2] Afterwards Lord Sydenham.
[3] Afterwards Sir Maurice Hankey.

The precautions were soon justified. When Balfour's Government fell in 1906, few of Sir Henry Campbell-Bannerman's Cabinet had grasped the principles by which the Committee of Imperial Defence worked. Their leader's attitude towards its problems was complacently supine. "The truth is," he wrote in January 1903, "we cannot provide for a fighting Empire, and nothing will give us the power. A peaceful Empire of the old type we are quite fit for." [1] The fate of the Committee therefore gave Balfour more anxiety than almost anything else in the political situation when he left office. He resembled the inventor of some delicate machine, obliged to entrust it to unskilled hands. He said to me in 1927: "As a matter of fact the Liberals never understood it properly,—and I believe Campbell-Bannerman really thought of abolishing it! However, it survived; I think Haldane saw the point of it better. But they went about asking this person and that person to sit on it, till there was a danger of some of these people thinking they had a right to be on it; there was a danger of it becoming a centre for Elder Soldiers—who are even more dangerous than Elder Statesmen."

He was nearing eighty himself when he talked thus. His own record on the Defence Committee testifies to the power of work he could develop in his middle life. For example, the year of the Tariff crisis, 1903, was also the year of his two important Reports on the Invasion of Britain, and Indian Defence, and of five other Memoranda from his pen. After his Government had fallen in December 1905, he completed one on the possibility of a raid by a hostile force on the British coast. The flexible rules that Balfour invented enabled him soon after the outbreak of the Great War to be summoned back to the Committee when his Party was still in Opposition. In the meantime it may be thought that the mere organisation of the Committee of Imperial Defence has been dwelt on here at disproportionate length. That would not have been Balfour's own view. He looked on it as constructive work of vital importance, quite apart from the results which became apparent when the supreme tests were applied to it in August 1914. If the new body had succeeded only in bridging the dangerous gap between expert knowledge and ministerial responsibility, the details of its procedure might be left to specialists. But it completed a development of our constitution required by the changing conditions of modern gov-

[1] Sir H. Campbell-Bannerman to Mr. Bryce. See *Life of Sir H. Campbell-Bannerman,* by J. K. Spender, Vol. II, p. 88.

ernment and the growth of departmental work. The long, slow evolution of the Prime Minister's office reached a definite point when the supreme responsibility for co-ordinating the measures required for the safety of the Empire was vested in one man, and a Department created under his direction. There was a real change in status, appropriately followed by a grant from the Sovereign of special precedence for the First Minister of the Crown. This also was arranged during Balfour's Premiership, and came into effect on the change of Government in 1905.

Opening the archives of a Prime Minister's daily life is like throwing up a window and suddenly letting all the noises of the street into a room. It is a pity that this startling sense of many things going on at once cannot be reproduced without too greatly confusing the narrative, for it is a very essential factor in the real life of the head of any Government. But not much imagination is needed for understanding how the foreign policy which Balfour and Lord Lansdowne directed between 1902 and 1906 fitted in with considerations of Imperial Defence. The discovery of defects in our military system, and the scientific study of our vulnerable spots, coincided with an awakening consciousness of our friendless position among the Great Powers.

Chiefly through Mr. Chamberlain's initiative, efforts had been made during the last year of Lord Salisbury's Government to bring about an Anglo-German alliance. These fell through. An alliance with Japan, concluded for five years, had however been signed before Balfour became Prime Minister. It was based on a common fear of Russian aggression in China. Balfour was not a principal negotiator of this Agreement, and indeed a Memorandum exists in which he argues the case against it on the ground that it might involve us in "fighting for our existence in every part of the globe against Russia and France, because France has joined forces with her ally over some obscure Russian-Japanese quarrel in Korea."

The terms of the Agreement, as finally concluded, provided for neutrality if one of the parties were attacked by another Power. Only an attack by two Powers bound the other party to come to the help of its ally. Thus Balfour's objection was removed, and eventually he became so convinced of the expediency of the Japanese Alliance, that its renewal was one of the things he determined to accomplish before his Government left office in 1905. By that time however our relations with France were on a very different footing from what they had been when he became Prime Minister.

The most decisive act of the Balfour Government in the sphere of foreign policy was the making of the Entente with France. The disagreeable discoveries made by the British nation during the Boer War were not confined to the shortcomings of our generals; they included a perception of the scarcely veiled glee with which every European Power watched our difficulties. Moreover a Bill to double the size of the German Navy was passed in 1900. The time for the great change-over from isolation was at hand.

It is impossible to be sure of how much Balfour and Lord Lansdowne foresaw of the ultimate consequences of the conversations with the French Ambassador, which began on April 6th, 1902, apparently at M. Cambon's initiative. Their primary object was to remove causes of friction in Siam and Morocco, parts of the world where British and French differences of interest were small in comparison with their common determination to prevent any other country obtaining a dominating position. Morocco led on to Egypt, which was first discussed in July 1903, when the French Foreign Minister, M. Delcassé, was in London, accompanying the President on a return visit to an immensely successful one paid by King Edward to Paris in May. Friendly feeling was mounting between the two nations, largely assisted by the popularity and tact of the King, who in every constitutional way smoothed the path for his Ministers. King Edward was a warm friend to the Entente with France, but Balfour always considered it a slur upon the memory of a monarch who never overstepped his constitutional position, to call him the author of the policy.[1] This was launched before the King's Paris visit. The idea of an Arbitration Treaty was first mooted in May. It was signed in October, and the French President told our Ambassador that he hoped it would be followed by another of greater importance and more varied scope.[2] In April 1904, a further stage was reached, and the Agreement concluded which put an end, as far as was humanly possible, to the potential causes of quarrel between ourselves and the French in every part of the globe—and these were many—where our interests clashed. At the end no question was left outstanding, except one concerning

[1] See Lord Newton, *Life of Lord Lansdowne*. Letter from Balfour to him, p. 293.

[2] See *British Documents*, Vol. II, p. 319.

native rights to land in the New Hebrides, upon which agreement could not at the moment be reached, and this small failure serves to convey a picture of the patience and diplomatic skill which went to the making of an Agreement that dealt with the major interests of the two greatest Mediterranean naval Powers, and the two largest Colonial Empires in the World.

Lord Lansdowne consulted Balfour at every step, but both the burden and the credit of the long negotiations fell to him.[1] But neither in Lord Lansdowne's *Life,* nor among Balfour's records, is much light thrown upon the amount of approval with which they viewed the naval and military "Conversations" between the French and British Staffs that began after the conclusion of the Entente—if indeed Lord Lansdowne and Balfour knew about them at all. There has been some ambiguity about their origins, but there is no doubt that the naval talks at least had begun before the Conservative Government left office in December 1905.[2] It was Sir Edward Grey, as Foreign Secretary in Mr. Asquith's Government, who reluctantly gave them official sanction, driven thereto by the crisis with Germany over Morocco which developed soon after he took office. Balfour would probably have viewed the development of the Entente implied by the conversations with less repugnance than did his successor, but it does not seem that the Anglo-French Agreement was a prelude to a military understanding in the view of either Government at the time it was made. Had it been so he would hardly have written, as he did to a friend in 1912: "It came upon me as a shock of surprise—I am far from saying of disapproval—when I found how rapidly after I left office the Entente had, under the German menace, developed into something resembling a defensive Alliance."

The French were naturally quicker than ourselves to take alarm about Germany's aggressive intentions. But it was only after the weakness of the Russian Empire was revealed by the Japanese War of 1904–1905 and enhanced by the Revolution which followed it, that the "German menace" became the dominating consideration in European politics. Balfour's continental policy was still in the Salisbury tradition of regarding Russia as the potential enemy in chief. But his Government was at great pains to avoid anything

---

[1] See *Life of Lord Lansdowne,* Chapter X.
[2] See *British Documents,* Vol. III, p. 171. Lord Grey's *Twenty-five Years,* p. 76 orig. edition, p. 139 cheap edition.

that might embitter German feelings, as is shown by the suppression of the more lively parts of a correspondence regarding the evacuation of Shanghai in 1902, published in a White Book of December in that year.[1] On this the British Cabinet took a firm line:

4.11.1902.

Mr. Balfour with his humble duty to Your Majesty begs respectfully to inform Your Majesty that at Cabinet to-day Lord Lansdowne raised the question of an answer to be given to a note of Count Metternich on the subject of the recent action of Germany in connection with the proposed evacuation of Shanghai. The Cabinet did not attempt to draft the answer; but it was agreed that Lord Lansdowne should point out to the German Ambassador that it was to be regretted that his Government should have approached the Chinese on such a subject without previous consultation with us; and to indicate (delicately!) that for the Russians to interfere with the sovereign rights of China in Manchuria; and for Germany to interfere with those rights in Shantung, and *then* to go the Chinese Government and say that *we* ought not to interfere in the valley of the Yangtsze was, to say the least, not neighbourly. . . .

Overlapping these differences with Berlin in the Far East was the blockade of Venezuela, which we undertook jointly with Germany on account of a long series of provocative acts against the subjects and the shipping of the two Powers on the part of the Venezuelans. The matter eventually went to an Arbitral Tribunal at Washington, where Great Britain obtained a settlement of her first line claims, but was far from receiving any return for the trouble occasioned by the incident.

The unpopularity of Germany both in this country and in America was shown by the comments on our joint action with her against Venezuela. Moreover the annoyance it aroused in the United States added to the diplomatic difficulties which arose over the settlement of the Alaskan Boundary dispute in 1903. Balfour's letters to Lord Lansdowne and to the King, on the subject of the Russo-Japanese War and its consequences, show the point of view from which British Ministers watched the destruction of the European balance of power, and the rise of a great naval Power in the Far East.

The Japanese declaration of war took place in February 1904. All through 1903 the aggressiveness of Russian demands in respect of

[1] *British Documents*, Vol. I, p. 138 *et seq.*

Manchuria and Korea had produced increasing tension, and on December 11th the British Cabinet discussed the possibilities of war. Balfour wrote to the King:

Lord Lansdowne was authorised to speak unofficially to M. Cambon, and point out to him that a war between Russia and Japan might draw *us* in; and that if we were drawn in, France might find it difficult to keep out in the face of her treaty obligations. It was impossible to contemplate anything at once so horrible and so absurd as a general war brought on by Russia's impracticable attitude in Manchuria. The present condition of the Russian Foreign Office—which is so well known to Your Majesty—adds to the danger of the situation;—and it seems almost possible that the Emperor of Russia, the advocate of peace and disarmament, may without knowing it become the occasion and author of a widespread conflagration. We must hope better things; but the lack of authentic information as to the real intentions of Russia, is undoubtedly a source of great anxiety....

Shortly after this Cabinet discussion Balfour fell ill with influenza while staying with Lord Derby at Knowsley. His meditations on his sick-bed were sent to Lord Lansdowne on December 22nd in the form of a Memorandum, drawn up in his own handwriting.

JAPAN AND RUSSIA

22.12.1903.

(1) I have asked Intelligence Departments for their forecast of military operations in case of war between Japan and Russia. In the meantime I submit provisionally following observations.

(2) Japan is weaker in Battleships than Russia.
She cannot in these circumstances either safely send an expedition to Korea, or keep up communication with it if sent.

(3) On the other hand, an invasion of Japan by Russia on any important scale is, I believe, impossible. A war therefore would not "smash" Japan in the sense of wiping her out as a military power; nor need it even greatly damage her fleet.

(4) Her fast cruisers would probably check any overseas expedition of the enemy; and if properly handled they could not be caught by the Battleships. Her Battleships would presumably not be allowed to risk themselves against overwhelming odds.

(5) A war therefore would not seriously affect Japan except in so far as it affected her through Korea. We of course care little for Korea except as it affects Japan. From every other point of view (except that)

there could be nothing better for us than that Russia should involve herself in the expense and trouble of Korean adventure—with the result that at the best she would have become possessed of a useless province, which would cost more than it brought in, which could only be retained so long as she kept a great fleet in the Far East, and a large army thousands of miles from her Home base, and which would be a perpetual guarantee that whenever she went to war with another Power, no matter where or about what, Japan would be upon her back.

(6) In these circumstances, while I would avoid giving any advice to Japan which would enable her to say hereafter that we had got her into war, I would *not* put pressure upon her of any kind to abate her demands. To tell her (as has been suggested) that she *must* be content with less than she asks in Korea, is to help Russia, to offend all the sentiments of the Japanese people, to enable the Japanese Government to transfer their well-deserved unpopularity to us. Japan knows her own affairs as well as we do; and inasmuch as, for reasons given above, I do not believe in her being "crushed" under any circumstances, I should let her work out her own salvation in her own way. Even if I am wrong in my military forecast, I am disposed to think it would be better to come in as a deliverer at a later stage than to thrust unpalatable advice upon a reluctant ally in a matter with which we have no immediate concern.

A. J. B.

22.12.1903.

The Memorandum was followed on December 28th by a letter to the King, in which Balfour expanded much the same points, especially the one concerning the advantage of a weakened Russia:

The interest of this country [he wrote] is now and always *Peace*. But a war between Japan and Russia, in which we were not actively concerned, and in which Japan did not suffer serious defeat, would not be an unmixed curse. Russia ... would have created for herself an implacable and unsleeping enemy. ... Mr. Balfour concludes from all this that she would be much easier to deal with, both in Asia and in Europe, than she is at present. For these reasons Mr. Balfour would do everything to maintain peace, *short* of wounding the susceptibilities of the Japanese people.

This letter and the Memorandum of December 22nd were written before the naval and military experts had delivered their forecasts, therefore Balfour's provisional views on policy were based on his personal conviction that Russia would not be able to crush Japan. This was not the universally accepted view at the time. It is said indeed that Admiral Fisher actually pointed out to Lord Lansdowne on the map the exact spot where Japan would be annihilated.[1]

Balfour's Memorandum was circulated to the Cabinet on December 29th, together with the comments upon it by several colleagues. From these it appears that Lord Lansdowne was not so bold a backer of Japan as the Prime Minister.

I attach, I think, more importance to averting war than you do [he wrote]. War involves for us a threefold risk.

(1) The possibility that our ally may be crushed.

(2) The possibility that we ourselves may become implicated, not on account of our treaty engagement to Japan, but because the British public will not sit still while the crushing is being done.

(3) The aggravation of our present financial difficulties, already grave enough.

For these reasons I should like His Majesty's Government to try its hand as a mediator, or at all events a friendly counsellor, rather than wait until it can appear on the scene in the rôle of a "deliverer."

On the whole, the Cabinet seems to have sided with Balfour against offering mediation. He kept in closest touch with the Foreign Office during the Christmas holidays, which he spent at Whittingehame, and on the day before Lord Lansdowne expected to receive from the Japanese Ambassador the announcement that Japan had reached the maximum point of concession to Russian demands, Balfour sent his colleague a note for guidance. Some of this is reproduced word for word in Lord Lansdowne's official account of the interview.[2] Balfour wrote:

To LORD LANSDOWNE,   29.12.03.

I hardly think it wise to go further than to say that we shall in all circumstances adhere to our Treaty obligations not merely in the letter but in the spirit; that it is hardly possible for us to take the responsibility of advising on the course that Japan ought now to pursue, since this must depend partly on the degree to which Japanese interests are menaced; partly on military considerations; partly on considerations connected with public opinion in Japan itself,—on none of which subjects

[1] See Lord Newton, *Life of Lord Lansdowne*, p. 307.

[2] See *British Documents*, Vol. II, p. 227, Lord Lansdowne to Sir Claude Macdonald in Tokyo.

is it possible for us to form an opinion which would warrant us in attempting to influence policy.

You might ask, if you thought fit, whether there was any diplomatic action, which the Japanese would like us to take in their interests, bearing in mind that our avowed friendship for Japan would prevent Russia regarding us in this matter as a disinterested party.

ARTHUR JAMES BALFOUR.

The Japanese Government made it clear that mediation would not be acceptable. They hinted however that a loan would be helpful; upon which Balfour wrote:

WHITTINGEHAME.

DEAR LORD LANSDOWNE,   *Dec.* 31*st*, 1903.

Russia and Japan

I do not think it is possible for us to find the £20,000,000 for Japan. It would be difficult at any time, since guaranteeing a War loan to be used against Russia is as near as possible an "act of war"; indeed, morally it *is* an "act of war." Apart from this, money market considerations render the transaction practically impossible. And observe if, by any unfortunate chance, we get dragged in, we shall require every shilling of credit for ourselves. I wish Russia had not so formidable a war chest.

I am greatly interested in Scott's [1] suggestion that it is the Tsar who is raising objections to meeting Japanese demands about Manchuria. It is, I suspect, very characteristic of that worthy, but not very able, advocate of universal peace that he should plunge the world into war on so obscure a point of honour.

I propose to go to Chatsworth on Monday. I could, though not of course without some inconvenience, travel to London Sunday night if you thought this really important. I could be available for a meeting of the Defence Committee at 12 to discuss the Russian-Japanese military problems. I still fail to see how the process of "crushing" is to be carried out. Nor am I disposed, without further argument, to admit that a defeat would necessarily "deprive Japan for years" of her utility in the Far East. This depends as much on her Army as her Navy. But all this must be thrashed out.

yours ever,
ARTHUR JAMES BALFOUR.

There was no purely Foreign Office question on which Balfour, while Prime Minister, kept a more continuous grip than the problems arising on the eve of the Russian-Japanese War. His final

---

[1] Sir C. Scott, our Ambassador at St. Petersburg.

Cabinet Memorandum on the subject goes to the root of British policy.

1. Our moral obligations under the Anglo-Japanese Treaty do not exceed our legal obligations. The latter we are bound to fulfil at all costs, in the spirit as in the letter. Every demand made on us beyond this should be considered solely in the light of British interests, present and future.

2. It is most dangerous to admit any other view. The Japanese would assuredly refuse to consider themselves bound to support us in any controversy which might arise in connection with the Indian frontier or Constantinople. If war with Russia suited them at such a moment, they will doubtless make it. If not, not. So it must be with us.

It has been suggested that if we take this view, and if, in consequence, Japan fights without an ally and is beaten, she will in revenge for our "abandonment" of her, throw in her lot with her former enemy and combine with Russia against us.

3. Such a course would be in the highest degree unreasonable. It is also, I venture to think, extremely improbable. Japan is divided from Russia by an antagonism of interests deep-rooted in the fundamental conditions of Far Eastern affairs. Her interests and ours, on the other hand, so far as can be foreseen, will continue to run on parallel lines. Harmony of interests, and that alone, gives stability to alliances: and so long as that harmony persists unchanged, an alliance once formed is not to be easily shattered by temporary misunderstandings, should such unhappily occur.

4. And why, on the present occasion, should they occur even if the worst comes to the worst? The original policy of the Anglo-Japanese Treaty depended essentially on the theory, openly avowed I think by Japan at the time, that she was a match for Russia alone, but not a match for Russia and another Power in combination. If this pretension be exaggerated—which I am not disposed to believe—the whole policy of the Treaty is open to serious criticism.

And criticism must develop into condemnation if the policy of the Treaty is so stretched as to imply something like a moral obligation to help Japan whenever she seems likely to be beaten by Russia. Then the Japanese Alliance would become not a guarantee of peace, but the inevitable occasion of war. It would be a standing international danger. For since, by hypothesis, Japan single-handed is not a match for Russia, we should *always* have to go to her assistance in case of hostilities between the two. France in such an event being bound to throw in her lot with Russia, the Government at Tokyo would be the arbiters of peace and war for half the civilised world!

Such a condition of things would be absolutely intolerable unless we controlled the foreign policy of Japan. Yet is anything more certain than that Japan would never be mad enough to entrust us with such a responsibility, and that if she did we should never be mad enough to accept it?

The Memorandum then repeats the arguments against the "crushing" of Japan, and goes on:

The way we ought to look at the question is this: Would Russia, as a world Power, be stronger all along the vast line of her frontier, from the Baltic to Vladivostok, if she added Corea to her dominions? I hesitate to express a decided opinion, but there are evident reasons against answering the question in the affirmative.

Russia's strong point is her vast population and the unassailable character of her territories. Her weak point is finance. . . .

Even if we assume Russia to get the best of it, we can by no means assume that she will come out of the fight stronger than she went in. Stronger in the Far East for many purposes she may perhaps be. But we have to fear her chiefly as (a) the ally of France; (b) the invader of India; (c) the dominating influence in Persia; and (d) the possible disturber of European peace. For these purposes she will not be stronger but weaker after over-running Corea . . . bound to the East by the necessity of watching Japan, she will be unable freely to take part in strategical combinations against Britain in the West. Though her value to France in a war with Germany might thereby be little affected, her value to France in a war with us would be greatly reduced and her whole diplomacy, from the Black Sea to the Oxus, might be weakened into something distantly resembling sweet reasonableness.

A. J. B.

December 29, 1903.

War was declared on February 10th, and a whole set of new problems unrolled themselves for Britain.

A Russian fleet was in the Black Sea, and the British Government were determined that it should stay there. Balfour was taking no risks on the question of the passage through the Straits, and even before war was declared he wrote to Lord Lansdowne:

WHITTINGEHAME.

My dear Lansdowne,   *Jan. 19th, 1904.*

A propos of my Minute of yesterday, would it not be well to give Scott full instructions as to the course he ought to take directly he hears of any symptoms indicating that the Black Sea Fleet is about to move?

I presume you would desire him to act somewhat as follows: On the first information that the Fleet is moving he should ask for explanations, and, if none are forthcoming, he should take a very serious tone, explaining that we could not view any breach of Treaty engagements with indifference. If, in spite of this, the Straits were forced, it is a question whether he ought not to leave St. Petersburg at once and break off formal relations, though of course without declaring war.

I think he ought to have his lesson well by heart, so that he will not be taken by surprise should the unexpected occur.

I suppose you would in like manner give O'Conor [1] our general view of the situation, and instructions as to the language he is to employ to the Sultan if the Bosphorus is threatened.

Willie Selborne [2] will have an adequate force in the Eastern Mediterranean; and I think he should prepare instructions to the Admiral of the Mediterranean Fleet so that *he* also may know exactly what is expected of him.

A circular telegraphic despatch should be in readiness to our Representatives at the Courts of all the Signatory Powers, justifying our action and urging them to aid us in maintaining the law of Europe.

I venture to bother you with all these suggestions because, if the necessity for action arises at all, it will probably arise with very little warning.

yours, etc.,
ARTHUR JAMES BALFOUR.

Before the spring of 1904 was over the superiority of the Japanese became evident. At the end of August the Russians determined, as a forlorn hope, to send the Baltic Fleet to the Far East. As neutrals we denied them coaling facilities on the way, a decision which helped to fray nerves already shaken by reverses. The Baltic Fleet set forth, met with some fishing vessels near the Dogger Bank, imagined the presence of Japanese torpedo-boats, fired, sank a British boat, killed and wounded several persons (including some Russians). This fantastic mistake brought Great Britain and Russia to the verge of war. It occurred on October 21st, and much excitement filled the days which elapsed before the Russian Government agreed to an international enquiry on a basis satisfactory to Great Britain.

On October 26th Balfour wrote to his Cabinet colleagues:

...Lord Lansdowne proposes to inform Count Benckendorff that I speak at Southampton on Friday; that it will be impossible for me

---

[1] Sir N. O'Conor, our Ambassador at St. Petersburg.
[2] Lord Selborne, then First Lord of the Admiralty.

to avoid touching on the subject, and not less impossible, when I do touch on it, to avoid saying one of two things: either that all our demands have been accepted, *or*, if I am not in a position to say this, then to hint—politely but not obscurely—that we cannot allow the criminals to vanish into the Far East without immediate trial. We must not, however, disguise from ourselves that such words falling from the lips of a Prime Minister sound very like a declaration of war and bring the country perilously near to overt hostilities. I regret, however, to say that I cannot at present see that any other course is consistent either with our national honour or with the fixed sentiments of the country.

I ought to add that it is possible that, if I understand the naval position rightly, the Gibraltar Fleet may not be adequately reinforced in time to meet the Russians off the coast of Spain, and that, if the worst comes to the worst, they may have to be pursued.

A. J. B.

Oct. 26th, 1904.

Friday, October 28th, the day of the Southampton speech, dawned without any satisfactory reply having come from the Russians. Feeling was running even higher among them than in England, and one rash word might have been fatal. Our Ambassador in St. Petersburg wrote afterwards that on the Thursday evening the betting had seemed to him about even between peace and war.[1] Balfour put off leaving London till the last possible moment, and meantime prepared as best he could for a speech which might announce the relief of tension, or alternatively that the British Empire was at grips with Russia. It was not until his train reached Southampton that the telegram was put into his hand announcing that agreement had been reached. Balfour always spoke of this day as racking even to his placid nerves. Miss Balfour described the meeting in a letter to another member of the family.

They listened with the most profound attention. I never felt it more than on that day. Arthur spoke more slowly than usual with more weighing of words, and yet with very few corrections of words or phrases. His speaking can never be really like Uncle Robert's, but it was more like than I had ever before noticed it to be. He spoke with extreme gravity and even solemnity, so that his manner was impressive as well as his information.

[1] *British Documents.*

As the winter of 1904 advanced, it became clear that the Powers interested in the integrity of China must be ready to influence a peace as difficult and delicate as the war itself. Port Arthur fell to the Japanese on January 1st, 1905, and soon afterwards President Roosevelt put out feelers for an exchange of views with the British Foreign Office.

The President's personal relations with Sir Mortimer Durand, the British Ambassador in Washington, were not very easy, and he wrote to his intimate friend, Sir Cecil Spring Rice, then British First Secretary at St. Petersburg, winding up by begging him to visit the United States unofficially.[1] It was decided that Sir Cecil should go, and Balfour drafted a letter to him, which however does not appear to have been sent. Perhaps it was thought that the visit was too unconventional for the Prime Minister to be officially made aware of it. The following is therefore copied from the unfinished draft:

Lansdowne has allowed me to see a private letter written to you by the President. It is extraordinarily interesting, and, like all good letters, gives a most vivid picture of its author.

I do not propose to say anything about the many subsidiary points which it raises, much as I should like to do so. I go straight to what seems to me the underlying thought (hinted at rather than expressed), which the President seems to be turning over in his mind, and I can perhaps do so best by succinctly stating what I conceive to be the position in the Far East, and the best way of meeting the difficulties which the future may have in store both for us and the United States in connection with the integrity of China.

I. I am completely sceptical about the "Yellow Peril." The idea of Japan heading an Eastern crusade on Western civilisation seems to me altogether chimerical. Even if we can bring ourselves to believe (which *I* cannot) that any Japanese statesmen, present or future, could meditate so wild a project, it is sufficient to remark that Japan is never likely to have a Navy sufficient to meet the Fleets of the Christian world, who could therefore always cut her off from free communication with the mainland of Asia.

II. The real danger is not the remote and fantastic dream of a victory of East over West, but the very near and imminent peril of important fragments of China being dominated by more warlike and aggressive Powers.

[1] For President Roosevelt's letter see *The Letters and Friendships of Sir Cecil Spring Rice,* Vol. I, p. 441 *et seq.*

If America and ourselves were to enter into a Treaty, binding us jointly to resist such aggression, it would never, I believe, be attempted. Together we are too strong for any combination of Powers to fight us. I believe there would be no difficulty on this side of the Atlantic in the way of such a Treaty. The difficulty, I imagine, would be rather with the United States, whose traditions and whose Constitution conspire to make such arrangements hard to conclude.

I ought perhaps to add that there is a genuine difficulty connected with the strict maintenance of the integrity of China of which we have had some experience. It arises out of the necessity, which, with a Power like China, cannot always be avoided, of having to use force to compel either her, or States which are under her nominal suzerainty, to carry out their plain obligations. The Government at Peking is a master of obstructive tactics, and there is a point at which no foreign nation can submit any longer to have its just demands ignored. What, in such an event, is to be the machinery of coercion? It is hard to find any which does not involve at least the threat of a temporary occupation of Chinese territory. If the Chinese know that the threat cannot be carried out it will be made in vain. If it *is* carried out we must face the fact that a temporary occupation has a dangerous tendency to grow into a permanent one. Were it possible that coercion, when it became necessary, could be made international in its character, this danger would doubtless be avoided. But such a scheme seems to involve an international machinery which it would be difficult to create and—in view of international jealousies in that part of the world—still more difficult to work.

I only mention this as a point which may have to be considered, but which is quite subordinate to the main issue—that of securing Anglo-American co-operation.

III. I rather gather that the President feels considerable anxiety about the character of the arrangements likely to be made at the end of the war. He anticipates the possibility that pressure may be put on Japan to accept terms of peace which will suit neither her, nor the United States, nor us. It may be worth remembering that even if the War should last beyond the quinquennial term of the Anglo-Japanese Treaty, and even if the British Government then in office were unwilling to renew it, the instrument itself explicitly provided for its own continuance during the continuance of hostilities. From this it follows that until peace is arranged no material pressure can be put upon Japan by any foreign Power, other than Russia, without bringing us into the field. If Russia, in the later steps of the war, were to be so successful as to bring Japan to her knees, the victor might extort what terms he pleased, and the Anglo-Japanese Treaty would provide no remedy. This contingency is not thought very probable either here or in America.

But on the Continent it is commonly regarded as certain, and in my judgment it might be worth while for the United States and Britain to consider what terms they would regard as inimical to their interests, and how they can best prevent Russia indemnifying herself for the moral and material cost of the war by appropriating a large slice of Chinese territory. It is significant in this connection to note that she has already notified that China has broken her neutrality.

Anglo-American co-operation over the Far Eastern situation did not prove possible. For one thing Great Britain's alliance with Japan made her neither able, nor willing, to press for sacrifices contrary to what Japan considered to be in her own interests. Nevertheless the two Governments were in touch through Sir Cecil Spring Rice, whose correspondence with President Roosevelt was known to nobody "except the two Balfours and Lord Lansdowne."[1] The Peace of Portsmouth (New Hampshire), negotiated under the President's auspices, acknowledged Japanese rights in Korea, but obliged her to evacuate Manchuria. Public opinion in Japan had expected more reward for the victory that had bled the country white. There was rioting in Tokyo when the peace terms were published on August 29th. The Government which concluded them would have fallen but for the popular approval that greeted the renewal of the Anglo-Japanese Alliance of 1902 on terms which placed Japan on a par of power with Britain in Eastern Asia.

The objects of the new Treaty, to run for ten years, were defined as the maintenance of peace in Eastern Asia and India, preservation of the independence and integrity of China, of the principle of the "open door," and of mutual defence of the territorial rights and interests of Japan and Britain in Eastern Asia. This involved the possibility of armed assistance by the other Party, if either Korea or the Indian frontier were attacked. Balfour evidently believed more strongly than did the military experts in the value of the last provision.[2] A letter to the King gives his line of thought:

9.6.1905.

Mr. Balfour with his humble duty to Your Majesty begs respectfully to say that the discussions of the proposed Japanese treaty which have

[1] See *Letters and Friendships of Sir Cecil Spring Rice*, Vol. I, p. 485. Mr. Gerald Balfour was personally more intimate than his brother with Sir Cecil.

[2] See *British Documents*, Vol. IV, p. 138, for a somewhat critical Memorandum by the British General Staff.

extended over several Cabinets have now resulted in the preparation of a draft Treaty for the consideration of the Japanese Government.

The main difficulties which had to be dealt with were (1) that the guarantees of assistance by Japan to Britain, and by Britain to Japan, had to cover not merely the case in which the territories of the two Powers were attacked, but also the case in which adjacent territories were threatened. Japan, for example, must be able to call upon us to aid her if Corea were invaded; while we, in like manner, should claim her assistance if the same danger threatened Afghanistan.

(2) The assistance to be given by Britain could hardly be in the shape of a *military* force. The public would be somewhat alarmed, if we were under a treaty obligation to land soldiers in Corea, perhaps at the same moment that they might be urgently required in India.

(3) The naval force which in time of peace the Powers are to keep in Eastern waters demands careful consideration, and (4) the number of troops which Japan should send for the defence of India raises points which cannot be determined by military considerations alone, but involve questions of home politics as well. There is, for example, a real danger that, if a Radical Government came into power, they would reduce our army below the limits of safety; and this danger will be greatly augmented if they think they can rely on an unlimited supply of men from Japan. In the opinion of Your Majesty's present advisers it is not consistent either with the security or the dignity of the Empire that the defence of any part of it should depend mainly upon a foreign Power, however friendly and however powerful. We have therefore endeavoured to frame the Treaty (or rather the Notes which will be exchanged when the Treaty is signed) in such a manner as to make Japanese assistance in the defence of India bear a fixed relation to the efforts *we* make to send adequate forces to the front.

It remains to be seen what view the Japanese Government will take of our proposals. Mr. Balfour is sanguine that a satisfactory agreement may be come to.

The Anglo-Japanese Treaty completed the contribution of Balfour's Government to that all-round reinforcement of British security which held first place in his thoughts while he was Prime Minister.

The circumstances in which he and Lord Lansdowne decided to renew the Japanese Alliance afford in themselves the best proof of their motives. Before the Treaty was signed in August 1905, peace had been practically concluded on the basis of Japanese victory over Russia. But that outcome was by no means certain until after the battle of Tsushima in May, whereas the negotiations had been opened, on British initiative, in January. On May 16th, on the very eve of the decisive battle, Balfour wrote to the King that

Lord Lansdowne was instructed to make it clear (to the Japanese Minister) *before* the issue of the coming naval battle is known, that we are wedded to the principle of the Alliance. It would be altogether unworthy of Your Majesty's advisers to permit the Japanese to suppose that we are mere "waiters on fortune"—only prepared to assist the successful.

Chapter XVIII

CURZON AND KITCHENER

Lord Curzon and the Cabinet. Balfour's correspondence with Lord Curzon. Tibetan policy. The controversy over Indian Army Administration. Balfour argues the case with Lord Curzon. Lord Curzon resigns.

THE private relationships of members of the same Government may act like oil on the bearings of the political machine, or, alternatively, like grit. The co-operation of Balfour with Lord Lansdowne in the long and delicate diplomacy of the Entente and the Japanese Alliance is an example of the first; the reverse is shown in the friction with Lord Curzon over Indian affairs, for in this case the fact that Balfour's Ministry was full of the Viceroy's intimate friends merely imported personal distress into a difficult situation, without facilitating agreement.

This was largely due to Lord Curzon's own unbending character, but its effect upon Balfour was strong, though perhaps subconscious. The elimination of unnecessary pain or distress, mental or physical, was a part of his philosophy of life to which he clung with passion. The mortification which Lord Curzon suffered, and caused his friends to suffer, through his offended feelings was so far outside Balfour's own experience that he classed it among the preventable forms of pain. Moreover the intrusion of such personal emotions into public life was an assault upon his own barriers which he could hardly regard with patience. Nor could he, in this case, defend himself by his favourite method of standing aloof. He was one of the group of Ministers bound to Lord Curzon, and to one another, by affection and lifelong knowledge of each other's weaknesses and strengths. As friend and as Chief he had a part to perform. He disliked the necessity in either capacity, and the double rôle was intensely distasteful; he played it with half a heart. As one of the most devoted of his colleagues once remarked: "Arthur could never bring himself to dip his hands into dirty or troubled waters." This reluctance inspired much of his correspondence as Prime Minister with the Viceroy, and more than once brings a touch of comedy into the gloom of a curious exhibition of human nature.

Three and a half years of Lord Curzon's first term of office in India had passed when Balfour became head of the Government at home. They were the happiest and the most successful, and the Cabinet had appreciated the greatness of the Viceroy's achievements with a more intelligent interest than perhaps he gave them credit for. Lord Curzon's study of Oriental problems had been so profound, and his views on British policy in Asia were so decided, that he hardly admitted the right of others to hold opposite views. Balfour however was by no means the only member of his Government who had formed opinions on those matters. It could scarcely be otherwise while Russia was looked upon as the greatest military Power in the world—as she was until within a few months of the time when Balfour's Government ceased to be responsible for the safety of the Empire. Facts, as well as the traditions of his training, still dictated to the Prime Minister the distrust of Russia which he had imbibed from Lord Salisbury, when as his Private Secretary at the Berlin Congress he had watched the British Plenipotentiaries call check to Russian ambition in the Near East. Since then he had seen her domination spreading over Asia and drawing ever nearer to the Indian frontier. He and his Cabinet shared Lord Curzon's anxieties for that vital line. But Lord Curzon was persuaded that its safety could only be ensured by vigorous and immediate British penetration of the closed regions beyond. Hence his desire to place a British Resident permanently at Lhasa, and to exert pressure upon the Amir of Afghanistan for a treaty which would bring Kabul into closer contact with the Government of India. The Cabinet dreaded the entanglements, even more than the expense, which this forward policy would entail. Thus began a conflict of wills which reached its climax on questions of reform in the administration of the Indian Army.

When Balfour became Prime Minister however none of the major struggles had developed, but there were strained relations on minor points, and he had only been at the head of the Government for a few days when he felt compelled to cable to Lord Curzon, suggesting the withdrawal of a Despatch on the question of whether the expenses of the Indian guests at King Edward's Coronation should be paid by the Home or the Indian Government. He wired the strong hint that the document "read too much like the indictment of one colleague by another." The Viceroy refused to withdraw it, and the India Office gave way, the Government being in fact not unsympathetic with Lord Curzon's view on this particular point. But the ever unyielding attitude was having its inevitable effects at home, and Lord George Hamilton, then Secretary of State for India, began to feel the dread which became a familiar symptom whenever a communication arrived from the Viceroy.

Balfour's cable had crossed a charming congratulatory letter from Lord Curzon to the new Prime Minister. "For myself," it ran, "I have never doubted for one moment during the many years in which I have been privileged to be your friend and follower, that you ought to be, and would be, Prime Minister, and I rejoice that the post has fallen to you while you are in the plenitude of your powers...." Then follows a passage, the unconscious humour of which cannot have escaped the person addressed: "I hope that you will find time to assert that real control over the Cabinet and the business of the entire Government which is reported to have steadily weakened in recent years, and to have been on the decline ever since the days of Sir Robert Peel...." The letter then enters at some length into the vexed question of Coronation expenses, and ends: "Good luck to you, old boy, in all that you undertake and do, and may God bless you in your noble task.—Your ever affectionate, Curzon."

This was no doubt, in some ways, a slightly embarrassing letter to respond to at the moment, but never did the Nemesis of the lazy correspondent fall more swiftly than on Balfour. Had he written by return Lord Curzon could just have received his reply before a new cause of disagreement arose, this time on the refusal of the Cabinet to meet the Viceroy's wish to announce a remission of taxation at the Coronation Durbar. It was thought undesirable to associate the King's name with taxation, but Lord Curzon took the refusal greatly to heart, and cabled straight to the King's Secretary, Sir Francis Knollys, invoking the aid of the Sovereign to reverse the Cabinet's decision. The Cabinet was deeply incensed; official communications passed at the end of November 1902, but it was not till December 12th that Balfour wrote a private letter to Lord Curzon for the first time since he became Prime Minister. It was a remarkably characteristic letter, in its plain speaking, as well as in the warm charm with which it covers up negligences.

Dec. 12th, 1902.

MY DEAR GEORGE,

Truly I am severely punished for the dilatory manner in which I carry on my private correspondence! Had I written to you, as week by week I intended to do for these many years, [*sic,* months?] in answer to your delightful letter, I should not now find myself in the position of having to make my first epistolary communication to you on a subject respecting which we unfortunately disagree. But I am not going to argue it, I am only going to dogmatise. I cannot really assent to your view that because the position of the Sovereign was (in your view) affected by the course to be taken at the Durbar in reference to taxation, you were therefore justified in carrying on an independent correspond-ence on a point of high policy without the knowledge or assent of your colleagues....

However I regard all this as ancient history. What is not ancient history is our admiration for your great services as Indian administrator. You seem to think that you are injured whenever you do not get exactly your own way! But which of us gets exactly his own way? Certainly not the P.M. Certainly not any of his Cabinet colleagues. We all suffer the common lot of those who, having to work with others, are sometimes over-ruled by them. I doubt whether any of your predecessors have ever received so large a measure of confidence from either the S. of S. or the Home Government. I am ready to add that probably none have ever deserved that confidence more; but do not let any of us forget that there cannot be a greater mistake committed by a British statesman than to interpret any difference of opinion as a per-sonal slight, or as indicating any want of confidence among colleagues.

Dear George, I do assure you that no one has marked with greater pride or greater pleasure your triumphant progress, and the admirable courage, energy and sagacity with which you have grappled with the immense difficulties of your task, than your old friend and colleague.

I have differed from you on this point or that point; I may have (who knows) to differ from you on others. But nothing will for a moment diminish either the warmth of friendship or the enthusiasm of my admiration.

yours ever,

A. J. B.

The taxation question was finally settled by means of a form of words proposed by Lord Curzon himself. Matters of greater importance, especially in respect of policy in Tibet and Afghanistan, were under discussion, when, early in 1903, Lord Curzon proposed the renewal of his Viceroyalty for a second term. He made the suggestion first of all in a letter to Balfour, dated February the 5th. This was answered in March, but not conclusively, for reasons which might have persuaded anyone less imperious than Lord Curzon that the hesitation was not due to lack of consideration for him. Balfour's letter opens with high praise of his work, but goes on:

> If your plan of resigning the Viceroyalty and being reappointed after an interval, were adopted, it might be completely frustrated by a Ministerial crisis in the middle of your holiday, and even short of this, objection might be felt to your reappointment on the eve of a General Election which turned against us.

Lord Curzon took umbrage at the phrase "your plan," and wrote with offended dignity on April 30th. Six weeks passed, during which a spate of letters poured upon certain other Ministers, and nerves wore thin; but in the end the question of the renewed Viceroyalty was settled according to Lord Curzon's suggestion. Then Balfour unsheathed his pen:

My dear George,   *June 18th, 1903.*
You will have gathered from my telegram that the obstacles to the lengthening of your term of office or rather the creation of a supplementary term have been overcome....
So much for business. Now I am going to enter a very humble protest against your epistolary style! You and I are old and devoted friends, why should you adopt towards me the tone of your last communication? I mean your letter of April 30th. In it you speak with apparent indignation of my having described the scheme for prolonging your Viceroyalty as "your plan" and "your suggestion." Why of course it was your plan and your suggestion. Look back at your letter of Feb. 5th, in which it was first broached. But why should it not be your plan? I think it is a very good one, and am certain that the person responsible for it had no reason to be ashamed of his handiwork, and no one thinks that your desire to stay on (and whatever you may say, it is and ought to be, your desire) is prompted by any motive whatever except the good of India.... But why should the man who volunteers upon a service of difficulty, if not of danger, quarrel with those who describe the enterprise as "his plan"? You have often reproached my slackness as correspondent and I plead guilty to the charge. I admit that I always take up my pen with the utmost reluctance and lay it

down with a sigh of satisfaction. But I sometimes think that the weakness has its good side. You do not share it; but are you not sometimes tempted to use your extraordinary readiness of composition in a way which does not facilitate the co-operation of those who should find it specially easy to work together, since they are not only colleagues but life-long friends? Differences of opinion among these there must occasionally be. It is much more difficult to conciliate those differences by correspondence than by speech. Even if we were sitting together round a Cabinet table we might not absolutely agree; still more difficult is absolute agreement when we are separated by thousands of miles. But do remember that so far as the Cabinet is concerned you have had an absolutely free hand in Indian administration, that we have admired you and supported you through your most honourable labours, and that if we have differed and perhaps still differ about certain questions of foreign policy, this is neither due to weakness of purpose on our part nor to any want of regard for you.

Well, this is a long screed from one who is no letter writer; but (if things go awry) it may be the last I shall address to you as P.M. Hence perhaps its abnormal proportions. But whatever the fortunes of the minority or the Party, at all events you have the satisfaction of knowing that your Indian administration has added great lustre to a Government which I believe will be thought in time to come to have done much for the country; and as this is so, why should I wrangle with you over questions of style.

My dear George, take care of your health,
and, Believe me,
yours ever,
ARTHUR JAMES BALFOUR.

This letter succeeded in evoking that side of Lord Curzon's character which explains the long-suffering love borne him by his friends. He answered instantly.

VICEREGAL LODGE,
SIMLA.
July 8th, 1903

MY DEAR ARTHUR,

I am much obliged for your letter of June 18. I am sorry that you were offended with the style of my letter of April 30. When I wrote it—and I did not write it in a hurry, for I kept yours for ten days—I was hurt not at the style but at the tone of yours to which it was a reply, and which seemed to treat me grudgingly. I thought that I was submitting to a sacrifice—and I think that if you had five years of the strain in India you would think so too.... Your letter seemed to imply that the Govt. were doing me a great favour.... I dare say I did you a complete injustice; but honestly this was in my mind and it coloured my answer.

As regards correspondence in general, I write freely to the Sec. of State and other friends. I do not know how they use my letters. Sometimes I know that things that I never meant to be seen by anyone else have been shown and have done harm. I am very defenceless in this respect, but I think it a sound rule never to be offended at anything in a letter which one was not meant to see....

I think you assume too readily that because in the discharge of my duty I sometimes put forward advice in respect of Foreign Affairs, which is not accepted by the Cabinet at home, therefore I am seriously offended, or there is a grave discrepancy between our respective principles and points of view....

I have another point of view. I think it the duty of Ambassadors, Proconsuls, Governors, etc. to be a little ahead of the Governments whom they advise. The inclination of the latter is always to go slow, sometimes unnecessarily slow. The way has to be shown to them, even if they decide perhaps quite rightly not to take it....

Some of the things that I have put forward and that you have rejected—e.g. Tibet—will of a surety come; and my only discredit will have been to be a little previous.

Apart from these small differences, my dear Arthur, which are the incidents of public life, I have never been indifferent to the support which has on many occasions been given to me by the Government, and which I am confident that, within reason, I may always be hopeful of receiving from yourself.

yours ever,

CURZON.

The mood of this letter was unhappily recurrent rather than constant. The second term of office was filled with bitterness to a proud and thwarted spirit. The Prime Minister was criticised even at the time for sanctioning the renewal by friends more fitted perhaps to realise the strain which India put upon the Viceroy. Balfour himself afterwards acknowledged that it had been a mistake. But in the summer of 1903 the struggle between Lord Curzon and Lord Kitchener over control of the Indian Army had not developed, and against the controversies with the Cabinet must be set the vast labours for Indian reforms for which the Home Government had nothing but admiration. It would at that moment have seemed a strong order to recall a Proconsul of Lord Curzon's calibre against his own will.

Between the time of taking the decision in June 1903, and Lord Curzon's visit to England in the summer of 1904, he had to a certain extent forced his own policy upon the Cabinet with regard to Tibet. In this case, as in that of Afghanistan, Lord Curzon worked for closer contact, penetration, establishment of permanent influence, at almost any cost, as the only means, in his view, of countering the intrigues of Russia.

A British Mission, under Colonel Younghusband, advanced upon Lhasa, where it did not penetrate without the use of force. It ended by demanding conditions from the Tibetans which would have committed Great Britain to keeping a control over the country for seventy-five years. These terms, imposed by Colonel Younghusband, were promptly repudiated by the Cabinet, to the intense mortification of Lord Curzon, who was in London at the time. Every step in the whole affair had really been against the Government's will, although a telegram sanctioning the advance of the Mission into the interior of Tibet (under strict conditions which were afterwards broken) had been drawn up by Lord Lansdowne with Balfour's approval, and sent during the days of confusion which accompanied the Cabinet crisis over fiscal policy in 1903. Lord George Hamilton's resignation then caused a change at the India Office, and Mr. Brodrick was transferred from the War Office to the vacant post. At the first meeting of the reconstructed Cabinet the telegram about Tibet was challenged and would have been withdrawn, had it not been too late.

The Afghanistan question also involved despatch of a British Mission to Kabul, which again was insisted upon by Lord Curzon, and reluctantly agreed to by the Government. The history of the episode is summed up by Balfour in a letter to the King:

16.2.05.

Mr. Balfour with his humble duty to Your Majesty begs respectfully to say that Cabinet yesterday adjourned at 1.30 and met again at 6 o'clock in Mr. Balfour's room at the House of Commons. The main topic was Afghanistan,—and Mr. Balfour has seldom taken part in discussion more anxious and more prolonged.

There can unfortunately be no doubt that the Indian Government has under-rated the Amir's sense of his own importance, his exaggerated opinion of the value which the alliance is to us, and his extreme reluctance to admit us into Afghanistan even for purposes immediately connected with the defence of that country against Russia. Animated by these sentiments he has refused to modify in our favour the old Treaties and Engagements entered into by his father; he has behaved with considerable discourtesy, and has shown himself utterly impracticable. In these circumstances the Government of India want to *withdraw* the Mission, believing that the Amir will get alarmed and will accede to our demands. The Indian Council *here,* on the other hand, believe that the withdrawal will have no such effect; that the Amir will go on without a treaty, free therefore to make what arrangements he pleases with Russia and to foment what disturbances he pleases on our own frontier. They think that this will be regarded as a most serious diplomatic defeat all over the Middle East, that it will cause unrest, or worse, among the Afridis, and may encourage Russian intrigues and aspirations. They urge therefore that the Amir's offer to renew, without altering, the engagements of his father should be accepted and they point out that these engagements gave us for 20 years comparative peace on the North-west frontier.

This choice which the Cabinet has had to make between the opposing policies has been a most painful one. They are fully aware of the feelings with which Lord Curzon will see his advice overruled; and they greatly dislike opposing the authorities on the spot. On the other hand they find it difficult to believe that the Government of India are not *still* making the same mistake as to the Amir's real temper of mind as they have made throughout the negotiations, and they would view with dismay a game of "bluff" between us and him in which he would come out successful. They remember that each step on the road to Lhassa was to be the "last,"—though it was not till Lhassa itself was reached that the Lamas gave in. In Mr. Balfour's judgment the Amir will never really show himself "malleable" until he has been thoroughly frightened by the Russians,—and the Russian defeats by the Japanese have encouraged the idea in his ill-balanced brain that *he* can go and do likewise.

The case Mr. Balfour has been endeavouring to explain is fully set forth in the telegram Mr. Brodrick proposes to send to the Viceroy, which contains the main reasons why the Cabinet are of opinion that it is the Indian Council here, and not the Government of India, which in this particular case offer the best advice.

Lord Kitchener's appointment to be Commander-in-Chief in India had been made, like Lord Curzon's to be Viceroy, during the Salisbury Government, even then not without some heartburnings at home about the possible consequences of setting these two natural autocrats to work together in a distant Continent. But the Indian system of Army administration was quite out of date, and not only

Lord Curzon himself, but Lord Lansdowne and Lord Roberts, had urged the appointment of Lord Kitchener to put it right. After a year's intensive study, Lord Kitchener put forward a reorganisation scheme, to cost ten million pounds. This had the practically unanimous support of the Viceroy's Council, and of the Council of India in Whitehall. The Defence Committee and the Cabinet became seriously alarmed about a system which had allowed things to reach a point of inefficiency requiring such immense sums to be expended with the complete assent of those responsible for the unpreparedness.

Lord Kitchener had discovered what he believed to be the root of the trouble—namely, the dual control of Army matters between the Commander-in-Chief and the military member of the Viceroy's Council. Before he had been three months in India he wrote a private letter to a common friend of his own and of the Prime Minister, ominous of what was coming.

CALCUTTA.

25.1.03.

...Curzon is all that one could wish and as kind as possible; but the system by which a Member of the Council is made responsible for the administration of the Army, independent of the C.-in-C., while the latter has only executive functions, is extraordinary. What it comes to is this; a machine is handed over to the C.-in-C. for him to work by turning the handle, but he must not interfere in any way with the defects in the complicated machinery.

I asked Curzon why he liked to keep up such a farce, and his answer was—"if the C.-in-C. had anything to do with the machinery he would become too powerful, so to keep him down we take his power away and run another man as well; between the two the civil elements get control." He assured me that, though perhaps not logical, the system worked very well, and he was satisfied with the results. Lord Dufferin said just the same when he was Viceroy. When one sees however the deplorable state of the organisation of the Army, I am astonished at the satisfaction expressed....

As to power, I do not want more power outside the Army, but I do want power to do good in the Army; if I am incapable why appoint me; if I fail get rid of me; but why keep on a dead level of inefficiency or drift backwards because you won't trust the person you appoint to do good? ...

I am sorry to say under the present system I find initiative for good in the administration of the Army is so choked that it ceases to be workable. Human nature again; I suppose one ought to be able to work, but there it is. . . .

And again, in November of the same year, Lord Kitchener wrote to the same correspondent:

The system of putting the really important parts of the army under a separate administration is simply monstrous, and full of the utmost danger in war time. I have an army without any means of feeding, mounting or supplying it. For this I have to trust to a totally distinct and separate Dept. of Govt., which is, I firmly believe, very inefficient, and certainly knows nothing of the requirements of war.

When war comes disaster must follow, and then I suppose the soldiers will be blamed. . . .

Balfour had by this time made up his own mind, for in December he wrote a long letter to Lord Kitchener on problems of frontier defence in which he remarked:

I have not touched on questions of Indian Army administration, but my personal conviction is (at least as at present advised) that the existing division of attributes between Commander-in-Chief and the Military Member of Council is quite indefensible.

This remained his opinion when, after Lord Curzon reached England in May 1904, discussions began in Defence Committee and in Cabinet. They were disastrously interrupted by Lord Curzon's own bad health, and by the serious illness of his wife, and no final decision on the dual-control question was taken. But it became clear that Lord Curzon was the only person consulted who thought no change in the system necessary at all. In the meantime Lord Kitchener telegraphed his resignation in September. He was however persuaded to withdraw it, and the incident had at least the effect of hastening the decision of the Government on the question.

The dispute was by this time the absorbing topic in the political and social world to which the principal parties belonged, and various friends were trying to pour oil on the troubled waters. Balfour wrote to one of them at this stage:

One of the most unlucky sides of all this business is that George Curzon's visit here, from which I had hoped so much, has largely lost its value, firstly by his perpetual illness, and then by poor Mary Curzon's desperate struggle with death. . . . This rendered difficult, and indeed impossible, the full personal discussion of all the questions which press for solution. I was up to my eyes in work at the end of the Session, . . . and before the Session was over he had vanished to Walmer. However, "there's no use crying over spilt milk!" . . .

I frankly admit that I am now rather puzzled as to what ought to be done. . . .

What he did do was to make a final appeal to Lord Curzon:

Nov. 3rd. 1904.

. . . There is another matter on which we have had some conversation already, but on which I am still most anxious to press my views on you —I mean the question of military organisation in India.

There are aspects of this on which I should never think of putting my judgment against yours. You necessarily have an experience of the working of the existing system to which I cannot pretend. But there are some general considerations whose value seems to me to be almost independent of local circumstances or special knowledge, which we cannot afford to forget.

Hitherto India, under our rule, has never really been threatened by an external enemy. The fear of Russian invasion stretches over many generations of Indian Administrators, and goes back to a time when, as far as I can judge, an invasion would have been wholly impracticable. No one however can say that it is impracticable now; and with the evidence of the magnitude of the Russian forces which can be accumulated and supplied at the end of a single railway 7000 miles long, we have to recognise that since the extension of Russian railways to the Afghan border, the problem of Indian Defence is wholly different from that which had to be faced even 15 or 20 years ago.

This being so, we have sent out as Commander-in-Chief a soldier who certainly commands a greater amount of confidence than any other English General, Lord Roberts excepted. He takes the strongest view as to the impossibility of efficiently conducting a war with the present organisation of the Indian military system, and I feel perfectly confident that he will not consent to stay in India if that system remains unmodified. I feel also certain that if he resigns, he will make public the ground of his resignation, and that the ground will be the one I have stated.

Now, putting aside for the moment the intrinsic merits of the question, how is such a contingency to be met?

You will remember that at our meeting in my room at the House of Commons to discuss this question, there were present yourself, Brodrick, Lord Roberts, Godley, Lee Warner and myself. Of these six, you and Lord Roberts—the latter mildly—were in favour of retaining the present dual system; Brodrick, Godley, Lee Warner and I were all strongly in favour of abolishing it. This, you will say, only shows that whatever view may be held by those who do not know India by personal experience, those who do know it are agreed in deprecating any fundamental change. Grant that this be so, I should still venture to say that if Kitchener resigned because he found it impossible to work the dual system, it would be found that the vast weight of opinion in this country would agree with him, and of however little value might be the opinions of Brodrick, Godley, Lee Warner and myself, we should in this respect be found very representative of our countrymen.

In these circumstances, I do not believe it to be possible to let the question rest where it is. Closer examination into the system might show that you and Lord Roberts were right, and in that case you would stand absolved for refusing, and Kitchener condemned for desiring, to introduce any fundamental change. But if no step be taken,—if no Commission be appointed to reconsider the military organisation in relation to the changed circumstances of India;—if Kitchener thereupon resigns; and if, to crown all, we become involved in serious hostilities with Russia, I believe that both at home and in India an impossible situation would be created.

I therefore do very earnestly suggest that the subject should not be allowed longer to drift; and that we should make up our minds to modify, or, at all events, thoroughly to re-examine, the present relations between the Commander-in-Chief and the Military Member of the Council....

In the spring of 1905 the Government, acting on the advice of a Committee of great Indian experience, decided on a rearrangement of the ultimate military responsibility in India, which in the main conformed to the Commander-in-Chief's desires. Lord Curzon fought a desperate battle against the verdict, and though he ultimately acquiesced in it, a further dispute on a point arising out of it caused him to send in his resignation, which Balfour accepted with a promptitude that was not the least tragic touch in this most personal drama of high politics.

A few months later Balfour's own Government fell. The controversies related in this chapter added not a little to the harassments of its closing year.

Chapter XIX

THE LAST TWO YEARS OF CONSERVATIVE GOVERNMENT

1905

Discontents within the Party. Balfour's Parliamentary tactics. Mr. George Wyndham's resignation and its causes. The eighteen-pounder gun. "Chinese Slavery." Balfour's defeat in Manchester. Balfour's first meeting with Dr. Weizmann. The rise of the Labour Party.

THE Prime Minister laid down the Government's fiscal policy in his Sheffield speech of October 1903. Never has a Party leader's "lead" been more anxiously awaited, and seldom can it have evoked less enthusiasm, at any rate at first hearing. The Free Trade Unionists distrusted it, the "whole-hoggers" found it lacking. The bulk of the Party, who immediately found themselves dubbed "little piggers," were gloomily aware that here was no very inspiring slogan for the constituencies. The Opposition were jubilant, and Sir Henry Campbell-Bannerman and Lord Rosebery hastened to renew the political relations which had for some time past been broken off between them. Possibly some Liberals really thought, what they all said, that when Balfour rejected the taxation of food as a practical possibility, he was merely wanting in courage. The same mistake was shared by the Free Trade Unionist paper, the *Spectator,* which made the following prophecy, prefacing it with the words *sunt lacrimae rerum:*

> Whatever else may happen, Mr. Balfour's day as a great British statesman is over. No turn in the political kaleidoscope can restore to him the confidence of the country.

Nevertheless, before the end of 1904, F. C. Gould, the shrewdest as well as the wittiest political caricaturist of his day, was reversing the gibes with which he enlivened the *Westminster Gazette.* Mr. Chamberlain, depicted at first as the Mayor of the Palace, had now become the suppliant at Canossa. Neither attitude represented the facts. The significance lies in the admission that a body of opinion was rallying to Balfour's position, as time revealed the unripeness of the public mind for Mr. Chamberlain's crusade.

Nevertheless the middle path was beset with pitfalls to right and left, and some idea of the Parliamentary skill and resource required of the commander can be got by seeing how his most trusted lieutenants floundered when he was absent from his place. It happened that when the House met for the first time after the Sheffield speech, in February 1904, the Prime Minister was laid up with influenza. The Opposition were naturally unwilling to postpone their attack for his return. The six-day Debate on the Address which opened on February 8th was conducted from the Ministerial Front Bench much as one of Napoleon's battles might have been if Napoleon himself had been absent from the battlefield. Balfour's brother Gerald, President of the Board of Trade, to whom it fell to make the first exposition of the Sheffield policy given to the House of Commons, transmitted faithfully the Prime Minister's arguments. But he was less convinced than his brother of the immediate impracticability of Colonial Preference, and he could not conceal this opinion under the fire of questioning. Otherwise his speech contented the Unionist Free Traders better than the Chamberlainites. These on the other hand were delighted by the tone in which the new Colonial Secretary, Mr. Alfred Lyttelton, pleaded that the door should not be closed upon Preference. The suspicions thus aroused in the Free Traders were increased by the fact that Mr. Austen Chamberlain took no share in the Debate. Finally the Home Secretary, Mr. Akers Douglas, failed lamentably in an appeal to Party loyalty. He struck the wrong note with a quavering finger, and the upshot was that some twenty-seven Unionists went into the Opposition Lobby, and seven others abstained from voting. The Amendment to the Address was rejected by 327 to 276. More important than the figures was this initial shake to morale and discipline, from which the Unionist Party in the House of Commons never really recovered before the crash of the General Election of 1906. Had the leader himself been able to expound his own policy on this occasion it is conceivable that he might have kept the ranks of his followers unbroken; but in that case the House of Commons would not have witnessed the exhibition of Parliamentary resourcefulness with which Balfour met every fiscal motion of the next two years. It began by a calm acceptance of facts as they stood.

He had only been back in his place a few days when, on March 9th, a revolt of over a hundred Chamberlainite "whole-hoggers" compelled him at the last moment to withdraw an Amendment to one of the Opposition's "wedge-driving" Motions. This Amendment, though tabled in the name of a private member, was known to have been drafted in the Whips' Office, and its fate seemed to reveal a breakdown of authority so humiliating that resignation must soon follow.

Balfour however had no more idea of renouncing office because of the tantrums of the Party wings than has a good horseman of turning back because of the vagaries of a troublesome mount. Matters were in hand which he was not prepared to leave unfinished to the mercy of the Opposition. In that very month of March 1904, the Committee of Imperial Defence was being built into the Constitution, and vital questions of Army Reform were coming to a head. At the Foreign Office Lord Lansdowne and M. Cambon were entering upon the final stage of the negotiations which were to lead to the Entente Cordiale. Balfour's preoccupation with the security of the Empire at this date was enhanced by his hearty distrust of the Liberal handling of foreign policy or military affairs. In both these spheres things required to be done, before he was ready to relinquish power. The Government, which had been nine years in office, which had revolutionised Education, and waged a long and costly war, was bound in any case to fall at the next General Election. Balfour was determined to work while it was day, and to prolong the day, if possible, until the work was done. The odium attaching to a Government suspected of clinging to office was no doubt thereby added to the causes of the defeat of 1906, but even if Balfour had foreseen that utter rout he would not have tried to avert it at the price of resignation in 1904. He was less obsessed by the tariff controversy than most of his colleagues and his followers; not that it was possible to distract himself from it for long. But the general tone of his correspondence reinforces the impression that he felt it an interruption of more fruitful meditations. His own views on the subject had been crystallised in the *Notes on Insular Free Trade,* and the Sheffield policy. Following with an attentive eye the reactions of the country to Mr. Chamberlain's campaign, he was confirmed in his original judgments. He

did make one slight movement towards Mr. Chamberlain's standpoint in a speech at Edinburgh in October 1904, when he pledged
himself, if the Conservatives were returned to power, to summon a
Colonial Conference, whose conclusions however should not come
into force until after another General Election had been held. This
plan, whatever its defects, eased the immediate situation for those
supporters of the Government inside and outside the Cabinet, who
were looking eagerly for some advance in the direction of Colonial
Preference. It was inevitable that the "hot-gospellers" of both wings
should believe the Prime Minister to be perpetually capitulating to
the other side. After every fiscal debate his letter-bag was filled with
expostulations from some quarter of his own camp against the
Parliamentary tactics by which he had preserved the appearance
of a united front. The device of moving the Previous Question
sufficed for some time. At last the Opposition thought they had
cornered him with a series of Resolutions which embodied a specific
condemnation of Mr. Chamberlain's programme, as well as of Balfour's own Retaliation policy, and the Conference proposals of his
Edinburgh speech. The Whips reported that the "Previous Question" would not hold the Party against each and all of these Resolutions. It was obviously necessary to treat them all in the same way.
Balfour, after consultation with the Cabinet, therefore announced
from the Treasury Bench his intention of walking out before the
first Division was taken, and invited his followers to do likewise.
He waited to listen to the indignant protests of Sir Henry Campbell-
Bannerman, and then "with smiling countenance, languorous grace
and lingering step, he fared forth, followed in single file by his
colleagues on the Treasury Bench,"[1] and in due course by the
occupants of the benches behind. Etonians among them must surely
have been irresistibly reminded of the exit of Sixth Form from
Chapel.

This strategic retreat was repeated on other nights during the
week of March 1905, when the fiscal Motions were successively
taken. The Opposition advertised it as an exhibition of the Prime
Minister's total loss of control, but in fact it showed the reverse.
Seldom has a leader made more exacting demands upon his following than Balfour, when he forbade the Preferentialists to strike a
blow for their faith on this occasion. Such drafts upon loyalty are
neither presented nor honoured when confidence in leadership has

[1] See Sir Henry Lucy, *The Balfourian Parliament*, p. 376.

fled. Yet it is only right to observe that without the unwavering support of Mr. Chamberlain's own son the Prime Minister could hardly have carried the thing through. Had the Chancellor of the Exchequer shrunk now from the sacrifice of personal feeling involved for him in the refusal to accept battle on the fiscal Motions, irrevocable schism must have appeared in the Conservative ranks, and the General Election been forced on at the bidding of the Liberals.

Those who lived in daily contact with Balfour never ceased to marvel at his capacity for carrying his burdens piecemeal. He was greatly helped by the power of sleep which goes with Cecil blood. He refreshed himself also by his favourite form of reading whenever a chance occurred. For instance, during an attack of phlebitis in the autumn of 1904, he wrote to Professor Pringle Pattison.

Nov. 16th, 1904.

I am most grateful to you for the proof of your review of Pragmatism in general and Dewey in particular. Though very exceptionally hard-worked in the region of public affairs, my close confinement has given me enough leisure to look, more or less perfunctorily, through Dewey's book, some of Schiller's Essays, and the articles in this quarter's "Mind" so that I shall approach your review not in total ignorance of the controversy.

Nevertheless in the last year of his Premiership he probably came nearer to experiencing that feeling of the "last straw" so familiar to most of us than at any other time in his career. The heavy feverish colds, which were the chief ailments of his middle life, often kept him from his place in the House of Commons in 1905, and colleagues remember an unusual sense of strain which impelled them to save him troubles as far as they could.

On March 2nd, 1904, Balfour received the resignation of the Chief Secretary for Ireland, Mr. George Wyndham. This was the climax of a series of events which brought upon him a poignant mixture of political anxiety and personal distress. The facts were much misrepresented, even after the story was accurately told in Mr. Wyndham's biography after his death.[1] Suspicion that something was being kept back was undoubtedly fostered by Balfour's refusal to publish the private letters which passed between himself, Mr. Wyndham, and other Ministers. Balfour felt strongly that such correspondence must never be liable to publication under pressure.

[1] See *Life and Letters of George Wyndham.*

Therefore the very urgency with which it was demanded in the House of Commons confirmed him in his determination not to produce it. He preferred to run the risk of its being supposed that there was something he wanted to hide. But the lapse of twenty years removed the objection on the score of public interest, and he had determined to print in his own Autobiography the letters which were actually published after his death in the *Quarterly Review*.[1]

It was difficult however to persuade him that any good object would be served by so doing. When reminded that there might still be people who believed that both he and Mr. Wyndham had been disloyal to the cause of Unionism in Ireland, and that he had left his Chief Secretary to bear the penalty alone, he answered with the rare flash of anger in his eye: "I am not interested in changing the opinion of anybody who thinks that."

The story begins when Balfour, forming his Cabinet in 1902, included Mr. Wyndham, who was already Chief Secretary for Ireland. The most important part of the programme of constructive Irish policy, planned ever since Balfour's own tenure of the Chief Secretary's office, was then at last on the way. A Land Purchase Bill was to be the chief measure of the Session of 1903. Mr. Wyndham threw into it all the nervous energy of his enthusiastic nature. "Overengined for his hull" is his biographer's description of him. At a crucial moment, before the Bill was ready, his Permanent Under-Secretary resigned for reasons of health. Mr. Wyndham fixed his choice of a successor upon Sir Anthony MacDonnell, an Irishman and a distinguished Indian Civil Servant who had lived all his life out of Ireland, but was known to be a convinced Home Ruler. When Mr. Wyndham wrote to Balfour asking permission to offer Sir Anthony the post, Balfour warned him of this danger:

Is it not true [he wrote on August 26th, 1902] that he would excite the most violent suspicion among your friends; that everything you did against the Orange extremists would be put down to his advice; while even the most rigorous action you might take against the Nationalists would, on his account, be regarded as mere tinkering and compromise?

But Mr. Wyndham insisted. The Prime Minister yielded at last, rather against his better judgment. There were powerful reasons. The Land Purchase Bill was a most intricate piece of legislation.

[1] See *Quarterly Review*, January 1932. "The Wyndham-MacDonnell Imbroglio." There can be found the full correspondence on which the briefer account given in this chapter is based.

No other Permanent Official available had Sir Anthony's qualifications for working it out. And Balfour, fresh from his own co-operation with Mr. Morant in the Education Act, knew well what might depend upon the difference between first-rate and second-rate expert assistance.

All went well until the Bill was through. But afterwards it appeared that when Sir Anthony accepted the Irish appointment, he had sought from Mr. Wyndham, and believed that he had been given, a freedom of initiative for policy not normally accorded to permanent officials in Great Britain. Nevertheless the action which presently brought on the storm was not consciously taken by Sir Anthony without the knowledge of his Chief. Work on the Land Purchase Bill had brought him into contact with Lord Dunraven and other leading Irishmen, whose views went much further in the direction of Home Rule than those of the Government which Sir Anthony served. They founded the "Irish Reform Association," and worked out a programme of "Devolution," transferring some measure of control over finance and legislation from Westminster to Dublin. With this Sir Anthony was in open sympathy. The draft of the scheme which he helped to frame was written on Dublin Castle note-paper, and he fully believed that the Chief Secretary knew all about what he was doing during the summer of 1904. But in fact Mr. Wyndham had not taken it in. Like many brilliant men he was a better talker than he was a listener, and markedly so at this period, when overwork was bringing him to the verge of a nervous breakdown. His biographer says that "artificial stimulants and bursts of violent physical exercise only ran up the overdraft. All he wanted was to get away and have a complete rest." He went off to Germany as soon as the House rose; but a few weeks' holiday was not enough to restore his health. While he was away Sir Anthony wrote to him twice, mentioning his co-operation with Lord Dunraven in the Devolution scheme. These references were however inserted casually near the end of long letters, full of administrative detail and by a truly singular omission the writer kept no copies. Mr. Wyndham never really mastered their contents, and most unfortunately mislaid both the letters. They were only rediscovered after his resignation. Mr. Wyndham was utterly taken by surprise when, on his way home from Germany, he read in *The Times* the text of the Dunraven Devolution scheme, and a leading article attributing the "insidious project" to "an influential clique in Dublin

Castle of which Sir Anthony MacDonnell is regarded by numbers of Irish Unionists as the head." The Chief Secretary instantly wrote to *The Times* a repudiation of the whole thing, and as soon as Sir Anthony realised that he had been acting without authorisation he dissociated himself from the proceedings of the reformers. But the mischief was done. The Ulstermen smelt danger, and worked themselves into a suspicion that not only the Chief Secretary, but Balfour himself, had "sold the pass" to the Home Rulers. Saner opinion in the Unionist Party pressed strongly that Sir Anthony MacDonnell should be got out of Ireland.

The possibility of his resuming his place on the Indian Council was discussed by the Cabinet and rejected, for both Balfour and Lord Lansdowne agreed with Mr. Wyndham's view, expressed in a letter to Balfour, on November 24th, 1904:

I cannot press MacDonnell to leave Ireland now. To do so would injure me in my own eyes to such a point that I should almost cease to be useful as a Minister. . . . I could not be silent in a Debate on his removal, and if I spoke I could not say that he had ever disobeyed my instructions, or acted disloyally to me.

Balfour agreed with this point of view, and probably the Cabinet would have dissuaded Sir Anthony from returning at once to the Indian Council. But in fact he was determined to retain his Irish post, unless he was dismissed, until (as he wrote) he could "leave it with honour and dignity." He was angry, and his feelings were not soothed by an *aide-mémoire* addressed to him by the Cabinet in December 1904, which concludes thus:

The Government therefore disapprove of your having assisted Lord Dunraven in formulating proposals which include these purposes. The Government believe that you assisted Lord Dunraven in ignorance of the view which we take of such proposals, and are convinced that you acted without disloyalty to your official superiors.

Thus the Cabinet took a course, unusual in respect of a Civil Servant, but facing squarely the facts of the case. They did not consider that Sir Anthony had knowingly done anything to merit dismissal, but they were not prepared to defend the whole of his action. As soon as Parliament met in February 1905, the Ulstermen opened fire on Sir Anthony, and the speech of one of them, on February 16th, brought Mr. Wyndham to his feet. He had felt his position difficult from the time of the Cabinet's *aide-mémoire,* and he was far from well. His long, rambling explanations failed to silence the suspicions that, somewhere in the Ministry, the principle of Unionism had been tampered with. Sir Henry Campbell-Bannerman made the first of many demands for the correspondence bearing on the MacDonnell appointment. Balfour's reply was a warm vindication of the personal honour of all concerned. But seven Ulstermen, and some English Unionists, abstained from the Division, and next day Mr. John Redmond, the Irish Nationalist leader, moved the Adjournment to enquire into the terms on which Sir Anthony held his appointment. Balfour argued that these were the same as with every permanent head of a Government department, and that they are "aiders, advisers and suggesters to their Chief, but always bound to follow the rulings of the Government they serve." But unluckily Lord Lansdowne in the House of Lords had described Sir Anthony as having "greater opportunities for initiative than he would have expected in the ordinary course." This was a divergence which the Opposition quickly seized, and the third night of the debate still left it ambiguous who was to blame for Sir Anthony's misunderstanding of his powers. At this point Mr. Wyndham's nerves gave way. He left London, and wrote to Balfour on March 2nd asking that his resignation should be accepted. Four more letters followed in the next three days. All show that their writer was in no physical condition for office at the moment. Mr. Wyndham's family were in Balfour's most intimate circle; and he knew enough about the state of his friend's health to be aware that he must not press him to go on just then. He put the facts to the House in the way Mr. Wyndham wished:

His principal reason [for resignation] is not ill-health, though I frankly admit I do not believe that he would at present be able to support all the labours ... of a great administrative office.

His principal reason is that he is of opinion that the controversy which has recently taken place ... has greatly impaired, if not wholly destroyed, the value of that work which he could do in the office which he has so long held.

Mr. Wyndham's next letter began:

DEAREST ARTHUR,

I am forever indebted to you for your statement, which I think quite perfect....

By May 9th he was well enough to make his own personal state-ment in the House. But of course the Opposition did not let the matter drop. They continued to press for the correspondence, and the Ulstermen ran more hot than ever on Sir Anthony's trail. One of them roundly told the Prime Minister that he had as much reason to resign as Mr. Wyndham. After this the Liberal attacks developed into accusations that Mr. Wyndham had been thrown to the wolves. Sir Anthony MacDonnell, still retaining his Irish post, betrayed a sense of grievance, and openly stated that he had letters in his possession which the Government would not desire to see published. Gossip and calumny spread and the fall of Balfour's Government in December 1905 did not stop the Irish tongues. In August 1906, Balfour was again urged to publish the letters, this time by his own ex-colleague, Mr. Walter Long, who had succeeded Mr. Wyndham at the Irish Office. Balfour wrote in reply (September 1906):

I gather that the loyalists in Ireland are good enough to suppose that either Sir Anthony or some other person possesses documents which would indicate that I have, or had, leanings towards views on Irish Administration other than those which I have consistently advocated in my public speeches.

The suspicions are contemptible; the documents are non-existent; and my own instinct would be to treat the whole affair with contempt. But I see you take a different view. You think that much harm is being done (which I do not deny), and that this harm would be checked if a certain number of private letters were published....

He refused. But he drafted a long letter to the Irish Unionists, intended for publication, but withheld at the advice of colleagues who thought it would only embitter the situation. And so perhaps it might have done. There was force in the criticism that Balfour had rebuked the Ulstermen alone for a distrust which was wide-spread within the Party. Mr. Austen Chamberlain emphasised that point, and added that "the draft...above all shows a complete failure to grasp the serious nature of the situation, and an entire want of appreciation of what is being said or thought in Unionist circles everywhere."

Here was candour! The reaction of the Party leader to the gravest criticism that could be levelled against one in his position was as characteristic of himself as was the plain speaking of the colleague whose loyalty had stood every call he had made upon it through three trying years. Not a touch of personal feeling ruffled his reply, which showed that his dormant powers of personal resentment had been roused at last, not against his correspondent, but by the lack of trust in the Party ranks.

I do not at all minimize the gravity of the crisis.... But it is not quite so clear to me as it is to you that the best way of dealing with it is to treat it as if it had justification.... I think it perfectly outrageous that I, for instance, should be suspected of tampering with Home Rule upon evidence on which you will not hang a cat. If I seem to tolerate or condone such relations as this suspicion implies between a Leader and his Party by concealing the views which I really entertain, I am not sure that I do not go some distance towards justification of the attacks which have been made upon my colleagues and myself....

Now you may be right in thinking that your method in dealing with this is the best.... But do not suppose that I have allowed what I admit are my own views as to the way in which the late Government have been treated by the Party to be clearly apparent on the face of the letter without also thinking that this may be the best way of dealing with the situation. I will write again.

Yours ever,

ARTHUR JAMES BALFOUR.

In the end he deferred to the views of his colleagues, dealing with the matter only once, vigorously but briefly, in a speech made in Manchester on October 23rd, 1906.

Possibly none of the advisers who deprecated the immediate expression of his indignation would have acquiesced so easily in suppressing its manifestations, had the attacks concerned themselves. Possibly his readiness to be guided in this by opinions he did not share, was due to his indifference to what people thought of him. Possibly, if he had followed his instincts at this opportunity, the distance between him and the rank and file, which Mr. Austen Chamberlain deplored, might have been diminished. These are speculations. But it was a pity that certain followers were denied the knowledge of the light in which their tittle-tattle struck their Chief.

Surely Irish Unionists may occupy themselves more profitably than in debating how far the oft-repeated professions of their Leaders are to be trusted. This way lies certain disaster. Proneness to suspicion is not only one of the most contemptible of failings, it is also one of the most dangerous.... And our perils are not small. We are blessed with a Government which threatens Ireland with measures avowedly leading to Home Rule.... If, with this and other dangers threatening us, we Unionists can do no better than chew the cud of imaginary wrongs, we shall thoroughly deserve the fate which will assuredly overtake us.[1]

In carrying on the story of events arising directly out of the MacDonnell affair the narrative has outrun the date of the General Election of January 1906. A little more remains to be said about the final year of office.

The signature of the Japanese Treaty in August 1905 had removed one reason for the delay of the General Election. The others seemed to be concerned with Party tactics, the expediency of an autumn Election, and the pros and cons of resignation or dissolution. Balfour's correspondence in the summer shows how conflicting advice poured upon him from every quarter of the Conservative camp. Some colleagues, more concerned with getting their own work done than with the state of the Party, urged meeting Parliament again in 1906. Party managers on the whole wanted an autumn Election in 1905. Balfour listened to them all, and chose his own date— December 4th, 1905—for resignation. He explained in a speech a week later why he had taken this course while still unbeaten in any important Division in the House of Commons. His Government, he said, would have been bound to bring in a Redistribution Bill if it stayed in office, and, in the absence of the stimulus of an accompanying Franchise Bill, the Party had not the "unanimous vigour" required to carry such a measure, owing to the "continued habit of mutual recrimination on the fiscal question." So much for his reasons for quitting office. His motives for holding on so long are less easily explained, but a chance remark of his threw a new light upon one of them in after years. He made it after the War, to Major Edward Lascelles, then his Private Secretary, and husband of his niece Joan. They had been talking of the electoral defeat of 1906, and Major Lascelles asked him why he had carried on through 1905, when factions were obviously bringing the Party into increasing discredit. Balfour cited the argument of the Japanese Treaty, and—after a pause of deep thought—he added that one other thing

[1] This Memorandum is reproduced in full with the other documents in the *Quarterly Review* of January 1932.

had weighed with him greatly, although he believed he had mentioned his anxiety to nobody. This was the matter of the 18-pounder gun. Major Lascelles appreciated the interest of this observation, for these were the guns which were first fired in earnest in Flanders in August 1914.

After the experiences of the South African campaign, the Cabinet had determined to undertake without further delay the tremendous operation of re-arming the Artillery with quick-firing guns. This revolution—only second in importance to the change from smoothbore to rifling forty years earlier—was imposed upon all military nations at the turn of the nineteenth century by the advances made in the application of the quick-firing principle. A change-over of weapons is a dangerous adventure, both from the political and technical point of view. It may be as fatal to undertake it too soon as too late. After the enterprise was decided upon in 1901, more than two years were spent in working out the designs. In 1903 the Special Committee were on the verge of a unanimous recommendation of two types—a 13-pounder for the Horse Artillery, an 18-pounder for the Field Artillery. Four batteries of this equipment were ready when a "Minute of Dissent" was put in. The smaller gun was giving better results in trials, and the 18-pounder was criticised as falling between the two requirements of mobility and power. It was suggested therefore that both Horse and Field Artillery should be armed with the 13-pounder, firing a 14½-lb. shell. Uniformity of type would have great advantages, especially in the British Empire, where field artillery may have to work over all sorts of country, and often with mounted troops. Expert opinion was divided. The Special Committee stuck to their original recommendations, but the War Minister, Mr. Arnold Forster, was not satisfied, called for the individual views of other officers, and finally referred the question to the Prime Minister:

WAR OFFICE,
15th July, 1904.

DEAR MR. BALFOUR,

I send herewith the paper on the new Field Gun about which I spoke to you. If you have leisure, I beg you will read it. Perhaps you will be more moved by the remarks of my colleagues than I am, I hope so. If you are not I think it might be worth while to bring the matter up before the Committee of Imperial Defence. I think you will admit that I am in a difficulty. All my technical advisers are dead against me, and yet, on my conscience I believe they are wrong.

I shall be delighted to find that you agree with them and not with me, because my mind will be at ease, which at present it is not.

Believe me,

Yours very truly,

H. O. ARNOLD FORSTER.

Balfour had been following the technical aspects of the question. When appealed to, he came down on the side of the Special Committee and the 18-pounder gun. The way seemed clear after this, but difficulties arose with the Departments and the manufacturers. The orders were only actually placed on Christmas Eve 1904. Before then, articles had appeared in the newspapers attacking the Government for the delay, and *The Times* had one on December 15th evidently inspired by a well-informed correspondent. Mr. Arnold Forster was worried by the criticism, and drafted a defence. Balfour wrote to him:

CHATSWORTH.

Jan. 5th, 1905.

I think your Memorandum on Guns powerfully written, and very interesting. I am not sure, however, that you would be well advised in publishing it,—at all events for the present: and for the following reason: The Opposition, . . . are without doubt going to do their best to make this gun question the theme of an attack on you and upon the Government. To make public your whole case now is to give them a month, or more, to get up their reply. Your Office is, and always has been, leaky. It has not always been loyal to its Chief; and any information that could be twisted into a reply to your arguments would certainly be supplied to the Opposition critics.

Moreover, it is almost impossible for you to give your whole defence. There is, for example, no reference in your proposed letter to an episode which struck me rather painfully when you told me about it towards the end of October: I mean the delay due to the difficulty which both Woolwich and the private firms had found in providing nickel steel which would stand the tests, and the ignorance in which you were kept both of the *fact* of the consequent delay and of its cause.

The people who profess to have private information from the War Office do not hesitate to assert that the consideration given—and, in my opinion, most properly given—to the scheme of the Ordnance Committee, which requires the field gun to be of a different calibre from the horse artillery, was a blameworthy cause of delay. Can this be substantiated against all comers?

Do you not think, by the way, that you unduly deprecate our old field guns? Many of them, no doubt, have greatly deteriorated from use in the South African War: but this is not true of the guns in India, which are those most likely to be required if hostilities broke out. And I have some doubts whether the old 15-pounder, if in good order, is a materially less effective weapon than the present German or Japanese gun. On this point, however, I speak with diffidence.

Of course, my objection to the publication of your letter, which I do not wish to press against a strong conviction of your own, does not extend to statements in speeches by yourself or other members of the Government, to the effect that our critics are under a complete misapprehension as to what has really occurred in connection with the new gun.

Yours ever,
ARTHUR JAMES BALFOUR.

Balfour had written to King Edward on December 29th, 1904 expressing his relief that the order for the guns was given at last. If this had been the end of the story it would be difficult to explain his remark to Major Lascelles about the connection between his anxiety over the guns and the date of a General Election a year later. But the correspondence shows the eager interest with which he followed the inevitable technical troubles of the first experiments, and he wanted to see them through. The trials had been made with fuses manufactured by Krupp. The change to English measurements caused delay. King Edward himself was the unconscious cause of the discovery of a serious weakness. He wanted to see the first batteries, and two of them came up by road from Woolwich to Buckingham Palace on May 15th, 1905. When they returned, half the tubes in which the ammunition was carried in the limbers had given way. The guns had come successfully through their travelling trials on Dartmoor, and at first the accident seemed inexplicable. It was due to the long trot over the granite setts of the Old Kent Road—a kind of test that might otherwise never have been made till the guns were jolting over the pavé on the road to Mons.

The chronic disagreements of the Liberal leaders happened to be in acute phase when Balfour resigned office in the first week of December, and he was held to have shown much tactical skill in his choice of time and method in laying down office. As a matter of fact, once he had made up his mind not to confront the perils of a Redistribution Bill, the advantages of resignation over dissolution were obvious. Sir Henry Campbell-Bannerman would then be forced to form an Administration and a policy before the appeal to the country. Optimists hoped that the first might prove impossible. The right wing group, led by Mr. Asquith, Mr. Haldane, and Sir Edward Grey, were known to disagree with Sir Henry on Imperial policy, and an effort was actually made to eject him from the leadership in the House of Commons, Sir Edward Grey refusing at first to take office unless the Prime Minister designate took a peerage.[1] But he thought better of it, and by December 12th the new Ministry was in office with Sir Edward Grey as Foreign Secretary, Mr. Asquith Chancellor of the Exchequer, Mr. Haldane War Minister, and Mr. Lloyd George President of the Board of Trade. The difficulties of redeeming pledges in respect of Education and Home Rule now loomed near enough to cause many Liberals to warn their leader not to be caught in Balfour's trap. But Sir Henry Campbell-Bannerman had a shrewder instinct for the temper of the country. He knew that from his point of view "it was all right."[2]

Few on either side expected that the Unionists would be given a new run of power. No one on either side expected that the great Party which had ruled, with one brief interval, for twenty years, would be returned a leaderless remnant of 157.

This was the scale of the disaster which befell Conservatism at the end of Balfour's Premiership. What were its causes?

Apart from the armoury of lesser weapons which a Government that has been long in office puts into the hands of its enemies, the Liberals had the Education Act and the Food Tax cry. The opposition of the Nonconformists to the Act had not been allowed to die down in those parts of the country where it was possible to keep it alive, and the price now to be paid in votes for this great and lasting piece of legislation was very heavy. When the strength of the Free Trade feeling in the country is also considered, it seems probable that the Liberals might have won a sufficiently decisive victory in honourable warfare without the aid of the cry of "Chinese Slavery."

Indentured Chinese coolies had been introduced into the South African gold-mines early in 1904 to supplement a scarcity of native

---

[1] See *Life of Sir Henry Campbell-Bannerman*, Vol. II, p. 193 *et seq.*
[2] *Ibid.*, Vol. II, p. 204.

labour, which, in the opinion of the British Government, neither could, nor should, be made good by the employment of white men working side by side with Kaffirs. The Chinese contracts were for three years, and were made voluntarily in knowledge of the conditions, which included enclosure in large compounds during the period of service, and repatriation at the end. The cry of "Slavery" had at once been raised by the Opposition, but was allowed to drop until about the middle of the year 1905, when it was effectively used in bye-elections. By this time more than 40,000 Chinese were at work on the Rand. Sir Henry Campbell-Bannerman pledged himself in his first speech after taking office on December 21st to "stop forthwith the recruitment of and embarkation of Chinese coolies." [1] The announcement was greeted with "a storm of cheers." But it was shortly discovered to have been "somewhat rash," [2] and the promise was modified in a further speech on January 9th, the eve of the polls. Sir Henry was "somewhat loth to part with the idea of a clean cut," [3] but the Law Officers had reported difficulties about cancelling the licences for 14,500 additional coolies, now embarked, or embarking, from China. It could not be done without legislation, and to legislation the Cabinet was extremely averse. [4] So it was settled that existing licences must stand. As for the 47,000 Chinamen, who, in the opinion of the Government, were in a state of "slavery," it was decided to leave the responsibility for their fate to the Government of the Transvaal. This body was however not in existence, as the new South African Constitution had not yet been passed. In the meantime pictures of Chinamen in chains, of Chinamen being flogged and kicked, covered the hoardings all over the country. "What hypocrisy is this?" exclaimed Balfour. "If I thought," he said, "that we were really staining the great anti-slavery traditions of this country, do you suppose that I would for a moment remain a member of a Government who intended indirectly to perpetuate it? That is what they mean to do. They have the power now ... to put an end to the whole system. They do not mean to do it. They do not dare to do it, and what they mean to do is to ride off on the idea that they can throw the responsibility on somebody else,

[1] See *Life of Sir Henry Campbell-Bannerman*, Vol. II, p. 228.
[2] *Ibid.* Also *Life of Lord Oxford and Asquith*, Vol. I, p. 178.
[3] See *Life of Sir Henry Campbell-Bannerman*, Vol. II, p. 230.
[4] *Ibid.*

when, if it be slavery, they are the people, and the only people, who can prevent it." [1]

"If and when they revoke the Ordinance," he said a day later, "they will indeed show that they have the courage—of the placard. ... The whole charge of slavery is a mere electioneering dodge. When the Election is over it will be forgotten like other electioneering dodges." [2]

The word "slavery" was repudiated as soon as possible after the Election, Sir Henry Campbell-Bannerman explaining that he had always been careful in his use of it. "I have said that it was 'tainted with slavery'," he told the House of Commons, "and I repeat that. I have said that it had many of the characteristics of slavery, and I repeat that. Beyond that I have never gone." [3]

Balfour had no seat in the House of Commons at the moment when this piece of casuistry was offered it. His opinion of the Chinese Slavery episode is therefore contained chiefly in the Manchester speeches. One of the difficulties for the Conservatives at this Election was the lack of a constructive policy on the part of the enemy. Balfour remarked in a letter written in 1911 that "the greatest victory at the polls ever won by any Party was won upon no policy at all—C.-B.'s victory in 1906." The strongest swimmer is helpless in the undertow of the ebbing tide. Balfour experienced the new sensation of fighting a losing battle. His spirits rose to the stimulus. He delivered the best platform speeches of his life, during the ten grim January days in which Manchester rain pelted unceasingly upon Manchester cobble-stones. His headquarters were, as usual, in the Queen's Hotel. Through the green-painted pillars of that Victorian portico the stream of pressmen, Party organisers, supporters, and busybodies passed continually in and out. Upstairs, in the suite of first-floor rooms, Balfour's sister and his secretaries guarded his moments of quiet. Yet it was to this place, and under these circumstances, that one visitor was summoned for a conversation, which in years to come was to bear fruit undreamed of by them both, and to set its impress upon history, in the Balfour Declaration of 1917, pledging the British Government to promote the establishment of a National Home for the Jews in Palestine.

[1] Speech in Manchester, January 9th, 1906 (*Manchester Courier*).
[2] Speech in Manchester, January 10th, 1906.
[3] See *Life of Sir Henry Campbell-Bannerman*, Vol. II, p. 231.

The first meeting between Balfour and Dr. Chaim Weizmann was a prelude to that story.

Balfour's interest in the Jews and their history was lifelong. It originated in the Old Testament training of his mother, and in his Scottish upbringing. As he grew up, his intellectual admiration and sympathy for certain aspects of Jewish philosophy and culture grew also, and the problem of the Jews in the modern world seemed to him of immense importance. He always talked eagerly on this, and I remember in childhood imbibing from him the idea that Christian religion and civilisation owes to Judaism an immeasurable debt, shamefully ill repaid. His interest in the subject was whetted in the year 1902 by the refusal of the Zionist Jews to accept an offer of land for settlement in British East Africa, made to them by his own Government through Mr. Chamberlain, then Colonial Secretary. This episode roused in him a curiosity which he found no means to satisfy. He had no contacts with Zionist Jews, who were few and far between in England then, and non-existent in the social circles to which Balfour's Jewish friends, such as the Rothschilds, belonged. His Chairman in Manchester was however a Jew, Mr. Dreyfus, and to him, in 1905, Balfour mentioned his wish to fathom the reasons for the Zionist attitude to the East African offer. Mr. Dreyfus told him that there was at that moment in Manchester one of the younger leaders of the Zionist movement, a Russian Jew, Chaim Weizmann by name, who had recently settled in England and held a post as lecturer in organic chemistry at the Victoria University. Balfour asked to see him, and in the midst of the election turmoil an interview was arranged, timed to occupy a quarter of an hour or so. It lasted an hour and a quarter. Both participants described it to me many times afterwards, in a way that showed the unusual sympathy which sprang up, almost at first sight, between two leaders, widely separated by every material circumstance of life and tradition.

The young scientist, born and bred in the tragic surroundings of Russian Jewry, had no great belief in his powers to explain the motive forces behind the dawning Jewish national revival to the Conservative leader, on whom Fortune had showered almost every one of her richest gifts. Still less did Dr. Weizmann expect to convince the British politician of the spiritual necessity that drove the Zionists to make contact again with the soil of Palestine, and forbade them to accept escape through settlement on any other spot

ARTHUR JAMES BALFOUR

on earth. He certainly did not anticipate any particular result from the conversation. The offer of Balfour's Government had been rejected, gratefully but decisively, by the section of Zionists among whom Dr. Weizmann was already a leader. That Government had just fallen from power. Yet he had not been ten minutes in Balfour's presence before he found himself striving his utmost to break down the obstacles of his, as yet, imperfect command of English, and expound the Zionist consciousness of historical right.

"I began to sweat blood to make my meaning clear through my English. At the very end I made an effort, I had an idea. I said: 'Mr. Balfour, if you were offered Paris instead of London, would you take it? Would you take Paris instead of London?' He looked surprised. He: 'But London is our own!' I said: 'Jerusalem was our own when London was a marsh.' He said: 'That's true!' I did not see him again till 1916."

Thus Dr. Weizmann described to me their first meeting. Imagination supplies more. When Balfour's attention concentrated on something that really held it, he would look at the speaker with a steady expectant gaze. His eyes seemed then like windows to his inner self through which one had only to look to find perfect comprehension. To evoke that particular expression was an experience even for those who were familiar with it. For a stranger in a strange land it was an unforgettable moment.

Balfour for his part told me often about the impression the conversation made on him.

"It was from that talk with Weizmann that I saw that the Jewish form of patriotism was unique. Their love for their country refused to be satisfied by the Uganda scheme. It was Weizmann's absolute refusal even to look at it which impressed me."

The conversation of which this is a fragment took place at a date when Zionism itself, and Balfour's understanding of it, had both been put to practical tests. The story of the meeting with Dr. Weizmann in Manchester is no digression, but an integral part of the narrative of Balfour's life during the General Election. He turned, then, very characteristically, for relaxation, to a subject which interested him alike as a political philosopher, a student of history, and a statesman; but also as a statesman temporarily freed from responsibility.

The train of reflection was started in 1906 by the contact of two singularly magnetic personalities, and Balfour pursued it for the next few years, intermittently no doubt, but with the ardour he reserved for his speculative moments. The more he thought about Zionism, the more his respect for it, and his belief in its importance, grew. His opinions took shape before the defeat of Turkey in the Great War transformed the whole future for the Zionists. The policy of the "Balfour Declaration" of 1917 has been attributed to various motives, worthy and unworthy, on the part of British statesmen. The long-standing sympathy of the then Foreign Secretary was a factor which is too commonly left out of account.

To return to Manchester. Polling in every Division of the City took place on January 13th. By eight o'clock the Conservative Club was thronged with a company, slightly apprehensive no doubt of coming shocks, but utterly unprepared for the series of blows which began with the announcement of Mr. Winston Churchill's victory over Mr. Joynson-Hicks in the North-west Division. News of two more defeats came quickly after, and then the staggering news that Balfour was out. His Liberal opponent, Mr. Horridge,[1] had polled 6,403 to his 4,423. One by one the defeated candidates reached the friendly shelter of the Club and faced the bewildered supporters. The nine Manchester seats, of which only one had been Liberal, did not return a single Conservative. Two had gone to Labour, and the other six were Liberal gains. Balfour and his sister were almost the last to arrive at the Club, and the crowd in the Hall pulled themselves together and gave him a victor's reception. He made two speeches that evening, the second at Ardwick in the other end of the constituency. It was the first time he had to face a most painful experience, the bitter disappointment of his workers. "The very salt of the political earth," he called them that night. "They are that without which politics cannot flourish. They indicate the self-sacrificing energy in the great cause, which ... has but little echo or fame, but is nevertheless the base and the root of all that is valuable in our public representative life of this country."

Next day he left Manchester, never again to return to it as one of its members. A whole programme of appearances in other parts of the country had of course been arranged for the Party leader. He was in Nottingham on the 15th, Glasgow on the 18th, where he followed on the heels of the new Prime Minister, who had let himself go in exultation.

England and Scotland alike showed the same overwhelming re-

[1] Afterwards Sir Thomas Horridge, a Judge of the King's Bench.

versals. Balfour's brother, Gerald, had lost his seat in Leeds; Alfred Lyttelton, the Colonial Secretary, was unseated at Leamington. Five of the seven Glasgow Divisions were about to go Labour or Liberal —Unionist Free Traders holding two. London had slumped heavily. Birmingham alone held firm, and with its surrounding county seats eventually increased its Unionist strength.

Election speeches seldom bear resurrecting. Only one passage in Balfour's Glasgow reply to what he called the Prime Minister's "war-dance" is worth noticing, in its warning of a future which would forbid the economies and reductions of taxation lavishly promised. The references to "a Power who thinks it can blackmail you to any extent it pleases, or bring you to your knees" were only beginning to be pointed in the minds of his audience (the Algeciras Conference was sitting in that very January).

"God forbid," he went on, "that such a moment should come under any Government, especially under the present Government; but if it comes, mark my words, the success of our diplomacy, our power of at once holding our just rights, and yet avoiding war, depends in the last resort on the relative strength of our Navy, and for the advocates of peace to be also the advocates of retrenchment in this regard is to make themselves the apostles of a creed essentially contradictory with itself."

The defeat of 1906 is the end of the first Volume of Balfour's *Life,* in a real, as well as in a literal sense. Through his private letters and his speeches of the period there seems to run the sense of a future pregnant with change, in which he would have new parts to play. No physical fatigue, no lack of energy dimmed that instinct now. Released from the Election campaign his attention leapt to that part of the political field where forces were gathering really worthy of study. The fifty-one Labour Members who would sit in the new House seemed to him a far more interesting portent than the triumphant hosts who had rallied for the last time to the old Liberalism of his own youth.

After the Nottingham speech he went to Whittingehame for one day before proceeding to Glasgow. He found waiting for him a note from Lady Salisbury which ran thus:

"My dear A. J. B.,
     D——n. D——n. D——n."

He answered:

MY DEAR ALICE,

I am delighted at the pithiness and vigour of your language. I am horribly ashamed at feeling a kind of illegitimate exhilaration at the catastrophe which has occurred. It has made me more violently and pleasurably interested in politics than I remember having been since the Home Rule Bill. If I read the signs aright, what has occurred has nothing whatever to do with any of the things we have been squabbling over the last few years. C.–B. is a mere cork, dancing on a torrent which he cannot control, and what is going on here is the faint echo of the same movement which has produced massacres in St. Petersburg, riots in Vienna, and Socialist processions in Berlin. We always catch Continental diseases, though we usually take them mildly....

Thus ended the first phase, the phase that began in 1880 when the offspring of the House of Cecil, almost against his own will, made up his mind to take politics seriously. Twenty-five years had passed since he had seen Benjamin Disraeli watching his approach up the long avenue at Hatfield. Twenty-five more years were to run before he resigned the Seals of Office for the last time into his Sovereign's hands. Those twenty-five years were to span as stirring a career, and bring him to as high a position in the Councils of the Empire, as ever fell to the lot of an elder statesman.

James Balfour = L

James Maitland Balfou

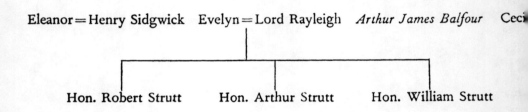

Eleanor = Henry Sidgwick   Evelyn = Lord Rayleigh   *Arthur James Balfour*   Ceci

Hon. Robert Strutt   Hon. Arthur Strutt   Hon. William Strutt

Ruth = William Balfour of Balbirnie   Eleanor = Hon. Galbraith Cole   Mary

Blanche = Edgar Dugdale   Frank = Hon. Phyllis Goschen

Eleanor Maitland

.ady Blanche Gascoigne Cecil

rancis   *Gerald* = Lady Betty Lytton   Alice   Eustace = Lady Frances Campbell

Eve   *Robert* = Jean Cooke-Yarborugh   Kathleen = Richard Oldfield
              |
          Gerald

n = Hon. Edward Lascelles   Alison = Arthur Milne   Oswald

Index

Printed in the United States
121635LV00007B/33/A

9 781432 558987